Individual Development and Social Change

EXPLANATORY ANALYSIS

Individual Development and Social Change

EXPLANATORY ANALYSIS

Edited by

JOHN R. NESSELROADE

College of Human Development
The Pennsylvania State University
University Park, Pennsylvania
* and*
Max Planck Institute
* for Human Development and Education*
Berlin, Federal Republic of Germany

ALEXANDER VON EYE

Max Planck Institute
* for Human Development and Education*
Berlin, Federal Republic of Germany

1985

ACADEMIC PRESS, INC.

(Harcourt Brace Jovanovich, Publishers)

Orlando San Diego New York London
Toronto Montreal Sydney Tokyo

ACADEMIC PRESS, INC.
Orlando, Florida 32887

United Kingdom Edition published by
ACADEMIC PRESS, INC. (LONDON) LTD.
24/28 Oval Road, London NW1   7DX

Library of Congress Cataloging in Publication Data

Main entry under title:

Individual development and social change.

    Includes index.
    1. Developmental psychology--Methodology--Addresses,
essays, lectures. 2. Social change--Methodology--Address-
es, essays, lectures. I. Nesselroade, John R.
II. Eye, Alexander von.
BF713.5.I53   1984   155   84-16769
ISBN 0-12-516620-0 (alk. paper)

PRINTED IN THE UNITED STATES OF AMERICA

85 86 87 88   9 8 7 6 5 4 3 2 1

Contents

Contributors

Numbers in parentheses indicate the pages on which the authors' contributions begin.

Marietta L. Baba (1, 265), Department of Anthropology, Wayne State University, Detroit, Michigan 48202

Jochen Brandtstädter (243), Department of Psychology, University of Trier, 5500 Trier, Federal Republic of Germany

David L. Featherman (213), Department of Sociology and Institute on Aging, University of Wisconsin, Madison, Wisconsin 53706

H. Jörg Henning (295), Studiengang Psychologie, Universität Bremen, D-2800 Bremen 33, Federal Republic of Germany

Klaus Hüfner (51), Freie Universität Berlin, D-1000 Berlin 33, Federal Republic of Germany

David A. Kenny (343), Department of Psychology, University of Connecticut, Storrs, Connecticut 06268

Erich W. Labouvie (31, 189), Center of Alcohol Studies, Rutgers, The State University, New Brunswick, New Jersey 08903

Richard M. Lerner (155), College of Human Development, The Pennsylvania State University, University Park, Pennsylvania 16802

Jens Naumann (51), Max Planck Institute for Human Development and Education, 1000 Berlin 33, Federal Republic of Germany

John R. Nesselroade (189), College of Human Development, The Pennsylvania State University, University Park, Pennsylvania 16802; and Max Planck Institute for Human Development and Education, 1000 Berlin 33, Federal Republic of Germany

Georg Rudinger (295), Psychologisches Institut der Universität Bonn, Bonn, Federal Republic of Germany

Rolf Steyer (95), Department of Psychology, University of Trier, 5500 Trier, Federal Republic of Germany

Alexander von Eye (125), Max Planck Institute for Human Development and Education, 1000 Berlin 33, Federal Republic of Germany

Bernard P. Zeigler (1, 265), Department of Computer Science, Wayne State University, Detroit, Michigan 48202

Preface

The linking of conceptions of individual development and social change is one of the rapidly emerging activities of developmentalists. The attempt to integrate what may seem to be quite distinct perspectives has considerably more history and substance, however, than one sees in many of the topics that become prominent for a time and then fade away. Although each discipline's members have their own views on the interactive nature of individual development and social change, social and behavioral scientists such as Baltes, Brim, Cattell, Featherman, Lerner, Neugarten, Riley, and Schaie, to name a few, have labored intensively and long to breathe new life into conceptions of the interactive relationships among developing persons and their social contexts. As a result, truly interdisciplinary discourse and collaboration is no longer an abstraction to warm the heart; it is becoming a realization that fires the imagination. The sense of excitement that important new discoveries await us on the boundaries between the developmental disciplines, including the biological, is keen indeed.

Probably at no time in our history has the challenge been more pressing to improve our theoretical formulations and methodological tools for apprehending the nature of individual development and social change. Whether one's concern is focused on the shaping of educational practices in school systems in developing nations or on improving the quality of life in retirement communities in an economy dominated by concern for national defense, there is an urgency of novel proportions underlying our quest for knowledge. The articulation of concepts and principles concerning the interrelationship between individual development and social change is not without risks, however. If one takes this subject matter seriously, that very subject matter is a constant reminder that conclusions reached, however valid at the time, are likely to be of quite limited generality.

This volume represents a convergence of three lines of emphasis now visible in developmental research and theory building. The three are (1) the life course as a focus for the study of development and social change, and their interrelationships; (2) the life-span orientation to the study of individual development, with its acknowledgment of the salience of contextual features for understanding development; and (3) the growth of methodological innovations that provide more appropriate and powerful ways of exploiting data gathered to describe and explain developmental change processes. Various kinds of cohort analysis, for example, illustrate the application of methodologies for the exploitation of data containing information about developing individuals in a changing society.

Through the mechanism of paper sessions and discussion (and some editorial prompting), we have endeavored to bring together knowledgeable representatives of a variety of perspectives and to engage them in dialogue with each other to produce a more integrated and coherent articulation of their positions than would typically occur in disciplinary settings. In this way, we have sought to help the study of human development capitalize on the products of a number of disciplines, representing both European and North American perspectives. Individually, the chapters are a set of position statements or perspectives on substantive and methodological issues pertaining to the study of individual development and social change phenomena. Collectively, the chapters represent a guide to engaging in the study of development and change without separating the developing entity from its changing context. To render this message in other terms, we will ignore a tired old metaphor in favor of its concrete referent: If one's interest is in studying the baby, it is important to know when to throw out the bathwater, because there is much to be learned while the infant is in the tub.

We owe a great deal to many individuals. First, we are grateful to the authors, who labored so diligently to prepare and revise their contributions. Second, we wish to thank the Max Planck Institute for Human Development and Education (Berlin, Federal Republic of Germany) for supporting the preparation of the volume from its inception. We are especially pleased to acknowledge help of Doris Anderson, Amy Michele, and Sylvia Stolle, who assisted with the final preparation of manuscripts. Third, we thank Robert L. Burgess, Jeffrey Kurland, and Robert G. Reynolds for their help in reviewing some of the manuscripts. Fourth, we are grateful to Athena Droogas and Kathy Lenerz for preparation of the subject index. Finally, we are very thankful to our families and colleagues, who provided us with a supportive version of the social and intellectual context that profoundly influences the development of a volume such as this.

1

Evolution and Innovation in Sociocultural Systems: A Punctuated Equilibria Model

MARIETTA L. BABA

BERNARD P. ZEIGLER

I. Introduction

How does major cultural change originate and unfold over time? Through the gradual assimilation of incremental change within the fabric of a continuing system? By local innovation and broad diffusion via trade routes and other communication pathways? Through imposition by an economically powerful society upon a less developed system? Cultural anthropologists, with some notable exceptions, have traditionally postulated such mechanisms as the motive forces driving culture change. Indeed, there is little doubt that these mechanisms often play a key role in mediating cultural evolution. But other mechanisms may also be in operation at the same time — mechanisms which are, perhaps, more crucial determinants of the locus, mode, and tempo of evolutionary change.

This chapter proposes and elaborates upon one such potential mechanism; it seeks the locus of innovation in uniquely constituted groups of

INDIVIDUAL DEVELOPMENT
AND SOCIAL CHANGE:
EXPLANATORY ANALYSIS

1

individuals — individuals who are marginal to the stable, dominant systems from which they emerged. It is from the evolutionary paradigm of punctuated equilibria (Eldredge & Gould, 1972) that we draw our central analogy. Rather than seek an explanation for the emergence of new life-forms in the gradual accumulation of beneficial genes in an existing species, this theory seeks mechanisms by which unique combinations of genes are formed in small, peripheral populations, each of which then "tests its mettle" against the rigors of a new environment. In like manner, we seek the cultural locus and mode through which human bearers of new ideas can test these ideas in a multitude of cultural experiments. Just as successful new combinations of genes may be identified by the rapid growth of the peripheral isolate and the emergence of a new species which may then radiate to fill whole new ecozones, so the successful cultural innovation is known through its rapid develoment and possible transformation of the culture in which it sprang to life.

This chapter reviews the contribution of modern evolutionary anthropology to the definition of culture and the characterization of cultural levels or grades and then critically analyzes the conceptual background in which modern anthropology conducts its studies. Exclusive adherence to a narrow form of phyletic gradualism fails to seek systematic explanatory relationships for cultural advance, although evolutionary anthropology has documented the existence of cultural grades. Against this background, the anthropological contribution of Sahlins and Service (1960) and the punctuated equilibria paradigm of Eldredge and Gould (1972) inspire the present work.

In the main body of this chapter, the punctuated equilibria hypothesis is presented and modified for interpretation as a mechanism to explain cultural advance. This mechanism is then elaborated in the context of two examples of techno-economic transformation. The punctuated equilibria model provides an account consistent with that of Flannery (1969) for the evolution of agriculture in the Near East. The model is also consistent with the modern process of technological innovation in which the innovator – entrepreneur and the small, science-based firm may be responsible for the technological transformation of twentieth-century industry.

The ideas presented in this chapter are not intended to suggest that Darwinian selection is anything other than a primary evolutionary force. Furthermore, the argument that strict adherence to phyletic gradualism may unnecessarily limit our understanding of evolution should not be taken as an indictment of Darwinian theory or as a total rejection of gradualism. Recent developments in the literature clearly point out the need to refine and integrate the modes of phyletic gradualism and punctuated equilibria within a general evolutionary framework that can ultimately enhance our knowledge of life's history on earth (e.g., see Schoch, 1982, p. 360). The authors also wish to emphasize that this chapter is not intended as a presentation of formal, empirically testable deductions regarding the punctuated equilibria model or of data which might be used to test such deductions. Our approach is intended to explore the possible applicability of the punctuated equilibria perspective to future studies of culture change and to suggest the potential contribution of this model to the theory of cultural evolution.

Because the ideas presented here have not been rigorously tested, it is not yet possible to determine whether punctuated equilibria is simply a metaphor for certain types of social change or whether it is a fundamental mechanism of cultural evolution. The chapter does propose research paths along which the anthropologist, ethnographer, psychologist, and systems modeler can pursue the issues that have been identified.

II. The Contributions and Limitations of a Darwinian Approach to Culture Change

The expectations of theory color perceptions to such a degree that new notions seldom arise from facts collected under the influence of old pictures of the world. New pictures must cast their influence before facts can be seen in different perspective.

[Eldredge & Gould, 1971, p. 83]

One of the most significant intellectual events in modern anthropology has been the infusion of evolutionary theory from the biological sciences. This process was initiated by Darwin's formulation of the theory of natural selection and was reinvigorated during the 1950s following the modern evolutionary synthesis of selection theory and population genetics. The evolutionary perspective asserts that there are laws of social change and that the forces described by these laws have produced cultures at several levels of techno-economic productivity (White, 1943, 1945, 1949, 1959).

The explanatory power of an evolutionary framework proved extraordinarily potent in a discipline noted for atheoretical empiricism during the first century of its formal existence (Harris, 1968). This framework has had important implications for the anthropological research program and for the application of more robust methodological tools in sociocultural investigation.

Prior to the advent of evolutionary anthropology, there was no generally accepted definition of culture that described the systematic relationship of cultural components and related the functioning of these components to energy capture and energy–resource flow (Harris, 1968). Culture was

Table 1.1

Evolutionary Series of Cultural Systems

Techno-economic productivity	Socio-organizational complexity
Post-industrial	Modern state
Industrial	Archaic state
Advanced agriculture	Chiefdom — hierarchical
Agriculture-pastoralism	Chiefdom — egalitarian
Incipient agriculture	Tribal level
Hunting and gathering	Band level

loosely defined as a collection of learned patterns of thought and behavior characteristic of a particular population (e.g., Wissler, 1929; Murdock, 1961). Such a normative and particularistic definition did not readily lend itself to the production or organization of a data base from which models could be developed (Flannery, 1967; Watson, LeBlanc, & Redman, 1971). Evolutionary anthropology, by contrast, defines culture as a uniquely human adaptive system designed to capture, harness, and distribute environmental energy and resources for the survival and well-being of its carriers (Steward, 1949, 1955). Following this definition, major components of all cultural systems are described as (1) the techno-economic base that captures materials and energy from an environment; (2) the social structure that organizes individuals to carry out energy production, environmental exploitation, and resource distribution activities; and (3) the ideology that constitutes a set of ideas and values that rationalize and motivate social behavior and the relations of production (White, 1949).

Perhaps the most significant impact of evolutionary theory on the study of human culture was the discovery that cultural systems, much like biological species, represent differing grades of development. These grades are hierarchically ordered according to their level of efficiency and productivity in the capture, distribution, and utilization of energy (Sahlins & Service, 1960; White, 1943, 1959). Table 1.1 lists two generally accepted series of cultural advance arranged according to level of techno-economic productivity and socio-organizational complexity. Following is a list of traditional measures of *quantum cultural advance,* which, for the purposes of this chapter, is defined as techno-economic developments that both require and permit major new forms of social organization as a result of improved energy capture, distribution, and/or utilization.

1. Absolute energy capture
2. Ratio of energy capture to energy expended in capture
3. Systematic complexity (number of components)
4. Systematic integration (linkages between parts)

A. EVOLUTIONARY ETHNOGRAPHY

More than three decades of anthropological fieldwork have now been guided by a Darwinian paradigm of evolution, producing a rich literature describing the reality of culture at varying grades of techno-economic productivity (Fried, 1952, 1967; Lee, 1968; Mintz, 1956; Rappaport, 1968; Service, 1955, 1962; Wolfe, 1957, 1966). The vast majority of ethnographic investigations emerging from the evolutionary school of anthropology thus far have focused upon (1) static, structural–functional descriptions of the ecological niches occupied by cultures at varying stages of evolutionary advance and (2) dynamic adjustment of specific cultures to changing environmental contexts. While these studies have confirmed the existence of energetically defined cultural grades, they generally have lacked concern for the processes of innovation and forces involved in de novo[1] advance to new levels of sociocultural integration.

For students of culture, techno-economic transformation and major sociopolitical reorganization have been viewed primarily as a function of contact between two cultures at different stages of development, with change occurring as the result of forced domination of one system by the other. In such cases, the less advanced system was exposed to new economic pressures or was compelled to participate in the economic structure of the dominant system (e.g., Murphy & Steward, 1955). Studies of this type relegate quantum change to a phenomenon conceived by the deus ex machina of intercultural contact.

How quantum cultural innovations arise, why they occur, and what systemic relationships may be operative during each change are some of the major questions which may be raised concerning the process of evolution. Such questions have been seriously investigated only by archaeologists (particularly those influenced by systems theory), who have concentrated upon the origin of major cultural innovations that produced new grades of social organization (e.g., Flannery's "broad spectrum revolution" in the Near East, 1969; Carneiro's origin of state-level civilizations in the New World, 1970). For such investigations, the most fascinating questions have centered on new quantum developments in the techno-economic base and on the resulting transformation of sociopolitical systems, settlement patterns, and population density. One reason for archaeologists' concern with processes of

---

[1] For the purposes of this essay, de novo is defined as the original invention of an idea, artifact, structure or process within a particular cultural context. The term de novo implies that the new entity was invented within the cultural context in which it appears and was not borrowed or transplanted from another cultural system. De novo entities may, of course, be invented independently in two separate cultures, entirely without diffusion or borrowing.

change may be the nature of their discipline, which views culture over tens of thousands of years. Trends leading to major social change may leap more readily to view from this telescopic perspective than when viewed from the microscopic perspective of ethnographers, who typically witness change over a much shorter period of time.

Among cultural anthropoloists, Sahlins and Service have contributed significantly to the modern school of evolutionary theory championed by Leslie White. Their collection of essays entitled *Evolution and Culture* (1960) explicitly challenges ethnographers to apply three laws of general cultural advance to the study of modern societies. Of these three laws, two deal with the origins of quantum social change (the Principle of Stabilization and the Law of Evolutionary Potential), while the third treats change as a function of culture contact (the Law of Cultural Domination). Although Sahlins and Service's book is required reading for many undergraduates, subsequent generations of fieldworkers have not taken up the challenge; for the most part, they apply only the Law of Cultural Domination in their exploration of social change.

B. DARWINIAN BIASES

One factor that may have contributed to the failure of ethnographers to consider processes which account for the emergence of cultural innovation is the presence of certain biases inherent in the Darwinian perspective. Darwinian selection has been the dominant paradigm in evolutionary biology for more than 100 years. Darwin's own discussion of selection theory and the interpretation of this theory by evolutionists that followed included some very distinctive notions regarding the tempo, mode, and locus of evolutionary change — notions which have had an important influence on evolutionary anthropology.

1. TEMPO OF EVOLUTION

Darwinian selection has been viewed by many students of evolution as a gradual, step-by-step process linking ancestors and descendents through an unbroken chain of transitional, intermediate forms (see Eldredge & Gould, 1972). According to this viewpoint, evolution is a "stately unfolding" of change over time; small, incremental steps of change lead imperceptibly to new forms of life. All parts of the life system slowly adjust to modified conditions, and sudden leaps or saltations are not expected.

Anthropologists have also expected cultural change to occur in a gradual fashion. Indeed, "evolutionary" change in the social sciences has come to mean gradual, incremental change and is contrasted with "revolutions" during which rapid, disruptive shocks cause serious social and economic imbalance. Such rapid shocks are viewed as aberrant phenomena and are not typically the subject of mainstream research. In the process of focusing upon gradual, incremental change, anthropologists may have inadvertently missed some evidence that supports quantum social transformation.

2. MODE OF EVOLUTION

Darwinian theory asserts the primacy of selection as the creative agent of change (Gould, 1982). Selective forces operate on the basis of relative "adaptive fits" between organisms and specific ecological contexts. From such a selectionist paradigm, the small-scale adjustments or "adaptive strategies" of living societies in response to environmental change would be identical with processes generating macrolevel transformations to new grades of organization. In the cultural application of this paradigm, a study of cult formation as an "adaptive" response to economic domination by a foreign power or an investigation of "adaptive" social structure shifts associated with the forced transition from food-gathering to market economies would be treated as theoretical examples of cultural evolution.

Yet while natural selection and adaptive shifts in environmental pressure are important parts of cultural evolution, other forces may be at work in the emergence of true cultural innovation. In macrolevel change, selection may exert its creative influence in concert with both stochastic processes and dynamic relationships inherent within sociocultural systems. These additional forces may be sufficiently different from those of gradual adaptive change to warrant the hypothesis that new quantum developments cannot be reduced to the action of microlevel selection or to adaptive responses to environmental change.

3. LOCUS OF EVOLUTION

Darwin's work emphasized gradual change in large, interbreeding populations that occupy contiguous geographical space. The focus was upon the *entire* species and its change *as* a species over time. Darwin did not select certain parts of species as the lead agents of change nor did he look to certain parts of a species' geographical range as the primary site of change. Evolutionary change swept up all interlocked demes in its path.

Anthropologists also perceive intact cultures as the primary units of evolution and search for patterns of change which may originate anywhere within these units. If certain parts of a culture fail to change, this failure is viewed as a "maladaptive" phenomenon (Turnbull, 1972). If the cutting edge of change regularly originates in specific parts of the system, then a holistic focus on total patterns may filter out significant transformation events.

C. PHILOSOPHICAL BIASES

The choices made by evolutionary ethnographers in selecting research topics and their focus on change as a consequence of culture contact may also be influenced by philosophical biases in modern Western thought. Gould and Eldredge (1977) noted this:

> The general preference that so many of us hold for gradualism is a metaphysical stance embedded in the modern history of Western cultures: It is not a high-order empirical observation, induced from the objective study of nature. The famous statement attributed to Linnaeus — *natura non facit saltum* (nature does not make leaps) — may reflect some biological knowledge, but it also represents the translation into biology of the order, harmony and continuity that European rulers hoped to maintain in a society already assaulted by calls for fundamental social change. (p. 145)

Furthermore, evolutionary theory was reintroduced into the discipline in the late 1940s and early 1950s, a period during which anthropologists were sensitive to the links between nineteenth-century evolutionary anthropology (e.g., the work of Lewis Henry Morgan) and the writings of Marx and Engels. In the McCarthyist era of the early 1950s, evolutionists might have unconsciously (or consciously) chosen the comparatively safer course of describing systematic relationships within cultures at varying grades of advance rather than focusing upon the forces which drive evolution from one stage to another. The latter approach might well have led to considerable discomfort for scholars, since the official state philosophy of the Soviet Union was (and is) founded upon "dialectical materialism" — a theory of quantum social transformation that seeks the motive force of change within systemic relationships.

III. Paradigm Shift: The Punctuated Equilibria Model

> *The importance of peripheral isolates lies in their small size and the alien environment beyond the species border that they inhabit — for only here are selective pressures strong enough and the inertia of large numbers sufficiently reduced to produce the "genetic revolution" that overcomes homeostasis.*
>
> [Eldredge & Gould, 1972, p. 114]

In his book *On the Origin of Species by Means of Natural Selection,* Darwin noted that new species can arise only as the result of two processes: (1) phyletic evolution, whereby a total population is transformed to a new state and (2) speciation, in which an ancestral lineage splits into more than one descendent line. However, Darwin may have blurred the distinction between these processes in much of his own work by holding that speciation and phyletic evolution both occur as the result of slow, gradual adjustments of populations in contiguous geographic regions (Mayr, 1959).

Darwin's gradualistic vision of lineage-splitting shares certain features with the sympatric model of speciation, a model which has not been the preferred view of modern population genetics (Eldredge & Gould, 1972).[2] Most contemporary biologists and geneticists favor the allopatric model of speciation. In the allopatric model, subpopulations "bud off" the main ancestral species and enter new and frequently marginal geographic regions. The establishment of reproductive barriers between the main population and the "spin-off" groups, together with the pressure of different selective forces operating in frontier environments, creates conditions favorable to the emergence of distinctive gene pools and eventually to the formation of new species.

Since 1970 some paleontologists have begun to question the Darwinian conception of evolution as a gradual process and have advanced the model of punctuated equilibria to explain some perplexing "anomalies" in the fossil record. Eldredge and Gould have suggested that the famous "gaps" in the fossil record may not be the result of imperfect preservation of prehistoric life forms but may reflect the actual process by which most evolution has taken place (Eldredge, 1979; Eldredge and Gould, 1972; Gould and Eldredge, 1977). According to Eldredge and Gould, proper emphasis upon the process of speciation over the past 3 billion years generates a new paradigm of evolutionary change.

The punctuated equilibria model holds that most evolutionary change is concentrated in very rapid spurts of speciation, a process occurring most frequently in small, peripheral populations existing at the geographic margins of habitation for the group in question. According to this paradigm (which draws some of its features from the allopatric model of speciation), the main body of a population will remain genetically stable over long periods of time because of the homogenizing forces of gene flow and the operation of homeostatic mechanisms in developmental and genetic systems (Gould, 1982). The main population will experience minor fluctuations in gene frequency but will not demonstrate the long-term directional change associated with speciation.

---

[2] Mayr (1963) notes that the sympatric model of speciation is actually pre-Darwinian. This model holds that an interbreeding population will develop isolating mechanisms *within* a single geographic region as the result of ecological forces. The sympatric view may be contrasted with the geographic, or allopatric, model of speciation. This latter model holds that "a population, which is geographically isolated from its parental species, acquires during this period of isolation characters which promote or guarantee reproductive isolation when the external barriers break down" (Mayr, 1942, p. 155).

Genetic stability of large ancestral populations is usually attributed to one or both of the following mechanisms:

1. Gene flow among interbreeding demes, which exerts a homogenizing influence "to counteract local ecotypic adaptation by breaking up well-integrated gene complexes" that might otherwise tend to form new species (Mayr, 1963); and
2. Developmental and genetic homeostasis, or self-regulation, in which natural selection acts to favor heterozygotes rather than extreme genetic types (Lerner, 1954; see Gould, 1982).

Developmental homeostasis (or ontogenetic self-regulation) occurs because heterozygotes possess a greater ability to stay within the range of canalized development; genetic homeostasis means that populations with a larger number of heterozygotes will display a greater overall reproductive fitness.

The locus of change in the punctuated equilibria model is the small, isolated subpopulation which "buds off" the main ancestral body to form a deme at the margins of the ancestral species' geographic region. Peripheral isolates form as the result of "population push" from the optimal environment inhabited by the ancestral group and move into a variety of suboptimal microenvironments. The spin-off population is genetically variable but small enough to constitute a unique nonrepresentative sample of the total ancestral gene pool. The advantages of a small, unique gene pool reside in the heightened possibility of successful new genetic recombinations and the ability to increase the frequency of a favorable gene very rapidly. The isolate population carries with it most of the genetic features that may eventually become hallmarks of a new species status, although these features may exist in very low frequency at the outset.

Genetic isolation of the spin-off group must persist until enough change has taken place to ensure that gene flow will not occur between the isolate and the ancestral species. Genetic isolation, and the reduced genetic variability of the isolate, disrupts the homeostatic equilibrium which prevented speciation in the ancestral population. It is the unique combination of genes, freed from homeostatic restraint and within the context of a stressful new environment, that permits speciation to occur.

Isolate formation may be viewed as the establishment of genetic experiments. Certain ancestral populations will continually spin off, or peripheralize, isolates, with each possessing a unique gene pool and entering a relatively new microenvironment. A number of futures are possible for any given isolate, including extinction, resorption into the main body, survival at a low level of density, and successful speciation followed by increasing density and range. Stochastic processes determine which few unique gene pools will succeed. Most experiments will surely fail, and it will be difficult to predict success. Where gene pools are well matched to the demands and opportunities provided in marginal microenvironments, speciation will occur very rapidly.

The theory of punctuated equilibria focuses closely upon the process of evolutionary transformation. Why species do or do not emerge, the mode by which speciation takes place, the location of a locus or cutting edge of genetic change within a population — these are the key questions addressed by the punctualist model. This approach sharpens the focus of research upon specific *loci* of change and specific *modes* of change rather than pointing to all living populations and all forms of adaptation as probable sites of and processes critical to evolution. Such a sharpening of focus may improve the testability of evolutionary hypothesis and help to satisfy some of the objections which have been raised concerning the "nonfalsifiability" of Darwinian hypotheses.

IV. A New Paradigm of Sociocultural Innovation

A. THE CONTRIBUTION OF SAHLINS AND SERVICE

> *Evolution is usually diagrammed as a tree with the trunk representing the "main line" of progress, as though the advance from the highest form at one stage to the new form at the next were phylogenetically continuous. It is an inappropriate and misleading picture, however, and the recognition of the discontinuity of advance is an important element in the understanding of some major problems.*
>
> [Sahlins & Service, 1960, p. 97]

Sahlins and Service's book, *Evolution and Culture* (1960), is an important contribution to the theory of quantum social change. This treatise identifies two key rules governing change in cultural systems that foreshadow the central premises of punctuated equilibria introduced by Eldredge and Gould nearly a dozen years later. Sahlins and Service call these rules the *Principle of Stabilization* and the *Law of Evolutionary Potential.* These rules represent a significant break from Darwinian tradition in cultural studies and suggest a different mode, locus, and tempo of evolutionary change.

The Principle of Stabilization asserts that "a culture at rest tends to remain at rest" (Sahlins & Service, 1960, p. 54). The authors note the following:

A culture is an integrated organization of technology, social structure and philosophy adjusted to the life problems posed by its natural habitat and nearby and often competing cultures. The process of adjustment or adaptation, however, inevitably involves specialization, a one-sided development that tends to preclude the possibility of change in other directions, to impede adaptive response to changed environmental conditions. While adaptation is creative, it is also self-limiting. The tendency toward stability is, empirically speaking, thoroughly familiar to anthropologists. The his-

> toric, archaeological, and ethnographic records attest to numerous instances of the
> persistence, "survival," or "inertia" of cultural traditions, particular cultures and
> elements or traits. (pp. 53–54)

This corollary of the Principle of Stabilization is well demonstrated by the numerous field studies of "adaptive" evolution mentioned earlier in which the successful adjustment of cultural components to external pressure without development of true technological or social innovations is documented. Sahlins and Service themselves suggest several examples of the operation of this principle, including the stability of food procurement techniques at the end of the Pleistocene in Europe, the adaptation of the Siberian Yakut to northeastward migration, and the elaboration of wampum use by the Iroquois to maintain confederacy organization.

The Principle of Stabilization may represent an original anthropological contribution to evolutionary theory. The notion that central populations tend to remain genetically stable over long periods of time does not appear to have been a prominent concept in evolutionary biology in the late 1950s nor did the authors borrow this perspective from the then-embryonic field of systems theory. Rather, it appears that Sahlins and Service developed this principle as a result of observing records of human behavior.

Sahlins and Service moved beyond recognition of cultural stability to define the locus of true cultural innovation. The Law of Evolutionary Potential states:

> The more specialized and adapted a form in a given evolutionary stage, the smaller is
> its potential for passing to the next stage. Another way of putting it which is more
> succinct and more in conformity with preceding chapters is: Specific evolutionary
> progress is inversely related to general evolutionary potential. (p. 97)

Several important corollaries of the Law of Evolutionary Potential are identified by Sahlins and Service. These include:

1. *The local discontinuity of progress.* As the result of stability, ancestral lines will not typically give rise to new forms of organization. The emergence of new grades of development is more likely to occur in areas that are removed or separated from the ancestral type.
2. *The privilege of backwardness.* Cultural innovation is more likely to be created or adopted by societies or groups that are not as energetically advanced as the dominant cultural form of the time. Such "backward" groups may have more to gain from the adoption of new social or economic structures and less vested interest in the current dominant structure.
3. *The direct relationship between rate of change and extent of discontinuity.* The more rapid the process of change, the more distance will separate dominant ancestral populations from those less dominant groups engaged in innovation.

The operation of these corollary principles is described in a number of fascinating examples, including the occurrence of a socialist revolution in Russia, the development of a cult of youth in the People's Republic of China, and the rapid development of a strong industrial economy in the United States.

The Principle of Stabilization and the Law of Evolutionary Potential closely parallel basic concepts in the punctuated equilibria model developed by Eldredge and Gould. The Principle of Stabilization is similar to the punctualist tenet of genetic homeostasis in central populations. "The norm for a species during the heyday of its existence as a large population is morphological stasis, minor non-directional fluctuation in form, or minor directional change bearing no relationship to pathways or alteration in subsequent daughter species" (Eldredge & Gould, 1972, p. 117). While Sahlins and Service did not identify specific mechanisms of social homeostasis, the punctuated equilibria model provides some useful insights into such causes and mechanisms (punctualist contributions in this area were discussed in Section III).

Sahlins and Service's Law of Evolutionary Potential also bears some resemblance to the punctualist notion that speciation occurs in small subpopulations which are isolated from the main ancestral body. However, in their analysis of those cultural loci holding most potential for change, Sahlins and Service used the criterion of specialization, or narrow adaptation to a particular niche, as a marker of low innovative potential. Sahlins and Service argue that narrow adaptation to a specialized niche would militate against change that might allow the exploitation of a new resource base, while the generalized ability to exploit a variety of resources might permit creative new economic techniques to be developed and adopted. This essentially Darwinian argument emphasizes relative "adaptive fit" to environmental conditions as the most important factor contributing to evolutionary success. While this adaptive scenario may indeed emerge as an important consideration in particular cases of culture change, we will argue here that the distinction between specialized and generalized adaptive strategies may not be the single most critical marker denoting potential for quantum transformation.

B. THE PUNCTUALIST MODEL OF CULTURAL EVOLUTION

[The] underlying "rules" which seem to govern the behavior of entities so diverse as a digital computer, living organism, or a sociocultural system are more than simple analogies. Delineating the similarities among these different kinds of systems is . . . a form of generalizing or of abstracting basic realities.

[Watson et al., 1971, p. 65]

Important parallels between evolutionary processes in biology and cultures have long been noted (Huxley, 1956; Sahlins & Service, 1960). Some writers suggest that these similarities may actually be homologies (Roosevelt, 1910). Culture is, after all, a biobehavioral extension of the earth's dominant life form and thus may be subject to the influence of certain basic developmental laws that affect all life as we know it. Indeed, general systems theorists examine behavior and structure at all levels of complexity for underlying systemic principles. The ubiquitous application of certain mathematically isomorphic models (such as the second-order differential equation system) across a wide range of disciplines (from physics to physiology and ecology) attests to the existence of underlying unities (Rappaport, 1972). Although the existence of isomorphisms in biological and cultural phenomena have been noted (Weinberg & Weinberg, 1974), the early age of general systems theory as an analytic tool suggests that it may be more productive to explore both the positive and negative aspects of such analogies (Bunge, 1981) rather than attempt to force phenomena into the same mold.

Within the restrictions that must govern application of all analogue models, the concept of punctuated equilibria may serve as a framework for developing a new paradigm of sociocultural evolution. This paradigm draws not upon gradualism and "adaptive fit" but utilizes concepts derived primarily from population genetics and from systems theory to explain homeostasis and its functioning in groups of varying size and structure. These concepts may provide a more robust analytic tool in the explanation and prediction of modern social change. The major features of a new punctualist paradigm of cultural evolution are described in the remainder of this section.

Formation of Peripheral Isolates. The cutting edge of cultural evolution may be forged through the action of social subsets, or small organizational forms, which have been "peripheralized" through the "push" of forces within a larger, more dominant organizational system. Peripheral isolates in human cultures may be formed as economic, social, and political pressures within the optimal environment generate sufficient motive force to trigger "out-migration" and exploration of "marginal environments." Such "environments" are not simply spatially defined but may include exploration in the worlds of new ideas, technologies, and sociocultural lifestyles. The most important consideration here is that the isolate group should exist in an environment at the boundary of the dominant group's sphere of influence that is less favorable than that of the dominant group. For human societies isolation may, therefore, be geographic (e.g., colonization of a frontier), economic (e.g., developing nations in the world market system), or philosophic (e.g., sectarian religious or political ideologies).

The initiation of human peripheralization probably involves forces of "motivational pull" as well as "push." Indeed, a most interesting exploration would center upon the common characteristics of cultural innovators that form the leadership of such isolates. For example, it has long been noted that frontier-opening human populations frequently contain a disproportionate number of "super-fit" individuals (i.e., individuals with greater-than-average physical stamina or intellectual capabilities) (Tanner, 1978). A partial cause of this nonrepresentative sample may be that the frontier experience attracts individuals with certain physical and mental characteristics. In the optimal environment, these individuals may not have received adequate challenge or stimulus or they may have experienced sociopsychological stress from actions associated with the display of their physical and/or mental prowess.

It is clear that the individuals who form the core of peripheral isolates manage somehow to escape the norms of canalization which restrict the behavior of their less-adventurous colleagues. The "sociological deviance" of such individuals must, therefore, be considered in a new light; from a punctualist perspective, such deviants may be an indispensable ingredient in the innovation formula and attempts to normalize their behavior probably reflect the force of social inertia.

Size and Variability of Peripheral Isolates. From a punctualist perspective, innovating peripheral groups in human populations are expected to fall within a certain size range — large enough to provide the "critical mass" of knowledge and resources necessary to maneuver in the suboptimal region, but small enough to permit the many advantages associated with flexibility (i.e., rapid rearrangement and/or increase of advantageous components or activities). The innovating human isolate should derive from its parent group most of the basic knowledge, concepts, skills, and resources requisite for major new forms of organization or technology. The isolate group — because of small size, random factors, and hostile environmental pressure — will then recombine these concepts and resources in totally new ways, triggering quantum social change.

Isolation of the Peripheral Population. In human societies, the model predicts that it will be necessary for isolate groups to maintain a separate identity from the parental population until major innovation is well consolidated and has proved successful (i.e., the isolate group has proved capable of self-maintenance and is more productive and efficient than the ancestral form). The punctualist model predicts that too close an interaction between the isolate form and its ancestor before quantum change has been stabilized will lead to resorption and a dampening of innovative action.

Buffering of Subpopulations versus Exposure of Peripheral Groups.
Large, dominant organizations will possess a varied array of strategic resources that will tend to shelter all of the subgroups operating within the
primary system. Frontier-opening isolates, however, will be cut off from
such protection and will have to stand or fall on the basis of their inherent
abilities. The direct exposure of peripheral groups to harsh external conditions without benefit of extensive buffering mechanisms means that most
human peripherals will not be able to withstand isolation for periods long
enough to consolidate real change. Most human peripheral groups will fail
to survive in the suboptimal zone and will either disintegrate, be resorbed
into the main population, or continue to struggle along at very low densities.

Stochastic Nature of Success. Dominant sociocultural systems will inadvertently generate a continual flow of isolate-forming subgroups. Each
isolate will constitute a unique "social experiment" and most of these will
ultimately fail to achieve lasting change. Success may not be predicted on
the basis of forecasting models which consider only a few variables. The
future success of such groups will depend upon an extremely complex interplay of individual attributes (especially the knowledge-related characteristics
of the participants), external forces, and random factors. While the mode
and locus of change may be predictable, the future of any particular isolate
certainly cannot be predicted given the current state of knowledge in the
social sciences.

Rapid Change in Suboptimal Areas. The model predicts that quantum
cultural shifts will occur in very short periods of time, somewhat akin to the
"qualitative leaps" predicted by Hegelian dialetics or the "socialist revolution" yearned for by Marxist–Leninists. Once stasis has been disrupted and
a new homeostatic balance has been achieved by the isolate, it will be impossible to stuff the quantum change back into its cultural womb. A successful
innovation will assert itself and, where human culture is concerned, the true
innovation is very likely to change the rest of the world as well. The ability of
human innovation to permeate and transform older systems is one of the
most important distinctions between social change and genetic change associated with speciation.

V. Examples of Punctuated Equilibria
in Techno-economic Change

An important tradition in evolutionary anthropology has been a theoretical and empirical emphasis upon techno-economic components of cultural
systems. Such components were viewed by Leslie White (1949) and Julian

Steward (1955) as critical subsystems linking human populations to their environments through energy and resource flow and serving as the "base" for other system components that organize and rationalize the techno-economic mode of production. Too frequently, perhaps, the evolutionary school has concentrated exclusively upon the role of techno-economic subsystems as the motive force driving change throughout cultural systems without paying proper attention to the positive feedback cycles that may originate within socio-organizational or ideological subsystems and serve as an "initial kick" to major systemic change. For example, the emergence of state-level societies does indeed require a minimal food production base, but the forces that stimulate state formation may be closely tied to acts of mutual aggression and the establishment of political alliances between groups in circumscribed environmental regions (Carneiro, 1970). A new form of techno-economic base is not necessarily required for the support of state-level civilizations, although the formation of states often has a profound impact on food production systems.

The systems approach to cultural anthropology provides a framework that demonstrates the importance of relationships between cultural components, permitting escape from the sterile notion of material determinism and enabling researchers to analyze dynamic interactions of techno-economics, social structure, and value subsystems, all of which must participate in quantum change to new grades of organization. Within the framework of a systems approach, techno-economic subsystems may continue to serve as a useful focus of investigation. While such subsystems are not the sole determinants or markers of new organizational grades, change within the techno-economic base has set the stage for major cultural advance throughout the history of humanity, and certain forms of social organization are quite impossible without an adequate energetic foundation (e.g., industrial capitalism could not arise de novo in a hunting and gathering society).

Two cases of techno-economic change that illustrate some of the primary features of a punctuated equilibria paradigm will be presented in the next section. This discussion is not meant to serve as a test of the model. Rather, the purpose of presenting these examples is to demonstrate the potential applicability of the punctualist paradigm.

A. ORIGIN OF FOOD PRODUCTION IN THE NEAR EAST

The transition from hunting and gathering to food production was a profound techno-economic transformation in the development of human culture. This revolutionary change, which occurred independently in the

Old and New Worlds around 10,000 B.C. and 4000 B.C., respectively, provided the foundation for stable, sedentary communities, for substantial increases in population density, and for complex forms of sociocultural organization.

Archaeologists have concentrated an enormous wealth of physical and intellectual resources on discovering the processes by which agriculture emerged. A prominent hypothesis advanced by Kent V. Flannery (1969) to explain plant production shares many features with the punctuated equilibria model. Although the archaeological evidence is not entirely conclusive, Flannery's hypothesis is consistent with the majority of archaeological data now available.

Flannery was influenced by the work of Lewis Binford (1968), who argued that causes cited earlier as the impetus for agricultural innovation (e.g., Childe's use of climatic change, 1937/1951) were inadequate and unsupported. Binford was particularly unimpressed with Braidwood's notion (1975) that domestication began in the Hilly Flanks region of the Fertile Crescent where potential domesticates already existed. Although there is evidence that hunting and gathering groups did exploit the rich environments in which future domesticates grew wild (and indeed these people gathered wild cereal grains and probably understood seed germination), Binford asserted that populations would not be likely to adopt a new economic system in the absence of severe pressure to do so. Rather, the hunters and gatherers in optimal ecological zones would maintain their population densities at carrying capacity, thus relieving the pressure to adopt new economic modes, by "budding off" daughter populations to surrounding areas. Binford suggested that the origins of agriculture might be found in the marginal environments invaded by the daughter groups that were pushed out of the optimal zone.

Flannery (1969) built upon Binford's arguments, noting that extant hunting and gathering populations can easily extract sufficient calories from wild foods "without even working very hard." Even the !Kung of the Kalahari Desert may be able to obtain an average of 2100 calories per person per day through the efforts of an average 3-day workweek (Lee, 1968). Flannery cited the field experiment performed by Harlan and Zohary (1966) in which Harlan, equipped with only a flint-blade sickle, was able in 1 hour to gather 1 kg of edible wheat from wild stands in the Hilly Flanks. Flannery judged that during the 3-week period in which wheat must be harvested in the Hilly Flanks a family of experienced gatherers could collect an entire year's supply of cereal. Such abundance, argued Flannery, would generate tremendous inertial forces that would preclude agricultural innovation in this rich and diverse environment.

On the other hand, the Flanks are bordered by less favorable environments that could receive overflow population from the optimal zone. Flannery contended that it was in the surrounding marginal areas, lacking wild forms of grain, that human populations first began the regular cultivation of plants and domestication of animals.

According to Flannery, population pressure and varying resource availability in the preferred environment would propel groups of hunters and gatherers into the marginal regions. When climatic conditions were less favorable, population pressure would be strong and continuous, causing bands to flow from the optimal core area into peripheral zones. Increasing population density in the marginal environment would be a strong incentive to experiment with new production techniques. Groups existing under such conditions and possessing knowledge of wild cereals and their domesticable properties would have attempted to recreate the lush stands of wheat growing wild on the Hilly Flanks by sowing seeds obtained from the ancestral population (Flannery, 1965).

Once such experiments proved successful, selection would favor groups that expanded cultivation and concentrated energy on sowing, tending, and reaping cereal grain crops. Flannery (1969, 1973) suggests that, during this period of increasing cultivation, humans themselves became selective agents for rapid genetic changes in the cereals (e.g., by selecting grains with tough rachises and brittle husks, both necessary characteristics of high-yield domesticated cereal crops). Removal of these plants from their native environment also subjected them to new selective pressures and resulted in genetic changes such as polyploidy, thereby producing the domesticated cereal types of modern times. These genetic changes increased the yield of grain crops, establishing agriculture as a superior techno-economic system and contributing to its rapid adoption by other groups and diffusion to contiguous regions.

The parallels between Flannery's hypothesis and the punctuated equilibria model are striking. These parallels include:

1. Systemic inertia of ancestral populations;
2. Population "push" leading to the spin-off of peripheral isolates into marginal zones;
3. Quantum change originating in the marginal area;
4. Peripheral group carrying all basic components necessary for development of a new economic system; and
5. Very rapid change and re-establishment of homeostasis at a new level of organization.

This example of techno-economic transformation, which developed under the influence of Flannery's system-thinking, demonstrates the value of evolutionary vision that reaches beyond phyletic gradualism. Innovation

was not bound within the confines of a slow, adaptive response to environmental change (see Childe, 1937/1951) nor did change occur in the region of
surplus resources where Braidwood (1975) logically expected it. While
population pressure in the central zone was an important environmental
stimulus to innovation, the unexpected genetic changes which humans
wrought in the cereal grains were probably an equally important, if not the
critical, trigger to a massive positive feedback cycle that continually re-
warded increasing investments in agricultural activity. Thus a complex
interplay of population dynamics, environmental conditions, human creative vision, and random factors combined to generate a qualitative economic shift that changed the history of life on earth.

There are some important differences between this example of human
innovation and the events which trigger speciation, but even these differences only serve to highlight other parallels. For example, genetic change is
conditioned by the new, unique combination of genes in subgroups invading
marginal zones, while quantum change in culture will depend upon the
availability and utilization of knowledge-related attributes. Yet, as in the
case of speciation, the hunter–gatherer bands invading suboptimal zones
were "preadapted" to innovation. The assumption of preadaptation is
derived from data available on extant hunter–gatherer populations; such
groups typically understand that seeds generate plants, and they may even
sow some seeds in order to make stands more accessible to human collection
(Flannery, 1965). In fact, there is evidence (Hole & Flannery, 1967; Solecki,
1964) that preagricultural people already possessed some of the technology
requisite for cereal grain consumption (e.g., grinding stones and storage pits).

The idea that wild plants grow from seeds which can be sown to produce
more plants was a discovery whose precise origin among hunting and gathering people will probably never be determined. Like genetic mutations, such
ideas probably arose repeatedly and in many different places. The ultimate
utility of such an idea was conditioned by the existence of environmental
"pull," just as a new mutation will only confer selective advantage under
special environmental conditions.

Future archaeological research in the Near East might test the validity of a
number of predictions generated from the punctualist framework. For
example, the punctualist perspective predicts:

1. The initially smaller size of marginal bands invading peripheral zones
   compared to typical hunting and gathering bands in the Hilly Flanks;
2. Weaker links (e.g., trade) between peripheral bands and the ancestral
   group than between bands within the ancestral population; and
3. An array of alternative futures for spin-off populations, including resorption, or continuing marginal survival in the suboptimal zone with
   a hunter–gatherer economy.

Archaeologists themselves can formulate stronger and more appropriate hypotheses for testing on the basis of the punctualist paradigm. Transformation in human societies is dependent upon knowledge generation and knowledge reproduction subsystems (i.e., the creation of new ideas, the original synthesis of knowledge, new applications of knowledge, dissemination of information). Although such subsystems do deposit remains in the fossil record (technologies, settlement patterns, population densities), it is evident that the fullest appreciation of knowledge-related processes involved in quantum change will only be gained by field observation of extant human societies. Therefore, the next example focuses upon contemporary techno-economic change.

B. TECHNOLOGICAL INNOVATION IN MODERN INDUSTRY

I believe quite simply that the small company of the future will be as much a research organization as it is a manufacturing company, and that this new kind of company is the frontier for the next generation.

[Edwin Land, founder of Polaroid, 1946; see Jacobs, 1982, p. 35]

Technological innovation is a primary motive force driving modern industrial economies (Kelly & Krantzberg, 1978). Industrial innovation — including the generation of new ideas, the development of prototype models, and the commercialization of new products and processes — is the force that generates productivity improvement, holds down costs, and stimulates market demand. All of these effects contribute to economic growth and the creation of new jobs.

In the United States, technological innovation is both a serious economic problem and an exciting socioeconomic phenomenon. On the one hand, sluggish productivity growth in several basic manufacturing industries (e.g., steel, motor vehicles, textiles) has riveted the attention of federal policy-makers on the failure of these industries to adopt existing technological innovations and develop new technology-based products. These basic industries are virtually stagnant, creating very few new jobs and frequently failing to record a profit. On the other hand, many observers of modern American life have proclaimed that the nation has entered an era of technological revolution (Boulding, 1964; Drucker, 1970; Toffler, 1970). This claim is based upon burgeoning technological change in the areas of telecommunications, information processing, artificial intelligence, and genetic engineering. The so-called high technology industries operating in these fields display strong growth profiles; such industries are vigorous competitors in the international market, they show impressive performance in the areas of employment and return on investment, and they are aggressively developing and commercializing ingenious products that are already altering the nature of our entire society (Joint Economic Committee, 1982).

While technological change has always been an essential component in the process of industrial development, it appears that the current technological revolution may be driven by a new type of company. These new advanced technology firms are *science-based.* Science-based firms are distinct from firms in more traditional industries in a number of ways. First, they place a high priority upon research and development (R&D) and invest a disproportionately large percentage of their revenue in such activities relative to other areas such as marketing and production (Jacobs, 1982). Science-based companies employ large numbers of Ph.D.s and skilled technicians; in fact, scientists and inventors are frequently founders and owners of such firms. Secondly, recent investigations (Freeman, 1974; Tornatzky et al., 1982) suggest that such firms display higher research productivity than non-science-based firms with large in-house research and development operations (e.g., they generate a larger number of patents per dollar of research and development expenditure). Such firms also have been found to contribute a disproportionately large share of seminal inventions (Hamberg, 1964; Jewkes, Sawers, & Stillerman, 1958; U.S. Dept. of Commerce, 1967).

Science-based firms also differ from traditional industries in their use of a business strategy that uniquely combines "technology push" and "market pull" considerations. Naturally, the scientific entrepreneurs owning and managing these companies are motivated to maximize return on investment, but they are usually seeking something more than profit alone. Frequently, they have been personally involved in the development of a radically new product concept and their marketing strategy is a means of realizing their vision that this new concept will succeed and may even "change the face of the earth" (Jacobs, 1982). Partly as a result of this vision and drive, small science-based companies often take risks that other businesses will not dare. In many cases, these risks have paid off and small, scientifically oriented firms have been responsible for major contributions in the establishment of whole new industries in fields ranging from radio and chemicals to office copiers to semiconductors and amorphous materials (Freeman, 1971; Jacobs, 1982; Shimshoni, 1966, 1970).

The emergence of a new type of industrial organization and the important impact of these firms on modern socioeconomic structure and the quality of life may indeed warrant the view that science-based firms constitute a significant cultural innovation. Although we stand only upon the threshold of the "technological revolution" and cannot foresee the ultimate effects of computer technology, artificial intelligence, and gene-splicing upon future generations of humanity, it is conceivable that in retrospect the science-based industrial organization will be judged a critical agent of quantum transformation in the economy, social structure, and value systems of modern culture. Such speculation is even more fascinating when the emergence of science-based firms is viewed from the perspective of a punctuated equilibria model of culture change. We will now describe the major features of a punctualist view of technological innovation.

Technological Inertia in the Large Company. Homeostatic forces in large, mature firms, even those with substantial in-house R&D operations, may prevent such organizations from developing and exploiting radical new product concepts (Tornatzky et al., 1982). Recent investigations show that large firms typically will not commercialize a product if it has only a narrow, specialized market (Freeman, 1974; Jacobs, 1982). Such companies require the lure of large markets to justify R&D expenditures, so that a radical new technology with profound potential but a small initial market niche will not meet quarterly "bottom line" objectives and will be ignored by company decision makers. In fact, large companies may actually suppress their own R&D results or buy and sequester the rights to new products developed elsewhere in order to ensure that the product does not reach the marketplace (Freeman, 1974).

These considerations suggest that in large companies, even those that are technology-based, decision making is concentrated in the hands of individuals whose focus of concern is return on investment rather than technological innovation per se. Such organizations have enormous capital investments in existing product lines and more attention is probably paid to the profitability of these lines with an avoidance of new, high risk ventures (Freeman, 1974; Jacobs, 1982). While such companies typically employ scientists and possess sophisticated R&D facilities, the objective of such operations is more likely to be improvement of existing products rather than development of entirely new product concepts.

Formation of the Small Science-based Firm. Major technological advance may be forged by small groups of scientists who are both "pushed" and "pulled" out of large research organizations to enter unstable, high risk market niches. A substantial body of literature shows that many new advanced technology companies emerge as a result of spin-off from existing firms (Joint Economic Committee, 1982). In fact, entire new industries frequently begin in this way (Jacobs, 1982). Typically, scientists, engineers, and technicians working in a large industrial laboratory or in a number of different research establishments (e.g., a government laboratory or university) will develop an idea for a product which they are unable to commercialize within their employing organizations. Financial policy in their home operation or regulations governing entrepreneurial behavior of employees may "push" these inventors out of the place in which their idea was developed. "Motivational pull" is another factor contributing to the formation of such companies. The founding group of inventors often have "a solution in search of a problem" (i.e., they have developed an exciting new technology which as yet has no market). The inventors decide to leave their home company, lured by the personal profit that will accrue to discovery of an appropriate "problem" (i.e., market) for their product concept. Significantly, such individuals frequently have personality attributes that motivate them to achieve success through the development of unique ideas (Jacobs, 1982; Tornatzky et al., 1982).

In keeping with the punctualist paradigm, the founders of small science-based firms generally carry with them most of the basic technical knowledge and concepts needed to develop new products. It is also important to note that the "microenvironments" entered by these groups of entrepreneurs are generally hostile, being characterized by lack of critical resources (capital availability), predator stress (threat of acquisition by a large company), and strong competition from other groups of entrepreneurs.

Size and Variability of the Small Firm. Although the small science-based company must possess a "critical mass" of variable skills and resources (ideas, technical expertise, marketing skill, and venture capital), it must also remain small enough to realize a number of important advantages associated with small, "organically" (vs. mechanistically) functioning organizations (Kelly & Krantzberg, 1978; Tornatzky et al., 1982). Clearly, the number of owners and workers in small research-oriented companies is less than the number of such individuals in large firms and gives a nonrepresentative sample of employees in large manufacturing establishments. The high concentration of Ph.D.s, technicians, inventors, and entrepreneurs in science-based firms has been noted previously. Yet in spite of, or perhaps because of, the concentration of a few unique skills in a small number of highly motivated individuals, these companies display several significant advantages over traditional manufacturing establishments.

Recent investigations have shown that small firms are able to maneuver more quickly in markets in which technology is rapidly changing; they can make decisions, reorganize priorities, and change strategies more rapidly than large bureaucratized companies. Such advantages are likely to derive from the close and informal association of owners, scientists, and marketing experts that facilitates communication and permits the close coordination and rapid trial of new strategies necessary for tight maneuvering in turbulent markets. In fact, the physical proximity and personal relationships of scientists, inventors, and business people in the small firm effectively "couples" the typically diffuse stages of the innovation process (i.e., invention, prototype development, and marketing) and may significantly reduce the time normally required to move an idea from the formative stage to the marketplace.

Isolation, Exposure, and Success. The spin-off of inventors and entrepreneurs from industrial R&D departments, government laboratories, and universities causes a loss of protective buffering and more direct exposure and trial of the new group's capabilities. In large organizations, research groups are at least partially supported by general corporate funds that flow from revenue-generating operations. Short- or intermediate-range periods of low productivity for such groups do not usually result in their dissolution or in the firing of individuals. Large corporations are able to continue support for such research groups from the massive financial resources that are available. When a group of individuals leaves the corporate nest, however, they lose the protective financial buffering of a large financial empire and must survive or fail on the strength of their own skills in the marketplace. Immediate and direct exposure to the market effectively eliminates most small companies in a very short period of time — 90% of all small firms declare bankruptcy within their first four years of operation (Dun & Bradstreet, 1980).

Unlike peripheral demes, however, successful small firms may face an increasing danger of resorption or premature splitting. Large corporations are constantly scouting for aggressive young firms to acquire and for successful inventors and entrepreneurs to hire. Young science-based firms also experience splits of their own as individual partners decide to take the ideas and run. The peripheral field for advanced technology companies is thus tremendously unstable, and only a very few of these business "experiments" survive to become truly innovative forces.

Rapidity of Uptake. The punctuated equilibria model predicts that those few successful experiments in technological innovation will experience rapid growth and diffusion. New technologies may totally replace older ones within a generation or, even more spectacularly, whole new industries can be spun off from ancestral organizations (Jacobs, 1982). The success and expansion of human innovations will differ significantly from that of newly evolved species, which are prevented from sharing their unique genetic "discoveries" with ancestral populations by the action of isolating mechanisms. Cultural innovations are distinct because they are capable of rapid uptake by organizations other than the one giving them birth, including uptake by parental groups which may be totally transformed in the diffusion process.

VI. Conclusion

One of the virtues of the evolutionary view is that, more than any other perspective, it makes the concerns of cultural anthropology directly relevant to modern life in the future. As Tylor once put it, it is the "knowledge of man's course of life, from the remote past to the present," the study of the evolution of culture, that will enable us to forecast the future. The modern social sciences, now that they are almost exclusively nontemporal, or functional, have not been able to help us to judge the future and thus guide our actions and deliberations in relation to modern political problems. The past-as-related-to-the-future has long since been left to dogmatic Marxists or to the more respectable but nevertheless equally non-scientific "universal" historians, such as Brooks Adams, Spengler, Huntington, and Toynbee.

[Sahlins & Service, 1960, p. 94]

Anthropologists and other social scientists have tended to view change as a diffuse phenomenon, occurring continuously and affecting all components of sociocultural systems. Cultures have been viewed as gradually evolving through internal adjustment to structural strain, through imperfect and incomplete enculturation processes, or as a result of adaptation to external pressures and cross-cultural diffusion. In this chapter, we have drawn a distinction between the gradual fluctuations required to maintain homeostasis and the change that disrupts an equilibrium state and leads to the emergence of new forms of socioeconomic organization. The punctuated equilibria model views the peripheral isolate as a primary vector of quantum culture change. This paradigm has the power to organize and rationalize what would otherwise appear to be disparate facts about prehistoric and contemporary technological innovation processes.

Many questions are raised by this analysis. To what extent can it be formalized in mathematical or computerized form? In a later chapter (see Chapter 10, this volume), Zeigler and Baba develop a rationale for systems modeling and simulation of sociocultural research hypotheses. Modeling and simulation of isolate formation may enable social scientists to test the futures of social experiments conducted under varying conditions and determine the markers of evolutionary potential.

What type of research program must be formulated to adequately test the validity of the punctualist paradigm? Perhaps more so than for any other field of social investigation, quantum change requires a unified, interdisciplinary approach to data gathering and analysis. Archaeology is well suited to the investigation of major changes that have taken place in the past. The punctuated equilibria model can be applied to analyses of several prehistoric transformations, including the shift from prehominid economies to the hominid hunting mode, the development of agriculture in the New World, and the emergence of the nation-state. Historians can also contribute to this investigation through exploration of quantum change in the recent past (e.g., the development of modern industrial economy). In the study of current social transformation, anthropologists, linguists, sociologists, and psychologists may determine whether the punctualist paradigm is applicable to processes of change beyond the techno-economic domain. How do language shifts occur? How and where are major new forms of social organization prototyped and pioneered? Is the inventor–entrepreneurial personality a constant factor in social change? What other personality types or individual roles are critical in the process of social innovation?

What are the policy implications of punctuated equilibria? If large dominant systems are heavily committed to an established homeostatic equilibrium, then there will probably be inherent systemic biases against radical innovation. As culture evolves and dominant ancestors become larger and more powerful, systematic inertia may actually inhibit or prevent successful splitting of isolate groups. The dominant organizational form will certainly maintain structural–functional relations which heavily favor the present equilibrium state, creating pervasive, diffuse, and unconscious prejudice against the isolate and rendering its viability all the more doubtful. Subtle biases against innovation may be found in exploring the socioeconomic environment in which small science-based firms operate. Small companies are disproportionately affected by federal regulations and corporate tax structure, and they face notorious difficulties in obtaining start-up capital from traditional financial institutions. Corporate co-optation strategies are also growing in strength as large companies seek new ways to attract and hold entrepreneurs and inventors within their organizational domains (Robert S. First Conference, 1982). Finally, and perhaps most significantly, small R&D firms developing radical new technologies (e.g., in amorphous material or solar technologies) may find their most lucrative markets within developing Third World nations or other non-Western economies. This raises a serious question regarding the ability of mature industrial economies in the West to adopt and implement such innovative technologies.

If the punctuated equilibria model truly highlights a locus, mode, and tempo of change inherent in many life systems, then governmental policy modifications may not be able to significantly alter the pattern of inertia and spin-off described in the examples presented above. However, it is possible that ancestral systems will discover ways and means to infuse innovation and nudge inertial systems toward critical goals and objectives. Government can act to limit homeostatic mechanisms and to enhance countervailing tendencies toward innovation. Antimonopoly suits and affirmative action programs for small business may be examples of such tendencies toward disruption of homeostasis. Constitutionally guaranteed liberties also give license to sociocultural and ideological experimentation. Universal education enhances the potential of individuals to creatively exploit this license by increasing the likelihood that new ideas will be generated by the few and tolerated by the many.

At this point, we are surely not in a position to propose policies that will promote quantum advance based on validated models. However, even now the punctuated equilibria paradigm may sensitize social policymakers to issues and opportunities not perceived from the conventional Darwinian perspective. New species, once established, cannot be collapsed back into their ancestral population because of stringent genetic barriers. Cultures, however, have always been susceptible to penetration by new ideas, and we may yet learn to perform quantum leaps as humanity continues to make itself.

Acknowledgments

The authors wish to express their deepest appreciation to Linda Darga, at Children's Hospital in Detroit, Michigan, for her critical review and constructive commentary. Thanks are also due Patricia Schneider and Mary Mayberry for their expert assistance in the preparation of several manuscripts which culminated in this chapter.

References

Binford, L. R. Post-Pleistocene adaptations. In L. R. Binford & S. R. Binford (Eds.), *New perspectives in archeology.* Chicago: Aldine, 1968.
Braidwood, R. J. *Prehistoric men.* Glenview, Ill.: Scott, Foresman, 1975.
Boulding, K. E. *The meaning of the twenty-first century.* New York: Harper & Row, 1964.
Bunge, M. Analogy between systems. *International Journal of General Systems,* 1981, *7*(4), 221–224.
Carneiro, R. A theory of the origin of the state. *Science,* 1970, *169,* 733–738.
Childe, V. G. *Man makes himself.* New York: New American, 1951. (Originally published, 1937.)
Darwin, C. *On the origin of species by means of natural selection.* London: John Murray, 1959.
Drucker, P. K. *Technology, management and society.* New York: Harper & Row, 1970.
Dun & Bradstreet. *Quarterly Failure Report* (Dun's Statistical Review). First-Fourth Quarters, 1980.
Eldredge, N. Alternative approaches to evolutionary theory. *Bulletin of the Carnegie Museum of Natural History,* 1979, No. 13, 7–19.
Eldredge, N., & Gould, S. J. Punctuated equilibria: An alternative to phyletic gradualism. In T. M. Schopf (Ed.), *Models in paleobiology.* San Francisco: Freeman, Cooper, 1972.
Flannery, K. V. The ecology of early food production in Mesopotamia. *Science,* 1965, *147,* 1247–1256.

Flannery, K. V. Culture history vs. culture process: A debate in American archeology. *Scientific American,* 1967, *217*(2), 119–122.

Flannery, K. V. Origins and ecological effects of early domestication in Iran and the Near East. In P. J. Ucko & G. W. Dimbleby (Eds.), *The domestication and exploitation of plants and animals.* Chicago, Aldine, 1969.

Flannery, K. V. The origins of agriculture. *Annual Review of Anthropology,* 1973, *2,* 217–310.

Freeman, C. F. *The role of small firms in innovation in the United Kingdom since 1945.* (Report to the Bolton Committee of Inquiry on Small Firms, Research Report No. 6). London: HM Stationery Office, 1971.

Freeman, C. F. *The economics of industrial innovation.* Middlesex, England: Penguin, 1974.

Fried, M. Land tenure, geography and ecology in the contact of cultures. *American Journal of Economics and Sociology,* 1952, *11,* 391–412.

Fried, M. *The evolution of political society.* New York: Random House, 1967.

Gould, S. J., & Eldredge, N. Punctuated equilibria: The tempo and mode of evolution reconsidered. *Paleobiology,* 1977, *3*(2), 115–151.

Gould, S. J. Darwinism and the expansion of evolutionary theory. *Science,* 1982, *216,* 350–387.

Hamberg, D. Size of firm, oligopology and research: The evidence. *Canadian Journal of Economic and Political Science,* 1964, *30*(1), 62–75.

Harland, J., and Zohary, D. Distribution of wild wheats and barley. *Science,* 1966, *153,* 1004–1080.

Harris, M. *The rise of anthropological theory.* New York: Crowell, 1968.

Hole, F., & Flannery, K. V. The prehistory of southwestern Iran: A preliminary report. *Proceedings of the Prehistoric Society,* 1967, *33*(9), 147–206.

Huxley, J. S. *Evolution: The modern synthesis.* New York & London: Harper, 1943.

Huxley, J. S. Evolution, cultural and biological. In W. L. Thomas, Jr. (Ed.), *Current Anthropology.* Chicago: University of Chicago Press, 1956.

Jacobs, M. The physicist as entrepreneur. *Physics Today,* January, 1982, pp. 34–40.

Jewkes, J., Sawers, D., & Stillerman, R. *The sources of invention.* New York: Macmillan, 1958.

Joint Economic Committee of the United States Congress. *Location of high technology firms and regional economic development.* Washington, D.C.: U.S. Govt. Printing Office, 1982.

Kelly, P., & Krantzberg, M. *Technological innovation: A critical review of current knowledge.* San Francisco: San Francisco Press, 1978.

Lee, R. B. What hunters do for a living. In R. B. Lee & I. DeVore (Eds.), *Man the hunter.* Chicago: Aldine, 1968.

Lerner, I. M. *Genetic homeostasis.* Edinburgh: Oliver and Boyd, 1954.

Mayr, E. *Systematics and the origin of species.* New York: Columbia University Press, 1942.

Mayr, E. Isolation as an evolutionary factor. *Proceedings of the American philosophical society,* 1959, *103,* 221–230.

Mayr, E. *Animal species and evolution.* Cambridge, Mass.: Harvard University Press, 1963.

Mintz, S. Canamelar, the sub-culture of a rural sugar plantation proletariat. In J. Steward (Ed.), *The people of Puerto Rico.* Urbana: University of Illinois Press, 1956.

Murdock, G. P. Evolution in social organization. In *Evolution and anthropology: A centennial appraisal.* Washington, D.C.: The Anthropological Society of Washington, 1959.

Murphy, R., & Steward, J. Tappers and trappers: Parallel processes in acculturation. *Economic Development and Culture Change,* 1955, *4,* 335–355.

Rapoport, A. The uses of mathematical isomorphism in general systems theory. In G. J. Klir (Ed.), *Trends in general systems theory.* New York: Wiley, 1972.

Rappaport, R. A. *Pigs for the ancestors: Ritual in the ecology of a New Guinea people.* New Haven: Yale University Press, 1968.

Robert, S. First Conference on Technology Transfer and Innovation, 1982. In M. Hooker (Chair), Roundtable Session on Industry–University Research, Washington, D.C., Sept. 13–14, 1982.

Roosevelt, T. *Biological analogies in history.* New York: Oxford University Press, 1910.

Sahlins, M. D., & Service, E. R. *Evolution and culture.* Ann Arbor: University of Michigan Press, 1960.

Schoch, R. M. Letters to the editor. *Science,* 1982, *220,* 360.

Service, E. Indian–European relations in colonial Latin America. *American Anthropologist,* 1955, *51,* 411–425.

Service, E. *Primitive social organization.* New York: Random House, 1962.

Shimshoni, D. *Aspects of scientific entrepreneurship.* Unpublished doctoral dissertation, Harvard University, 1966.

Shimshoni, D. The mobile scientist in the American instrument industry. *Minerva,* 1967, *8*(1), 59–89.

Solecki, R. S. Shanidan Cave, a later Pleistocene site in northern Iraq. *Report of the VIth International Congress on the Quaternary,* 1964, *4,* 413–423.

Steward, J. H. Cultural causality and law: A trial formulation of the development of early civilization. *American Anthropologist,* 1949, *51,* 1–27.

Steward, J. H. *Theory of culture change: The methodology of multilinear evolution.* Urbana: University of Illinois Press, 1955.

Tanner, T. M. *Focus into man: Physical growth from conception to maturity.* Cambridge, Mass.: Harvard University Press, 1978.

Toffler, A. *Future shock.* New York: Random House, 1970.

Tornatzky, L. G., Eveland, J. D., Boylan, M. G., Hetzner, W. A., Johnson, E. C., Roithman, D., & Schneider, J. *The process of innovation: Analyzing the literature.* Washington, D.C.: National Science Foundation, 1982.

Turnbull, C. *The Mountain People.* New York: Simon & Schuster, 1972.

U.S. Department of Commerce. *Technological innovation: Its environment and management.* Washington, D.C.: U.S. Government Printing Office, 1967.

Watson, P. J., LeBlanc, S. A., & Redman, C. L. *Explanation in archeology.* New York & London: Columbia University Press, 1971.

Weinberg, D., & Weinberg, G. M. Biological and cultural models of inheritance. *International Journal of General Systems,* 1974, *1*(2).

White, L. Energy and the evolution of culture. *American Anthropologist,* 1943, *45,* 355–356.

White, L. A. History, evolutionism and functionalism: Three types of interpretation of culture. *Southwestern Journal of Anthropology,* 1945, *1,* 221–248.

White, L. A. *The science of culture.* New York: Grove, 1949.

White, L. A. The concept of evolution in cultural anthropology. In *Evolution and anthropology: A centennial appraisal.* Washington, D.C.: The Anthropological Society of Washington, 1959.

Wissler, C. *An introduction to social anthropology.* New York: Holt, 1929.

Wolfe, E. Closed corporate peasant communities in Mesoamerica and central Java. *Southwestern Journal of Anthropology* 1957, *13,* 1–18.

Wolfe, E. *Peasants.* Englewood Cliffs, N.J.: Prentice–Hall, 1966.

2

Sequential Strategies as Quasi-experimental Designs: Possibilities and Limitations in Explanatory Analysis*

ERICH W. LABOUVIE

I. Introduction

Almost 20 years ago Schaie (1965) introduced the use of sequential methods to the field of developmental psychology. He proposed the application of three designs defined in terms of pairwise combinations of the three time variables of age (A), cohort (or time of birth) (C), and time of measurement (T) in order to identify different sources of individual change. This marked the beginnings of a growing awareness by developmental psychologists that patterns of individual development do not only exhibit cultural differences but are also subject to social – historical changes (Baltes, Reese & Lipsitt, 1980). At the same time it also indicated an increasing need to

* Preparation of this chapter was in part supported by National Institute on Alcohol Abuse and Alcoholism Grant AA 3509-05.

INDIVIDUAL DEVELOPMENT
AND SOCIAL CHANGE:
EXPLANATORY ANALYSIS

31

gather empirical evidence about individual and social change in a way which, compared with conventional cross-sectional and longitudinal designs, would facilitate descriptive and explanatory analysis and interpretation.

Whether or not the application of sequential methods does in fact advance causal analyses of developmental change phenomena has been the subject of an ongoing debate (Adam, 1978; Baltes, 1968; Buss, 1973; Cattell, 1970; Horn & McArdle, 1980; Labouvie, 1975; Schaie & Baltes, 1975; Schaie & Hertzog, 1982; see also Labouvie & Nesselroade, Chapter 7, this volume). Sequential methods, like more conventional ones, fall into the category of quasi-experimental designs. That is, although comparisons are based on samples of individuals thought to be randomly selected from one or more subpopulations, random assignment of subjects to different levels of age, cohort, or time of measurement is impossible (Schaie, 1977). This chapter focuses on three specific issues which are relevant to an explanatory analysis of social and individual change but have largely been neglected so far. The first problem concerns the choice of a concept of social change that is logically consistent with the empirical application of sequential strategies. Compared with the formulation of various concepts and models of individual development (e.g., Overton & Reese, 1973; Reese & Overton, 1970), the concept of social–historical change has received relatively little systematic attention by developmental psychologists. It will be argued here that the application of sequential strategies, while neutral with regard to strong or weak conceptions of individual development, imposes certain logical constraints on one's notion of social–historical change.

The other two problems to be considered here are directly related to aspects of the empirical implementation of sequential methods. If one surveys previous studies in which these methods were used (e.g., Baltes, Baltes & Reinert, 1970; Baltes & Reinert, 1969; Nesselroade & Baltes, 1974; Schaie, Labouvie & Buech, 1973; Schaie & Strother, 1968a, 1968b), two common features become evident. First, the studies share the absence of experimental manipulations (e.g., Labouvie, 1978). Second, as observational studies they are limited to an empirical assessment of psychological characteristics and behaviors of individuals. No attempts are made to include measures of either biological–maturational (e.g., hormonal levels, neurophysiological status) or environmental–experiential factors (e.g., intellectual stimulation, parental child-rearing style, stressful life events) that are advanced by developmental theories as potential sources of individual change and development (e.g., Longstreth, 1968). Thus, after presenting a concept of social change which is consistent with the use of sequential strategies, we will explore the question of whether and how these methods may gain in explanatory usefulness if they are expanded to include (1) experimental manipulations and (2) the assessment of variables beyond the realm of individual psychological characteristics and behaviors.

II. Models of Individual Development and Social Change in the Context of Sequential Strategies

It is generally accepted that empirical facts are conceptual in nature (Weimer, 1979). In our view, however, that statement in itself does not clarify how and to what extent a particular design may constrain the conceptual use of the empirical evidence it provides. We do not believe that it implies such a strong link between developmental theory and design as was suggested, for instance, by Schaie (1977). According to Schaie, an irreversible decrement model of aging requires the use of cohort-sequential designs, a stability model requires the use of cross-sequential designs, and a decrement with compensation model requires the use of time-sequential designs. We suspect that such links between theory and design, if established in empirical practice, are more likely to foster identity foreclosure than identity formation in the course of theory development, just as ahistorical conceptions of individual development relied for a long time only on simple cross-sectional and longitudinal designs.

The empirical evidence obtained with sequential strategies is typically based on *aggregates of observations,* with individuals representing the observational and experimental units of interest (Kirk, 1982). In the most general case, an observation may include measures of an individual's psychological characteristics and behaviors B_i, measures of his or her biological – maturational characteristics H_i, and measures of his or her physical, social, and cultural environment and experience E_i. Following common scientific practice, individuals are both sampled and observed independently of one another. This prescription for experimental independence was introduced in connection with the classical experimental approach in order to reduce the chance that the target relationship(s) between dependent and independent variables would be confounded and thus to maximize internal validity. In other words, to the extent that experimental independence is obtained, it can be assumed that a subject's behavior is not influenced by the behavior of other subjects included in the experiment.

What, then, are the implications of this methodological feature for the study of individual and social change in the context of sequential strategies? As far as the study of individual change and development is concerned, sequential methods provide relevant empirical information regardless of whether one adopts a strong or a weak conception of human development (e.g., Schaie & Hertzog, 1982). The resulting evidence is typically used to obtain an empirical description of "average" individuals and "average" change patterns as well as of individual deviations around those averages.

As far as the study of social – historical change is concerned, the results of sequential strategies are used to discover change patterns in the distributional characteristics (e.g., central tendency, dispersion) of B_i, H_i, or E_i in respective populations. However, given the fact that individuals represent observational and experimental units, the empirical evidence can provide only a demographic description of social change and necessarily excludes any conception of social change which is based on groups or systems as relevant observational and experimental units. Although such demographic descriptions may be rejected as primitive and irrelevant by some sociologists (see, e.g., Naumann and Hüfner, Chapter 3, this volume), it would be erroneous to conclude that distributions that are obtained from aggregates of independently sampled and observed individuals reflect only those processes and antecedents that operate independently across individuals. In actual observational studies where individuals are typically sampled from finite populations within relatively narrow geographic boundaries, the resulting distributions are equally likely to reflect the operation of common and more broadly defined antecedents and processes (see also Lerner, Chapter 6, this volume). Thus, we would argue that a demographic description of social change is not completely trivial and without scientific merit. Instead, it becomes important to formulate theoretical models that are consistent with, though not necessarily limited to, a demographic conception of social change.

The essential elements of one such model are presented in Table 2.1. It is derived from the *variation – selection model* which has been proposed to account for cultural differences in patterns of individual development (Campbell, 1966; LeVine, 1969). Individuals and their environments, viewed as two interacting systems, are characterized in terms of (1) interaction-relevant features, (2) "planned" selection processes, and (3) "unplanned" selection processes.

Interaction-relevant features of systems may be subdivided somewhat arbitrarily into demands and opportunities. From the perspective of individuals, demands may, for instance, include environmental norms, expectations, and values, while opportunities are found in environmental resources, facilities, and capabilities. From the perspective of environments, demands involve individual needs, expectations, preferences, and values, and opportunities encompass individual resources, skills, and abilities. Obviously, the distinction between what constitutes demands as opposed to opportunities is a relative one, and depends on how a particular system values its own and other systems' features. For instance, a particular environmental norm or value (e.g., law and order) may be viewed by some individuals as a constraint

Table 2.1

Person – Environment Interactions: Elements of a Variation – Selection Model

Element	System	
	Individual	Environment
Interaction-relevant features	Individual needs, expectations, goals, values, skills, capabilities, etc.	Environmental demands, norms, values, goals, opportunities, facilities, resources, etc.
Planned selection processes	Individual value functions and optimization principles	Environmental value functions and optimization principles
Unplanned selection processes	Side effects of individual planned selection processes	Side effects of environmental planned selection processes
Variation in features and selection processes	Variation across individuals and time	Variation across space and time

and so a demand, but by others as an opportunity. Or in turn, a particular individual need (e.g., need for change) may constitute a demand and liability in some social environments, but a resource and opportunity in others. Finally, and most important, all interaction-relevant features exhibit variability across individuals, environments, and time.

According to systems theory, a system's interactions with other systems are not completely random but instead selective (e.g., Laszlo, 1972).[1] In other words, the behavior of individuals and environments involves purposeful actions that operate as planned selection processes. According to Marney and Schmidt (1976), such planned selection processes can be characterized in terms of (1) value functions and (2) optimization principles of the system being considered. In general, the value functions of a system will involve one or more of its own features (e.g., individual level of arousal) as well as features of the systems it is interacting with (e.g., level of environmental noise). Associated optimization principles, whether simple or complex, are always aimed at controlling or manipulating the variability in value functions; that is, they are aimed at controlling the variability in valued features (e.g., the range of levels within acceptable limits, the direction and amount of change in levels).

Planned selection processes, like interaction-relevant features, will also

[1] Developmental psychologists have generally emphasized the structural aspects of general systems theory. Process-oriented features of the theory that share similarities with the orientation of action theory (Chapman, 1982) have, by and large, been neglected.

exhibit variability across individuals, environments, and time, either with regard to their value functions, their optimization principles, or both. Furthermore, every planned selection process is likely to be associated with a number of unplanned ones simply because the values for which a system selects are likely to covary with a number of other features. In other words, every planned selection process is likely to produce unplanned side effects.

Variability in both interaction-relevant features and planned selection processes — and the existence of side effects as well as other factors (e.g., choice of means to implement a planned selection process) — will tend to generate slippage between the desired and/or anticipated goal and the actual effect of any selection process. For instance, parents may plan to raise their child according to a selection process aimed at maximizing certain intellectual abilities and personality traits. However, even if both parents can be assumed to operate consistently across time, the child is likely to encounter other environments operating according to different selection processes and thus the effectiveness and outcome of the parental actions will be jeopardized. In turn, the occurrence of slippage and of unanticipated side effects may cause a system to revise its own planned selection processes by changing either value functions, optimization principles, or both. For instance, after observing unwanted side effects of their child-rearing program, the parents may decide to change their maximization principle to one aimed only at ensuring the attainment of minimally acceptable levels of valued abilities and traits in their child.

We believe that the general variation – selection model as just outlined has the potential to provide a useful theoretical guide for the explanatory analysis of individual development and social change within the empirical context of sequential strategies. First, the model is an interactional one, emphasizing not only that individual development is shaped by environments but also that environments are shaped and changed by individuals, with the latter representing the seeds for social change at the individual level (see Lerner, Chapter 6, this volume). An extension of the model to population statistics and a demographic notion of social change is straightforward.

Second, the model suggests that individual development and social change be viewed as open-ended processes, a perspective quite consistent with that of life-span developmentalists (Baltes et al., 1980). That is, variability in interaction-relevant features and in planned selection processes, presence of unplanned or unanticipated side effects, and slippage between intended and actually achieved effects are all likely to ensure that developmental stability and person – environment congruence (e.g., Windley & Scheidt, 1980; Lerner, Chapter 6, this volume) are observed as only local and temporary rather than universal and permanent phenomena.

Third, the model provides a conceptual basis for the design of experimental manipulations in connection with the use of sequential strategies. More specifically, the variation–selection model suggests an approach to experimentation as the controlled simulation of individual and environmental selection processes by simulating value functions or optimization principles or both.

Fourth, we believe that this model can bridge the gap between a demographic concept of social change and those notions that are based on a consideration of larger units. More specifically, we think that historical change at the level of social groups, programs, institutions, organizations, and cultural meaning systems can be conceptualized equally well in terms of variability in interaction-relevant features and planned selection processes. However, given the fact that the study of individual change and development requires a focus on individuals as observational and experimental units, the question remains whether and how the resulting descriptions of the sociocultural environment can be "individualized" in order to permit an empirical assessment of its relationships to individual behavior. To the extent that such descriptions are either viewed to represent only components of an individual's distal environment or linked to the behavior of "average" individuals, they obviously fail to provide some crucial information for a causal analysis as attempted by developmentalists. In comparison, descriptions of the environment provided by a demographic notion of social change are more readily amenable to an analysis at the level of individuals (see Featherman, Chapter 8, this volume).

III. Empirical Applications of Sequential Strategies

As stated above, previous discussions and empirical applications of sequential methods have not considered the inclusion of either experimental manipulations or the empirical assessment of biological–maturational and environmental–experiential factors. Therefore, it is not only quite appropriate but desirable to explore some of the potential advantages as well as problems associated with such an expansion.

A. PURPOSES OF EXPERIMENTATION:
WHAT IS VERSUS WHAT CAN BE

According to Wohlwill (1973a) and McCall (1977), the bulk of developmental research has relied too much on an experimental approach. In fact, Wohlwill goes so far as to question the general utility of an experimental approach for the study of individual development. For his part, McCall defines the role of experimentation in connection with a distinction between two basic questions, one focusing on what can be (what can cause what) in the context of controlled experimental conditions, the other on what is (what causes what) in the context of naturally occurring conditions. The distinction is certainly a useful one. However, it can be argued that it is misleading to equate it with the distinction between an experimental and an observational approach. Instead, if the two questions are seen as opposite ends of the same continuum, it is quite obvious that experimentation can be, and actually is, used in connection with both questions.

When experimentation is used primarily for the purpose of exploring what can be, it is carried out with little regard for what is. In other words, the researcher is not concerned with the question of whether the experimental situations he creates resemble in quantity or quality those that are found in the natural environment of the organisms studied. As demonstrated by the natural sciences, the "what can be" approach is important in contributing to our knowledge and understanding of phenomena. Furthermore, the "what can be" of today may become the "what is" of tomorrow, as is illustrated by technological progress. When viewed in this context, sequential methods primarily provide a plan for systematic replications of one's experimental manipulations across independent instances, that is, across cohorts, times of measurement, or ages (see Table 2.2).

Experimentation may also be used in connection with a strong emphasis on what is. In that case, it reflects an explicit interest in modeling or simulating both similarities to and deviations from what is in order to better understand its workings. For instance, Werner's (1957) principles of orthogenesis and microgenesis can be viewed as a theoretical foundation for developmentally relevant simulations of what is. When seen from this perspective, sequential strategies provide not only a description of what is as the standard of comparison for one's simulations but they also become a means for simulating individual and social change through experimental manipulations. It is unimportant whether such manipulations represent short- or long-term interventions (see Baltes & Goulet, 1971), although in practice it will be easier to maintain experimental control (and achieve internal validity) over short periods of time.

The following discussion will be limited to considering issues that pertain only to the use of sequential strategies for simulation purposes. First, we will deal with the question of how sequential methods can or should be used to describe what is in terms of (1) the variables that are selected for empirical assessment, (2) the framework that is chosen to represent the temporal characteristics of those variables, and (3) specific issues of internal validity in connection with the description of demographic social change. Second, we will consider the problem of defining more explicitly the sense in which experimental manipulations do or do not simulate what is.

Table 2.2

Sequential Methods as Designs for Experimental Replications

Replication variable	Experimental condition	Time variable
Time-sequential		
Time of measurement	E_1	$A_1, A_2, A_3, \ldots$
$(T = 1, 2, \ldots)$	E_2	
	⋮	
Cross-sequential		
Cohort	E_1	$T_1, T_2, T_3, \ldots$
$(C = 1, 2, \ldots)$	E_2	
	⋮	
Cohort-sequential		
Cohort	E_1	$A_1, A_2, A_3, \ldots$
$(C = 1, 2, \ldots)$	E_2	
	⋮	

B. SIMULATIONS OF INDIVIDUAL AND SOCIAL CHANGE

1. THE DESCRIPTION OF INDIVIDUAL AND SOCIAL CHANGE

Selection of Empirical Indicators. In the past, most developmental psychologists entertained a rather narrow view of the task of description by limiting themselves to an empirical assessment of the behaviors and psychological characteristics of individuals. From an explanatory point of view, however, it can be argued that such an approach to the task of description is highly inadequate, for unless one is willing to assume that later behavior is influenced only by earlier behavior, the empirical descriptions one obtains with such an approach are of minimal value for causal–analytic purposes. This is because other potential sources of intraindividual change, such as biological–maturational factors and environmental–experiential factors, are not charted empirically. Consequently, the resulting developmental descriptions remain of very limited usefulness for explanatory analyses such as those involving causal modeling (Bentler, 1980). Such descriptions are also rather uninformative for simulation purposes because they furnish little information about the features of those sources of change that we may want to simulate experimentally. Thus the information that is obtained is more likely to be used to support rather than to selectively reject a variety of developmental hypotheses and speculations.

A minimal description in the above sense is equally unsatisfactory for an explanatory analysis of social change. It emphasizes a notion of social change as a product or outcome rather than as a context and source of individual change. In our everyday language, however, we refer to social–historical change in terms of changes in our physical and social environment at least as often as we describe it in terms of behavioral and psychological differences between successive cohorts or generations. Thus, if the description of social changes in developmental patterns via sequential strategies is to lead to more than just speculation as to its sources, it will be necessary to demonstrate empirical relationships between historical changes in the physical and social characteristics of individuals' environments on the one hand and changes in the patterns of social–psychological development they exhibit on the other.

In sum, if the descriptive use of sequential strategies is to provide a meaningful empirical data base for explanatory analyses of individual and social change, it is, in our opinion, not sufficient to limit oneself to the observation of individual behaviors and characteristics. Regardless of whether one prefers a causal modeling approach in conjunction with observational studies or a simulation approach in the context of experiments, either approach becomes possible only if the descriptions of individual and social change are extended to include empirical indicators of individuals' environmental contexts.

Choice of Time Coordinates. Most of the controversy surrounding the use of sequential methods has centered around the question of how to choose a temporal framework for a given purpose in view of the fact that the three time-variables are bound together in an algebraic relationship (see Labouvie & Nesselroade, Chapter 7, this volume). According to Schaie and Baltes (1975), the description of individual development and its variability across historical time is best accomplished using longitudinal sequences with cohort and age as the temporal coordinates. However, their suggestion is much less compelling in view of the arguments presented above. If one is also interested in describing historical changes in individuals' physical and social environment as a potential source of the observed variability in individual development, the choice of an age–time of measurement system of coordinates is more convenient for a description of the former. However, this raises the question of how to link descriptions of individual change in a cohort–age matrix to descriptions of history-related environmental changes in an age–time of measurement matrix.

A developmental causal analysis requires the systematic mapping of individual behavior and its temporal features onto antecedents and processes and their respective temporal characteristics (see Labouvie & Nesselroade, Chapter 7, this volume). In order to accomplish this goal, it is necessary that

the conceptualization and empirical description of antecedents, consequents, and mediating processes be based on a common temporal framework. In other words, a cohort–age description of individual changes and
an age–time of measurement description of environmental changes are
difficult to relate to each other unless one or the other can be translated so
that both share the same system of time coordinates. To illustrate this point
more clearly, consider the following hypothetical example. Assume that
some environmental feature E (e.g., amount of intellectual stimulation)
represents an antecedent of behavior B (e.g., intellectual ability) with its
effect on B being mediated by a normative, cumulative process that is invariant across individuals and time. Further, assume that E can be characterized as a normative age- and history-graded antecedent (see, e.g., Baltes,
Cornelius, & Nesselroade, 1979) over some historical time interval
$[T_a, T_b]$. Thus, from a social change perspective, the temporal characteristics of E may be expressed in an age–time of measurement framework as:

$$E_i(A, T_m) = a_i T_m - b_i A$$

with $a_i > b_i > 0$ for individual i, or $E(A, T_m) = a.T_m - b.A$ for the population with mean$(a_i) = a.$ = constant, mean$(b_i) = b.$ = constant, var(a_i) =
constant, and var(b_i) = constant for the interval $[T_a, T_b]$. In other words, E
(amount of intellectual stimulation) is assumed to increase with historical
time T_m and to decrease with age A. Furthermore, the coefficients a_i and b_i
are assumed to reflect individual differences in both the amount and the
temporal change gradients of that stimulation.

As shown in Table 2.3, E can easily be rewritten in a cohort–age and a
cohort–time of measurement framework. Furthermore, using integral calculus to express the assumed cumulative, invariant nature of the mediating
process, the associated behavioral outcome B can also be presented in any of
the three different temporal frameworks. In our opinion, it would be inappropriate to suggest that only one of the three representations of E and B is
correct, while the other two are incorrect. Instead, all three are equally valid
as descriptions of the temporal features of E and B. As already suggested
above, a causal analysis of the relationship between E and B requires only
that both be based on the same temporal framework. However, we realize
that individual researchers' preferences for one or the other system of time
coordinates are likely to bias their conception of the mediating processes.

Although this example has been kept simple by assuming a single antecedent and a single invariant, normative process, it helps to illustrate several
important points. First, as is shown in Table 2.3, regardless of which of the
three systems of time coordinates is chosen, the temporal characteristics of
the behavioral patterns are not identical to those of the antecedent. If in
addition one were to attribute more complex temporal features to the me-

Table 2.3

Hypothetical Example: Three Mathematically Equivalent Representations of the Same Antecedent E and Associated Behavioral Outcome B^a

Antecedent E	Behavior B
Age–time of measurement: A, T_m	
$E_i(A, T_m) = a_i T_m - b_i A$	$B_i(A, T_m) = a_i T_m A - \frac{1}{2}(a_i + b_i)A^2$
Cohort–age: T_c, A	
$E_i(T_c, A) = a_i T_c + (a_i - b_i)A$	$B_i(T_c, A) = a_i T_c A + \frac{1}{2}(a_i - b_i)A^2$
Cohort–time of measurement: T_c, T_m	
$E_i(T_c, T_m) = (a_i - b_i)T_m + b_i T_c$	$B_i(T_c, T_m) = \frac{1}{2}(a_i - b_i)T_m^2 + b_i T_c T_m - \frac{1}{2}(a_i + b_i)T_c^2$

$^a T_m = T_c + A$. Average population patterns are obtained by replacing the coefficients a_i and b_i with their means $a.$ and $b.$

diating process, the likelihood of such an identity in temporal characteristics would become quite remote. In other words, the empirical identification of the behavioral patterns and their temporal attributes in any one of the three time frameworks tells us little besides whether they are similar or dissimilar for different individuals or groups of individuals. The identification of behavioral patterns by itself yields very little information about the temporal characteristics of either antecedents or mediating processes.

Second, according to our example the same antecedent may generate (1) intraindividual change within a given cohort, (2) interindividual differences in such change within a cohort, and (3) differences in change between cohorts. Thus different variance components (as identified through the application of analysis of variance in connection with sequential designs) may in fact be linked to the same antecedent. Put another way, the variance components of the behavioral patterns in relation to age, cohort, or time of measurement do not necessarily reflect different types of antecedents but merely different temporal aspects of the same antecedent. For instance, consider the case in which an environmental influence E on behavior B exhibits a steady change across a prolonged historical time interval (e.g., 100 years). Assume that an investigator chooses to compare birth cohorts that are defined in terms of a sequence of adjacent time intervals of moderate length (e.g., 10 years). Due to the assumed steady change in E, individuals belonging to the same cohort will exhibit differences in their developmental patterns of B. At the same time, the change in E will also produce differences in average cohort-specific patterns of B.

Third, if it is possible for the same antecedent to produce both within- and between-cohort variability in intraindividual change, the conceptual distinction between intra- and inter-cohort differences becomes vague, at least from a causal–analytic perspective. In line with Baltes's argument (1968), this ambiguity emphasizes the fact that the concept of birth cohort is not very useful in advancing developmental causal analyses. In addition, it suggests that any experimental simulation — whether of differential intraindividual changes in general or of social–cultural differences in such changes in particular — represents at the same time a simulation of potential social–cultural change. Furthermore, such simulation attempts do not have to be based on multiple-cohort designs to yield relevant information (although such designs are still desirable to obtain more complete descriptions of the "what is").

Fourth, although it is possible to represent without less of information the same empirical envidence in any of three different systems of time coordinates, an age–time of measurement framework is likely to be preferred by a social change perspective, while a cohort–age or cohort–time of measurement framework seems to be more convenient for an individual change perspective. As was already mentioned, as far as a causal analysis of individual development and change is concerned, a focus on individuals as the relevant observational and experimental units requires only that antecedents, consequents, and processes should be capable of being conceptualized and empirically described at the level of individuals with a common system of coordinates.

Internal Validity of Cohort Differences as Indicator of Social Change. Originally, the formulation of sequential methods was motivated to a considerable degree by concerns over the internal validity of cross-sectional age differences and the external validity of simple longitudinal age changes. With the use of multiple-cohort longitudinal sequences, however, the proposed solution for the problem of the external validity of simple longitudinal designs has turned into a problem of the internal validity of cohort differences. More specifically, it is questionable whether differences in cohort-specific developmental patterns that have been reported in previous empirical applications do reflect true differences in cohort populations. Given the notoriously poor sampling techniques and small sample sizes that are characteristic of developmental research, whatever cohort differences are observed could simply reflect differences in sampling procedures, differences in selective sampling biases (e.g., due to historical changes in volunteering behaviors), or differences in selective survival. It is obviously much more difficult and costly to establish the internal validity of empirical cohort differences as indicators of true demographic social change in a population than it is to establish the internal validity of intraindividual changes. As a consequence, it would seem advisable to interpret observed cohort differences with much greater caution than has been shown in previous work.

2. Experimental Manipulations as Simulations of Individual and Social Change

As was stated earlier, experimental simulations are aimed at producing varying degrees of similarity and dissimilarity between an experimentally controlled phenomenon and some selected aspect of the "what is." Such attempts can proceed along two lines, each with a different emphasis. In the more frequently used approach, the researcher specifies the target to be simulated in terms of selected characteristics of an individual's environment and proceeds to experimentally manipulate them as independent variables in order to identify their relationships to behavioral outcomes. In the second approach, the target to be simulated is defined in terms of individual behaviors and characteristics (the dependent variable); the researcher explores the range of independent variables, both qualitative and quantitative, that may produce behavioral patterns that are similar to or different from the specified target pattern (e.g., Baltes & Goulet, 1971). With either approach the researcher is faced with the problem of how to define and select experimental manipulations and conditions. To at least outline the complexity of that problem, we have chosen to consider two issues. The first has been grossly neglected by developmentalists; the second has been familiar to psychologists for some time.

Temporal Characteristics of the Sources of Change. Developmentalists have spent a great deal of time and effort describing the temporal characteristics of intraindividual changes in many different domains of behavior. By contrast, very little attention has been devoted to the task of describing the temporal characteristics of the presumed sources of those changes. In particular, the ability of developmentalists to conceptualize and empirically assess those characteristics is at a primitive stage and reminds one of the status of classical mechanics in physics. As is well known, classical mechanics, conceived as the study of the movement of objects in space, conceptualizes those objects as mass-points devoid of any spatial characteristics save location. In similar fashion, developmental psychology tends to conceptualize most sources of intraindividual change, whether experimental manipulations or naturally occurring events (including biological–maturational events), as event-points devoid of temporal characteristics other than their location along the time dimension (see Campbell & Stanley, 1966, for an example of the temporal representation, or lack thereof, of experimental interventions in the context of longitudinal quasi-experimental designs). According to Wohlwill (1973a), the temporal characteristics of interest to developmentalists have generally been limited to age of onset, duration, and age of termination, suggesting essentially a representation of events in terms of binary on-off sequences (see also Featherman, Chapter 8, this volume). This approach is also reflected in the common analytical practice of linking interindividual differences observed at one time to interindividual differences obtained at another time (via regression analysis, for instance), thereby quite successfully circumventing the problem of having to specify the temporal features of antecedents in any detail.

This approach may be satisfactory if one is primarily interested in short-term effects of short-term antecedents (measured in hours or days). It appears somewhat simplistic, however, if one is interested in the study of long-term phenomena (measured in years) such as, for instance, the effects of long-term age- and/or history-graded antecedents or the long-term outcomes of specific historical periods. Thus it would seem necessary to adopt a more sophisticated conceptualization and measurement of the temporal features of antecedents. For instance, when studying the development of social behavior in relation to parental child-rearing style (e.g., Baumrind, 1975), it may well be that certain temporal features (e.g., the timing, rate of change, and amount of change in increases or decreases in parental control or love over extended periods of time) are important in shaping the developmental course of social behavior through adolescence and early adulthood. As was just mentioned, the conventional empirical mapping of parental differences observed at one time onto individual differences in social behavior at some later time via regression analysis completely overlooks the potential relevance of the temporal features of antecedents. Finally, as our hypothetical example suggests, a more precise assessment of the temporal characteristics of both antecedents and consequents is necessary if one is interested in identifying the long-term temporal features of mediating processes.

The Concept of Experience. In their attempts to understand causal relationships between environmental sources and contexts on the one hand and individual development on the other, psychologists have proposed different notions of the concept of experience. In particular, experience has been defined either in terms of the stimulus conditions to which individuals are exposed or in terms of all the activities and behaviors elicited by those conditions (e.g., Moos, 1974; Wohlwill, 1973b). Conceptually, the class of elicited behaviors includes individual perceptions and appraisals of the stimulus conditions (i.e., perceived environment) as well as the target behaviors or dependent variables to be measured.

As far as the empirical assessment and manipulation of experience is concerned, it will generally be easier, more convenient, and more precise to define it in terms of stimulus conditions or events. However, such an approach is probably not acceptable to those developmentalists who believe that at least some of the behaviors elicited by the stimulus conditions are equally or perhaps even more important for a causal analysis of individual change in the target behaviors of interest. Taken together, the two notions of experience suggest a strategy that is entirely consistent with the points made earlier in connection with the task of describing the "what is." That is, in order to be able to specify as precisely as possible how and in what sense a particular experimental manipulation simulates the "what is," it is necessary to describe it both in terms of stimulus properties and a range of elicited behaviors, including relevant covert behaviors (for instance, see Bandura's microanalysis of self-efficacy, 1982). Thus, the task of measuring a representative sample of elicited behaviors becomes crucially important. Of course, it presupposes the formulation of a theoretical framework that will provide a specification of the population of relevant elicited behaviors.

IV. Conclusions

When evaluating the potential utility of sequential designs for explanatory analyses, it is useful to distinguish between an individual change and a social change perspective. As far as the first approach is concerned, cohort $\times$ age and cohort $\times$ time of measurement designs provide relevant information regardless of whether one adopts a weak or a strong conception of human development. In particular, both will facilitate explanatory analyses as long as the selection of concepts and empirical indicators is not limited to the realm of individual behaviors and psychological characteristics B_i but instead extended to include environmental sources E_i and biological–maturational sources H_i. Such an extension is necessary not only for a meaningful application of causal modeling techniques but also for an experimental approach that focuses on the simulation of the sources, rather than the outcomes, of individual change.

From a social change perspective, on the other hand, the use of sequential strategies tends to impose certain conceptual constraints. In particular, the empirical evidence that is obtained through sequential strategies is based on aggregates of independently sampled observations (taking individuals as the observational units). Therefore, the resulting notion of social change is primarily a demographic one that emphasizes historical changes in the population distributions of the B_i, E_i, and H_i. That limitation, in turn, becomes important as far as issues of internal validity are concerned. More specifically, to the extent that sampling techniques are poor and cohort samples small, the internal validity of cohort differences as an indicator of social change is highly questionable.

Finally, we have proposed a variation – selection model as a potentially unifying framework for the explanatory analysis of individual change and of social change in the context of sequential strategies. In addition, such a model can provide a conceptual link to alternative conceptions of social change.

References

Adam, J. Sequential strategies and the separation of age, cohort, and time-of-measurement contributions to developmental data. *Psychological Bulletin,* 1978, *85,* 1309–1316.

Baltes, P. B. Longitudinal and cross-sectional sequences in the study of age and generation effects. *Human Development,* 1968, *11,* 145–171.

Baltes, P. B., Baltes, M. M., & Reinert, G. The relationship between time of measurement and age in cognitive development of children. *Human Development,* 1970, *13,* 258–268.

Baltes, P. B., Cornelius, S. W., & Nesselroade, J. R. Cohort effects in developmental psychology. In J. R. Nesselroade & P. B. Baltes (Eds.), *Longitudinal research in the study of behavior and development.* New York: Academic Press, 1979.

Baltes, P. B., & Goulet, L. R. Exploration of developmental variables by simulation and manipulation of age differences in behavior. *Human Development,* 1971, *14,* 149–170.

Baltes, P. B., Reese, H. W., & Lipsitt, L. P. Life-span developmental psychology. In M. R. Rosenzweig & L. W. Porter (Eds.), *Annual review of psychology* (Vol. 31). Palo Alto, Calif.: Annual Reviews, 1980.

Baltes, P. B., & Reinert, G. Cohort effects in cognitive development of children as revealed by cross-sectional sequences. *Developmental Psychology,* 1969, *1,* 169–177.

Bandura, A. Self-efficacy in human agency. *American Psychologist,* 1982, *37,* 122–147.

Baumrind, D. Early socialization and adolescent competence. In S. E. Dragastin & G. H. Elder, Jr. (Eds.), *Adolescence in the life cycle: Psychological change and social context.* New York: Wiley, 1975.

Bentler, P. M. Multivariate analysis with latent variables. In M. R. Rosenzweig & L. W. Porter (Eds.), *Annual review of psychology* (Vol. 31). Palo Alto, Calif.: Annual Reviews, 1980.

Buss, A. R. An extension of developmental models that separate ontogenetic changes and cohort differences. *Psychological Bulletin,* 1973, *80,* 466–479.

Campbell, D. T. Variation and selective-retention in sociocultural evolution. In H. R. Barringer, G. I. Blanksten, & R. W. Mack (Eds.), *Social change in developing areas: A re-interpretation of evolutionary theory.* Cambridge, Mass.: Schenkman, 1966.

Campbell, D. T., & Stanley, J. C. *Experimental and quasi-experimental designs for research.* Chicago: Rand McNally, 1966.

Cattell, R. B. Separating endogenous, exogenous, ecogenic, and epogenic component curves in developmental data. *Developmental Psychology,* 1970, *3,* 151–162.

Chapman, M. Action and interaction: the study of social cognition in Germany and the United States. *Human Development,* 1982, *25,* 295–302.

Horn, J. L., & McArdle, J. J. Perspectives on mathematical/statistical model building (MAS-

MOB) in research on aging. In L. W. Poon (Ed.), *Aging in the 1980s.* Washington, D.C.: American Psychological Association, 1980.

Kirk, R. E. *Experimental design: Procedures for the behavioral sciences.* Monterey, Calif.: Brooks/Cole, 1982.

Labouvie, E. W. An extension of developmental models: Reply to Buss. *Psychological Bulletin,* 1975, *82,* 165–169.

Labouvie, E. W. Experimental sequential strategies for the exploration of ontogenetic and socio-historical changes. *Human Development,* 1978, *21,* 161–169.

Laszlo, E. *Introduction to systems philosophy: Toward a new paradigm of contemporary thought.* New York: Gordon & Breach, 1972.

LeVine, R. A. Culture, personality, and socialization: An evolutionary view. In D. A. Goslin (Ed.), *Handbook of socialization theory and research.* Chicago: Rand McNally, 1969.

Longstreth, L. E. *Psychological development of the child.* New York: Ronald Press, 1968.

Marney, M., & Schmidt, P. F. Evolution of scientific method. In E. Jantsch & C. H. Waddington (Eds.), *Evolution and consciousness: Human systems in transition.* Reading, Mass.: Addison–Wesley, 1976.

McCall, R. B. Challenges to a science of developmental psychology. *Child Development,* 1977, *48,* 333–344.

Moos, R. H. Systems for the assessment and classification of human environments: An overview. In R. H. Moos & P. M. Insel (Eds.), *Issues in social ecology.* Palo Alto, Calif.: National Press Books, 1974.

Nesselroade, J. R., & Baltes, P. B. Adolescent personality development and historical change: 1970–72. *Monographs of the Society for Research in Child Development,* 1974, *39*(1, No. 154).

Overton, W. F., & Reese, H. W. Models of development: Methodological implications. In J. R. Nesselroade & H. W. Reese (Eds.), *Life-span developmental psychology: Methodological issues.* New York: Academic Press, 1973.

Reese, H. W., & Overton, W. F. Models of development and theories of development. In L. R. Goulet & P. B. Baltes (Eds.), *Life-span developmental psychology: Research and theory.* New York: Academic Press, 1970.

Schaie, K. W. A general model for the study of developmental problems. *Psychological Bulletin,* 1965, *64,* 92–107.

Schaie, K. W. Quasi-experimental research designs in the psychology of aging. In J. E. Birren & K. W. Schaie (Eds.), *Handbook of the psychology of aging.* New York: Van Nostrand Reinhold, 1977.

Schaie, K. W., & Baltes, P. B. On sequential strategies in developmental research and the Schaie-Baltes controversy: Description or explanation? *Human Development,* 1975, *18,* 384–390.

Schaie, K. W., & Hertzog, C. Longitudinal methods. In B. B. Wolman (Ed.), *Handbook of developmental psychology.* Englewood Cliffs, N.J.: Prentice–Hall, 1982.

Schaie, K. W., Labouvie, G. V., & Bucch, B. V. Generational and cohort-specific differences in adult cognitive functioning: A fourteen-year study of independent samples. *Developmental Psychology,* 1973, *9,* 151–166.

Schaie, K. W., & Strother, C. R. A cross-sequential study of age changes in cognitive behavior. *Psychological Bulletin,* 1968, *70,* 671–680. (a)

Schaie, K. W., & Strother, C. R. The effects of time and cohort differences on the interpretation of age changes in cognitive behavior. *Multivariate Behavioral Research,* 1968, *3,* 259–294. (b)

Weimer, W. B. *Notes on the methodology of scientific research.* Hillsdale, N.J.: Erlbaum, 1979.

Werner, H. The concept of development from a comparative and organismic point of view. In D. B. Harris (Ed.), *The concept of development.* Minneapolis: University of Minnesota Press, 1957.

Windley, P. G., & Scheidt, R. J. Person-environment dialectics: Implications for competent functioning in old age. In L. W. Poon (Ed.), *Aging in the 1980s.* Washington, D.C.: American Psychological Association, 1980.

Wohlwill, J. R. *The study of behavioral development.* New York: Academic Press, 1973. (a)

Wohlwill, J. F. The concept of experience: S or R? *Human Development,* 1973, *16,* 90–107. (b)

3

Evolutionary Aspects of Social and Individual Development: Comments and Illustrations from the World System Perspective

JENS NAUMANN
KLAUS HÜFNER

I. The Context of Development and the Development of Context

Recently Urie Bronfenbrenner set out on a journey through time (1982). He wanted "to trace the evolution of the concept of environment in systematic research on human development" (p. 2). Since he was unable to find a reasonably reliable road map, he took a Land Rover (with a built-in compass, of course) and drove right across that rather unexplored part of historico-psychological country: "In contrast to other branches of psychology—notably experimental—there has been no systematic historical account of the progressive growth of empirically-based knowledge about human development" (p. 2), the closest approximations being two concise but comprehensive historical surveys of child development as a total field, namely, Sears

INDIVIDUAL DEVELOPMENT
AND SOCIAL CHANGE:
EXPLANATORY ANALYSIS

(1975) and Hartup (1978) (Bronfenbrenner, 1982, p. 2). We propose to start with a summary of his travel account and then compare it with some "aerial photographs" of the region. One set of "photographs," provided by the John Meyer Chopper Company (presented in the next section), consists of beautifully detailed shots taken from the highest altitude at which the helicopters of this pushy little firm are licensed to operate. We try to put these shots into perspective by comparing them with a second set of "pictures" we took on flights with the fast and ever higher flying Parsons Jets, regularly providing service between "Western Past" and "Western Present." Admittedly those latter shots are somewhat blurry due to the fact that, in contrast to the daring pilots of the Chopper Company who hover dangerously close to the fuzzy demarcation line of the world system's perspective, the chief pilot of the Parsons Jets usually steered clear of the troubled and diffuse downstream zones of present day modernization. Instead, he preferred to map out in ever more detail the many separate streams originating in the hilly past of Western Civilization and their meandering and confluences on the sixteenth- to nineteenth-century plateau.

In a nutshell, Bronfenbrenner supplied the following account of evolutionary landmarks (for a simplified graphic presentation see Figure 3.1). The baseline is provided by studies — old and new — that focus on the impact that genetic factors and, more generally, the human organism have on

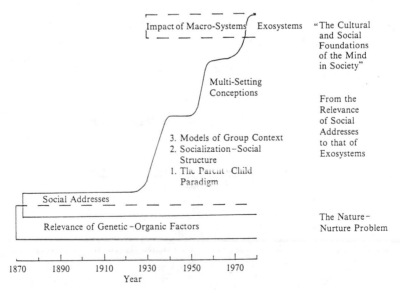

Figure 3.1   The individual and the environment: Bronfenbrenner's description of evolving concepts of human development studies.

the individual's development. In these studies the implied conception of "social" environment often tends to be very restrictive. In discussions by Galton (1876), Spearman (1914), Burt (1972), and Jensen (1980), it "may be described as a definition by exclusion; that is, the environment becomes that portion of the variance that cannot be explained by genetic factors under conditions in which major potential sources of environmental influences are not taken into account . . ." (Bronfenbrenner, 1982, p. 9). Still, Galton was the first to systematically draw attention to the social position of the family, to family structure, and to family functioning, all sources of influence which were taken up again in detail more than fifty years later.

Bronfenbrenner's account concentrates on the stepwise introduction of wider concepts of social environment on the one hand and on more sophisticated concepts of the developing personality on the other. The ancestor of what he calls the very important *social addresses-paradigm* is a survey conducted by the Pedagogical Society of Berlin (Pädagogische Verein in Berlin, 1870) to investigate the differential impact of urban–rural origin on the knowledge of children. But what the outcome actually showed was the existence of marked sex differences and the importance of preschool or kindergarten experience. In analytical terms, the paradigm consists of a comparison of children living at different social addresses:

> Although the social addresses become more sophisticated, this century-old model continues to characterize the majority of investigations being conducted today on the role of environmental factors in human development. . . . First, the model may be characterized as child-centered in the sense that no one else's behavior is being examined except the child's. Second, the model is unidirectional, with the child being a passive recipient and product of environmental influences. Third, no explicit consideration is given . . . to intervening structures or processes through which the environment might affect the course of development. (Bronfenbrenner, 1982, p. 7)

Returning to our opening metaphor, we can conceive of the period from the 1870s to the mid-1920s as making for easy travel over terrain having only a limited increase in analytical sophistication regarding the child's social position and that of its family. But the 1930s (actually extending to the present) presented a steep hill of three types of dynamic paradigms. First, *the parent – child paradigm,* originally explored by David Levy and Percival Symonds, focused on the details of familial patterns of child rearing and personality development. Second, a wide array of studies on *socialization and social structure* systematically improved the crude social addresses to make possible more complete assessments of the impact of socially differentiated family milieus on children's development. (Surveys conducted in 1932 for the White House Conference on Child Health and Protection, summarized in Anderson, 1936, are identified as the forefather of a long series of investigations of socialization and social class). Third, a family of studies Bronfenbrenner calls *models of group context* primarily investigated the impact of institutionally routinized (and restricted) treatments of children and eventually led to the first experimental early intervention as a research strategy (Skeels, Updegraff, Wellman, & Williams, 1938). In assessing the growing impact of more sophisticated theoretical models of the individual in interaction with his or her environment as the most important spur to the field, Bronfenbrenner cited especially the work of Freud, Piaget, and Lewin, and to a somewhat lesser extent Clark Hull.

While these three paradigms continue to play an important role in the present, beginning in the 1950s they were supplemented by studies using a multi-setting conception of the environment (with formal schooling playing an increasingly important role). Bronfenbrenner describes the underlying model as a system of settings "containing the developing person" and calls it a "mesosystem" (1982, p. 42).

In the 1970s two extensions of the concept of human development seemed slowly to emerge. The first involved extending the concept of the "developing subject" to include the adult personality with the traditional child and adolescent personality as primary foci of attention. The normal personality was seen as a nonstatic, developing system influenced by prior experience and acquired modes of coping with life's challenges, yet also open for new learning. Thus, the "life-course" entered the stage. The second extension had to do with specifying the relevant environment. Bronfenbrenner speaks of "exosystems" as those parts of the environment "beyond the behavioral world of the developing person. . . . Among the most powerful exosystems are those agencies and institutions, both in the private and public sector, that design and administer policies affecting the well-being and functioning of families, schools, social service programs, and other socialization settings" (Bronfenbrenner, 1982, p. 44).

Although Bronfenbrenner does not explicitly state the connection, we submit that the type of relevant man-made, non-face-to-face social environment to which his term "exosystem" refers links up with what he considers the "dramatically different paradigm of the role of culture in human development" (p. 22) followed by the Soviet psychologists Vygotsky and Luria. The general thesis of Vygotsky's *Mind in Society* (1978) and Luria's *Cognitive Development: Its Cultural and Social Foundations* (1976) was that the evolution of cognitive processes in the individual is shaped by the definitions of reality in the wider social context and is influenced by planned and unplanned large-scale social changes. Quite tellingly, these works were banned for 40 years in the Soviet Union but were finally published in Russian and in English in the middle 1970s.

Interesting and "true" as Professor Bronfenbrenner's account of his intellectual travel is, it somewhat lopsidedly emphasizes a sample of succeeding generations of empirical studies as a means of reconstructing, on the one hand, broader concepts of the "context of development." The "development of context," on the other hand, enters the story rather metaphorically as an "affair" between the research community and Clio, the muse of history, an affair that is wrongly held to be illicit. We go a step further and propose that, illicit or legitimate, the bonds between conceptions of the individual and social development not only have been and continue to be strong but are also likely to be even more heavily emphasized in the future.

More specifically, we would like to submit the following thesis: The social sciences — partly ahead of, partly behind empirical trends in the real world — are increasingly being challenged to make explicit and reconceptualize their models of social change and modernization. From a mode of thinking in the dichotomy of (Western) modern societies (of the liberal – capitalist or the socialist – Marxist variety) versus traditional societies we will have to move to an open, dynamic conception accommodating the emerging world system of societies (Parsons, 1977a) or world society (Luhmann, 1975). Instead of expecting traditional societies to change in the direction of the static and "finalized" conception of a modern society, a more generalized concept of modernization would allow and require a decentered assessment of trends and strains in modern societies by no longer treating them as "the end of the road."

Human development studies in particular, and psychology in general, will certainly be affected by this overall reorientation of the social sciences. This is likely to happen along the lines roughly indicated by each discipline's development in the overall body of the social sciences. A glimpse of these interdependencies is given implicitly in Bronfenbrenner's account. In fact, to the extent that psychology has been part of the social (and cultural) sciences, it has been involved in the effort to conceptualize human action systems as an analytical subsystem of the human condition, where the action systems articulate with their environments but are not identical with them (see Figure 3.2, based on Parsons & Platt, 1973 and Parsons, 1978). Of course, one salient aspect of psychology has been its constant affinity for determining the organic base of the individual, but the thrust of psychology's own development over the past one hundred years or so has clearly been to conceptualize the human individual as part of a social and cultural context not reducible to the physical and biological laws of nature. In that sense, psychology and the other social (and cultural) sciences were, and are, allies vis-à-vis images of the world based on too-sweeping generalizations of insights regarding the structure and evolution of organic systems. Such modes of thought were particularly popular in the latter part of the last century in the wake of the success of the natural sciences, especially Darwin's theory of biological evolution. Seen from a present-day perspective, the history of

Figure 3.2 The human condition. The shaded part is expanded in Figure 3.3a. Source: based on Parsons and Platt, 1973; Parsons, 1978.

empirical studies in the field of human development is a small part of the long intellectual journey towards the conceptualization of the triad of culture, social systems, and individual which, in one way or another, is employed in most types of current reasoning about action systems (see Figures 3.3a and 3.3b). Legion are the descriptions and analyses of empirical systems, historical and current, that try to elucidate the relationships between the individual and all or parts of his or her sociocultural environments. Numerous, and often contradictory, are the interpretations of the long-term changes in these relationships and the primacy and interdependencies of the various subcomplexes. However, overwhelming evidence suggests that, seen from a long-term evolutionary perspective, the cultural systems (symbolic systems) are for the action system what the genetic pool is for the organic systems of species. "Cultural innovations, especially definitions of what man's life *ought* to be, thus replace Darwinian variations in genetic constitution" (Parsons, 1964/1967, p. 495).

But cultural systems, which are no more an individual matter than a genetic pattern, do not implement themselves; they have to be shared among a plurality of individuals and have to be made to bear on social structures. Thus, internalization by individuals and institutionalization in social systems are prerequisites for the maintenance — and, even more, the further development — of cultural systems at any level of complexity. While this formulation brings both "material and social factors" and "man" back into an analytical perspective that might otherwise be charged with being too idealistic, at the same time it highlights another aspect of the importance of cultural patterns for social evolution. Unlike variations in the pools of biological genes that depend on the slow processes of the organic evolution of species for their dissemination, cultural patterns are subject to diffusion

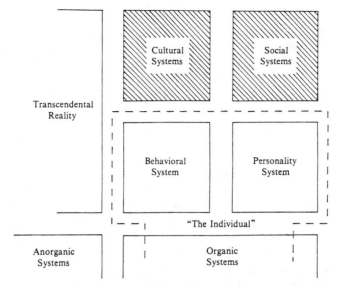

Figure 3.3a Action systems and their environments: The "triad" of cultural systems, social systems and "the individual." The shaded parts are expanded in Figure 3.3b.

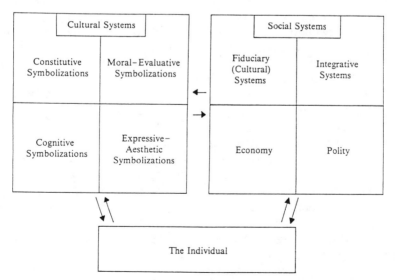

Figure 3.3b The triad: Differentiating the cultural and social systems.

mainly through individual and social learning. Thus the particular constellation of factors that facilitated the emergence of a cultural innovation and its often slow process of initial institutionalization in a particular society does not necessarily set the pace and conditions for subsequent diffusion processes (for further discussion see Baba & Zeigler, Chapter 1, this volume).

To put the basic theoretical premise of our paper more succinctly, we propose to view Bronfenbrenner's history of empirical human development studies as a mirror reflecting some aspects of the "institutionalization of individualism" as an integral part of more general processes of sociocultural development. The starting point of this perspective is that, simply as organic systems, there have always been individual members of the human species or different human populations. However, the extent to which individual personalities, given organic constraints, are allowed to or are normatively expected (even forced) to develop depends on a complex interplay of the structures and characteristics of cultural and social systems vis-à-vis each other and the individual. Undifferentiated cultural systems (i.e., those that explain and legitimate every aspect of life on the basis of an all-encompassing constitutive–religious perspective) cannot justify the existence of differentiated social rules and arrangements, both of which constrain the complexity of personality structures. Seen in this theoretical perspective, the historical changes experienced by today's developed countries have, in a circular way, been caused by a number of important structural changes in the triadic cultural systems–social systems–individual that released formerly constrained development potentials. The structure of the cultural systems has been changed by the emergence of differentiated cognitive, moral–evaluative, and expressive–aesthetic symbolizations in addition to religious ones. The changes thus produced have led to differentiation and specialization of social structures that in stepwise fashion have created and reinforced "institutionalized individualism" as a culturally legitimated and socially anchored image of the human individual, an image which stresses equality, dignity, and independence and legitimates a this-worldly instrumental activism.

We want to provide some theoretical arguments and empirical evidence for the hypothesis that the evolutionary trend towards a stronger institutionalization of individualism is in fact continuing. Seen from a world systems perspective, this trend is not just a process of diffusing a completed and stable "Western" conception of the individual but rather a process of upgrading that conception, a process requiring further generalization and abstraction of the underlying cultural constructs. This process of cultural generalization and abstraction is not confined to the cognitive realm but seems to receive its dynamics from upgrading processes in the moral–evaluative and constitutive realm. As such this trend clearly also affects the so-called developed countries or regional societies. In fact, common social science wisdom would hold that developed countries would develop faster in this respect, accommodating more easily the pressure of cultural and social systems to transcend the traditionally preponderant national context and to encompass the emerging characteristics of world society. From a current world system perspective, we consider this assertion an empirically open question.

II. Toward Worldwide Institutionalized Individualism: The Trend at the State Level

Let us start with a summary of content analyses done by John Meyer and his associates on the constitutions of the independent countries in the world between 1870 and 1970 (Boli-Bennett, 1979; Boli-Bennett & Meyer, 1978). Figure 3.4 shows the composite scores for the constitutional definitions of citizen rights, citizen duties, and state jurisdiction. Figure 3.5 presents the mean scores on indicators for the constitutional definition of the right to education, the duty to be educated, childhood as a distinct stage, state control of education, and state responsibility for children. Figure 3.6 displays the development of a summary index for constitutional definitions of childhood for three groups of countries, essentially, the rich, the intermediate, and the poor. The overall results can be summarized in the following way:

1. There is a marked trend, particularly after 1930, to spell out in more detail and in wider domains both citizen rights and collective responsibilities (Meyer and his associates prefer to use the term "state" for the collectivity). This overall trend is the same for "old" states (independent at 1870) and succeeding generations of new countries and the same for rich and poor. If anything, particularly in the case of childhood indicators, the younger and poorer countries tend to be ahead in the process of constitutionally codifying the mutual, individual, and collective rights and obligations. Technically, this leads to negative correlations between specifications of conceptions of the desirable and measures of the available state resources and level of economic development.

2. Implicit in the citizen rights and state jurisdiction indicators (Figure 3.4) and explicit in the childhood phase (Figures 3.5 and 3.6), there is an overall trend of specifying conceptions of the desirable minimum conditions for the individual's life over the entire life-course (Meyer, 1981).

> The dominance of the ideology of differentiated and state-managed childhood reflects the rise of both individualism and the rationalized nation–state. The individual's status in society increasingly takes the form of membership (citizenship) in the nation and the state: the individual becomes as much an agent of the collectivity as of personal or subgroup interests. (Boli-Bennett and Meyer, 1978, p. 810)

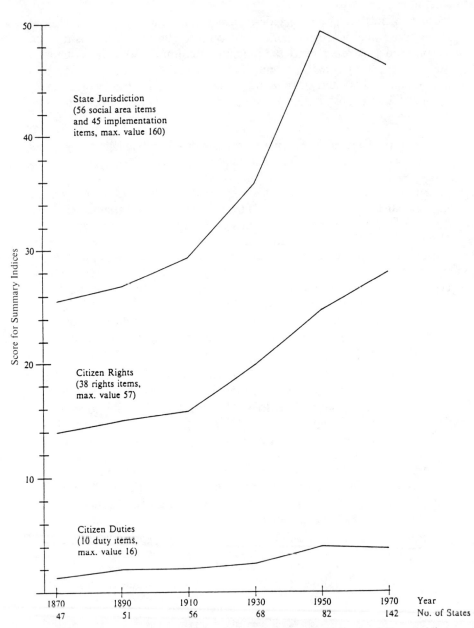

Figure 3.4 Composite score for the definition of individual and collective rights and obligations in state constitutions. Source: based on Boli-Bennett, 1979, p. 227.

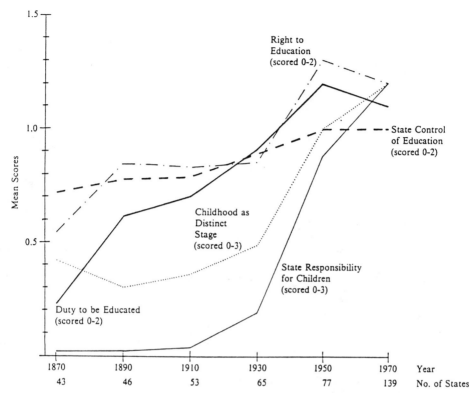

Figure 3.5 Mean scores on indicators for constitutional differentiation of childhood, 1870 – 1970, all countries. Source: based on Boli-Bennett and Meyer, 1978.

Citing the type of data we have summarized, Meyer and his associates frequently refer to the emerging world system. They trace its origin and evolution back to the fifteenth century, the beginning of modern colonialism and the establishment of capitalism:

> Following Immanuel Wallerstein . . . we conceive of the modern world system as an 'effective division of labor', a world economy, in which fundamental commodities are produced and exchanged. [Chase-Dunn and Rubinson, 1979, p. 276. From J. W. Meyer & M. T. Hannan (Eds.), *National Development and the World System: Educational, Economic, and Political Change, 1950–1970*. Chicago: The University of Chicago Press. © 1979 by The University of Chicago.]

While we do not deny the importance of the economic subsystem, either alone or in conjunction with changes in the political system, we hold that its importance as the prime mover is exaggerated (at least in the sense that the cultural prerequisites for such a continued functional primacy are insuffi-

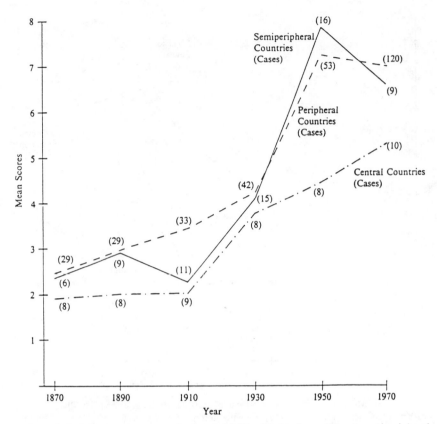

Figure 3.6 Mean scores on constitutional childhood index for peripheral, semiperipheral, and central countries, 1870–1970. Central countries command more than 3%, semiperipheral between 1 and 3%, and peripheral countries less than 1% of world trade. Source: based on Boli-Bennett and Meyer, 1978.

ciently clarified). Further, the institutional and organizational developments "above" the nation–state level, with its more than 35-year history, never explicitly enter the story. But that is, of course, typical for mainstream sociology and, to a somewhat lesser extent, even for the generalist tradition of Parsons.

In the remainder of this section we will first comment at a more technical level on Meyer's data, essentially justifying his and our thesis that the term "institutionalized individualism" (which is usually meant to characterize modern liberal–capitalist states in contradistinction to socialist countries, the rest of the world, and the past) indeed properly characterizes the direction of trends in the current world system. We shall then refer to a set of evolutionary universals suggested by Parsons that describes in greater breadth the dimensions of modernization captured in Meyer's indicators and, at the same time, provides an abstract theoretical formulation for some institutionalization trends at the world system level to which we turn in the third section. We close this second section with some remarks on what seem to us pervasive ideological currents of the last decades underlying the spur to worldwide modernization and institutionalized individualism.

The weakest point in Meyer's analysis is that his variables for the content analysis of constitutions simply measure the total number of provisions referring to, for example, the rights and duties of the citizen and the state. If more sophisticated indicators of the trend towards institutionalized individualism had been devised, the same material — namely, constitutions — would have yielded a more differentiated pattern that agreed more closely with common conceptions of the stratification patterns of the world system. This would hold true particularly if the scores were sensitive to those cases in which the constitutional provisions of individual and collective rights and responsibilities with regard to cultural and political diversity and freedom are explicitly or implicitly restricted (by institutional provisions for a one-party system, for a state religion or ideology, etc.). True, even with sophisticated indicators this procedure would not adequately represent the situation of individual cases such as the Republic of South Africa and its "internal satellites," the homelands, for the simple reason that the apartheid system is only indirectly anchored in that country's constitution. Nor could Saudi Arabia, one of the few countries of the world without a constitution, be adequately included. But it would certainly differentiate substantially between different groups of "central" and "semiperipheral countries" (along the Western liberal and socialist axis) and it would, in all likelihood, allow some differentiation within the group of peripheral Third World countries.

If such an ordering of countries were correlated with data on economic and demographic trends, the opposite of Meyer's findings is likely to result. Does this mean that the indicators and the analyses are invalid with regard to both the emerging and changing ideological reality and, even more important, the socioeconomic reality? Not quite. One of the serious shortcomings of (quantitative) research on comparative development is its socioeconomic reductionism, which is aggravated by its methodological bias towards cross-sectional or short-period time-series analyses. (Of course, reasonably reliable, or at least usable, economic and demographic data for the peripheral and semiperipheral countries have only become available during the last two or three decades.) The results of this reductionism and methodological bias should be well known but unfortunately are not. They consist in the discovery, description, and "explanation" of usually huge (and often growing) disparities between indicators of socioeconomic development for the countries of the world. One can say even less about psychological and sociopsychological issues relevant to the world system because of the lack of data and interest in them. Very often such analyses, and more generally, the empiricist socioeconomic outlook, completely miss the point. Fascinated by differences in current or recent socioeconomic indicators, many analysts become insensitive to coexisting underlying trends of increasingly shared patterns of cognitive and moral – ideological orientation and social organization which, to a considerable extent, co-determine the measurable differences in socioeconomic development and the conflicts arising over them.

In a sense, then, Meyer's analyses of certain provisions of constitutions are a methodological proxy for capturing long-term trends of the ideological and social dynamic of the developing world system, in particular the trend towards institutionalized individualism. There are, of course, other proxies which can be analyzed and interpreted in essentially the same way, such as the absolute and relative growth of school enrollments in the recent decades all over the world (Meyer, Ramirez, Rubinson & Boli-Bennett, 1977/1979; World Bank, 1980). There is also a wealth of legal – historical studies corroborating the overall trend while at the same time "explaining" in a more differentiated way its sociocultural setting and describing in detail the slow process by which efforts to institutionalize individualism coexist, interpenetrate, and partially substitute for different forms of religiously based "customs" and customary law (see Kouassigan, 1974; Tarazi, 1978; Levasseur, 1976; Gasse, 1971).

On the technical level of constitutional provisions, Meyer's data roughly capture confounded aspects of the social modernization process. In a very general way, this process can be characterized as overcoming religiously legitimated kinship bonds as the primary form of social organization. Parsons has suggested the following five "evolutionary universals" of social modernization. They capture different dimensions of restraining as well as supplementing the formerly all-pervasive relevance of the religiously based kinship complex (Parsons, 1967):

1. *Bureaucratic organization:* the institutionalization of universalistic rules by the establishment of an authority of office technically anchored in hierarchical organizations. In an evolutionary perspective closely associated with governmental functions (but not confined to the political realm in the narrow sense), it is a prerequisite to supplementing and controlling kinship-based orientations and criteria of action.

2. *Money and market complex:* the emancipation of economic resources (land, capital, labor) from ascriptive bonds such as kinship expectations, the obligations of loyalty to (feudal) political groups, and the submission to detailed religious imperatives, thereby increasing the legitimate range and

flexibility of combinations of the economic factors of production, range of products, and demand.

3. *Generalized universalistic legal order:* the emergence of codified norms and formalized procedural rules, administered by independent courts and changeable only as the result of due political process as an emancipation of customary law from its embedment in religious tradition on the one hand and its subjection to the arbitrariness of worldly rulers on the other.

4. *The principle of democratic association:* this principle implies elected leadership and fully enfranchised membership in freely accessible associations. Just as bureaucratic organization is not confined but intimately linked to the political realm, this universal is primarily meant to replace hereditary rights of access to and maintenance of leadership positions by institutionalizing leadership functions in the form of elective office. The widening of franchise to include "all normal members" in collective decision making will tend to widen the domain of political issues, potentially affecting diverse patterns of prerogatives and functional specialization which have evolved with social stratification based on the differentiation of classes of kinship units closed by rules of endogamy and the principle of heredity.

5. *Specialized cultural legitimation:* the availability of differentiated cultural justifications once the taken-for-granted fusion of the social structure with the mythical–religious symbolization of a monistic world is left behind. This presupposes at once both the evolution of the systems of cultural symbolization and the institutionalization of the culture-oriented legitimizing function in the fiduciary subsystem. While for long periods of history and a wide range of cultures and societies this relationship was essentially confined to constitutive systems of religious symbolization closely interwoven with the social structure, "Western modernization" has been characterized by a process of abstraction from and generalization of the religious symbolizations, leaving room for the development of more autonomous (but not completely independent) ethical, aesthetic, and cognitive cultural systems and their respective institutionalization.

In accounting for the visible worldwide trend toward institutionalized individualism, Meyer emphasizes the relevance of a general ideology of modernization in connection with the economic subsystem and state bureaucracies for the last three or four decades. We think that more thought should be given to that ideology of modernization because it seems to embrace far more than state-administered economic growth and welfare programs. Moreover, in addition to causing the growth of the number of state bureaucracies and their functional domains, this ideology accounts for two very important phenomena: (1) the amazing post-World War II institutionalization of international organizations and (2) other anchors of the increasing transnational interpenetration of social systems. To put it in a nutshell, the economic "multis" are not the only organizations besides state bureaucracies and international organizations to explicitly "carry" processes of transnational interpenetration. Churches, private charities, and Amnesty International, for example, exemplify noneconomic, nongovernmental organizations that belong to the fiduciary subsystem but are *not* primarily cognitively oriented. Further, since cultural systems and social systems are *not* the same, attention has to be paid to processes of generalizing and upgrading cultural systems lest the proliferation of states and individuals and the processes of *value change* in individuals and in fiduciary organizations be misinterpreted as segmentation, disintegration, or regression when, in fact, they are attempts to cope with the strains of upgrading.

We see the response to the challenge of fascism as the greatest recent push toward an upgrading of the constitutive and moral complexes of Western societies, with far-reaching consequences for the emergence of the present world system. In a sense, fascism, with its racist base, brought to the fore a highly generalized theory of kinship-based social and cultural stratification and evolution (in that sense, as in other more specific contexts, a "modern" ideology). As "applied sociocultural Darwinism" it married the idea of the nation – state with a conception of "sociocultural" differences based on differing racial capacities and tried to delineate the stratification within the spectrum of the truly or fully human from the essentially humanoid or subhuman species (Mazrui, 1968). This type of reasoning, linking the sociocultural definition of "we-ness" to some kind of kinship bond symbolized by commonly shared "blood" and an explicit or implicit definition of the "others" as super- or subhuman species (not related to "us"), is, of course, as old as humanity and survives in some forms in the most modern societies. For instance, the easiest way to join present-day modern societies as a member is to be born a national; this way is closely followed by marrying into the kinship unit. But there is also a trend — from an evolutionary perspective, a very important one — toward specifying conditions under which "joining" and "leaving" is conceived of as an individual's voluntary association with or disassociation from the particular collective solidarity group called "nation" (Parsons, 1977b). No wonder fascism struck a chord of consensus and accorded with social practices of discrimination and their cultural legitimation in *all* the nonfascist, mostly "Western" countries that eventually joined together in the war alliance of the United Nations. One should remember in this connection the discrimination in the United States and elsewhere against Jews (a "light-skinned race") and also the discrimination in the United States and European colonial empires against members of various nonwhite races who were considered to be even further down the scale of humanoid gradation.

But a powerful ideological counteroffensive developed, emphasizing those centuries-old themes of "equality" and "fraternity" (solidarity) and "freedom". Of course, these values had, in general terms, a long history of successful institutionalization in Western societies, from the religious notion of the equality of souls before a Christian God—a God conceived as the Lord of all mankind and not just a particular tribe or race—to the equally religiously based notion of the responsible freedom of the individual vis-à-vis a God accessible without the mediation of a bureaucratized hierarchy. This was followed by the secularized interpretations of the universalistic ideologies of individual human rights, equality, and dignity from the Enlightenment up to the modern "civil religion" type of conceptions (socialist or Western–liberal style) of what man ought to be (Bellah, 1966). The thrust of these ideologies indeed stresses the worth and dignity of equal individuals, irrespective of kinship ascriptions and sex, and stresses also "responsible freedom," which is freedom *within* a morally defined and restricted order of orientation and criteria *with respect to* social structures legitimated in these terms.

From a moral viewpoint, this conception of responsible freedom calls for and at the same time restricts the collective structuring of action systems and constitutes the legitimation for the organization of collective political leadership: "the party," the political system, the state, the international–transnational community. Thus the moral framework of legitimation does not simply provide the rock-bottom base for the grounding of collective political organizations but rather is some kind of autonomous measuring rod of the extent to which collective political organizations live up to the conceptions of the desirable.

The consequences of moral upgrading emerging as a response to the challenge of fascist fundamentalism were far-reaching and operated on a number of different levels. On the international level, one result was the establishment of the United Nations system as a generalization of the ideology and the institutional mechanisms of a modern political system. On the internal state level it supplied, in the case of the United States, a spur to the process of extension of full citizenship to various minority groups besides the Jews, eventually even reaching the black Americans. Externally, it made the United States the "Western" champion of decolonization, putting it in the situation of ideologically joining forces with the socialist camp in its moral support of the colonial world that increasingly challenged the European colonial powers. In the case of the European colonial powers, notably France and Britain, it led to some 15 years of effort to include incrementally the nonmetropolitan, nonwhite colonial subjects in some form of a generalized and extended citizenship status (for a contemporary account of French efforts see Thiam, 1953). That process was speeded up both by "assimilated" Asian and African intellectuals (often teachers) working within the system and by "wars of national liberation" under leaders who rejected the "tokenism" of colonial adjustments.

With some notable exceptions, the colonial system had broken down by the early 1960s. But the "failure" of strategies to transform yesterday's colonial empires into modern political units was accompanied by the emergence and diffusion of the concept of *development,* an amazing upgrading and generalization of "Western" (i.e., "liberal" *and* "Marxist") conceptions of progress. Quite revealing conceptual and ideological realignments had taken place or were under way. In the 1950s, the static notion of "backward" or "underdeveloped" countries, implicitly connected to notions of cultural relativism which in turn were closely interwoven with the idea of the racial and ethnic grounding of culture, personality, and social systems, slowly gave way to the open concept of development. This concept of development, it should be noted, was not an extension of organismic analogies of the unfolding and growth of inherently given natural potentials but rather was the generalization of the ideology of instrumental activism of responsible individuals and collective units in either the Western–liberal or the socialist variant of modernization. Thus, after World War II socialist ideas of the purposeful and accelerated construction of modernity (which before World War II had the status of a deviant experiment in the form of the USSR) found functional equivalents in Western–liberal conceptions of the welfare state and its active interventions designed to promote further economic and social development. Moreover, differently accentuated amalgams of these two strands of ideologies were generalized so as to apply to the rest of the countries of the world and to the world as a whole (the "First Development Decade" being proclaimed in 1961). It should be noted that this process of generalization and abstraction of values and normative conceptions, measured by John Meyer and others on the technical level of diffusion of norms, particularly in the period from 1950 to 1970, is not just an "extension of sameness" but, rather, implies a pluralistic widening of concepts of legitimate diversity and variety. (Mazrui, 1976, has provided a further elaboration of these ideas.)

The ideological upgrading in response to the challenge of fascism seems to have reached a plateau in the period dating roughly from the early 1960s to the middle 1970s. On the politico-ideological front the strains of the Cold War confrontation between the liberal–capitalist and the socialist proponents of modernization subsided (in spite of, or even to some extent because of, the Vietnam War) and made the period of détente possible. Linked to this, but not identical with it, were two important trends in the constitutive system. First, the ecumenical orientation between and within the three major families of Christian churches with regard to the major non-Christian faiths grew in importance. Second, the churches became increasingly ready to acknowledge the legitimacy of a wider spectrum of political responses to the pressing economic and social problems of our times. Within the Roman Catholic Church this trend was symbolized by Pope John XXIII and Vatican II and was, in fact, both part of the move of the Roman Catholic Church toward a stronger ecumenical orientation and a step toward a reduction of the ideological cleavages vis-à-vis socialist movements, parties, and states.

In the 1970s, however, particularly in the second half of the decade, more and more signs of increasing strain became observable; they were partly identical with certain dimensions of the worldwide push toward moderniza- tion in the 1950s and 1960s and partly due to the limits of that process, limits that so far cannot be overcome.

One aspect of these strains is the world economic crisis, triggered by the repeated oil price hikes after 1973, which is the most visible part of the challenge of restructuring economic North – South relations and the growing evidence for the ever more limited scope and feasibility of nationally re- stricted economic policy making. In a sense, this world economic crisis is the result and the expression of the dilemma characterized by "the limits to growth" coexisting with the desperate need for further rapid growth.

While economic and social progress for the countries of the North meant a historically exceptional growth in per capita income and consumption dur- ing the last three-and-a-half decades, for most countries of the South it meant a (very limited) improvement in living conditions, leading to an unprece- dented drop in mortality and thereby to unequalled overall population growth (see Figure 3.7). Strange as it may look at first sight, the accelerating world population explosion of the post-World War II decades is the most valid indicator of the unprecedented modernization push in the Third World, and at the same time it is a striking example of the potentially destabilizing influence that the (human) organic factor (i.e., population in the biological sense) is able to exert on action systems. While the present standards of per capita consumption in the developed world (given present day and prospective technology) by themselves endanger — ceteris paribus — the chances of survival of the species, the Third World as a whole has claim to a fairer (i.e., a rapidly growing) share of present and future resources (*The Global 2000 Report to the President,* 1980). In the meantime, large, if not absolutely increasing, numbers of "human organisms" in the Third World are victims of an extreme form of alienation. Analytically, they are socialized neither into the "modern" or "modernizing" sector nor into the remnants of the "traditional" sector but rather into the ranks of the present- day form of the "lumpenproletariat" as extremely deracinated and alienated products of social change — and not as subjects of development.

While on the surface the tactical skirmishes of modernization seem to

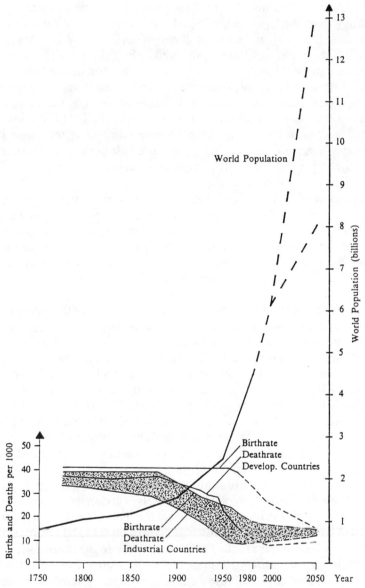

Figure 3.7 Population development of the world: Birthrates, deathrates, 1750–2050. For developing countries, unadjusted birth- and deathrates are shown. Industrial countries includes the USSR and Eastern Europe. Source: based on World Bank, 1980, p. 85.

follow the same patterns as the political debates in the 1970s, the strategic assessment of the situation has slowly but profoundly changed. The optimistic and forward-looking stance of the 1960s generally gave way to an increasingly critical perspective that challenged some of the basic premises of the ideological and political trends of the last decades. In a number of important instances the critical reassessment led to preponderant feelings of disenchantment, despair, deception, and futility and resulted in regressive trends of political and moral – ideological fundamentalism. The Khomeini regime symbolizes the relevance of this fundamentalist undercurrent for the Third World while the Reagan administration represents its counterpart in the First (and Second) Worlds as the visible tip of an iceberg consisting of revived conservatism in other Western countries and, with changed signs, the hawks in the socialist countries. While the Khomeini regime symbolizes its opposition to the evil consequences of modernization by fighting the "Great Satan" (this designation of the United States tellingly underlines the constitutive religious base of political radicalism), the U.S. administration has rediscovered the mood, the theory, and the practice of the "crusade" against the "godless" socialist regimes. This attempt to return to a fundamentalist de-generalization of values, which in essence is supposed to serve as a basis for legitimation of policies along traditional lines of cleavage, should certainly not be taken lightly. However, the existence and relevance of counter-movements should not be discounted. To a still-small extent this counter-movement, most visible in the Western – liberal countries, either forms part of the established or newly emergent ("Green") parties or is part of the churches (as traditional forms of institutionalization of noncognitive fiduciary functions) or peace movements, ecological groups, and lay international charities.

III. The Institutionalization of Individualism at the World System Level

Looking at the history of the institutionalization of the United Nations system from a sociological perspective is revealing for two reasons. First, up to the present day there are theoretical and ideological patterns of arguments treating individual states and their relations to each other in exact parallel to human individuals in a modernizing sociocultural setting. In that sense the post-World War II period of organizing the community of states is a quick motion picture of secular trends in social organization and cultural legitimation that are usually discussed at the level of national societies. Second, there is a supplementary trend, particularly visible since the late 1960s, to conceive of the human individual as an actor in the world system who has legitimate rights and claims vis-à-vis the world community on top of and beyond those of states as collective actors.

A. STATES AS "INDIVIDUALS"

The term "international organization" has a number of meanings and connotations. In older usage it referred, for example, to the secular trend of emerging action patterns in the international relations of states, whether in the form of customary international law, treaties (mostly bilateral) or contract law, or rudimentary procedural regulation of usually ad hoc types of multilateral diplomatic conferences. Before World War I the most important, if not the sole, type of legitimate actors in this action system were the "civilized states," that is, the states of European descent as contrasted with "barbarian" collectivities.

More recently the term increasingly has been restricted to mean either International Governmental Organizations (IGOs) or International Non-Governmental Organizations (INGOs), both relatively new phenomena. The International Telegraph Union (today a specialized agency of the UN system under the name of International Telecommunication Union), founded in 1865, was the first IGO. In 1874 it was followed by the Postal Bureau, which today is a specialized UN agency called the Universal Postal Union. These organizations were confined to limited technical functions.

The first international organization in a general political domain that was meant to be "universal" was the League of Nations, established after World War I. By 1939, the beginning of World War II, the number of IGOs, both universal and "regional," had increased to 87. After World War II the United Nations system was founded, once again with universalistic pretensions; the total number of IGOs, including particularistic ones, jumped to 120 and reached a level of over 200 in the early 1960s. By 1970, the total number of IGOs and INGOs was about 3000. IGOs and INGOs, together with other actors, including most recently the human individual, are today considered to be "subjects" of international law and thereby actors in the international system.

In this section we will confine our comments essentially to universal IGOs, that is, the UN system. What we want to illustrate are, first, some aspects of these organizations as attempts to organize the *polity* of the community of member states, and, second, certain aspects of these IGOs as *bureaucracies* of the rational–legal type pretending to an autonomous "authority of office".

In the preamble and the first articles of the Charter of the United Nations, the general purposes and principles are declared: "We, the People of the

United Nations, are determined to reaffirm faith in fundamental human rights, in the dignity and worth of the human person, in the equal rights of men and women and of nations large and small." Member states promise, inter alia, (1) to practice tolerance and live together in peace and as good neighbors, and (2) to employ international machinery for the promotion of the economic and social advancement of all peoples.

In accordance with the overall normative conception, the United Nations is "based on the principle of sovereign equality of all its Members" (Article 2.1 of the charter) in spite of the enormous social stratification of the community of states. The most visible procedural manifestations is the principle of "one state, one vote." These are the basic ideological premises for the United Nations proper (the all-purpose political center) and the various functionally specialized autonomous agencies which, in contrast to the situation at the time of the League of Nations, are an expression of the overall extension of the concept of political domain and legitimate collective responsibility (see Figure 3.8).

The number of sovereign and equal states grew from 51 founding member states in 1945 to 157 member states in 1981, a growth that was to a considerable extent furthered, if not "caused," by the existence of the UN system (see Figure 3.9). Over the years this growth process slowly shifted the relative weight of votes away from the Junkers of world society, the feudally privileged, to the majority of the more recently enfranchised members from the lower social strata.

As always, there are a number of different ways of defining and measuring social stratification among the members of a societal community. We propose here to look at the assessment scale of UN member states for the regular budget of the UN (see Table 3.1). The same or similar scales are used by most specialized agencies; the scale is based on a number of indicators of the absolute and relative wealth of the members. (For the absolute size of regular budget appropriations for 1981, see Table 3.2.)

In 1970, one state (the United States) contributed 31.5% and the top 15 "upper-class" states together contributed 83% to the regular budget, whereas 69 "lower-class" member states contributed a combined total of only 2.85% (in the range of 0.04–0.05% of the assessment scale).

In 1980 a similar situation prevailed: The United States contributed 25% and the 18 upper-class states together contributed 86% to the regular budget, compared to a 1.36% contribution of by now 94 lower-class states (which are in the range of 0.01–0.05% of the assessment scale).

It is in the General Assembly of the United Nations and the equivalent plenary bodies of the other agencies that the principle of "one state, one vote" finds its clearest institutionalization. The rules of access to the mostly smaller main organs, commissions, and committees tend to be a combination of formal acknowledgment of special prerogatives and responsibilities

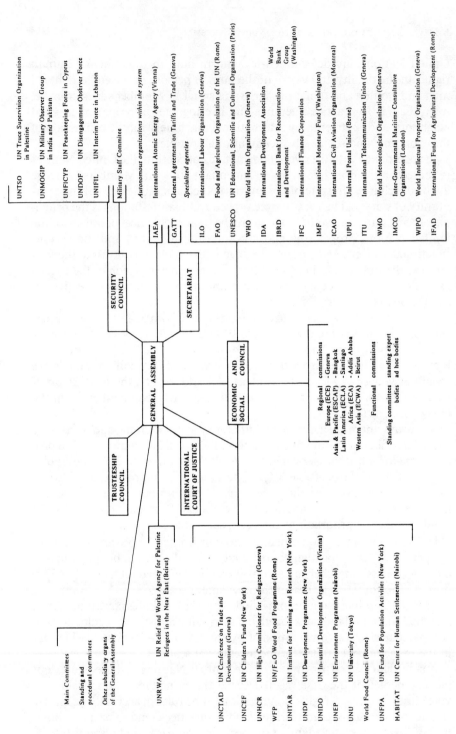

Figure 3.8 The United Nations system. Source: UNITAR, 1980.

UNTSO   UN Truce Supervision Organization in Palestine
UNMOGIP   UN Military Observer Group in India and Pakistan
UNFICYP   UN Peacekeeping Force in Cyprus
UNDOF   UN Disengagement Observer Force
UNIFIL   UN Interim Force in Lebanon

Military Staff Committee

Autonomous organizations within the system

IAEA   International Atomic Energy Agency (Vienna)
GATT   General Agreement on Tariffs and Trade (Geneva)

Specialized agencies

ILO   International Labour Organization (Geneva)
FAO   Food and Agriculture Organization of the UN (Rome)
UNESCO   UN Educational, Scientific and Cultural Organization (Paris)
WHO   World Health Organization (Geneva)
IDA   International Development Association
IBRD   International Bank for Reconstruction and Development
IFC   International Finance Corporation
World Bank Group (Washington)
IMF   International Monetary Fund (Washington)
ICAO   International Civil Aviation Organization (Montreal)
UPU   Universal Postal Union (Berne)
ITU   International Telecommunication Union (Geneva)
WMO   World Meteorological Organization (Geneva)
IMCO   Inter-Governmental Maritime Consultative Organization (London)
WIPO   World Intellectual Property Organization (Geneva)
IFAD   International Fund for Agricultural Development (Rome)

TRUSTEESHIP COUNCIL

SECURITY COUNCIL

GENERAL ASSEMBLY

SECRETARIAT

INTERNATIONAL COURT OF JUSTICE

ECONOMIC AND SOCIAL COUNCIL

Regional commissions
Europe (ECE) - Geneva
Asia & Pacific (ESCAP) - Bangkok
Latin America (ECLA) - Santiago
Africa (ECA) - Addis Ababa
Western Asia (ECWA) - Beirut

Functional commissions

Standing committees standing expert bodies ad hoc bodies

Main Committees
Standing and procedural committees
Other subsidiary organs of the General Assembly

UNRWA   UN Relief and Works Agency for Palestine Refugees in the Near East (Beirut)

UNCTAD   UN Conference on Trade and Development (Geneva)
UNICEF   UN Children's Fund (New York)
UNHCR   UN High Commissioner for Refugees (Geneva)
WFP   UN/FAO World Food Programme (Rome)
UNITAR   UN Institute for Training and Research (New York)
UNDP   UN Development Programme (New York)
UNIDO   UN Industrial Development Organization (Vienna)
UNEP   UN Environment Programme (Nairobi)
UNU   UN University (Tokyo)
World Food Council (Rome)
UNFPA   UN Fund for Population Activities (New York)
HABITAT   UN Centre for Human Settlements (Nairobi)

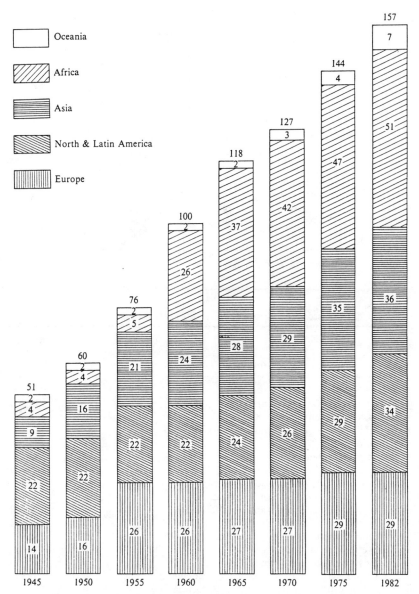

Figure 3.9   Increase of United Nations membership, 1945–1982 (July), by geographical regions.

Table 3.1

Ranges of the UN Assessment Scale, 1970 and 1980[a]

Assessment level (%)	Number of member states		Assessment (subtotals)	
	1970	1980	1970 (%)	1980 (%)
15.01 – 32.00	1	1	31.50	25.00
6.01 – 15.00	2	4	21.20	35.25
3.01 – 6.00	5	3	20.00	11.19
1.01 – 3.00	7	10	10.20	14.67
0.51 – 1.00	10	8	7.25	5.65
0.21 – 0.50	13	13	4.60	4.65
0.06 – 0.20	19	19	2.40	2.23
0.04 – 0.05	69	94	2.85	1.36
	126	152	100.00	100.00

[a] Source: Hüfner, 1983.

Table 3.2

Personnel and Expenditures of the UN System, 1978[a]

Organization	Personnel	Expenditures (in millions of dollars)
UN (United Nations)	14,350	926,500
WHO (World Health Organization)	4,275	333,300
FAO (Food & Agriculture Organization)	4,279	288,600
UNESCO (UN Educational, Scientific, & Cultural Organization)	3,301	188,200
ILO (International Labor Organization)	2,751	150,200
IAEA (International Atomic Energy Agency)	1,563	65,300
ITU (International Telecommunication Union)	598	62,900
ICAO (International Civil Aviation Organization)	988	52,200
WMO (World Meteorological Organization)	356	34,200
GATT (General Agreements on Tariffs & Trade)	216	15,372
WIPO (World Intellectual Property Organization)	192	14,400
UPU (Universal Postal Organization)	130	10,600
IMO (International Maritime Organization)	219	9,100
IFAD (International Fund for Agricultural Development)	80	5,100[b]
World Bank/IDA (International Development Association)	5,260	240,037[b]
IMF (International Monetary Fund)	1,482	95,107[b]
IFC (International Finance Corporation)	265	16,179[b]
	40,305	2,507,295

[a] Source: United Nations, Department of Public Information, 1979, pp. 37–38.
[b] Not including grants and credits.

related to a member state's rank in the social stratification and the principle of free elections based on majority vote. This arrangement requires candidates to campaign for support and obliges the incumbent to act not only for himself but on behalf of his constituency. The most obvious, and in this formal way unique, example for the persistence of a "hereditary right" to leadership positions is the 5 "permanent members" of the Security Council (out of a total of 15) who, in addition, have the right to veto any majority position on matters of substance. Another acknowledgment of social rank is the formal (and informal) reservation of seats for representatives of the lower classes. In many instances this practice has eventually led to the upper-class members becoming a minority. Another prominent exception to the generally pervasive egalitarian principle of the right to equal representation and opportunity to participate in discussions and voting is the World Bank Group. The voting power of the members of the Board of Governors of the World Bank is distributed according to the number of "shares" of the "capital stock" the member states (represented by their governors) hold. The "Great Satan" holds more than 20% of the votes and can, in combination with a few of the medium-sized shareholders, easily mobilize a blocking minority of a third of the votes (for a detailed analysis in favor of further weighted voting formulas see Newcombe, Wert, & Newcombe, 1971).

A salient feature of the development of the UN system has been the enormous growth of issues and functional areas held to legitimately fall within the very general mandate of the UN proper and the extensive interpretation of the mandate of the various specialized agencies. This trend became particularly evident in the 1960s and 1970s. The extension of the franchise to the lower class supported and reinforced the "development issue," which was originally conceived mainly as the "catching up" of segmented lower-class state units but increasingly came to be seen as a complex of interdependencies in which local situations, trends, and decisions manifestly or potentially both depended on and influenced the actions or nonactions of others. Without the strengthening of the cognitive and moral conceptualization of "mankind on spaceship Earth" (or take any other functionally equivalent formulation), the UN system would have crumbled under the permanent clashes of interests and flagrant violations of its principles. But then, what is the UN in functional terms? Is it a fiduciary subsystem — a new church — concerned with the formulation and construction of counterfactually valid values and norms? Or is it a polity, designed for the production of decisions with binding power on its members?

It was always meant to be both a fiduciary subsystem and a polity. On the one hand there were, right from the beginning, all the careful checks and balances designed explicitly to restrict the consequences of majority decisions on dissenting minorities or individual states. The veto was the most extreme form of such control and the status of resolutions as unenforceable, nonbinding recommendations was the most common form. Binding decisions, then, consisted of the residual category of decisions about the internal structure and activities of the organizations. However, majority and particularly consensual unanimous decisions and declarations were and are still declared to have a moral weight and, as such, are deemed to be, or at least to contribute to, international law. In that sense they are considered a separate "source" of international law in addition to contractual – treaty law, customary law, and the learned *communis opinio.* Still, there have been remarkable, though foreseeable, shifts and changes in the appreciation of the "binding" character, the moral relevance, and the law-making aspect of UN decisions.

In a sense, the socialist camp of the Junker states has, over the decades, been consistent in its distant and skeptical attitude vis-à-vis the UN system. These socialist states essentially view the UN as a technical arrangement to facilitate governmental contacts that involves and binds the member states only with their explicit consent. From this position results a hostile attitude vis-à-vis theoretical, ideological, and practical assessments and trends regarding the organizations of the UN system as distinct actors (as "full subjects" of international law besides states) with "implied powers" which unfold in the historical process. In practical terms this has meant, inter alia, that the socialist camp has done the least to support the emergence of the infrastructure of the system in the sense of a bureaucracy of the rational – legal type (Tunkin, 1969; Osakwe, 1972; Rubinstein & Ginsburgs, 1971).

The Western camp of the Junker states (on the level of state bureaucracies and with changing bearers of the ideological banner) has been the most inconsistent UN constituent. From a general position of hailing the procedural, factual, and moral advantages of the democratic character of the system in the 1950s, it changed to practicing for a little more than a decade low-key but financially effective resistance to both the letter and spirit of the mechanisms and has, in quite evident factual alliances with the socialist camp, spent much of the 1970s bemoaning the "tyranny of the majority" and keeping the growth of effective institutionalization of worldwide cooperation at about the level it had reached in the 1960s (Falk, 1975; Moynihan & Weaver, 1978; Schiff, 1974; Stoessinger, 1973).

The Third World, or "Group of 77" as it came to be called in the process of setting up the UN Conference on Trade and Development in the 1960s (by the middle 1980s actually numbering some 120 states), has consistently pressed for a strengthening of the system, supported by the UN bureaucracy and the largely invisible networks of pressure groups in the richer Western countries. In this connection the concept of implied powers has played an important role. In one interpretation it is linked to the law-making function of the system. In pre-World War II times international law consisted largely of "customary law" as it had evolved over the centuries. Most of it had not even been properly codified and existed only as principles and rules distilled in scholarly works from the course of history and common patterns of treaties. In contrast, the last two or three decades has seen an unprecedented growth in positive, codified international law, mostly in the form of treaty law, part of which is conventions that have to be ratified by a minimum number of states before becoming binding upon them and part counterfactually valid norms of existing international law for the rest of the international community. Given the historical changes and the comparatively advanced present day level of international organization, the question has risen as to whether decisions of representative UN bodies on general principles designed essentially to direct the legal and political developments in areas either not covered by customary law or in need of basic revision have the status of international law (Alexandrowicz, 1973; Dupuy, 1975; Hohmann, 1982; Virally, 1965). Is there such a thing as "instant customary law" created by one, two, or some other number of repeated decisions on the same matter? With what types of majority?

More specifically, is there a law of international develoment, and are there principles and rules requiring developed states to effectively contribute to bilateral and multilateral development efforts? Does the 0.7% of GNP (gross national product) requirement as a financial contribution of the Junker states to the development effort of the lower classes and the world, with the consent of the Junkers being declared as necessary in the First, Second, and Third Development Decades, have by now the status of a lawful tax (even if cases of tax evasion are bound to happen)? Is it permissible to infer from the existence of numerous valid and binding conventions on human rights — the most vocal champions of which used to be the "Great Satan" and his Moscow counterpart — that there is a "human right to development"? That inference, which is actually made by large numbers of states and numerous scholars, would strengthen the link between Urie Bronfenbrenner's exosystems and individuals through international law. This would, of course, transcend the preferred type of empirical research and make World Bank literature (World Bank, 1980, 1981) compulsory reading for psychologists.

Another meaning of "implied powers" that has a closer connection to the concept of authority of office in a bureaucracy should be mentioned. The UN Charter and the founding instruments of the specialized agencies are very timid in specifying decisions with binding powers vis-à-vis the community of member states. However, the members of the organizations are fairly free to decide, by majority rule, internal matters of structure and activities of the organizations which, once decided upon, should in principle be financed via the regular budget to which members are obliged to contribute qua members. The logic of these stipulations has made sense against the background of the old, narrow conception of the typical output of political organizations as consisting exclusively of the production of binding rules for the members. Once you have limited the possibility of producing such rules, you can be generous with regard to alternative ways of nonproduction. But what happens when the general ideology changes to include as legitimate outputs of political organizations diverse forms of direct services and assistance to members of the community, provided by and channeled through the political organization and their newly established service units? Such services cost much money; in effect, they are far more costly than "rule production." Do such activities and the requisite structures, staff, and money fall within the legitimate, implied powers of organizations with a general, worldwide mandate that requires their members qua members to abide by majority decisions? The majority of countries thought and think so. The Junkers, of course, had to pay lip-service to the idea, but at the same time always found reasons to reject specific proposals. The result was a series of near stillbirths of "programs" (see the dotted line in Figure 3.10; see Vashti-Kamara & Plano, 1974; Plasil-Wenger, 1974). The Junkers resisted the establishment of new specialized agencies by declaring their unwillingness to ratify the respective conventions suggested by the lower-class majority. By referring to the concept of "implied powers" the lower-class majority nevertheless imposed them on a mini-scale as "programs," forcing the Junkers to pay symbolic amounts for these programs via their regular contributions. To become fully or even halfway "operational" these programs have regularly depended on voluntary contributions which have or, more often, have not come forth. In addition, very often such voluntary contributions have been linked to specific stipulations and expectations of the donors.

Let us close this section with some remarks on the Secretariat of the UN (and the specialized agencies). According to the charter, the UN Secretary-General and the staff "shall not seek or receive instructions from any government or from any other authority external to the Organization" (Article 100); furthermore, "the paramount consideration in the employment of the staff . . . shall be the necessity of securing the highest standards of efficiency, competence, and integrity" and the recruitment of staff shall take place "on as wide a geographical basis as possible" (Article 101).

The Secretary-General of the United Nations has a dual capacity as the executive head of an organization, namely the United Nations, and as the primus inter pares in the administration of the entire UN system. This implies the rather difficult coordination of the UN specialized organizations and the funds and voluntary programs of the UN, of which the Secretary-General is the chief administrator.

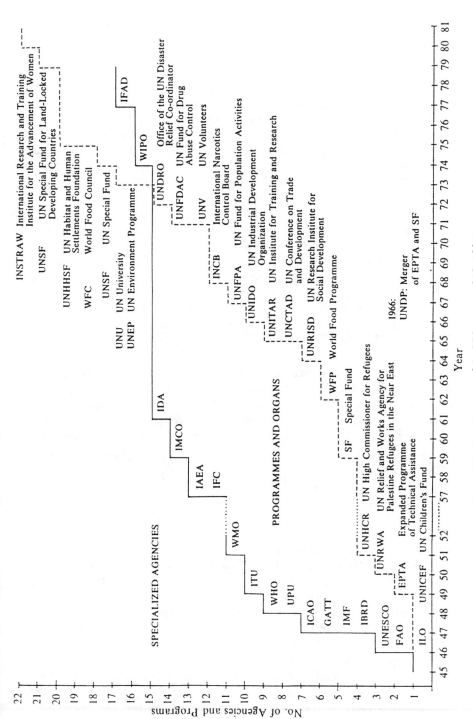

Figure 3.10 Development of the UN system, 1945–1981.

The UN Secretariat comprises all of the international personnel who serve the organs and subsidiary organs of the UN. In 1978 the UN Secretariat consisted of about 14,300 staff members (the figure for 1970 was 10,600), of which about 40% belonged to the professional and field service category and the rest to the general services category. In addition to the overall figure of 14,300 staff members, there were 2,000 experts who served under the UN Regular Technical Assistance Program, UN Funds-in-Trust Projects, and the UNDP (UN Development Program). For the entire UN system over 40,000 staff members were employed in 1978 (the figure for 1970 was 33,000) (see Table 3.2); this staff was serving in 180 different localities all over the world.

The Secretariat is, of course, under considerable internal and external pressure with regard to recruitment and promotion, and in broader terms with respect to its international character and independence. The same is true for the bureaucracies of the specialized agencies. At present, there exists a rather chaotic system of recruitment guidelines, often contradictory and in various respects not in accord with the spirit of the UN Charter. Since it is not infrequent that member states express reservations or even objections to the recruitment of certain individuals, the present situation has made it extremely difficult for the Secretary-General to adhere to the principles laid down in the charter (for details see Finger & Mugno, 1975; Meron, 1976). Nevertheless, recent conflicts between the General-Director of UNESCO (UN Educational, Scientific, and Cultural Organization) and socialist member states clearly indicate that the administrative heads of the UN system continue to work for an independent international civil service.

B. THE WORLD SYSTEM AND THE HUMAN INDIVIDUAL

The United Nations and its specialized organizations are international *governmental* organizations; their members are sovereign nation states. This fact could lead to the conclusion that the normal human individual in his or her personal capacity has neither access to the UN system nor is the immediate "target" of any policies. This conclusion, however, is no longer valid; trends toward the codification of international law and the formulation of international development strategies which bring in the individual play an increasingly important role.

The classical forms of international law as it addresses the relations between state actors, remain, of course, in the center of the legal activities of the UN system. But in addition to law and treaty making and codification processes designed to revise old structures or to put new problems into legal frameworks (for instance, the law of the sea, the law of outer space), a remarkable growth of international private law can be observed. An example is the growth in international law relating to the activities of multinational companies.

Furthermore, certain trends in the field of human rights codification should be noted. The Charter of the UN contains, as mentioned earlier, the reaffirmation of "faith in fundamental human rights, in the dignity and worth of the human person, in the equal rights of men and women and of nations large and small". "Promoting and encouraging respect for human rights" and "assisting in the realization of human rights and fundamental freedoms" are phrases appearing, with some variation, in different contexts in the charter. Moreover, there exist two articles in which all member states pledge to take joint and separate action in cooperation with the organization for the achievement of "universal respect for, and observance of, human rights and fundamental freedoms for all without distinction as to race, sex, language, or religion" (Articles 13 & 15). Still, the charter remains vague in its provisions and it contains the often-quoted domestic jurisdiction clause which proclaims that nothing in it "shall authorize the United Nations to intervene in matters which are essentially within the domestic jurisdiction of any state" (Articles 2 & 7). One of the significant changes in the process of international human rights codification is, however, the growing tendency toward nonapplication of the domestic jurisdiction clause because human rights have ceased to be considered "essentially within the domestic jurisdiction of states"—a trend sharply criticized by many states, especially those charged with human rights violations. In other words, neither the vagueness and generality of the human rights clauses for the charter nor the domestic jurisdiction clause have prevented the UN from considering, investigating, and passing judgment on concrete human rights situations (for surveys see Rowe, 1970; Vasak, 1980).

When the UN charter was being drafted in the 1940s, there was a general agreement among the founders of the UN that an International Bill of Human Rights be proposed to supplement the human right provisions of the charter through the establishment of a Commission on Human Rights with procedural provisions for following up complaints. As a first result, on December 10, 1948, the UN General Assembly adopted the Universal Declaration of Human Rights which proclaims in Article 26, Section 1 that "everyone has the right to education. Education shall be free, at least in the elementary and fundamental stages. Elementary education shall be compulsory." Although the Universal Declaration is not, as such, a legally binding document, it has exercised a powerful influence both at the national and international level. In many new nation-states provisions of the Universal Declaration have been incorporated, in their original wording, into the national constitutions. At the international level, the Economic and Social Council (ECOSOC) of the UN passed several resolutions which led after 1971 to a step-by-step improvement of the procedure and to rules for the admission of complaints ("communications"). Since then the Commission on Human Rights has had the power to deal with "gross violations" and "consistent patterns of violations" communicated to the commission by *individuals* and *nongovernmental organizations* (like Amnesty International). This development put new life into the human rights norms as laid down in the Universal Declaration (Fonseca, 1975; Guggenheim, 1973).

The other two parts of the old project of an International Bill of Human Rights were adopted by the UN General Assembly on December 16, 1966, and came into force in 1976: (1) the International Covenant on Economic, Social and Cultural Rights and (2) the International Covenant on Civil and Political Rights (together with the Optional Protocol to the Covenant on Civil and Political Rights). These two covenants are legally binding treaties. Article 13 of the first covenant is wholly devoted to the right to education. As of July 1, 1981, 69 national states had ratified the first covenant, 67 the second one. By the same date 26 states had ratified the Optional Protocol, whereby they recognize the competence of a new international organ, the Human Rights Committee, to receive and consider communications from *individuals* who claim to be victims of a violation of the covenant.

On December 14, 1960, the UNESCO General Conference adopted the Convention Against Discrimination in Education and a recommendation containing similar substantive provisions. The convention entered into force on May 22, 1962; as of December 31, 1980, 38 states had ratified it. The UNESCO convention restates two principles of the Universal Declaration, namely the prohibition of any kind of discrimination (Article 2) and the right of every person to education (Article 26). The purpose of the UNESCO convention is, therefore, not only to eradicate all forms of discrimination but also to ensure that further steps are taken toward increasing the equality of educational opportunity and treatment. Article 1 of the convention states that

> the term "discrimination" includes any distinction, exclusion, limitation, or preference which, being based on race, colour, sex, language, religion, political or other opinion, national or social origin, economic condition, or birth, has the purpose or effect of nullifying or impairing equality of treatment in education, and in particular:
> (a) of depriving any person or group of persons of access to education of any type or at any level;
> (b) of limiting any person or group of persons to education of an inferior standard;
> (c) subject to the provisions of Article 2 of this convention, of establishing or maintaining separate educational systems or institutions for persons or groups of persons; or
> (d) of inflicting on any person or group of persons conditions which are incompatible with the dignity of man. (UNESCO, 1981, p. 4)

Member states must submit periodic reports which are examined in accordance with a procedure established by the UNESCO Executive Board in 1965. Furthermore, in 1968 a protocol became effective that instituted a Conciliation and Good Offices Commission responsible for seeking the settlement of any dispute which may arise between states or other parties to the UNESCO convention mentioned above.

In 1976 the UNESCO Executive Board adopted a procedure which, though similar to that of the ECOSOC, goes much further in the procedure to be followed in the examination of cases and questions submitted to UNESCO concerning the exercise of human rights in the sphere of its competence. According to that procedure, states, individuals, groups of individuals, and nongovernmental organizations are entitled to address communications to UNESCO about violations of human rights in education and other fields of its competence, provided that the authors are either victims of the violations or have "reliable knowledge" about human rights violations. The procedure distinguishes between "cases" (individual and specific violations of human rights) and "questions" (massive, systematic, or flagrant violations of human rights committed de jure or de facto by a state or resulting from an accumulation of individual cases forming a consistent pattern). Also important is the fact that the procedure includes no requirement that the author of the communication should be in any particular ascriptive relationship, in terms of nationality or residence, vis-à-vis the state charged with the violation. The communication must indicate whether "an attempt" has been made to exhaust available domestic remedies. It does not, however, require, as is the case in most other international procedures, the previous exhaustion of all domestic remedies. Therefore, the UNESCO procedure has been characterized as only "half way" applying the restrictive traditional judicial rules. Finally, a striking departure from the ECOSOC procedure on "gross violations" should be noted. In relation to questions of "massive, systematic or flagrant violations of human rights and fundamental freedoms . . . falling within UNESCO's field of competence," confidentiality is no longer demanded; on the contrary, such questions are to be considered by the UNESCO Executive Board and General Conference in public meetings.

Additional trends which relate the human individual to the world system in legal and functional terms have become salient since the middle of the 1970s. A milestone was the International Labour Organization's (ILO) tripartite world conference in 1976, which convened state representatives as well as representatives of national trade unions and employers' organizations to discuss a new leitmotiv of world society: "Employment, growth and basic needs: A one-world problem" (International Labour Office, 1976). The basic human needs approach as outlined in the ILO report asked for a reformulation and reorientation of traditional development strategies by including, as an explicit goal, the satisfaction of an absolute minimum level of basic needs. Two elements were included in the concept of basic needs, namely (1) certain minimum requirements of a family for private consumption such as adequate food, shelter, and clothing and (2) essential services provided by and for the community at large, such as safe drinking water, sanitation, and health and education facilities.

ILO stressed that a basic-needs oriented policy implies the participation of the people in the decision-making processes which affect them and should serve both as a means and as an end; further, the ILO policy asked for a redistribution of income and wealth. In addition, ILO emphasized that basic needs constitute the minimum objective of society, that the basic-needs concept is of universal applicability (although the relative importance of its components will vary from state to state, depending upon the level of development), and that the satisfaction of an absolute level of basic needs should be placed within the broader framework of fulfilling basic human rights.

This ILO document is one of the important landmarks of a trend in international discussions (and those in the transnational professional community) of economic and social development strategies to "go beneath" the state or functional system level (economic branches, functional sectors, organizations) and increasingly include "the individual." In fact, this trend is double-edged since it establishes at the same time the analytical and normative links between "the individual" and the world system level.

A number of quite different issues and problems (and, consequently, disciplinary and theoretical perspectives) contributed to the emergence of this trend during the last decade. For instance, the basic human needs debate previously referred to has to be seen in the wider context of the critical appraisal of the economic development strategies of the First Development Decade (the 1960s), strategies which were charged with an overemphasis on capital-intensive technologies in the modern, often export-oriented (agro-)industrial sectors and on unjustified optimism with regard to the "trickle-down" effects of economic growth. As a consequence, the problems of what came to be called "absolute poverty" and, more generally, of more equilibrated efforts to include the majority of the populations in modernization efforts came to the fore (Asher, 1971; Gordenker & Jacobson, 1970; Singer, 1978).

Another issue was the rising salience of the population explosion which, in turn, was closely connected with the debate about the availability of renewable and nonrenewable resources and problems of ecological equilibria. The world population issue, empirically and analytically "present" since about the end of the 1950s, moved to the political fore in the late 1960s to early 1970s. The national and also the world system consequences of the historically unprecedented rates of population growth came to be discussed on a large scale. The sharp controversies about the need and the legitimacy of population and family-planning policies that were designed to reduce the growth rates characteristic of the debate a decade earlier slowly but persistently gave way to more sober analytical and political efforts (for an assessment see UNFPA, 1980).

The World Development Reports of 1980 and 1981 (World Bank, 1980, 1981) are probably the most comprehensive summaries available of an empirically oriented, social science type of reasoning about human development issues linked with the wider problems of national and international socioeconomic development. To be sure, the reports primarily marshal theoretical and empirical evidence for the long-term effects of strengthening the institutionalization of individualism and plead for corresponding political and administrative actions, indirectly and cautiously assessing and criticizing current priorities of governments and international agencies. Of course, the implied bias of instrumental activism accounts for a comparative neglect of the theoretical and empirical arguments explaining the evolutionary origins of the current situation in Third World countries and the diversity of "nonmodern" forms of resistance to efforts to change it.

Connected with the aforementioned confluents making up the visible trend toward institutionalized individualism at the world system level, but technically centered on political and normative – legal aspects of this process, was yet another string of debates and controversies of the 1970s; the topic was the New International Economic Order (NIEO) and its links with the evolving conceptions of individual human rights and their international codification. The thrust of the original NIEO resolutions and declarations (United Nations, 1974a, 1974b) was to complement the free world market mechanisms with certain regulations and interventions meant to improve the position of the peripheral countries vis-à-vis those of the (Western) center. In the present connection, the protracted and continuing negotiations about the details of regulating various markets of raw materials and intermediate and final products need not concern us. What is important, however, is the fact that the original NIEO-level of analysis restricting the development and policy issues to the interstate level was soon generalized to include various intranational dimensions of development: internal income distribution, the need not only to develop export-oriented industries but to devise policies reducing mass poverty, meeting basic human needs, and safeguarding fundamental human rights.

In 1979, a report by the Secretary-General ascertained for the first time the existence of an emerging Right to Development which includes and combines individual human rights and rights and obligations of states (United Nations, Secretary-General, 1979). There have been forerunners (see for example, UNESCO, 1978) and there will continue to be many more efforts like the current ones of the UN Commission on Human Rights (United Nations, 1982) to translate the "soft law" of declarations and resolutions into the "harder" form of conventions and treaties, to transform "mere" moral rights and obligations into legally binding norms. While the international codification of the "first generation" of individual human rights (i.e., civil and political rights) was championed mainly by the Western countries and the "second generation" of rights (i.e., social and economic rights) by the socialist countries, the current "third generation" of rights — by now designated "solidarity rights" — is championed by the Third World. Not surprisingly, they meet with considerable resistance from the Junker states because rights also constitute obligations, and linking individual human rights to development to state rights to development in the present world system also constitutes third-party (state) obligations — and it still seems to be easier to live with defaults on moral obligations than not to abide by "the law."

IV. Conclusions

What does our long and abstract story boil down to? Aren't all these negotiations at the United Nations, including the efforts to institutionalize individualism, at best peripheral changes in what Bronfenbrenner (1982) would perhaps call "external exosystems"? To us these changes are not external but are proxies for internal changes of the world system which either go unnoticed or tend to be misinterpreted when traditional national perspectives are maintained. In analytical terms, the problem consists of conceptualizing in an adequate way the contemporary changes in cultural systems which call forth and legitimize the (still continuing) institutionalization of individualism in social systems and set the stage for and mold personalities. In this relationship, it seems to us, a silent revolution has been in the making during the last decades, and it is far more profound and general than Inglehart (1977, 1979) has identified in the changing value orientations of the people of Western countries. His excellent study identified a growing minority of people (more heavily represented in the younger age-groups and in the better-educated strata) with "post-materialist values." Members of this minority show markedly different opinions and action dispositions than do those belonging to the traditional "materialist" majority. While this study must be welcomed as a contribution toward a reopening of the debate about psychological correlates of modernization processes in industrialized countries, its theoretical and empirical bias should be noticed. There is no consideration of the possibility that Inglehart's conception of value change (even with *identical* items and scores) would have led to the *same overall*

patterns if data had been gathered on representative samples of the populations of socialist Second World countries. Nor is the possibility considered
that the *same patterns* would be found for certain portions of representative
population samples of Third World countries. Further, there is not the
slightest consideration of the possibility that a widening of the concept of
value change would have made it possible to tap dimensions of the silent
revolution even among the semiliterates and illiterates in representative
population samples of Third World countries. (For the unexplored challenge of such surveys see Hubscher, 1980 and Gallup International Research
Institutes, 1977.) What are the reasons for this bias in Inglehart's study (a
bias consistently showing up in the reaction of the scientific community as
well)? Not everything can be explained by the fact that the money and the
apparatus behind the data side of the enterprise is the European community
with its regular opinion pools. After all, one is free (within limits) to think
and read and write. The answer seems to be that, while social scientists are
likely to score high on the postmaterialist index of crude mass surveys, they
may at the same time score high on the materialist side of a more sensitive
instrument designed to measure their professional theoretical and empirical
orientations. Scored on the basis of his preferred authors and theoretical
orientation, Inglehart would be close to the materialist majority of "our
trade"; some of his "looser reasoning" about the origins and the likely
consequences of the silent revolution would, however, move him closer to
the postmaterialist minority, a typical intermediate value type.

   Our position in this paper has been radically postmaterialist. The silent
revolution, in our view, is a worldwide phenomenon which should perhaps
more appropriately be called the "educational revolution" in the world
system sense suggested by Meyer, Ramirez, Rubinson, and Boli-Bennett
(1977/1979), and theoretically explicated by Parsons (1971) and Parsons
and Platt (1973, especially Chapter 1). After the "industrial revolution" and
the "democratic revolution" which, starting in the seventeenth century,
created "modern society," we are today no longer witnessing the beginnings
but already some of the consequences of a socially generalized process of
cognitive and moral upgrading, a process heavily dependent on the spread of
modern formal education. This silent educational revolution does not substitute or replace the political or economic dynamics of modernization, but it
does affect them and it might even become the prime mover. The "new"
and the "old" priests, intellectuals, politicians, and, of course, scientists of
various backgrounds—in short, those entrusted with fiduciary responsibility for the adequate interpretation of the human condition—remain the
social agents mediating the relations between cultural systems and social
systems. Collectively, they define what "man ought to be." If nothing
more, looking at what happens in the United Nations system seems to be one

way to register world system trends which, when looked at from national
perspectives, either remain blurred due to that particularistic perspective or
become discernible and measurable only much later.

References

Alexandrowicz, C. H. *The law-making functions of the specialized agencies of the United Nations.* Sydney: Angus & Robertson, 1973.
Anderson, H. E. *The young child in the home.* New York: Appleton Century, 1936.
Asher, R. E. Development assistance in DD II: The recommendations of Perkins, Pearson, Peterson, Prebisch, and others. *International Organization,* 1971, *25,* 97–119.
Bellah, R. N. Religious evolution. In S. N. Eisenstadt (Ed.), *Readings in social evolution and development.* Oxford: Pergamon Press, 1966.
Boli-Bennett, J. The ideology of expanding state authority in national constitutions, 1870–1970. In J. W. Meyer & M. T. Hannan (Eds.), *National development and the world system: Educational, economic, and political change, 1950–1970.* Chicago & London: University of Chicago Press, 1979.
Boli-Bennett, J., & Meyer, J. The ideology of childhood and the state: Rules distinguishing children in national constitutions. *American Sociological Review,* 1978, *43,* 797–812.
Bronfenbrenner, U. *The context of development and the development of context.* Unpublished manuscript, Cornell University, 1982.
Burt, C. The inheritance of general intelligence. *American Psychologist,* 1972, *27,* 175–190.
Chase-Dunn, C., & Rubinson, R. Cycles, trends, and new departures in world-system development. In J. W. Meyer & M. T. Hannan (Eds.), *National development and the world system: Educational, economic, and political change, 1950–1970.* Chicago & London: University of Chicago Press, 1979.
Dupuy, R.-J. Droit déclaratoire et droit programmatoire: de la coutume sauvage à la 'Soft Law'. In Société Française pour le Droit International, *L'élaboration du droit international.* Paris: Pedone, 1975.
Falk, R. A. The American attack on the United Nations: An interpretation. *Harvard International Law Journal,* 1975, *16,* 566–575.
Finger, S. M., & Mugno, J. F. The politics of staffing the United Nations Secretariat. *Orbis,* 1975, *11,* 117–145.
da Fonseca, G. *How to file complaints of human rights violations.* Geneva: World Council of Churches, 1975.
Gallup International Research Institutes. *Human needs and satisfaction: A global survey* (Summary vol.). June 1977 (Princeton, N.J., mimeographed.)
Galton, F. The history of twins as a criterion of the relative power of nature. *Anthropological Institute Journal,* 1876, *5,* 391–406.
Gasse, V. *Les régimes fonciers africains et malgache: Evolution depuis l'indépendance.* Paris: Pichon & Durand-Anzias, 1971.
The Global 2000 report to the president. Published by the Council on Environmental quality and the Department of State. Washington, D.C.: Government Printing Office, 1980.
Gordenker, L., & Jacobson, H. K. Critical choices for the UN system: The second development decade. *Orbis,* 1970, *14,* 43–57.
Guggenheim, M. H. Key provisions of the new United Nations rules dealing with human rights petitions. *New York University Journal of International Law and Politics,* 1973, *6,* 427–454.

Hartup, W. W. Perspectives on child and family interaction: Past, present and future. In R. M. Lerner & G. B. Spanier (Eds.), *Child influences on marital and family interaction: A life-span perspective.* New York: Academic Press, 1978.

Hohmann, R. Recht auf Entwicklung in der internationalen Diskussion. *Vereinte Nationen,* 1982, *2,* 59–64.

Hubscher, F. Quand on ose interroger les Africains. *Jeune Afrique,* 31 Decembre 1980, 108–112.

Hüfner, K. *Die Vereinten Nationen: Ein Studien- und Arbeitsbuch.* Bonn: Deutsche UNESCO-Kommission, 1983.

Inglehart, R. *The silent revolution: Changing values and political styles among Western publics.* Princeton, N.J.: Princeton University Press, 1977.

Inglehart, R. Value priorities and socioeconomic change. In S. H. Barnes & M. Kaase (Eds.), *Political action: Mass participation in five western democracies.* Beverly Hills, Calif. & London: Sage Publications, 1979.

International Labour Office. *Employment, growth and basic needs: A one-world problem.* Geneva: Author, 1976.

Jensen, A. R. *Bias in mental testing.* New York: Free Press, 1980.

Kouassigan, G. A. *Quelle est ma loi? Tradition et modernisme dans le droit privé de la famille en Afrique noire francophone.* Paris: Pedone, 1974.

Levasseur, A. A. *The civil code of the Ivory Coast.* Charlottesville, Va.: Michie, 1976.

Luhmann, N. (Ed.). Die Weltgesellschaft. In N. Luhmann, *Soziologische Aufklärung 2.* Opladen: Westdeutscher Verlag, 1975. (Originally published, 1971.)

Luria, A. R. *Cognitive development: Its cultural and social foundations.* Cambridge, Mass.: Harvard University Press, 1976.

Mazrui, A. From social Darwinism to current theories of modernization: A tradition of analysis. *World Politics,* 1968, *1,* 69–83.

Mazrui, A. *A world federation of cultures: An african perspective.* New York: Free Press, 1976.

Meron, T. Staff of the United Nations Secretariat: Problems and directions. *American Journal of International Law,* 1976, *70,* 659–693.

Meyer, J. W. *The institutionalization of the life course and its effects on the self.* Unpublished manuscript, Max-Planck-Institut für Bildungsforschung, Berlin, F.R.G., 1981.

Meyer, J. W., Ramirez, F. O., Rubinson, R., & Boli-Bennett, J. The world educational revolution, 1950–1970. In J. W. Meyer & M. T. Hannan (Eds.), *National development and the world system: Educational, economic, and political change, 1950–1970.* Chicago & London: University of Chicago Press, 1979. (Originally published, 1977.)

Moynihan, D. P., & Weaver, S. *A dangerous place.* Boston: Little, Brown, 1978. (German edition: *Einspruch: Der UNO-Botschafter gegen die Weltpolitik der Anpassung.* Berlin: Ullstein Verlag, 1980.)

Newcombe, H., Wert, J., & Newcombe, A. Comparison of weighted voting formulas for the United Nations. *World Politics,* 1971, *23,* 452–492.

Osakwe, C. *The participation of the Soviet Union in universal international organizations.* Leyden: Sijthoff, 1972.

Der Pädagogische Verein in Berlin. Der Vorstellungskreis der Berliner Kinder beim Eintritt in die Schule. In *Städtisches Jahrbuch für Volkswirtschaft und Statistik* (Vierter Jahrgang). Berlin: Statistisches Bureau der Stadt Berlin, 1870.

Parsons, T. Evolutionary universals in society. In T. Parsons, *Sociological theory and modern society.* New York: Free Press, 1967. (Originally published, 1964.)

Parsons, T. Higher education as a theoretical focus. In H. Turk & R. Simpson (Eds.), *Institutions and social exchange.* Indianapolis, Ind.: Bobbs–Merrill, 1971.

Parsons, T. Comparative studies and evolutionary change. In T. Parsons, *Social systems and the evolution of action theory.* New York: Free Press, 1977. (Originally published, 1971.) (a)

Parsons, T. Some theoretical considerations on the nature and trends of change of ethnicity. In T. Parsons, *Social systems and the evolution of action theory.* New York: Free Press, 1977. (Originally published, 1975.) (b)

Parsons, T. A paradigm of the human condition. In T. Parsons, *Action theory and the human condition.* New York: Free Press, 1978.

Parsons, T., & Platt, G. *The American university.* Cambridge, Mass.: Harvard University Press, 1973.

Plasil-Wenger, F. UNIDO: Problem child of the United Nations family. *Journal of World Trade Law,* 1974, *8,* 186–199.

Rowe, E. T. Human rights issues in the UN General Assembly, 1946–1966. *Journal of Conflict Resolution,* 1970, *14,* 425–441.

Rubinstein, A. Z., & Ginsburgs, G. (Eds.). *Soviet and American policies in the United Nations: A twenty-five-year perspective.* New York: New York University Press, 1971.

Schiff, M. The United States and the United Nations: On a collision course. *Orbis,* 1974, *18,* 553–581.

Sears, R. R. Your ancients revisited: A history of child development. In E. M. Hetherington (Ed.), *Review of child development research* (Vol. 5). Chicago: University of Chicago Press, 1975.

Singer, H. W. Wirtschaftswachstum oder Bekämpfung der Armut? Dreißig Jahre Wandel im Entwicklungsdenken der Vereinten Nationen. In J. Naumann (Ed.), *Auf dem Weg zur sozialen Weltwirtschaft.* Berlin: R. Sperber Verlag, 1978.

Skeels, H. M., Updegraff, R., Wellman, B. L., & Williams, H. M. *A study of environmental stimulation: An orphanage preschool project.* Iowa City: The University of Iowa, 1938.

Spearman, C. The heredity of abilities. *Eugenics Review,* 1914, *6,* 219–237.

Stoessinger, J. G. *The United Nations and the superpowers: China, Russia & America.* New York: Random House, 1973.

Tarazi, S. el D. La solution des problèmes de statut personnel dans le droit des pays arabes et africains. *Recueil des Cours,* 1978, *159,* 351–463.

Thiam, D. *La portée de la citoyenneté française dans les territoires d'outre-mer.* Paris: Société d'Editions Africaines, 1953.

Tunkin, G. I. *The legal nature of the United Nations.* Leyden: Sijthoff, 1969.

UNESCO (United Nations Educational, Scientific, and Cultural Organization). *Expert meeting on human rights, human needs and the establishment of a new international economic order: Final report* (SS.78/Conf. 630/12). Paris: Author, 1978.

UNESCO (United Nations Educational, Scientific, and Cultural Organization). *Standard-setting instruments.* Paris: Author, 1981.

UNFPA (United Nations Fund for Population Activities). *Population facts at hand.* Saddle River, N.J.: Echo Productions, 1980.

United Nations. *Charta of economic rights and duties of states* (UN-Doc. A/Res/3281 [XXIX]), New York, Dec. 12, 1974. (a)

United Nations. *Declaration and programme of action on the establishment of a new international economic order* (UN-Docs. A/Res/3201[S-VI] & 3202[S-VI]), New York, May 1, 1974. (b)

United Nations. *Report of the working group of governmental experts on the right to development* (UN-Doc. E/CN.4/1489), New York, Jan. 25, 1982.

United Nations, Department of Public Information. *United Nations: Image & reality.* New York: UN, 1979.

United Nations, Secretary-General. *The international dimensions of the right to development as a human right in relation with other human rights based on international co-operation, including the right to peace, taking into account the requirements of the new international economic order and the fundamental human needs* (UN-Doc. E/CN.4/1334), New York, Jan. 2, 1979.

Vasak, K. (Ed.), *Les dimensions internationales des droits de l'homme.* Paris: UNESCO, 1980. (English version, in press.)

Vashti-Kamara, M., & Plano, J. C. *United Nations Capital Development Fund: Poor and rich worlds in collision.* Kalamazoo, Mich.: New Issues Press, Institute of Public Affairs, 1974.

Virally, M. Vers un droit international du développement. *Annuaire Français de Droit International,* 1965, *11,* 3–12.

Vygotsky, L. S. *Mind in society: The development of higher psychological processes.* Cambridge, Mass.: Harvard University Press, 1978.

World Bank. Part II: Poverty and human development. *World Development Report 1980.* Washington, D.C.: Author, 1980.

World Bank. Human development: A continuing imperative. *World Development Report 1981.* Washington, D.C.: Author, 1981.

4

Causal Regressive Dependencies: An Introduction*

ROLF STEYER

I. Introduction

Stochastic or nondeterministic causal dependence is one of the most important ideas in present scientific investigation. This can easily be seen from the fact that experimentation and almost the whole body of experimental design theory center around control techniques such as randomization, matching, and so forth, which are applied to assure "internal validity" (Campbell & Stanley, 1963; Cook & Campbell, 1979); that is, to prevent other variables from modifying the covariation between the dependent and the independent variables (see Bredenkamp, 1980). If internal validity can be assumed, a causal interpretation of the observed dependencies is permissible, although some authors try to avoid the word "causation" in this context. According to Bredenkamp (1980, p. 1), for example, the aim of experimentation is "to be able to interpret unambiguously the change of the dependent variable as a consequence of the change of the independent vari-

---

* Originally, the title of this chapter was "Causal Linear Stochastic Dependencies: An Introduction. Now (July 1984) I think the present title is more appropriate.

ables" [author's translation]. Fundamentally, internal validity represents an ideal situation in which the observed statistical dependencies are so pure or unconfounded that they can be causally interpreted, provided the variables are appropriately ordered with respect to time.

The idea of internal validity has undoubtedly been of great importance for the methodology of sciences like psychology because it has helped to bring about useful experimental, quasi-experimental, and nonexperimental design and control procedures. In this chapter, a stochastic formalization of this idea for dependencies of the kind that can be described by a conditional expectation is outlined. These dependencies include those described by analysis of variance, regression analysis, path analysis, common factor analysis, recursive structural equation, and logit-linear models. The implications of this theory concern both experiments and nonexperimental correlational studies. For the latter, we might add, a theory and explication of the concept of causal dependence is of crucial importance. Whereas in the randomized experiment there are few problems about interpreting an observed covariation between the dependent variable Y and the independent or treatment variable X, in nonexperimental and purely observational studies, the interpretational problems are often enormous.

In the last decade, causal modeling by structural equations has become a promising approach for a growing number of scientists because formalized and testable models have been introduced and a number of appropriate computer programs have become available (e.g., Jöreskog & Sörbom, 1981; Lohmöller, 1984). However, the model tests in structural equation models test only the *statistical* fit of the model. They do not test the hypothesis that the model describes the *causal mechanism* that generates the data. Some proponents of causal modeling even seem to believe that there is no problem in writing about causal models without defining the concept of causal dependence implicitly used (e.g., Bentler, 1980, p. 420):

> Obviously it is not necessary to take a stand on the meaning of "cause" to see why the modeling process is colloquially called causal modeling (with latent variables). The word "cause" is meant to provide no philosophical meaning beyond a shorthand designation for a hypothesized unobserved process, so that phrases such as "process" or "system" modeling would be viable substitute labels for "causal" modeling.

From my own point of view, it is quite obvious that a causal model does not have any meaning beyond that of a statistical model if there is no definition of causality used in the definitional context. In other words, a causal model, once it correctly describes the data, cannot be rejected in its *causal* status if there is no definition of the concept of causality used, for without it, one cannot deduce falsifying conditions that can be empirically tested. Hence, causal modeling should be based on a formal theory of causal dependence that gives meaning to the term "causal" as used in this context.

The aim of this chapter is, therefore, an explication of the formal difference between *descriptive* or *noncausal* and *explanatory* or *causal* regressive models. After some introductory examples, the basic concepts of the theory of causal and weak causal regressive dependence will be outlined, followed by some illustrative applications.

II. Introductory Examples

In this section, two examples are discussed in some detail. The first demonstrates that a definition of the term "causal effect" is not only of theoretical but also of much practical importance. The second is a paradigm for both causal and noncausal regressive dependencies. It shows that both kinds of dependence can correctly be described by a linear regression equation.

A. RETRAINING OF PAROLEES AND RECIDIVISM

Suppose the data in Table 4.1 to be collected in a large-scale study on the effectiveness of a retraining program with parolees, where the observed frequencies of recidivism are big enough to allow for an interpretation of the relative frequencies as probabilities. To decide whether or not the retraining program should be continued, the effectiveness of the program has to be evaluated. At first glance it seems that proponents of the program are unfortunate, because the conditional probability for "no recidivism" of those who had no retraining is

$$P(Y = 1 \mid X = 0) = P(Y = 1, X = 0)/P(X = 0) = .3/.5 = .6,$$

Table 4.1

Evaluation of a Retraining Program with Parolees[a]

	Retraining $X = 1$	No retraining $X = 0$	Pooled group
No recidivism $Y = 1$	.25	.30	.55
Recidivism $Y = 0$	.25	.20	.45
Pooled group	.50	.50	1.00

[a] Fictitious data, based on Novick (1980).

whereas the conditional probability for "no recidivism" of those who had the training is

$$P(Y = 1 \mid X = 1) = P(Y = 1, X = 1)/P(X = 1) = .25/.5 = .5.$$

Hence, opponents of the retraining program may claim that there is a *negative effect*

$$P(Y = 1 \mid X = 1) - P(Y = 1 \mid X = 0) = .5 - .6 = -.1 \qquad (1)$$

of the retraining. Consequently, a cancellation of the program would be reasonable.

However, proponents of the retraining program argue that it has a *positive effect* for both male and female parolees. In fact, the conditional probability for "no recidivism" of those males who had no retraining is

$$P(Y = 1 \mid X = 0, W = 0) = P(Y = 1, X = 0, W = 0)/P(X = 0, W = 0)$$
$$= P(Y = 1, X = 0 \mid W = 0)/P(X = 0 \mid W = 0)$$
$$= .075/.25 = .3,$$

(see Table 4.2), whereas the conditional probability for "no recidivism" of those males who had the retraining is

$$P(Y = 1 \mid X = 1, W = 0) = P(Y = 1, X = 1, W = 0)/P(X = 1, W = 0)$$
$$= P(Y = 1, X = 1 \mid W = 0)/P(X = 1 \mid W = 0)$$
$$= .3/.75 = .4.$$

Therefore, the effect of the retraining

$$P(Y = 1 \mid X = 1, W = 0) - P(Y = 1 \mid X = 0, W = 0) = .4 - .3 = .1 \quad (2)$$

is *positive* for males. The same is true for female parolees, because

$$P(Y = 1 \mid X = 1, W = 1) - P(Y = 1 \mid X = 0, W = 1) = .2/.25 - .525/.75$$
$$= .8 - .7 = .1. \qquad (3)$$

Thus, the proponents and opponents of the retraining end up with opposite conclusions. The latter would cancel the program, arguing that it has a negative effect (see Equation 1), whereas the former would continue it, arguing that it has positive effects (see Equations 2 and 3). Who is right and who is wrong? What is the actual effect of the retraining program?

In order to answer these questions we have to define what we mean by "effect"; that is, we have to introduce the distinction between *causal* and *noncausal* stochastic dependencies. This chapter is, therefore, concerned with the *formal properties which distinguish causal and noncausal stochastic*

Table 4.2

Evaluation of a Retraining Program with Parolees Conditional on Sex[a]

	Retraining $X = 1$	No retraining $X = 0$	Pooled group
A. Male parolees ($W = 0$)			
No recidivism $Y = 1$	.300	.075	.375
Recidivism $Y = 0$	.450	.175	.625
Pooled group	.750	.250	1.000
B. Female parolees ($W = 1$)			
No recidivism $Y = 1$	.200	.525	.725
Recidivism $Y = 0$	.050	.225	.275
Pooled group	.250	.750	1.000

[a] Fictitious data, based on Novick (1980). Equal probabilities are assumed for $W = 0$ and $W = 1$.

dependencies. However, the discussion will be restricted to those kinds of dependencies that may be described by conditional expectations $E(Y|X)$. It will be shown how these formal properties may help to answer the questions raised above.

A conditional expectation (or "true" regression) $E(Y|X)$ of the random variable Y given X is a random variable, the values of which are the conditional expectations $E(Y|X = x)$ of Y given $X = x$. For a mathematical definition of this concept and its formal properties (rules of computation), see the Appendix to this chapter. A nonformal introduction is given by Steyer (1984b). Equations on conditional expectations only hold with probability one, or *almost surely* (as). A conditional expectation $E(Y|X)$ is uniquely determined only if X is a discrete random variable. In these cases, we may write = instead of as=. For dichotomous variables Y with values zero and one, the conditional expectations $E(Y|X)$ are also denoted by $P(Y = 1|X)$ and called conditional probabilities of the event $Y = 1$ given X.

In the present example, the conditional expectation

$$E(Y|X) = P(Y = 1|X) = .6 - .1 \cdot X \qquad (4)$$

describes the dependence of Y (recidivism vs. no recidivism) on X (retraining no vs. retraining) for the pooled sex population. It contains both conditional probabilities $P(Y=1\,|\,X=1)$ and $P(Y=1\,|\,X=0)$ (see Equation 1) in one expression. Note that $E(Y|X)$ has the form of a simple regression equation. Similarly, given that $W=0$ and $W=1$, the conditional simple regression equations

$$E(Y|X,\ W=0) = P(Y=1\,|\,X,\ W=0) = .3 + .1\cdot X \qquad (5)$$

and

$$E(Y|X,\ W=1) = P(Y=1\,|\,X,\ W=1) = .7 + .1\cdot X \qquad (6)$$

(see Equations 2 and 3) comprehensively describe the dependencies of Y (recidivism vs. no recidivism) on X (retraining vs. no retraining) for the male ($W=0$) and female ($W=1$) parolees, respectively.

B. COINS AND ELECTROMAGNET

Before discussing formal properties that distinguish causal and noncausal regressive dependencies, let us consider another introductory example, one which is a paradigm for causal as well as noncausal stochastic dependencies. This example shows that both kinds of regressive dependencies can be correctly described by conditional expectations, parameterized as regression equations.

Suppose you were confronted with the hypothetical coin toss data presented in Table 4.3. At first sight you might be puzzled because of the stochastic dependence of the coin variables

$$Y_1 := \begin{cases} 1 & \text{if Coin 1 shows the metal side,} \\ 0 & \text{if Coin 1 shows the plastic side,} \end{cases}$$

and

$$Y_2 := \begin{cases} 1 & \text{if Coin 2 shows the metal side,} \\ 0 & \text{if Coin 2 shows the plastic side.} \end{cases}$$

Obviously, the joint probabilities do not equal the product of the marginal probabilities. For example, .53 is not equal to the product $.7\cdot.7$.

However, you cease to worry about the data once you realize that the coins, each of which has one metal and one plastic side, were tossed onto a plate that has the properties of an electromagnet that is on or off with the probability .5 each time the two coins are tossed. A scheme to explain the observed stochastic dependencies is depicted in Figure 4.1, where

$$X := \begin{cases} 1 & \text{if the electromagnet is on,} \\ 0 & \text{if the electromagnet is off.} \end{cases}$$

Table 4.3

Probabilities in the Coins and Electromagnet Experiment[a]

	Coin 2 shows		
Coin 1 shows	Metal side $Y_2 = 1$	Plastic side $Y_2 = 0$	Pooled condition
Metal side $Y_1 = 1$	.53	.17	.70
Plastic side $Y_1 = 0$	.17	.13	.30
Pooled condition	.70	.30	1.00

[a] The table shows probabilities in a fictitious coins and electromagnet experiment. Two coins, each having one metal and one plastic side, are tossed onto a plate that has the properties of an electromagnet, being on or off with probability .5.

In order to be sure that your explanation of the covariation of the two coin-tossing variables Y_1 and Y_2 is sufficient, you must look at the corresponding data of Table 4.4 for the two cases in which the electromagnet is either on or off. In fact, your expectation that Y_1 and Y_2 are stochastically independent, given a constant state of the electromagnet, is met. This can easily be seen from the fact that the joint conditional probabilities in this table are the product of the corresponding marginal conditional probabilities; for example, .25 = .5 · .5 (see Table 4.4, A) or .81 = .9 · .9 (see Table 4.4, B).

This example is useful not only because it is a paradigm of *stochastic* or nondeterministic *causal dependence* but also because it simultaneously involves a stochastic dependence that is intuitively *noncausal* and two stochastic dependencies that are intuitively *causal*. The causal dependencies are those of Y_1 on X and Y_2 on X, which can be described by the regression equations

$$E(Y_1 \mid X) = P(Y_1 = 1 \mid X) = a_{10} + a_{11}X = .5 + .4 \cdot X \qquad (7)$$

$$E(Y_2 \mid X) = P(Y_2 = 1 \mid X) = a_{20} + a_{21}X = .5 + .4 \cdot X. \qquad (8)$$

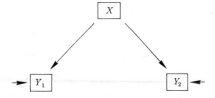

Figure 4.1 Causal scheme to explain the observed stochastic dependencies between the coin-tossing variables Y_1 and Y_2 by the electromagnet variable X.

Table 4.4

Conditional Probabilities in the Coins and Electromagnet
Experiment Given Constant State of the Electromagnet[a]

Coin 1 shows	Coin 2 shows		
	Metal side $Y_2 = 1$	Plastic side $Y_2 = 0$	Pooled condition
A. Electromagnet is off ($X = 0$)			
Metal side $Y_1 = 1$	.25	.25	.50
Plastic side $Y_1 = 0$	.25	.25	.50
Pooled condition	.50	.50	1.00
B. Electromagnet is on ($X = 1$)			
Metal side $Y_1 = 1$	.81	.09	.90
Plastic side $Y_1 = 0$	.09	.01	.10
Pooled condition	.90	.10	1.00

[a] The table shows conditional probabilities in a fictitious
coins and electromagnet experiment, given a constant state
of the electromagnet. Two coins, each having one metal
and one plastic side, are tossed onto a plate which has the
properties of an electromagnet, being on in situation A and
off in situation B. Situations A and B both occur with
probability .5.

The coefficients $a_{11} = .4$ and $a_{21} = .4$ are the effects of the electromagnet,
as is easily seen from the difference of the marginal probabilities of Table 4.4,
A and B. If the electromagnet is off, then for $i = 1, 2$,

$$E(Y_i \mid X = 0) = P(Y_i = 1 \mid X = 0) = .5 + .4 \cdot 0 = .5$$

(see Table 4.4, A), and if it is on, then

$$E(Y_i \mid X = 1) = P(Y_i = 1 \mid X = 1) = .5 + .4 \cdot 1 = .9$$

(see Table 4.4, B). The noncausal stochastic dependence is that of Y_1 on Y_2,
which also can be correctly described by a regression equation, namely,

$$E(Y_1 \mid Y_2) = P(Y_1 = 1 \mid Y_2) = b_{10} + b_{12}Y_2 = .5\overline{6} + .1905 \cdot Y_2. \quad (9)$$

If Coin 2 shows the plastic side ($Y_2 = 0$), then

$$E(Y_1 \mid Y_2 = 0) = P(Y_1 = 1 \mid Y_2 = 0) = .5\overline{6} + .1905 \cdot 0 = .5\overline{6} = .17/.30,$$

and if Coin 2 shows the metal side ($Y_2 = 1$), then

$$E(Y_1 \mid Y_2 = 1) = P(Y_1 = 1 \mid Y_2 = 1) = .5\overline{6} + .1905 \cdot 1 = .757 = .53/.70$$

(see Table 4.3).

Now that we have verified that not only Equations 7 and 8 but also Equation 9 are valid, the following question arises: *What are the formal differences between the intuitively causal dependencies described by Equation 7 and 8 and the intuitively noncausal dependence described by Equation 9?* Or, in other words, because a test of statistical fit of Equation 9 cannot lead to a correct rejection of the model described by Equation 9, *what are the hypotheses that have to be tested if one wants to reject Equation 9 as a causal model* (i.e., as a model that describes nonspurious or unconfounded dependencies)?

III. Causal and Weak Causal Regressive Dependence

In this section, the most important formal properties that distinguish causal, weak causal, and noncausal regressive dependencies will be introduced. First, however, the realm of applications of the proposed theory must be outlined. This realm comprises all those models that can be described by conditional expectations, which is the most adequate conceptual tool whenever we require an exact formulation of how the true mean of a random variable Y depends on the values of another, possibly multidimensional, random variable X. Therefore, it is worthwhile to become familiar with the rules of computation for conditional expectations listed in the Appendix.

A. REGRESSIVE DEPENDENCE

The theory of causal regressive dependence outlined in this chapter is concerned with those kinds of dependencies that can be described by specifying the functional form for the conditional expectation $E(Y \mid X)$ of a real-valued random variable Y given the n-dimensional random variable $X = (X_1, \ldots, X_n)$.

In reg-linear models, for example, $E(Y \mid X)$ is specified by

$$E(Y \mid X) \text{ as} = a_{Y0} + \sum_{j \in J} a_{Yj} X_j, \qquad J = \{1, \ldots, n\}, \qquad (10)$$

where the coefficients a_{Y0} and a_{Yj}, $j \in J$, are real-valued constants. If the random variables X_j represent quantitative properties, this is often called a *regression model.* If the variables X_j represent qualitative properties or group membership (see, e.g., Bock, 1975; or Moosbrugger & Steyer, 1983), it is also called an *analysis of variance model.*

In *logit-linear models,* where the dependent variable Y is dichotomous with $Y = 1$ or $Y = 0$, the conditional expectation $E(Y|X)$ is specified by

$$E(Y|X) \text{ as} = \frac{\exp(a_{Y0} + \Sigma_{j \in J} a_{Yj} X_j)}{1 + \exp(a_{Y0} + \Sigma_{j \in J} a_{Yj} X_j)}, \quad J = \{1, \ldots, n\}, \quad (11)$$

where again a_{Y0} and $a_{Yj}, j \in J$, are real-valued constants (see, e.g., Cox, 1970; Haberman, 1978, 1979; or Langeheine, 1980). In these cases, where Y is dichotomous with values zero or one, $E(Y|X)$ is also denoted by $P(Y = 1 | X)$ and called the conditional probability of the event $Y = 1$ given $X = (X_1, \ldots, X_n)$.

By specifying the conditional expectation $E(Y|X)$ of Y given X as in the reg- or logit-linear models, a proposition is made, concerning how the conditional expectations $E(Y | X = x)$ of Y given $X = x$ vary with the values x of X, where X is a possibly multidimensional random variable. If Y has more than two values, no proposition is made with respect to how the variance or other distributional properties of Y depend on X, although such propositions might be added, for example, on the conditional variance $V(Y|X) := E((Y - E(Y|X))^2 | X)$.

Because we do not require $E(Y|X)$ as$= Y$, the dependencies dealt with are nondeterministic or *stochastic* in general, allowing for an error or *residual* variable which is defined by $F := Y - E(Y|X)$, with variance $V(F) > 0$. The term *regressive independence* of Y on X will be used if $E(Y|X)$ as$= E(Y)$, indicating that the random variable X does not contain any information about the conditional expectations $E(Y | X = x)$ of Y given $X = x$, and the term *regressive dependence* will be used otherwise.

Sometimes models consist of several equations on conditional expectations. This is true for factor analysis as well as for recursive path analysis models. In the common *factor analysis model* (see Figure 4.2), Equation 10 is assumed for each manifest variable $Y_i, i \in I$. In this context the variables

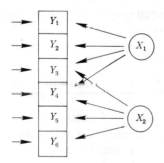

Figure 4.2 Path diagram of a factor analysis model with six manifest variables Y_i and two latent variables (factors) X_j.

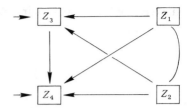

Figure 4.3 Path diagram for a recursive model with four variables.

$X_j, j \in J$, are the latent variables or factors and the coefficients a_{ij} are called the loadings of the manifest variables Y_i on the latent variables X_j. Usually an assumption on the independence of the residuals defined by $F_i := Y_i - E(Y_i | X)$ is added.

In recursive *path analysis models,* too, several equations on conditional expectations are needed to formulate the model assumptions. Consider, for example, the path diagram depicted in Figure 4.3. Models of this type can be described by specifying one equation for each dependent variable:

$$E(Z_3 | Z_1, Z_2) \text{ as} = a_{30} + a_{31}Z_1 + a_{32}Z_2 \tag{12}$$

and

$$E(Z_4 | Z_1, Z_2, Z_3) \text{ as} = a_{40} + a_{41}Z_1 + a_{42}Z_2 + a_{43}Z_3. \tag{13}$$

All other properties appearing as additional assumptions in the usual formulation of path analysis models (see, e.g., Brandtstädter & Bernitzke, 1976; Kenny, 1979; Hummell & Ziegler, 1976) can be derived from these two equations using the rules of computation for conditional expectations listed in the Appendix. These properties concern the residual variables defined by

$$F_3 := Z_3 - E(Z_3 | Z_1, Z_2) \quad \text{and} \quad F_4 := Z_4 - E(Z_4 | Z_1, Z_2, Z_3). \tag{14}$$

Equations 12 and 13 imply the usual assumptions of recursive path analysis models, namely,

$$C(F_3, Z_1) = C(F_3, Z_2) = 0, \tag{15}$$

$$C(F_4, Z_1) = C(F_4, Z_2) = C(F_4, Z_3) = 0 \tag{16}$$

$$C(F_3, F_4) = 0, \tag{17}$$

and

$$E(F_3) = E(F_4) = 0. \tag{18}$$

According to Equations 15 and 16, the covariances of the residuals with the corresponding predictors are zero, as well as the covariance of the two residuals (Equation 17) and their expectations (Equations 18). However, Equations 12 and 13 also imply

$$E(F_3 \mid Z_1, Z_2) \text{ as} = 0, \tag{19}$$

$$E(F_4 \mid Z_1, Z_2, Z_3) \text{ as} = 0, \tag{20}$$

and

$$E(F_4 \mid F_3) \text{ as} = 0, \tag{21}$$

properties which are in a crucial way stricter than the usual assumptions of path analysis, Equations 15 to 18. According to Equation 19, the *conditional* expectation — not just the (unconditional) expectation — of the residual F_3 given $Z_1 = z_1$ and $Z_2 = z_2$ is zero for all values z_1 and z_2, except for a set of values with probability zero. Equation 19 is not implied by Equations 15 and 18, but rather vice versa. The corresponding propositions are true, of course, for Equations 20 and 21. Equation 20 implies Equation 16 and Equation 21 implies Equation 17.

These propositions will now be proved in detail for the reader who wants to become familiar with the rules of computation for conditional expectations listed in the Appendix. We will first prove Equations 19 to 21. Equations 12 and 14 imply Equation 19, because

$$E(F_3 \mid Z_1, Z_2) \text{ as} = E[Z_3 - E(Z_3 \mid Z_1, Z_2) \mid Z_1, Z_2]$$
$$\text{(see Eq. 14)}$$

$$\text{as} = E(Z_3 \mid Z_1, Z_2) - E[E(Z_3 \mid Z_1, Z_2) \mid Z_1, Z_2]$$
$$\text{(see Eq. A.15)}$$

$$\text{as} = E(Z_3 \mid Z_1, Z_2) - E(Z_3 \mid Z_1, Z_2) \text{ as} = 0$$
$$\text{(see Eq. A.17)}.$$

Equation 20 is proved correspondingly. In order to prove Equation 21, we have to realize that F_3 is a function of Z_1, Z_2, and Z_3. Therefore, it is measurable with respect to the sigma-field generated by these three variables. (For a definition of the concept of measurability, see any introductory text on probability theory.) Hence, Equation A.17 can be applied once again, resulting in

$$E(F_4 \mid F_3) \text{ as} = E[E(F_4 \mid Z_1, Z_2, Z_3) \mid F_3] \qquad \text{(see Eq. A.17)}$$

$$\text{as} = E(0 \mid F_3) \text{ as} = 0 \qquad \text{(see Eqs. 20 and A.10)}.$$

Equations 15 to 17 now directly follow from the fact that $E(Y \mid X) \text{ as} = E(Y)$ implies $C(Y, X) = 0$ if the covariance $C(Y, X)$ exists. This completes the proof.

Note that Equations 12 and 13 do not *define* a causal model, but they may *describe* causal regressive dependencies. Conditions that allow a conditional expectation to be causally interpreted are treated in the following sections.

B. CAUSAL REGRESSIVE DEPENDENCE

The concept of *causal* regressive dependence is defined by two conditions, *preorderedness* and *invariance*. *Preorderedness* essentially says that $X = (X_1, \ldots, X_n)$ and that therefore each $X_j, j \in J, J = \{1, \ldots, n\}$, is antecedent to Y. *Invariance* means that for each potential disturbing variable W, the following equation holds:

$$E(Y \mid X, W) \text{ as= } E(Y \mid X) + h \circ W, \tag{22}$$

where $h \circ W$ denotes the composition of a numerical function h with W. Note that $W: \Omega \to \Omega''$ is a stochastic (or random) variable on the underlying probability space $(\Omega, \mathcal{A}, P)$ with values in the set Ω'' (usually $\Omega'' = \overline{\mathbb{R}}$), and that $h: W(\Omega) \to \overline{\mathbb{R}}$ is a function which maps the values of W into the set $\overline{\mathbb{R}}$ of real numbers enlarged by $+\infty$ and $-\infty$ ($W(\Omega)$ denotes the image of Ω with respect to W). Also note that $h \circ W$ is a real-valued random variable. The invariance condition states that, if any potential disturbing variable W is included as another conditioning variable, it only adds to $E(Y \mid X)$ in the equation for $E(Y \mid X, W)$, leaving $E(Y \mid X)$ *invariant*. (For formal definitions of "preorderedness" and "potential disturbing variables," see Steyer, 1984a.)

There are a number of situations in which Equation 22 holds. First, suppose, for example, that the conditional expectation of the random variable Y given X and W is the sum of a composition $f \circ X$ (where X may be multidimensional) and a composition $h \circ W$,

$$E(Y \mid X, W) \text{ as= } f \circ X + h \circ W. \tag{23}$$

This will be referred to as the *additivity* condition, a special case of which is the multiple regression equation

$$E(Y \mid X, W) \text{ as= } b_{Y0} + b_{YX}X + b_{YW}W.$$

The additivity condition also holds if, for example,

$$E(Y \mid X, W) \text{ as= } b_{Y0} + b_{YX}X + b_{YX^2}X^2 + b_{YW}W + b_{YW^2}W^2,$$

whereas it does not hold if, for example,

$$E(Y \mid X, W) \text{ as= } b_{Y0} + b_{YX}X + b_{YW}W + b_{Y(X \cdot W)}X \cdot W, \qquad b_{Y(X \cdot W)} \neq 0.$$

This last equation cannot be represented in the form of Equation 23 because of the multiplicative term $X \cdot W$.

If (i) this additivity condition (Equation 23) holds and (ii) X and W are stochastically independent, then Equation 22, which characterizes the invariance condition, is fulfilled.

In order to prove this proposition, let us suppose that the expectation $E(h \circ W)$ is equal to zero. Note that this does not restrict generality because, by subtracting its expectation, any composition $h' \circ W$ with an expectation not equal to zero can easily be transformed into a composition $h \circ X$ with the expectation zero. It now can easily be seen that conditions (i) and (ii) above imply Equation 22, because

$$E(Y\,|\,X) \text{ as= } E[E(Y\,|\,X,\ W)\,|\,X] \qquad \text{(see Eq. A.17)}$$

$$\text{as= } E(f \circ X + h \circ W\,|\,X) \qquad \text{(see Eq. 23)}$$

$$\text{as= } E(f \circ X\,|\,X) + E(h \circ W\,|\,X) \quad \text{(see Eq. A.15)}$$

$$\text{as= } f \circ X + E(h \circ W) = f \circ X \qquad \text{(see Eq. A.9),}$$

where, by assumption, $E(h \circ W) = 0$, and involving the theorem that the stochastic independence of W and X implies $E(h \circ W\,|\,X) \text{ as= } E(h \circ W)$. We may now substitute $E(Y\,|\,X)$ for $f \circ X$ in Equation 23, which yields Equation 22. This proves that the additivity condition together with the stochastic independence of X and W implies Equation 22, which characterizes the invariance condition. These two conditions make up the first situation in which Equation 22 is fulfilled.

In the second situation, suppose that W is *irrelevant* (see also Suppes, 1970) to the prediction of Y in that it contains no additional information on the conditional expectations $E(Y\,|\,X = x,\ W = w)$ of Y given $X = x$ and $W = w$. More precisely, suppose that

$$E(Y\,|\,X,\ W) \text{ as= } F(Y\,|\,X) \qquad (24)$$

In this situation too Equation 22 is fulfilled, because $h \circ W$ might be equal to 0. W's being a constant is a special case in which Equation 24 is true. Thus, the experimental control technique of *holding* potential disturbing variables constant can be based on the invariance condition. Note, however, that *holding* a variable W constant on one of its values w restricts the universe of discourse to the condition $W = w$. This touches the problem of external validity (see Campbell & Stanley, 1963; Cook & Campbell, 1979; or Steyer, 1983a).

The third and last situation in which Equation 22 is fulfilled is characterized by

$$E(Y \mid X) \text{ as} = Y, \tag{25}$$

where Y equals $E(Y \mid X)$, with probability one. In this case, too, $h \circ W = 0$ (see Equation 22).

Hence, causal regressive dependence requires neither that all of the variation of the dependent variable Y be explained by X (see Equation 25) nor that all influencing variables be known (see Equation 24). It is only required that all potential disturbing variables W behave as described by Equation 22. This equation is fulfilled if $E(Y \mid W, X) \text{ as} = E(Y \mid X)$ or if X and W are stochastically independent and additivity (Equation 23) can be assumed. The additivity condition is rather restrictive. Therefore, a weaker concept of causal regressive dependence will be proposed in Section III.D.

C. SIMPLE CAUSAL REG-LINEAR DEPENDENCE

In the case of a simple reg-linear dependence of Y on X that is characterized by the regression equation

$$E(Y \mid X) \text{ as} = a_{Y0} + a_{YX}X, \tag{26}$$

the invariance condition says that, for all potential disturbing variables W,

$$E(Y \mid X, W) \text{ as} = a_{Y0} + a_{YX}X + h \circ W.$$

Whatever the type of the composition $h \circ W$, the regression coefficient a_{YX} is left unchanged if the invariance condition holds.

Another remarkable property of the simple regression coefficient a_{YX} is that it is equal to the corresponding regression coefficient $a_{XY \mid W=w}$ of the conditional simple regression of Y on X given $W = w$:

$$E(Y \mid X, W = w) \text{ as} = a_{Y0 \mid W=w} + a_{YX \mid W=w}X,$$

provided the invariance condition holds. This is easily seen from the last equation, because, for $W = w$,

$$E(Y \mid X, W = w) \text{ as} = a_{Y0} + a_{YX}X + h(w),$$

where $h(w)$ is a constant so that we may define $a_{Y0 \mid W=w} := a_{Y0} + h(w)$ and $a_{XY \mid W=w} := a_{YX}$. Thus, Equation 26 and the invariance condition imply that a_{YX} is also the regression coefficient of the conditional simple regression of Y on X given $W = w$, where W is any potential disturbing variable. Therefore, we say that Y is *simply causally reg-linearly dependent on X* and that a_{YX} is the *simple causal reg-linear effect of X on Y, iff Y is causally regressively dependent on X and Equation 26 holds with $a_{YX} \neq 0$ ("iff" is an abbreviation for "if and only if").

D. WEAK CAUSAL REGRESSIVE DEPENDENCE

It may be argued that the kind of causal regressive dependence discussed above is unrealistically restrictive. Let us consider once again the invariance condition stated in Section III.B, saying that for all potential disturbing variables W,

$$E(Y \mid X, W) \text{ as} = E(Y \mid X) + h \circ W,$$

where $X = (X_1, \ldots, X_n)$. It can easily be seen that there are no multiplicative terms involving W and one or more of the random variables X_j, $j \in J = \{1, \ldots, n\}$. Therefore, the invariance condition excludes interactions in the analysis of variance sense of any order between the variables X_j and any potential disturbing variable W. This condition is a rather strict one that cannot be guaranteed to hold even in randomized experiments, where the term "causal" also seems to be appropriate in characterizing the dependence of Y on the treatment variables X_j which indicate membership in the experimental groups.

Therefore, we will now introduce a *weak* type of causal *regressive* dependence. This can be done by replacing the invariance by the *average condition,* which can be formulated as follows: For all potential disturbing variables W, the following equation holds with probability one for all conditional expectations $E(Y \mid X = x)$ of Y given $X = x$:

$$E(Y \mid X = x) = \int E(Y \mid X = x, W = w)P_W(dw), \qquad (27)$$

where P_W denotes the distribution of W. If W is a discrete random variable, this equation can be written

$$E(Y \mid X = x) = \sum_w E(Y \mid X = x, W = w) \cdot P(W = w), \qquad (28)$$

where the summation is across all values w of W. This average condition simply means that all conditional expected values $E(Y \mid X = x)$ will be the average of the conditional expectations $E(Y \mid X = x, W = w)$ of Y given $X = x$ and $W = w$, with probability one. Together with preorderedness, the average condition defines *weak causal regressive dependence* of Y on X.

A special situation in which Equation 27 is fulfilled is characterized by $E(Y \mid X, W) \text{ as} = E(Y \mid X)$. However, the importance of the average condition stems from the fact that it *is implied by the stochastic independence* of all potential disturbing variables W on one side and the n-dimensional variable $X = (X_1, \ldots, X_n)$ on the other side.[1]

E. RANDOMIZATION AND MATCHING

In a randomized experiment, the $X_1, \ldots, X_n$ are the treatment variables indicating the experimental group to which an experimental unit (the subject) belongs. *Randomization* implies that all potential disturbing variables W (representing any properties of the experimental units before the treatment) and the treatment variable $X = (X_1, \ldots, X_n)$ are stochastically independent. Therefore, the average condition holds in randomized experiments. Thus, weak causal linear stochastic dependence (or independence, if $E(Y|X)$ as$= E(Y)$) is guaranteed by randomization (for an example, see Section IV). Of course, *matching* serves the same purpose, but only for those potential disturbing variables W with respect to which the experimental groups are matched. Thus, the control techniques of randomization and matching can also be based on the theory being proposed.

F. TESTS OF CAUSALITY

However, and maybe more important, the theory of causal regressive dependence is also relevant for nonexperimental studies because both the *invariance* and the *average condition* may be tested once a potential disturbing variable W is observed. If neither holds, any causal hypothesis should be rejected for the model considered. If one or both of them hold, one may maintain the causal hypothesis (in either its weak or its strict form) as long as no potential disturbing variable is found for which the invariance and the average condition do not hold. Testing the average condition (see Equations 27 or 28) is a test of weak causal regressive dependence and testing the invariance condition (see Equation 22) is a test of causal regressive dependence (in the stricter sense). Of course, such tests make sense only if X is assumed to be antecedent to Y.

IV. Illustrative Applications

In this section, the discussion of the two examples of Section II will be continued and a third example will be given for an analysis of variance situation. These examples are intended to show how the invariance and

---

[1] For the proof, which is due to Robert Lang, University of Trier, see Steyer (1984a).

average conditions work to rule out wrong hypotheses of causal and weak
causal regressive dependence.

A. RETRAINING OF PAROLEES AND RECIDIVISM

We will now apply the invariance condition to the example, retraining of
parolees and recidivism, that was given in Section II. The stochastic dependence of Y (recidivism vs. no recidivism) on X (retraining vs. no retraining)
can correctly be described by

$$E(Y \mid X) = P(Y = 1 \mid X) = .6 - .1 \cdot X \qquad (29)$$

(see Equation 4). The question then arises: Does this equation describe a
causal regressive dependence?

In order to check for the *invariance condition,* we have to compute the
parameters of the equation

$$E(Y \mid X, W) = P(Y = 1 \mid X, W) = a_{Y0} + a_{YX}X + a_{YW}W + a_{Y(X \cdot W)}X \cdot W.$$

This equation is sufficient to describe the regressive dependence of Y (recidivism vs. no recidivism) on X (retraining vs. no retraining) and W (sex)
because X and W are dichotomous so that there are only four combinations
of values of X and W. If, by contrast, X were continuous, the equation for
$E(Y \mid X, W)$ might be much more complicated, involving more than four
parameters.

In order to compute the unknown coefficients a_{Y0}, a_{YX}, a_{YW}, and $a_{Y(X \cdot W)}$,
we must solve the four equations

$$P(Y = 1 \mid X = 0, W = 0) = .075/.25 = .3 = a_{Y0},$$

$$P(Y = 1 \mid X = 0, W = 1) = .525/.75 = .7 = a_{Y0} + a_{YW},$$

$$P(Y = 1 \mid X = 1, W = 0) = .3/.75 = .4 = a_{Y0} + a_{YX},$$

and

$$P(Y = 1 \mid X = 1, W = 1) = .20/.25 = .8 = a_{Y0} + a_{YX} + a_{YW} + a_{Y(X \cdot W)}$$

for the coefficients, with the conditional probabilities

$$P(Y = 1 \mid X = x, W = w) = P(Y = 1, X = x, W = w)/P(X = x, W = w)$$

$$= P(Y = 1, X = x \mid W = w)/P(X = x \mid W = w)$$

being obtained from Table 4.2. If $X = 0$ and $W = 0$, for example, this equation yields

$$P(Y = 1 \mid X = 0,\ W = 0) = .075/.25 = .3$$

(see Table 4.2).

Solving the four equations then results in

$$E(Y \mid X,\ W) = P(Y = 1 \mid X,\ W) = .3 + .1 \cdot X + .4 \cdot W,$$

which is not equal to

$$E(Y \mid X) + h \circ W = .6 - .1 \cdot X + h \circ W,$$

where $h \circ W$ is a composition of h with W. Whereas the coefficient $-.1$ of X in the equation for $E(Y \mid X)$ is negative, it is positive in the equation for $E(Y \mid X,\ W)$, and this contradicts the invariance condition.

Further computation reveals that the *average condition* also does not hold for $E(Y \mid X)$ because

$$E(Y \mid X = 0) = P(Y = 1 \mid X = 0) = P(Y = 1,\ X = 0)/P(X = 0) = .3/.5 = .6$$

(see Table 4.1) is not equal to

$$P(Y = 1 \mid X = 0,\ W = 0) \cdot P(W = 0)$$
$$+ P(Y = 1 \mid X = 0,\ W = 1) \cdot P(W = 1)$$
$$= .3 \cdot .5 + .7 \cdot .5 = .5.$$

(see Table 4.2). Hence, not only can the proponents of the retraining program reject the hypothesis that the causal reg-linear effect of the retraining is negative $(-.1)$, but they may even argue that the conditional causal reg-linear effect of retraining given sex is positive $(+.1)$ because

$$P(Y = 1 \mid X,\ W = 0) = .3 + .1 \cdot X$$

and

$$P(Y = 1 \mid X,\ W = 1) = .7 + .1 \cdot X$$

(see the equation on $E(Y \mid X,\ W)$). For both males and females, the conditional probability for "no recidivism" is greater for those receiving the retraining than for those not receiving it.

Of course, the new hypothesis of the proponents—namely, that .1 is the conditional simple causal reg-linear effect of X (retraining vs. no retraining) on Y (recidivism vs. no recidivism) given $W = 0$ (males) and $W = 1$ (females)—must be critically investigated too. Any evidence that the average condition does not hold within the sex groups will be sufficient to reject this new hypothesis in both its weak (average condition) and its strong form (invariance condition), because the invariance implies the average condition (for a proof, see Steyer, 1984a). Hence, if the average condition does not hold, we can conclude that the invariance condition also does not hold. The check for both conditions was carried through for didactic reasons only.

B. COINS AND ELECTROMAGNET

We will now continue the coins and electromagnet example given in Section II in order to illustrate once again how the invariance condition and the average condition work to rule out a wrong supposition of a causal regressive dependence. Suppose that one observes the regressive dependence of the first coin-tossing variable Y_1 on the second coin-tossing variable Y_2 (see Equation 9) and that one does not know about the electromagnet. Suppose, further, that Coin 2 (its result being represented by Y_2) is tossed before Coin 1 (its result being represented by Y_1). Because Y_2 is then antecedent to Y_1, it would initially make sense to assume that the regressive dependence described by

$$E(Y_1 \mid X_2) = b_{10} + b_{12}Y_2 = .5\overline{6} + .1905 \cdot Y_2 \qquad (30)$$

(see Equation 9) is a causal one.

However, one soon becomes dissatisfied with the first hypothesis because no physical explanation can be found for the causal mechanism of Y_2 influencing Y_1. One therefore looks for a third variable that might cause both Y_1 and Y_2 and account for the covariation between these two variables. Suppose that after some investigation the magnetic field is discovered and the magnet variable X is proposed as a candidate. Then the invariance condition tells how to falsify the first hypothesis that Y_1 is causally regressively dependent on Y_2.

Obviously, the magnet variable X is antecedent to both Y_1 and Y_2 because the electromagnet is on or off *before* the two coins are tossed. Hence, X is a potential disturbing variable with respect to the dependence of Y_1 on Y_2. According to its definition, the invariance condition for the dependence of Y_1 on Y_2 can be met only if the coefficient b_{12} of Equation 30 is identical with the coefficient a_{12} of the equation

$$E(Y_1 \mid Y_2, X) = a_{10} + a_{12}Y_2 + h \circ X.$$

From Table 4.4, however, the actual coefficient a_{12} can be computed; this results in

$$E(Y_1 \mid Y_2, X) = .5 + 0 \cdot Y_2 + .4 \cdot X.$$

In order to compute the coefficients occurring in this equation, the procedure described in detail in the last section must be used again, namely, solving the equations for the four conditional probabilities

$$E(Y \mid Y_2 = y_2, X = x) = P(Y = 1 \mid Y_2 = y_2, X = x)$$
$$= a_{10} + a_{12}y_2 + a_{13}x + a_{14}y_2 \cdot x.$$

Because the coefficient a_{12} is zero and not equal to $b_{12} = .1905$ (see Equation 30), the invariance condition is not met. Thus, this condition can be used to falsify the mistaken hypothesis that the regressive dependence of the first coin-tossing variable Y_1 on the second coin-tossing variable Y_2 is a causal one (in the strong sense).

We will show how the *average condition* may be used to reject the mistaken hypothesis that Y_1 is weakly causally regressively dependent on Y_2. According to the definition of the average condition, we must ask ourselves whether the equations

$$E(Y_1 \mid Y_2 = 0) = P(Y_1 = 1 \mid Y_2 = 0)$$
$$= P(Y_1 = 1 \mid Y_2 = 0, X = 0) \cdot P(X = 0)$$
$$+ P(Y_1 = 1 \mid Y_2 = 0, X = 1) \cdot P(X = 1)$$

and

$$E(Y_1 \mid Y_2 = 1) = P(Y_1 = 1 \mid Y_2 = 1)$$
$$= P(Y_1 = 1 \mid Y_2 = 1, X = 0) \cdot P(X = 0)$$
$$+ P(Y_1 = 1 \mid Y_2 = 1, X = 1) \cdot P(X = 1)$$

both hold. Using the data from Table 4.3 we obtain

$$E(Y_1 \mid Y_2 = 0) = P(Y_1 = 1 \mid Y_2 = 0)$$
$$= P(Y_1 = 1, Y_2 = 0)/P(Y_2 = 0)$$
$$= .17/.30 = .5\bar{6},$$

whereas the data from Table 4.4, A and B, and

$$P(Y_1 = 1, Y_2 = y_2, X = x)/P(Y_2 = y_2, X = x)$$
$$= P(Y_1 = 1, Y_2 = y_2 \mid X = x)/P(Y_2 = y_2 \mid X = x)$$

yield

$$P(Y_1 = 1 \mid Y_2 = 0, X = 0) \cdot P(X = 0)$$
$$+ P(Y_1 = 1 \mid Y_2 = 0, X = 1) \cdot P(X = 1)$$
$$= (.25/.5) \cdot .5 + (.09/.1) \cdot .5 = .7.$$

Hence, the average condition also is not met, and we can conclude that Y_1 is not weakly causally regressively dependent on Y_2. Since the invariance condition implies the average condition, the rejection of the average condition also implies the rejection of the invariance condition. Testing for both conditions was done for didactic reasons only.

C. EVALUATION OF THERAPY

The following example will demonstrate how the average condition can be used to rule out mistaken hypotheses of weak causal regressive dependence in an analysis of variance situation. It will also be shown that the average condition holds if the treatment variable X and the potential disturbing variable W are stochastically independent.

Consider the example outlined in Table 4.5. The conditional expectations $E(Y \mid X = x, W = w)$ of the dependent variable Y (indicating success of therapy) given $X = x$ and $W = w$ can be described by

$$E(Y \mid X, W) = 100 + 5 \cdot X + 0 \cdot W + 15 \cdot X \cdot W,$$

which is easily checked if X and W are held constant, yielding the four conditional expectations $E(Y \mid X = x, W = w)$ of Y given $X = x$ and $W = w$. Now suppose that we ignore W (the patient type) and ask whether

$$E(Y \mid X) = a_{Y0} + a_{YX}X = 100 + 8 \cdot X$$

(see the last column in Table 4.5) describes a weak causal regressive dependence. This would be the case (see the definition in Section III.D) only if $E(Y \mid X = 0) = 100$ equaled

$$E(Y \mid X = 0, W = 0) \cdot P(W = 0) + E(Y \mid X = 0, W = 1) \cdot P(W = 1)$$

$$= 100 \cdot .5 + 100 \cdot .5 = 100$$

(see the row "No therapy" in Table 4.5) and $E(Y \mid X = 1) = 108$ equaled

$$E(Y \mid X = 1, W = 0) \cdot P(W = 0) + E(Y \mid X = 1, W = 1) \cdot P(W = 1)$$

$$= 105 \cdot .5 + 120 \cdot .5 = 112.5$$

(see the row "Therapy" in Table 4.5). Obviously, these equations do not both hold in this example. Therefore, Y is *not* weakly causally regressively dependent on X.

Now consider Table 4.6, which differs from Table 4.5 only in that X and W are stochastically independent and therefore uncorrelated. Here, the average condition (see Section III) holds for W, because $E(Y \mid X = 0) = 100$ is equal to

$$E(Y \mid X = 1, W = 0) \cdot P(W = 0) + E(Y \mid X = 1, W = 1) \cdot P(W = 1)$$

$$= 105 \cdot .5 + 120 \cdot .5 = 112.5$$

(see the row "Therapy" in Table 4.6). Therefore,

Table 4.5

Therapy and Patient Type Nonorthogonal[a]

	Patient type A $W = 1$	Patient type B $W = 0$	Pooled group
Therapy	120	105	108
$X = 1$	(.10)	(.40)	(.50)
No therapy	100	100	100
$X = 0$	(.40)	(.10)	(.50)
Pooled group	104	104	104
	(.50)	(.50)	(1.00)

[a] Numerical example (fictitious data) for a modification of the reg-linear dependence of Y on X by a third variable W, where X and W are correlated and therefore not stochastically independent. The numbers in the 2×2 table are the conditional expectations $E(Y \mid X = x, W = w)$ of Y given $X = x$ and $W = w$. The numbers in parentheses are the probabilities for the four combinations of values of X and W. The model for patient type A is $E(Y \mid X, W = 1) = 100 + 20 \cdot X$, the model for patient type B is $E(Y \mid X, W = 0) = 100 + 5 \cdot X$, and the model for the pooled group (ignoring patient type) is $E(Y \mid X) = 100 + 8 \cdot X$.

Table 4.6

Therapy and Patient Type Orthogonal[a]

	Patient type A $W = 1$	Patient type B $W = 0$	Pooled group
Therapy	120	105	112.5
$X = 1$	(.25)	(.25)	(.50)
No therapy	100	100	100
$X = 0$	(.25)	(.25)	(.50)
Pooled group	110	102.5	106.25
	(.50)	(.50)	(1.00)

[a] Numerical example (fictitious data) for a modification of the reg-linear dependence of Y on X by a third variable W, where X and W are stochastically independent and therefore uncorrelated. The numbers in the 2×2 table are the conditional expectations $E(Y \mid X = x, W = w)$ of Y given $X = x$ and $W = w$. The numbers in parentheses are the probabilities for the four combinations of values of X and W. The model for patient type A is $E(Y \mid X, W = 1) = 100 + 20 \cdot X$, the model for patient type B is $E(Y \mid X, W = 0) = 100 + 5 \cdot X$, and the model for the pooled group (ignoring patient type) is $E(Y \mid X) = 100 + 12.5 \cdot X$.

$$E(Y|X) = 100 + 12.5 \cdot X$$

(see the last column in Table 4.6) may be interpreted as describing the weak causal regressive dependence of Y on X, as long as no other potential disturbing variable W is found for which the average condition does not hold.

Potential disturbing variables are defined in such a way that variables mediating between X and Y are excluded (see Steyer, 1983 or 1984a). In an experiment with subjects as experimental units and treatment variable X, potential disturbing variables are those variables only that represent properties of the subjects *before* or *at the time* of the treatment. Hence, if the data of Table 4.6 stem from a *randomized experiment*, all potential disturbing variables W and X will be stochastically independent. Therefore, the last equation will describe the weak causal regressive dependence of Y on X (see Section III).

V. Conclusion

The central aim of this chapter has been to show how it is possible to give meaning to the term "causal" as it is used in experimentation and in nonexperimental causal modeling. The discussion has been restricted to those stochastic dependencies that can be described by a conditional expectation, which is the formal concept catching the idea of a "true regression." This is why the term regressive dependence has been used. Two types of causal regressive dependencies, weak and strong, have been discussed. For either sort of dependency, the preorderedness condition must be fulfilled (the influencing variable X must be antecedent to the influenced variable Y). In addition, the crucial condition for *causal* regressive dependence of a random variable Y on a possibly multidimensional random variable X is the *invariance condition,* which postulates that, for all potential disturbing variables W, the following equation holds:

$$E(Y|X, W) \text{ as} = E(Y|X) + h \circ W.$$

By contrast, the crucial condition for *weak causal* regressive dependence is the *average condition,* which postulates that, for all potential disturbing variables W,

$$E(Y|X = x) = \int E(Y|X = x, W = w)P_W(dw)$$

holds for all values x of X, with probability one. This condition means that each $E(Y|X = x)$ is the average of the conditional expectations $E(Y|X = x, W = w)$ across the values w of W, with probability one. This average condition holds in randomized experiments.

The idea of an ideal randomized experiment has been so impressive that it seemed natural to many scientists to *define* causal dependence as a dependence observed in such an ideal experiment (e.g., see Wold, 1969). For many practical purposes such a definition is sufficient. However, as soon as one attempts to investigate topics that cannot be subjected to experimentation, such a definition no longer helps, because falsification of concrete causal propositions can only be achieved through experimentation.

The generally held belief that correlation does not prove causality is true, of course, and it remains true in light of the theory outlined. However, it has been made clear that a correlation or a regression equation *can* describe a certain kind of causal dependence. This explication of the concept of causality yields formal properties that can be investigated empirically and even falsified if the hypothesis of a causal or weak causal regressive dependence is actually wrong in the particular application under consideration.

In one of the examples in Section II, it was shown that the fact that a regression equation correctly describes the data does not imply that the parameters can be given a causal interpretation. For example, the model tests in the LISREL V program (Jöreskog & Sörbom, 1981) are tests of statistical fit. They test causal parameters only if one *presupposes* that the model is causal or that the structural parameters are "the fundamental parameters of the mechanism that generated the data" (Goldberger, 1973, p. 3). Thus these model tests are not the tests of causality that are necessary to test this presupposition. The theory of causal regressive dependence, however, allows one to deduce hypotheses for such tests of causality. Thus, it complements existing causal modeling procedures in a significant way.

Appendix

In this appendix are presented the definition of, and some theorems pertinent to, the conditional expectation $E(Y \mid \mathcal{C})$ of Y given the sigma field $\mathcal{C}$ that are frequently cited in this chapter. For an introduction to the concept and its background, see Bauer (1974), Breiman (1968), Gänssler and Stute (1977), or Loève (1977, 1978). A shorter and therefore more convenient name for $E(Y \mid \mathcal{C})$ is $\mathcal{C}$-*conditional expectation of* Y. The $\mathcal{C}$-conditional expectation of Y is a very general and useful concept. It is used, for example, to define the $\mathcal{C}$-conditional probability $P(A \mid \mathcal{C})$ of an event A as well as the $\mathcal{C}$-conditional variance $V(Y \mid \mathcal{C})$ and covariance $C(Y, Z \mid \mathcal{C})$ of stochastic variables. Special $\mathcal{C}$-conditional expectations are also obtained if $\mathcal{C}$ is the sigma-field generated by a stochastic (random) variable X, by a family $(X_j, j \in J)$ or sequence $X_1, \ldots, X_n$ of stochastic variables. In these cases, the notations $E(Y \mid X)$, $E(Y \mid X_j, j \in J)$, or $E(Y \mid X_1, \ldots, X_n)$ may be used.

The mathematical definition given below does not appeal very much to intuitive insight. Therefore, it might be helpful to recall that $E(Y|X)$ is a stochastic variable, the values of which are identical with the conditional expectations $E(Y|X=x)$ given $X=x$. Another way to think about $E(Y|X)$ is that it is a stochastic the values of which are the best predictions of Y given a value x of X. In many textbooks on applied statistics, the variable consisting of the best predictions of Y is denoted by $\hat{Y}$. $E(Y|X)$ may be thought of as the mathematical equivalent of $\hat{Y}$. Similarly, $E(Y|\mathcal{C})$ consists of the best predictions of Y based on the sigma-field $\mathcal{C}$. Note, however, that $E(Y|X)$ is defined without reference and restriction to a specific (regression) equation. It may also be thought of as a formalization of the notion of a "true regression."

DEFINITION 1. Let $Y:\Omega \to \overline{\mathbb{R}}$ be a numerical stochastic variable on the probability space $(\Omega, \mathcal{A}, P)$ with finite expectation $E(Y)$ or $Y \geq 0$ and let $\mathcal{C} \subset \mathcal{A}$ be a sigma-field. The stochastic variable $E(Y|\mathcal{C}):\Omega \to \overline{\mathbb{R}}$ is called the $\mathcal{C}$-*conditional expectation* of Y iff $E(Y|\mathcal{C})$ is $\mathcal{C}$-measurable and

$$E[1_C E(Y|\mathcal{C})] = E(1_C Y) \qquad \text{for all} \quad C \in \mathcal{C}. \tag{A.1}$$

Let $A \in \mathcal{A}$ be an event and 1_A its indicator function. $P(A|\mathcal{C})$ is called the $\mathcal{C}$-*conditional probability of* A iff

$$P(A|\mathcal{C}) := E(1_A|\mathcal{C}). \tag{A.2}$$

Let X be a $(\Omega', \mathcal{A}')$-stochastic variable on $(\Omega, \mathcal{A}, P)$. $E(Y|X)$ is called the X-*conditional expectation of* Y iff $\mathcal{C} = \mathcal{A}(X, \mathcal{A}')$ is the sigma-field generated by X and $\mathcal{A}'$ and

$$E(Y|X) := E(Y|\mathcal{C}). \tag{A.3}$$

Let $(X_j, j \in J)$ be a family of $(\Omega'_j, \mathcal{A}'_j)$-stochastic variables on $(\Omega, \mathcal{A}, P)$. $E(Y|X_j, j \in J)$ is called the $(X_j, j \in J)$-*conditional expectation of* Y iff $\mathcal{C} = \mathcal{A}[\cup_{j \in J}\mathcal{A}(X_j, \mathcal{A}'_j)]$ is the sigma-field generated by $[(X_j, \mathcal{A}'_j), j \in J]$ and

$$E(Y|X_j, j \in J) := E(Y|\mathcal{C}). \tag{A.4}$$

$E(Y|X_1, \ldots, X_n)$ is called the $(X_1, \ldots, X_n)$-*conditional expectation of* Y iff $\mathcal{C} = \mathcal{A}[\cup_{j \in J}\mathcal{A}(X_j, \mathcal{A}'_j)]$ is the sigma-field generated by $[(X_j, \mathcal{A}'_j), j \in J]$, where $J = \{1, \ldots, n\}$, $n \in \mathbb{N} = \{1, 2, \ldots\}$ and

$$E(Y|X_1, \ldots, X_n) := E(Y|\mathcal{C}). \tag{A.5}$$

Note that $E(Y|\mathcal{C})$ is the general concept. Hence, if propositions are true for $E(Y|\mathcal{C})$, then they also hold for $P(A|\mathcal{C})$, $E(Y|X)$, $E(Y|X_j, j \in J)$, and $E(Y|X_1, \ldots, X_n)$. Through the definition above, the $\mathcal{C}$-conditional expectation $E(Y|\mathcal{C})$ is uniquely determined only almost surely. Therefore, there are generally different versions of $E(Y\,|\,\mathcal{C})$, which are, however, equivalent, almost surely or with probability one. Equations on $E(Y\,|\,\mathcal{C})$ are therefore true only almost surely (as) in general.

Notice that there is a difference between the $\mathcal{C}$-conditional expectation $E(Y\,|\,\mathcal{C})$ of Y (i.e., the conditional expectation of Y *with respect to the sigma-field $\mathcal{C}$*) and the conditional expectation $E(Y\,|\,C)$ of Y *given the event C;* and, correspondingly, a difference between the conditional probability $P(A\,|\,\mathcal{C})$ of the event A *with respect to the sigma-field $\mathcal{C}$* and the conditional probability $P(A\,|\,C)$ of the event A *given the event C.* $E(Y\,|\,\mathcal{C})$ and $P(A\,|\,\mathcal{C})$ are stochastic variables, whereas $E(Y\,|\,C)$ and $P(A\,|\,C)$ are real-valued constants.

In the following theorem, a number of propositions on $E(Y\,|\,\mathcal{C})$ are gathered. Some of them are on conditions under which $E(Y\,|\,\mathcal{C})$ is equal to a constant function. In these and related contexts, the symbol for the function and the constant (its values) will be the same. The symbol a, for example, denotes not only a real-valued constant but also a function a: $\Omega \to \mathbb{R}$ taking the value $a \in \mathbb{R}$ for all $\omega \in \Omega$.

THEOREM 1. Let Y be a numerical stochastic variable on the probability space $(\Omega,\,\mathcal{A},\,P)$ with finite expectation $E(Y)$ or $Y \geq 0$. If $E(Y\,|\,\mathcal{C})$ is the $\mathcal{C}$-conditional expectation of Y, then the following propositions are true:

$$E[E(Y\,|\,\mathcal{C})] = E(Y). \tag{A.6}$$

$$E(Y\,|\,\mathcal{C}) = E(Y) \quad \text{if } \mathcal{C} = \{\Omega,\,\varnothing\}. \tag{A.7}$$

$$E[Y - E(Y\,|\,\mathcal{C})] = 0. \tag{A.8}$$

$$E(Y\,|\,\mathcal{C}) \text{ as} = Y \quad \text{if } Y \text{ is } \mathcal{C}\text{-measurable.} \tag{A.9}$$

$$E(Y\,|\,\mathcal{C}) \text{ as} = a \quad \text{if } Y \text{ as} = a. \tag{A.10}$$

$$E(Y\,|\,\mathcal{C}) \geq 0, \text{ almost surely,} \quad \text{if } Y \geq 0 \text{ almost surely.} \tag{A.11}$$

According to Equation A.6, the expectation of the $\mathcal{C}$-conditional expectation of Y is equal to the expectation of Y. Equation A.7 shows that the $\mathcal{C}$-conditional expectation of Y is equal to $E(Y)$ if $\mathcal{C} = \{\Omega,\,\varnothing\}$. According to Equation A.8, the expectation of the difference $Y - E(Y\,|\,\mathcal{C})$ of Y and its $\mathcal{C}$-conditional expectation is zero. Note that the difference $Y - E(Y\,|\,\mathcal{C})$ plays an important role in applications. It is called the *residual.*

Equation A.9 is often applied. Y is $\mathcal{C}$-measurable, for example, if $\mathcal{C}$ is the sigma-field generated by the $(\Omega_j,\,\mathcal{A}_j')$-stochastic variables $X_j, j \in J$, and $Y = X_j$, $Y = X_j \cdot X_k$, or $Y = X_j + X_k$, where $j, k \in J$. Hence, special cases of Equation A.9 are, for example,

$$E(X\,|\,X) \text{ as} = X,$$

$$E(X_i \mid X_j, j \in J) \text{ as}= X_i \qquad \text{if } i \in J,$$

$$E(X_i \cdot X_k \mid X_j, j \in J) \text{ as}= X_i \cdot X_k \qquad \text{if } i, k \in J,$$

and

$$E(X_i + X_k \mid X_j, j \in J) \text{ as}= X_i + X_k \qquad \text{if } i, k \in J.$$

The following theorem contains propositions on $E(Y \mid \mathcal{C})$, where Y is the weighted sum or the product of other stochastic variables. The notation $Y \leq Z$, almost surely, which occurs in Equation A.16, is an abbreviation for $Y(\omega) \leq Z(\omega)$ for almost all $\omega \in \Omega$.

THEOREM 2.   Let Y and Z be numerical stochastic variables on the probability space $(\Omega, \mathcal{A}, P)$ such that the $\mathcal{C}$-conditional expectations $E(Y \mid \mathcal{C})$ and $E(Z \mid \mathcal{C})$ are defined, and let $\mathcal{C}, \mathcal{C}_0 \subset \mathcal{A}$ be two sigma-fields. Then the following propositions are true:

$$E(Y \mid \mathcal{C}) \text{ as}= E(Z \mid \mathcal{C}) \qquad \text{if } Y \text{ as}= Z. \tag{A.12}$$

$$E(Y \cdot Z \mid \mathcal{C}) \text{ as}= Y \cdot E(Z \mid \mathcal{C}) \qquad \text{if } Y \text{ is } \mathcal{C}\text{-measurable}$$

$$\text{and if } E(Y \cdot Z) \text{ is finite.} \tag{A.13}$$

$$E[E(Y \mid \mathcal{C}_0) \cdot Z \mid \mathcal{C}] \text{ as}= E(Y \mid \mathcal{C}_0) \cdot E(Z \mid \mathcal{C}) \qquad \text{if } \mathcal{C}_0 \subset \mathcal{C}. \tag{A.14}$$

$$E(aY + bZ \mid \mathcal{C}) \text{ as}= aE(Y \mid \mathcal{C}) + bE(Z \mid \mathcal{C}) \qquad \text{if } a, b \in \mathbb{R}. \tag{A.15}$$

$$E(Y \mid \mathcal{C}) \leq E(Z \mid \mathcal{C}), \text{ almost surely}$$

$$\text{if } Y \leq Z \text{ almost surely.} \tag{A.16}$$

THEOREM 3.   Let Y be a numerical stochastic variable on the probability space $(\Omega, \mathcal{A}, P)$ such that the $\mathcal{C}$-conditional expectation $E(Y \mid \mathcal{C})$ is defined. If $\mathcal{C}_0 \subset \mathcal{C}$ is a sigma-field, then the following equations are true:

$$E[E(Y \mid \mathcal{C}) \mid \mathcal{C}_0] \text{ as}= E(Y \mid \mathcal{C}_0) \text{ as}= E[E(Y \mid \mathcal{C}_0) \mid \mathcal{C}]. \tag{A.17}$$

$$E[Y - E(Y \mid \mathcal{C}) \mid \mathcal{C}_0] \text{ as}= 0. \tag{A.18}$$

The sigma-field $\mathcal{C}_0$ will be a subset of the sigma-field $\mathcal{C}$, for example, if $\mathcal{C}$ is generated by the $(\Omega_j', \mathcal{A}_j')$-stochastic variables X_j, $j \in J$, and $\mathcal{C}_0$ by the $(\Omega_k', \mathcal{A}_k')$-stochastic variables X_k, $k \in K$, where $K \subset J$. Hence, special cases of Equations A.17 are

$$E[E(Y \mid X_1, X_2) \mid X_1] \text{ as}= E(Y \mid X_1) \text{ as}= E[E(Y \mid X_1) \mid X_1, X_2]$$

and

$$E[E(Y \mid X_j, j \in J) \mid X_k, k \in K] \text{ as}= E(Y \mid X_k, k \in K)$$

$$\text{as}= E[E(Y \mid X_k, k \in K) \mid X_j, j \in J],$$

where $K \subset J$.

Equation A.18 reveals that the $\mathcal{C}_0$-conditional expectation of the residual $F = Y - E(Y \mid \mathcal{C})$ is zero. This proposition on F is much stricter than that of Equation A.8, according to which the (unconditional) expectation of F is zero.

Acknowledgments

I want to thank Edgar Erdfelder and Joachim Funke for helpful suggestions on the first draft of this chapter.

References

Bauer, H. *Wahrscheinlichkeitstheorie und Grundzüge der Maßtheorie.* Berlin: de Gruyter, 1974.

Bentler, P. M. Multivariate analysis with latent variables: Causal modeling. *Annual Review of Psychology,* 1980, *31,* 419–456.

Bock, R. D. *Multivariate statistical methods in behavioral research.* New York: McGraw-Hill, 1975.

Brandtstädter, J., & Bernitzke, F. Zur Technik der Pfadanalyse: Ein Beitrag zum Problem der nichtexperimentellen Konstruktion von Kausalmodellen. *Psychologische Beiträge,* 1976, *18,* 12–34.

Bredenkamp, J. *Theorie und Planung psychologischer Experimente.* Darmstadt: Steinkopff, 1980.

Breiman, L. *Probability.* Reading, Mass.: Addison–Wesley, 1968.

Campbell, D. T., & Stanley, J. C. Experimental and quasi-experimental designs for research on teaching. In N. L. Gage (Ed.), *Handbook of research in teaching.* Chicago: Rand–McNally, 1963.

Cook, T. D., & Campbell, D. T. *Quasi-experimentation: Design and analysis issues for field settings.* Boston: Houghton Mifflin, 1979.

Cox, D. R. *The analysis of binary data.* London: Methuen, 1970.

Gänssler, P., & Stute, H. *Wahrscheinlichkeitstheorie.* Berlin: Springer, 1977.

Goldberger, A. S. Structural equation models: An overview. In A. S. Goldberger & O. D. Duncan (Eds.), *Structural equation models in the social sciences.* New York: Seminar Press, 1973.

Haberman, S. J. *The analysis of qualitative data I.* New York: Academic Press, 1978.

Haberman, S. J. *The analysis of qualitative data II.* New York: Academic Press, 1979.

Hummell, H. J., & Ziegler, R. Zur Verwendung linearer Modelle bei der Kausalanalyse nicht-experimenteller Daten. In H. J. Hummell & R. Ziegler (Eds.), *Korrelation und Kausalität, Band 1.* Stuttgart: Enke, 1976.

Jöreskog, K. G., & Sörbom, D. *LISREL V: Analysis of linear structural equation models by maximum likelihood and least squares methods.* Uppsala: University of Uppsala, Department of Statistics, 1981.

Kenny, D. A. *Correlation and causality.* New York: Wiley, 1979.

Langeheine, R. *Log-lineare Modelle zur multivariaten Analyse qualitativer Daten: Eine Einführung.* München: Oldenbourg, 1980.

Loève, M. *Probability theory I.* Berlin: Springer, 1977.

Loève, M. *Probability theory II.* Berlin: Springer, 1978.

Lohmöller, J.-B. *LVPLS 1.6 program manual: Latent variables path analysis with partial least-squares estimation.* Forschungsbericht 81.04. Munich: Fachbereich Pädagogik Hochschule der Bundeswehr, 1984.

Moosbrugger, H., & Steyer, R. Uni- und multivariate Varianzanalyse mit festen Parametern. In J. Bredenkamp & H. Feger (Eds.), *Enzyklopädie der Psychologie.* Serie Forschungs-methoden der Psychologie, Band 4. Göttingen: Hogrefe, 1983.

Novick, M. R. Statistics as psychometrics. *Psychometrika,* 1980, *45,* 411–424.

Steyer, R. Modelle zur kausalen Erklärung statistischer Zusammenhänge. In J. Bredenkamp & H. Feger (Eds.), *Enzyklopädie der Psychologie.* Serie Forschungsmethoden der Psychologie, Band 4. Göttingen: Hogrefe, 1983.

Steyer, R. *Causal linear stochastic dependencies: The formal theory.* In E. Degreef & J. Van Buggenhaut (Eds.), *Trends in mathematical psychology.* Amsterdam: North-Holland, 1984. (a)

Steyer, R. Conditional expectations: An introduction to the concept and its applications in empirical sciences. *Trierer Psychologische Berichte,* 1984, *11*(3), 1–24. (b)

Suppes, P. *A probabilistic theory of causality.* Amsterdam: North–Holland, 1970.

Wold, H. Mergers of economics and philosophy of science. *Synthese,* 1969, *20,* 427–482.

5

Structure Identification Using Nonparametric Models

ALEXANDER VON EYE

I. Structures

Typically, in empirical investigations in the social sciences n individuals are observed with regard to a set V of d variables. To study change processes, observations have to be repeated m times ($m \geq 2$). This leads to the well-known three-dimensional data matrix $X := \{a_{ijk}\}$, where $i = 1, \ldots, n$; $j = 1, \ldots, d$; and $k = 0, \ldots, m$.

The *structure* of the data in matrix X may be represented by the following two sets of properties:

1. the set S of elements in the structure; that is,
   a subset $\hat{V} \subseteq V$ of variables and/or
   a subset $\hat{N} \subseteq N$ of individuals and/or
   a subset $\hat{M} \subseteq M$ of occasions; $S := \{\hat{V}, \hat{N}, \hat{M}\}$;
2. the relations within S, for example, the associations between structural elements and/or the interactions within S.

The process of structuring data can be described simply as one of deriving statements about relations (e.g., correlations, associations, and dependencies; see Klix, 1971). The consequence of the structuring process may be described by both a positive and a negative characteristic. Positively, a well-defined structure increases the certainty concerning the common variation of the variables in S. The negative characteristic is the inverse of the positive: Superimposing a structure reduces the amount of variation that is possible in the case of complete independence of variables, that is, when no relations exist. The above characterization of a structure matches that given in systems methodology, in which a structural system is defined "as a set of 'elements,' 'parts' or 'subsystems,' along with a set of couplings or connections between these parts. . . ." (Cavallo, 1979, p. 92). It should be noted, however, that in mathematics proper the focus is most often on the relations between the elements and that their nature is of minor interest (see Eddington, 1956).

Closely connected with these characteristics is one of the most important features by which structures may be distinguished; namely, the *complexity of structures* (see Gaines, 1978; Klaus & Liebscher, 1979a, 1979b; Zalecka-Melamed & Zeigler, 1977). The complexity of a structure is a function of the number of elements in S, the number of states of these elements, and the number of relations within S. The greater the number of these parameters, the more complex the structure, and vice versa. To illustrate, let s_1 be the number of elements in S, s_2 the number of possible states of the elements, and s_3 the number of relations among the elements. It is generally assumed that the complexity C of a structure is directly proportional to s_1, s_2, and s_3: $C \sim s_1 s_2 s_3$. If it is possible to define a suitable constant c_C of proportionality, C becomes a quantitative measure of complexity: $C = c_C s_1 s_2 s_3$. Simple observation of this definition reveals that equal values of C can result from variations in s_1, s_2, and s_3. Thus, two or more structures can be characterized by identical values of C even if they differ in s_1, s_2, and s_3.

In addition to distinguishing among structures with regard to their complexity, cybernetics distinguishes between complex structures and *complicated* ones (see Klaus & Liebscher, 1979a). Complex structures contain only one kind of element. In contrast, complicated structures involve different kinds of elements.

Examples of complicated structures in the social sciences may be found in research on relations between and within variables in such different aspects of behavior as learning, motivation, and development. A structure which is composed only of relations among variables that are connected with learning processes can become complex but not complicated. Structures may become complicated if motivational or developmental variables are added to the structure. Similarly, and of special importance to the study of development and change, a structure becomes complicated if the relation between one group of variables is analyzed at more than one occasion; that is, even if the variables are the same, the structure becomes complicated by the addition of the time factor.

Examples of both complex and complicated structures involving different relations are rare in the social sciences. Even theories that define substantively differing kinds of relations between individuals across situations (e.g., speech patterns of school children in the company of peers as opposed to such patterns while with teachers or parents) are not true illustrations. Most often these relations have been measured with only one kind of similarity or association coefficient; for example, simple correlation coefficients or contingency measures. Such techniques are limited in their applicability, and perhaps even appropriateness, to the measurement of complicated structures. In the following section selected aspects of measuring relations between structural elements will be described, with special attention devoted to their assessment by nonparametric coefficients. (For parametric approaches with categorical variables see Mooijaart, 1982.)

II. Relations in Structures: A Formal Approach

The discussion of relations in structures will be restricted to two prominent topics; namely, the *order of relations* and the *distinction between associations and interactions* (a more general approach is presented in von Eye, 1981b).

A. THE ORDER OF RELATIONS

Elements of S (i.e., $s_1, s_2, \ldots, s_n$) are considered related to each other if there exists a mapping such that information about a subset of these elements also contains information about other elements. This relation r is symmetric if the common information remains unchanged when the order of related elements is changed. That is, r is symmetric if, in the case of two elements X_1 and X_2, $r(X_1, X_2) = r(X_2, X_1)$. The order of this relation i — and, therefore, its complexity — depends on the number of elements or sets that are involved. Permuting the number of elements, four cases can be distinguished. These cases are ordered hierarchically in such a way that the later cases contain the earlier ones as special cases.

1. A *first-order relation,* such as that described above, focuses analytical attention on the relation of two elements to each other.
2. A second form of a first-order relation, the *set – element first-order relation,* focuses on the relation of one element to a set of elements. In this case, too, relations may be symmetric or asymmetric. Consider,

for example, the situation in which a child adapts to the social situation at school. In this example both (simple) first-order and set–element first-order relations can be analyzed. With a simple first-order relation the relationship between the child and each single classmate is described successively. With a set–element first-order relation, the relationship between the child and the whole class is described. It is obvious that the latter description covers information that cannot be dealt with by compound analysis of all one-to-one relations.

3. In still a third possible first-order relation, the *set–set first-order relation,* analytical attention is devoted to the relationship of one set of elements to another. As with the previous two examples, this kind of relation can also be defined as either symmetric or asymmetric. A substantive example is the comparison of two sets of test items, each of which is considered a separate entity. It is apparent that repeated analysis of item–item or set–item relations deals with different sources of information.

4. The most general case, covering all possible *higher-order relations,* is employed when more than two single elements or more than two sets of elements are analyzed. Such higher-order relations include four principal manifestations:

   a. *In second-order relations of single elements,* a triplet of single elements is analyzed. As opposed to the $\binom{3}{2}$ first-order relations in all possible pairs of three variables or the set–element relations in the three possible one element–one set (containing two elements) combinations, just one relationship of three variables is analyzed. One example is the analysis of the relations that are possible when observing one person three times with respect to d cognitive variables. There are three possible first-order relations that involve two points in time. In addition, there is one second-order relation that expresses the degree of coherence within the triplet of all three points in time.

   b. *In second-order relations of set–element combinations,* any of the one element–two sets or two elements–one set combinations is analyzed. Because the order of sets and elements has no differentiating significance, the definition of symmetric relations involves only two distinguishable cases. Therefore, only the relations of element–set–set and element–element–set, or $r(e, s, s)$ and $r(e, e, s)$, may be obtained. The definition of asymmetric relations leads to 12 different combinations, beginning with $r(e, s_1, s_2)$ and ending with $r(s, e_2, e_1)$. Taking up the example of the child again, an element–set–set relation is analyzed when the coherence between this child and two subgroups of classmates (e.g., males and females)

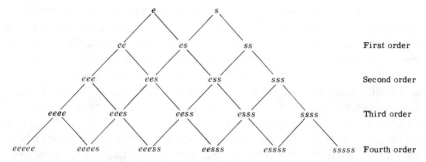

Figure 5.1   Application of the construction rule to obtain all possible symmetric nth-order relations.

is investigated.   Similarly, two single colleagues and one group of colleagues can be combined as a triplet and analyzed with respect to their element–element–set or second-order relation.

c. *Second-order relations of sets,* in which a triplet of sets is analyzed, is completely analogous to second-order relations of single elements.

d. Finally, *third- and higher-order relations* of single elements, element–set combinations, and sets may be analyzed.

The rule by which all possible symmetric nth order relations are constructed is depicted in Figure 5.1.   The rule consists of two steps that must be made in the correct order.   First, to get a new row (and order), add another e to the series of e's on the extreme left-hand side of the figure.   Second, moving stepwise from left to right, substitute an s for each e until no e remains.   This rule is equally applicable to all rows in Figure 5.1.   In order to get all possible asymmetric nth- order relations, all e's and s's have to be numbered and permuted in their positions.

B.   SOME CONCEPTS OF ASSOCIATION AND INTERACTION

In the analysis of systems and their structures, two main kinds of relations are analyzed: associations and interactions.   Unfortunately, there is no consensus on the meaning of either of these terms.   Some authors in statistics (e.g., Gokhale & Kullback, 1978, p. 13) define interaction so as to include virtually any kind of relation: ". . . we shall group all the concepts of association, dependence, etc., under the general term of interaction."   In contrast, a much narrower definition of interaction has been proposed by Lienert and colleagues (e.g., Krauth & Lienert, 1973; Lienert, 1978).   In their "interaction–structure analysis" (ISA) higher-order interactions are defined by dependencies (or directed relations) between two subsets of variables. According to these authors, first-order interactions describe the strength of a relation between one dependent and one independent variable while second-order interactions refer to sets of two independent variables influencing a third (dependent) variable (multiple ISA), to one variable affecting a set of two variables (multivariate ISA), or to a set of variables affecting another set of variables (canonical ISA). In this context the more general term is association. It is defined as a mapping such that knowledge of the properties of one subset of elements (or sets) informs predictions about properties of the remaining subsets of elements (or sets) in the target relation. On the basis of this definition, then, an interaction is an association between ordered (i.e., dependent and independent) variables. Compared to the analysis of variance (ANOVA) model, this approach is more general insofar as interactions are possible in the presence of only two elements (or variables). In ANOVA, at least three variables (two independent and one dependent) are needed before interactions are defined. Every other type of interaction in the Lienert and Krauth approach, however, has its analogue in ANOVA.

In this chapter, a third way of defining associations and interactions is adopted. This approach is based on the partitioning of the whole variation in S. As previously noted, the term *relation* will be used to subsume all statistical renderings of correlation, association, or interaction. The portion of the total variation that describes a given relation R is defined to be a compound of associations A and interactions I:

$$R := \{A_i, I_j\}, \ i, j \geqq 1. \tag{1}$$

That is, in the simplest case R is the sum of all associations and interactions. The consequence of this portrayal of relations is that a clear distinction between interaction and association is introduced in a nonparametric context. Just as interaction cannot be used as a general term subsuming association, neither can association be used to include interaction.

Associations. The main characteristic of relations that are termed associations is the previously noted predictability of properties of sets or elements from the properties of other sets or elements. This means that the analytic units in question must share a certain portion of information (or variation) to be considered associated with one another. One further ramification of this definition of association is that when the same sets or elements are analyzed the higher-order associations are independent of the lower-order associations. Consider the case of four elements, X_1, X_2, X_3, and X_4, that are analyzed with respect to their mutual associations. They may be grouped in $\binom{4}{2}$ pairs, $\binom{4}{3}$ triplets and $\binom{4}{4}$ quadruplets of elements. Because associations of different orders are characterized as independent, the measurement of any higher-order association should not be affected by the strength of any lower-order association (this issue will be discussed in more detail in Section II.C). Krauth and Lienert (1973) give a striking example of this characteristic in which three variables were strongly associated when their second-order association was computed but were not associated at all when they were combined as pairs.

In the study of development and change, an additional distinction — between directed and undirected associations — is important. As might be expected, when undirected associations are considered, the direction of the prediction of characteristics is not defined. Therefore, it can be inverted (in the case of simple first-order associations) or the order of the sets that are involved can be permuted (in the case of higher-order associations). Whereas undirected associations belong to the class of symmetric relations, directed associations are asymmetric relations. The reason for the latter assignment is that the inversion of the order of sets or elements in directed associations can change the meaning of the relation. For example, the phrase "the reinforcement accelerates the learning process" has a different meaning after inverting the order of the nouns into "the learning process accelerates the reinforcement." Another reason for their assigned asymmetry is that the formal description of directed associations does not always allow switching from $X_2 = f(X_1)$ to $X_1 = f(X_2)$.

Interactions. The second variety of relations, interactions, is the topic of this section. The meaning of an interaction is grounded in the concept of a higher-order association A. As stated above, this association is independent of all possible lower-order associations. This implies that a compound of all lower-order associations C_A cannot explain a larger portion of variation in a given relation than A itself: $C_A \leqq A$. This means that in A there is a first portion of variation that can be explained by lower-order associations and a second portion that is specific for the n-tuple in question (i.e., the interaction). Both portions must be conceptualized in such a way that they can cover from 0% to 100% of the total association. In Figure 5.2, for the quadruplet of elements X_1, X_2, X_3, and X_4, that partitioning of the whole relation into associations and interactions is depicted.

It follows from the decomposition of associations into portions describable by lower-order associations and interactions that only higher-order associations can be partitioned in this way. First-order associations cannot be decomposed because they involve the smallest number of elements that can be analyzed with respect to their relations. In this case, associations and interactions collapse, that is, for $n = 2 \rightarrow A = I$. As is the case with associa-

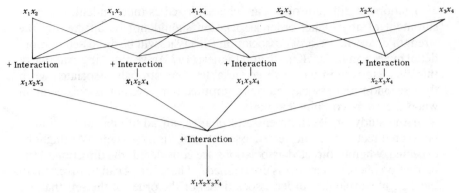

Figure 5.2 Partitioning of the relations in a set of four variables into associations and interactions.

tions, interactions may be considered as directed or undirected. In undirected interactions dependencies between variables are not taken into account; the order of variables is irrelevant for the interpretation. This may be appropriate, for instance, when items from a questionnaire scale are analyzed. If one is interested in that part of variation that characterizes these items as a whole, the interaction within a group of items should be independent of the order of items.

In the analysis of development and change, specific directions of interactions become important. The formulation of interaction terms can be restricted to a few substantively meaningful possibilities in which the order plays a substantial role. This may be illustrated by an example from "life-tree" research. In this area, the relevance of behavioral characteristics at a given stage (as determined by life events) for following stages is investigated. When events are analyzed that belong to different stages—for example, child-rearing techniques to which an individual was exposed in early childhood, kind of school career, or actual job satisfaction—it is obvious that only one directed interaction in each n-tuple of variables is of substantive interest.

Associations, like interactions, can be interpreted substantively in terms of the temporal order of these life stages. From the statistical point of view, however, temporally ordered data are often problematic. Von Eye and Brandtstädter (1981), for instance, showed that both the information-theoretic procedures proposed by Müller (1980) and some of the configural approaches discussed by Krauth and Lienert (1973) fail to account for the order of the variables in question. A specific inferential method to deal with hypotheses about the stage order has been proposed by Hildebrand, Laing, and Rosenthal (1977; see Froman & Hubert, 1980).

C. STATISTICAL ANALYSIS OF ASSOCIATIONS AND INTERACTIONS

The description of the statistical analysis of associations and interactions is restricted to two kinds of nonparametric procedures most relevant to the above definitions (for further nonparametric techniques see Henning & Rudinger, Chapter 11, this volume). The first procedure is the configural frequency analysis (CFA) of Krauth and Lienert (1973; Lienert, 1978). The second is the information theory constraint analysis of multidimensional contingency tables as discussed, for instance, by Broekstra (1979) and Krippendorff (1981).

1. χ^2 DECOMPOSITION

The "classical" Pearson χ^2 statistic as described by Siegel (1956) or Lienert (1973) is most often used to determine the differences between two or more variables with discrete categories. The χ^2 statistic is computed by applying the following formula:

$$\chi^2 = \sum_{i=1}^{\Pi c_i} (f_o - f_e)^2 / f_e, \qquad (2)$$

where $\sum_{i=1}^{\Pi c_i}$ denotes that the sum contains Πc_i elements, c_i is the number of categories of the ith variable, and f_e is the expected, f_o the observed value (for application rules and computational details, see the cited literature; for simplified formulas see Lienert & Wolfrum, 1980). In this context, the most important characteristic of Equation 2 is the fact that the resulting χ^2 refers to a number $d \geq 2$ variables. It is therefore an expression of the association within d variables as a whole. It is well known that parametric correlation coefficients — for example, the Bravais – Pearson r — can be expanded only up to $d = 3$. Higher-order correlations are not yet defined (see Lienert, 1981).

Since Equation 2 describes a d-tuple association, it can be used as an example of a measure of dth order relations as depicted in Figure 5.1. In the following pages the decomposition of χ^2 according to Figure 5.2 will be described. This decomposition is based on Lancester's (1969) definition of higher-order interactions and has been previously used by Krauth and Lienert (1973) for association structure analysis (ASA) within the framework of CFA. The following terms will be used in the description of the decomposition:

1. dth order association: $\chi^2(X_1, \ldots, X_d)$, and
2. dth order interaction: $\chi^2_{X_1, \ldots, X_d}$,

where $X_1, \ldots, X_d$ denotes the d variables that are involved in the analysis. To describe the relations furthest to the left in Figure 5.1 as associations by means of χ^2 statistics leads to the following expressions: $\chi^2(X_1, X_2)$, $\chi^2(X_1, X_2, X_3), \chi^2(X_1, \ldots, X_4), \chi^2(X_1, \ldots, X_5)$, and so forth. (For the analysis of sets of elements see Krauth & Lienert, 1973). Beginning with the second-order associations, decompositions become possible as depicted in Figure 5.2, so that the associations can be described as composed of

1. $\quad \chi^2(X_1, X_2, X_3) = \chi^2(X_1, X_2) + \chi^2(X_1, X_3) + \chi^2(X_2, X_3) + \chi^2_{X_1, X_2, X_3};$

2. $\chi^2(X_1, \ldots, X_4) = \chi^2(X_1, X_2, X_3) + \ldots + \chi^2(X_2, X_3, X_4)$
$\qquad - \chi^2(X_1, X_2) - \ldots - \chi^2(X_3, X_4) + \chi^2_{X_1, \ldots, X_4},$

3. $\chi^2(X_1, \ldots, X_5) = \chi^2(X_1, \ldots, X_4) + \ldots + \chi^2(X_2, \ldots, X_5)$
$\qquad - \chi^2(X_1, \ldots, X_3) - \ldots - \chi^2(X_3, \ldots, X_5)$
$\qquad + \chi^2(X_1, X_2) + \ldots + \chi^2(X_4, X_5) + \chi^2_{X_1, \ldots, X_5};$

and so on.

It should be noted that the signs change in the series of decomposition steps, and that the higher-order associations that are used as components can be used also in their decomposed form (see Lancester, 1969).

To describe structures one typically refers only to significant relation measures, that is, to significant interactions, associations, or (in ASA) "tuple-associations." Unfortunately, because of two related problems, it is not possible simply to compare the resulting χ^2 components with the tabulated critical values. The first problem results from the independence of the χ^2 tests. Sequential significance tests within one data set are rarely independent from one another. It follows that the actual significance level (i.e., the probability of making an α error) is higher than the nominal significance level. To avoid nonconservative decisions, Krauth and Lienert (1973) adopted the Bonferroni α-adjustment, which accounts for the number of significance tests t in a structure analysis. With this adjustment one obtains $\alpha^* = \alpha/t$ (for recent adjustment procedures see Lehmacher, 1981; Lindner, 1982).

The second problem results from the independence of the elements (variables) in question. The χ^2 decomposition of the Lancester (1969) type is based on the null hypothesis of total independence of all elements. Because it must be proved by means of substantive arguments, this condition is seldom demonstrated. Correlated elements can be conceived substantively as independent, whereas uncorrelated elements are sometimes necessarily dependent (e.g., in repeated measurement designs). This reflects both the difference between statistical and substantive concepts of dependence and problems inherent in the application of χ^2 decomposition procedures to empirical data sets (for further discussion see Section III of this chapter).

A notable characteristic of this χ^2 decomposition is the fact that ASA does not lead to higher-order relations that are independent from lower-order relations. When lower-order associations are significant, higher-order associations are also significant. On the other hand, higher-order associations can be significant even if lower-order associations are insignificant. As Krauth (1980) stressed, this can be a desirable property since the remaining part of dependency relationships in a data set might be of minor relevance, especially if most of the overall variation can be explained by first-order associations. However, it demonstrates the importance of the decomposition procedure to substantive interpretation; shallow inspection of significant higher-order associations could lead to misinterpretations.

2. DECOMPOSITION OF INFORMATION MEASURES

In order to complement the definition of association given in Section II.B, a second group of measures can be applied to structural analysis problems. This group has been called constraint or information analysis (Broekstra, 1977a, 1977b, 1979; Krippendorff, 1978, 1981). Although basic introductions to information theory in the social sciences are readily available (Attneave, 1959; Mittenecker & Raab, 1973), for readers not familiar with such statistics, an overview of the status of information theory in structural analysis research may be useful.

Information theory is concerned primarily with the measurement of input–output connections—the "information flow"—in communication systems. Elements of a system that communicate by transferring information can be treated as related to one another, since the definition of relations given in Sections II.A–II.C involves directed as well as undirected connections. Unlike the usual applications of information theory, in this context neither the unit of information transfer nor the type of transferred information is of interest. Thus, only the elements or sets that are related to each other and the strength of these relations are investigated. This, then, implies that information theory is used soley as a statistical tool with no additional substantive meaning.

As a consequence of the present specialized application of information theory, terms such as "bit," "entropy," and "redundancy" will not be used in the following description. Only those terms that refer to relations—that is, to associations and interactions—will be used. The first of these terms is *transinformation* or *transmission,* symbolized by T. Transinformation defines the amount of information shared by the elements or sets among which relations are being investigated. T can be used for any combination of sets and/or elements and is therefore directly comparable to the association χ^2 in Section II.C. Although further conceptual elaboration and computational details are available in the literature cited in this section, a more specific description of the two-element case is useful. In this case, T is

$$T(X_1, X_2) = H(X_1) + H(X_2) - H(X_1, X_2), \tag{3}$$

where $H(X_1)$ and $H(X_2)$ denote the amount of information in variables X_1 and X_2, respectively, and $H(X_1, X_2)$ is the total information covered by X_1 and X_2. If the latter term is small, then X_1 and X_2 overlap considerably, indicating that they are strongly associated with each other and that T is large. On the other hand, if the total information is large, then the total variation is enlarged by the second variable and T becomes small.

Analogously to χ^2, T can be expanded and decomposed so that formally equivalent expressions result ($T(X_1, \ldots, X_n)$) denotes associations, $T_{X_1, \ldots, X_n}$ denotes interactions):

1. $\quad T(X_1, X_2, X_3) = T(X_1, X_2) + T(X_1, X_3) + T(X_2, X_3) + T_{X_1, X_2, X_3};$

2. $T(X_1, \ldots, X_4) = T(X_1, X_2, X_3) + \ldots + T(X_2, X_3, X_4)$

   $\qquad - T(X_1, X_2) - \ldots - T(X_3, X_4) + T_{X_1, \ldots, X_4};$

3. $T(X_1, \ldots, X_5) = T(X_1, X_2, X_3, X_4) + \ldots + T(X_2, X_3, X_4, X_5)$

   $\qquad - T(X_1, X_2, X_3) - \ldots - T(X_3, X_4, X_5)$

   $\qquad + T(X_1, X_2) + \ldots + T(X_4, X_5) + T_{X_1, \ldots, X_5};$

and so on.

Here again, the higher-order associations (transmissions) can be expressed in their decomposed form. Significance tests for T values are possible on the basis of the following well-known relation:

$$\chi^2(T) \simeq 2 \cdot n \cdot \ln 2 \cdot T \simeq 2 \cdot n \cdot 1.3863 \cdot T, \tag{4}$$

where n denotes the sample size. Because interactions in information theory can become negative (see Kullback, 1968) relation 4 is valid only for association terms.

3. A SHORT COMPARISON OF χ^2 AND INFORMATION THEORY RELATION MEASURES

In the above description of two procedures that permit treatment of higher-order interactions and associations, the formal analogies were obvious. Both allow for the computation of structural characteristics that are disallowed by such methods as structural equation modeling. However, there are basic differences between the information theory and the χ^2 approaches that can contribute to different substantive interpretations of the same data set. These differences will be described in this section (see also von Eye, 1981a, 1982).

The first difference follows from the fact that the information theory transmission function is convex, whereas the χ^2 association measures are not. The convexity can be shown by constructing contingency tables that are increasingly extreme in their distributions; that is, matrices that are increasingly removed from the condition of having equal cell frequencies. In this case χ^2 increases as the distribution becomes more extreme. This trend continues until a distribution is reached for which the computation of a χ^2 coefficient makes no sense. (It should be noted that this statement holds true only for higher-order associations; first-order χ^2 values from two-way tables reach a maximum that cannot be exceeded.) Transmission measures, by contrast, reach a maximum that can be characterized by the following properties of square matrices:

1. the off-diagonal cells are empty; and
2. the frequencies in the diagonal cells are equally distributed.

In nonsquare matrices, the maximal T is restricted to $T = \min\{H(x_1), \ldots, H(x_n)\}$, if all variables reach their maximal H values. Constructing matrices with more extreme cell frequencies reduces the maximal T because the maximal H values of each variable are no longer attained.

For empirical data sets it is obvious that differences between T and χ^2 can lead to contrasting conclusions about structural characteristics. The interpretation of χ^2 values refers to deviations from equal cell frequencies; the more extreme the empirical distributions become, the larger the differences between the cell entries and the more clear-cut the assignment of single elements to cells on the basis of knowledge concerning their position in any of the variables.

The interpretation of T values, however, is based on two distinct sources of variation. There is, first, the actual amount of information covered by each variable, and, second, the common variation in all variables taken as a unique entity. It follows that, if the amount of information covered by at least one variable is small, the transmission within a set of variables can never be high. This case, however, is characterized by extremely unequal cell frequencies, and would therefore lead to large χ^2 values. High association, then, as measured by information theory T coefficients, signifies both (1) the possibility of assigning an element with a low error probability to a cell on the basis of knowledge concerning its position in any of the variables and (2) the fact that, although elements can belong only to very few of the cells of the contingency table, variation is not reduced.

Table 5.1

Matrices Reflecting the Differences between χ^2 and T
Associations

Cells	Matrices		
	I	II	III
111	5	10	1
112	5	0	0
121	5	0	0
122	5	10	0
211	5	10	0
212	5	0	0
221	5	0	0
222	5	10	39
$\chi^2(X_1, X_2, X_3)$	0.0	40.00	1601.03
$T(X_1, X_2, X_3)$	0.0	1.00	0.57
$\chi^2(T)$	0.0	55.45	18.71

In Table 5.1, three $2 \times 2 \times 2$ matrices are presented to demonstrate the differences between χ^2 and T associations (see von Eye, 1982). In matrices I and II χ^2 and T produce very similar results. In both cases the variation covered by each single variable is maximal. The difference between these matrices lies in the fact that whereas in matrix I it is not possible to assign one element to one of the cells on the basis of a given value in one variable, in matrix II it is. In matrix III such an assignment is also possible and, in addition, the probability of belonging to a cell other than 222 is close to $p = 0$. This reflects a more extreme frequency distribution, and therefore χ^2 is maximal. On the other hand, since for each variable the probability of falling in category 1 is $p = 1/39$, any given variable covers only a small amount of variation. Hence, T becomes small.

The second difference between χ^2 and T statistics emanates from the independence of higher-order interactions and lower-order associations and interactions. As described in Section II.C.1, higher-order associations in the χ^2 approach are necessarily significant when the lower-order associations of the same variables are significant, and, further, in the case of nonsignificance within the lower-order variable n-tuples, higher-order associations (and interactions) may still be significant. It follows that for the higher order interactions $\chi^2 = 0$ if all elements are independent, and $\chi^2 > 0$ if first- or higher-order relations exist.

As distinct from χ^2, higher-order information theory interactions can become negative (for formal descriptions and computational examples see, for example, Broekstra, 1976, 1977b), which is why they are excluded from significance testing. On the one hand, this characteristic may seem problematic, for it complicates the interpretation of the data structure. On the other hand, because negative interactions can always be interpreted as a portion of variation that is already covered by lower-order associations, they can provide important information about the kind of relations present in the data. Mittenecker and Raab (1973) describe negative interactions as a kind of correction for lower-order associations that have been included in the computations more than once.

Negative interactions reflected in T statistics can be valuable in the search for sources of relations in the analysis of development and change. It has been shown that spurious associations are the source of negative interactions. If, for instance, two variables are associated with one another only because they are in the same way dependent on a third variable, the interactions within the triplet of variables will be negative. More generally, negative information theory interactions can always be explained by spurious associations (for examples see Broekstra, 1976; von Eye, 1981a).

The discovery of dependence structures is also possible in the χ^2 approach, as Krauth (1980) pointed out. Given the assumption that certain associations or interactions are mediated by "regression" of the involved variables on other ones, analysis of subcontingency tables can reveal whether the interaction structure is the same for all categories of a given variable (or set of variables). However, in the χ^2 approach, dependency hypotheses have to be specified (which is not always an easy task), whereas the information theory approach provides some indicators of spurious associations.

Like negative interactions, spurious interactions can be analyzed. Although they are positive, they can also be due to spurious associations. Neither the χ^2 nor the constraint analysis approach provides immediate indicators of the presence of spurious interactions. Therefore, it is necessary to formulate dependence hypotheses for substantive reasons and to test each of them by holding variables constant or by analyzing subtables.

III. On the Detection of Structures

In the first two sections the focus was on general characteristics of structures and on two nonparametric methods to deal with structural properties of empirical data sets. In this section strategies for defining and detecting structures will be discussed. Here again the discussion will be based primarily on χ^2 and information theory tools (log-linear models are discussed by Henning & Rudinger in Chapter 11 of this volume; see also Bishop, Fienberg, & Holland, 1975; for prediction analysis see Hildebrand et al., 1977).

Two fundamentally different approaches to structure detection will be explicated, namely, hypothesis-free search and hypothesis-directed search.

A. HYPOTHESIS-FREE STRUCTURE
IDENTIFICATION

Frequently in developmental research one wants to know how much variation can be accounted for by nonlinear or higher-order relations. For example, after having identified developmental factors with traditional linear factor analysis, one might be interested in describing the variable structure under consideration of higher-order relations. In this example hypotheses about the structure may not exist. Hence, the application of hypothesis-free structure identification could be useful.

Hypothesis-free structure identification in empirical data sets can be defined as the measurement of associations and interactions without restrictions by prior theory-based statements regarding specific relations. This does not mean that this approach excludes substantive assumptions from structure search. On the contrary, such assumptions play a substantial role in at least two portions of the search process. Its first impact occurs during the selection of variables, persons, and occasions to be sampled in the investigation or in data analysis procedures. Even in "data snooping" approaches it is rather unusual to select variables that are not assumed to belong to the problem under investigation, or persons that are not assumed to show the behavior in question, and so on. Thus, to a certain extent, the determination of a research area entails the results of a structure search, even the results of a hypothesis-free structure search.

A second instance in which substantive assumptions play a role in hypothesis-free structure search is that of evaluating computational results. On the one hand, the respective results on relations may be prominent because of their statistical significance or the portion of variation they cover. Substantive considerations, however, become especially important when these prominent parts of the results are compared with theory-based search results or hypotheses concerning the "true" structure. In cluster analysis, for example, interpretations are often made by stressing the "plausibility" of clusters. In this case the results of a structure search are matched with implicit, unstated, or atheoretical hypotheses.

Following the decisions regarding selection of variables, persons, and occasions, the process of hypothesis-free structure identification can be described as consisting of three steps:

1. selection of one (or more) procedures that are assumed to match the interesting characteristics of inter-element relations; for example, χ^2,

information theory, cluster analysis, and heuristic and other procedures;
2. computation of all possible structural relations in a given data set; and
3. interpretation of results with respect to statistical measures, specific
   characteristics of the applied methods, previous results, structural hypotheses, or other results using the same data set.

The first step shows another example of the connection between substantive and statistical decisions; the choice between a relation-describing procedure as discussed in Sections II.C.1 – II.C.3, and a cluster analysis procedure,
or the choice between different similarity measures in cluster analysis, can be
based only on substantive reasons. When these reasons are not persuasive
enough to serve as decision aids, it is always possible to apply other methods
to the same data set and to compare the respective results. Examples of
reasons that lead to a decision for a specific procedure can be seen in the
assumptions regarding the dependence structure in a given data set. As
pointed out in Section II.C.3, both χ^2 and T statistics allow for the analysis of
dependence structures. One important difference is that, whereas in the
information theory approach, at least some of the mutual dependencies are
indicated, in the χ^2 approach specific hypotheses (or an excessive amount of
computational work) are needed to detect this type of relationship.

The second step above is the most critical one in hypothesis-free structure
identification. Depending on the number of variables, the number of possible relations may increase quite rapidly; this can be shown by simple computations. When n variables are given, one obtains

1. $\binom{n}{2}$ binary relations (since for $n = 2$, interactions and associations collapse, one gets $1 \cdot \binom{n}{2}$ only); and
2. $\binom{n}{3}$ associations and $\binom{n}{3}$ interactions in variable triplets, and so forth.

Altogether, one obtains $r = [2\Sigma_{i=1}^{n} \binom{n}{i}] - \binom{n}{2}$ nondirected associations and
interactions between variables. It should be stressed, however, that this is
the simplest case only, and is of minor relevance to the study of development
and change, an area in which possible directed relations and mutual dependencies must also be taken into account. However, unlike hypothesis-
guided research, the danger of getting many more relations than variables
increases.

There are three ways that this problem — a plethora of relations vis-à-vis
variables — attendant in hypothesis-free search structures can be minimized. First, it seems useful, even without specific substantive hypotheses,
to exclude from further attention all relations that are semantically or logically meaningless. Examples of such pseudorelations are influences of later
events on earlier events and effects of the social behavior of an adolescent on
his or her position in the birth order of a given family.

The second way in which the number of relations may be reduced is to restrict them to only one level. When applying this mode of analysis, it is assumed that the most important portions of the overall variation are covered by that level of relation actually chosen (usually first-order relations). It is apparent that factor analysis, scaling procedures, and cluster analysis are examples of techniques that use only first-order relations to describe one specific portion of the variation. Both first-order χ^2 and first-order T statistics can be applied in cluster analysis, as in single linkage algorithms (further examples are given in Vogel, 1975). An additional example can be seen in the application of the nonhierarchical CFA (see Krauth & Lienert, 1973, Chapter 2). Using this procedure, one tests whether the empirical frequencies in single cells in a given contingency table differ substantially from expected frequencies, with the latter computed under the assumption that the variables under investigation are independent of one another. A significantly over- (or under-) frequented cell can be interpreted as a positive (or negative) "local association" between all n variables, that is, as a local nth-order association.

A third way of reducing the number of relations is to fix statistical criteria — for example, a significance level — and to interpret relations at the highest possible order. If, for instance, three elements A, B, and C are correlated as pairs and as a triplet, it may be sufficient to interpret only the second-order correlation, since it covers both the bivariate and the additional triple portion of variation. The search for the highest significant order of relations can be conducted by either the ascending or the descending strategy. The former strategy begins with the lowest order of relations and, because higher-order relations can be significant even when lower-order relations remain weak, continues until *all* levels of relations are investigated. In contrast, the latter strategy begins with the highest possible order of relations. At each successively lower level, the relations between variables in nonsignificant higher-order relations can be neglected. So the number of tests required becomes smaller. Unless the so-called quasi-parametric case prevails, in which most of the variation is covered by first-order associations, it can be expected that in both cases the description of a structure involves relations of different orders.

In addition to these simple procedures, many other more sophisticated ones have been proposed; many of these may result in models that best fit a priori criteria for empirical data sets. The main purpose of these procedures, however, cannot be to prove the existence of a structure; rather, the objective is to facilitate the formulation of hypotheses in future investigations (see Wermuth, 1976; Victor, Lehmacher, & Van Eimeren, 1980; Krippendorff, 1981).

An additional problem is that of the independence of statistical tests.

When several statistical tests are applied to the same data set, each one must be considered as dependent on every other one. As was pointed out in Section II.C, adjustment of the significance level of α seems necessary to counterbalance nonconservative decisions about the strength of relations. Even in the case of a priori excluded relations in hypothesis-free structure identification, one does not know how many of the remaining relations are of specific interest. It follows that one has to choose the most extreme $\alpha^* = \alpha/r$. This necessity, however, reduces drastically the number of relation measures attaining significance. As an alternative one can either do without significance testing, as for example in cluster analysis, or renounce α adjustment, which has the effect of reducing the value of significance testing to that of a heuristic aid.

All these problems, however, do not devalue completely hypothesis-free structure identification. The main argument brought in favor of this strategy concerns the degree to which the information in a given data set is exhausted. Only by checking all possible relations, using different procedures that match different properties, can one be sure not to overlook a prominent structural characteristic. This is, then, quite naturally the main interest in hypotheses-free structure identification. It also can be important, however, for hypothesis testing, especially when the evidence for the hypotheses is weak, or when alternative hypotheses fit the data better than the hypothesis under study.

B. HYPOTHESIS-DIRECTED STRUCTURE IDENTIFICATION

Frequently in developmental research data are gathered in order to test specific hypotheses. For this situation statistical methods are needed that are tailored to match these hypotheses. Such methods will be discussed in the following sections from a nonparametric perspective.

1. HYPOTHESIS TESTING IN STRUCTURAL RESEARCH

The first problem to discuss in this section concerns the kind of hypotheses that can be dealt with in structure search using nonparametric statistics. With respect to Section II, a first group of hypotheses that permit the simultaneous analysis of one or more relations within a given data set can be identified. These relations, which must be specified a priori, constitute, together with the elements whose relations are analyzed, the structure under study. In the typical case, the hypotheses do not differentiate between subsets of elements, variables, or categories of variables. Therefore, they can be called *general hypotheses*. Restricting the predictions to subsets leads to *local hypotheses.* Such hypotheses refer to relations in groups of persons, occasions, or variables, or to relations in groups of persons at certain occasions in certain variables. The most specific local hypothesis involves one group of persons, at least two variables, and one occasion. In CFA such specific subsets of contingency tables are analyzed under the heading of "search for types" or "local associations" (see Krauth & Lienert, 1973).

Both general and local hypotheses can be stated in forms that differ in terms of the goals that are pursued. If one controls the α error (as is usually done in statistics), one attempts to determine whether an a priori-specified model can be *rejected* on the basis of a given empirical data set. On the other hand, one endeavors to find the model that fits the data best. In this case one should control the β error.

Examples of the hypothesis-rejecting type of statistical testing may be found in some information theory strategies of structure identification (cf. Broekstra, 1976, 1977b), as well as in CFA, ASA, and the prediction analysis of Hildebrand and associates (1977). "Model fitting" is attempted by, for example, the application of log-linear models or — in the parametric case — by the application of structural equation models (see Jöreskog, 1979; Steyer, Chapter 4, this volume). In Table 5.2 the distinctions between general versus local hypotheses and model rejection versus model fitting are displayed.

A hypothesis of Type I can be described as typical of investigations that apply the falsification approach. The hypothesis generated for testing involve the entire data set. They are maintained unless it can be proved that repeated applications of the same data collection strategy lead to clear rejections. It should be noted that the structural hypotheses do not necessarily contain only statements about relations between persons, variables, and occasions. It can also be predicted that certain elements remain unrelated, as is the case when one assumes that a given life event has no influence on later behavior.

A hypothesis of Type II has almost the same characteristics as a hypothesis of Type I. The only difference is the fact that only a proper subset of the data set is analyzed. When, for instance, one hypothesizes that the correlation between intelligence scores of adopted children and their adoptive parents decreases in the time interval between the (child's) ages of 4 and 20 — whereas for parents and their natural children no assumption regarding such a decrease exists — then it is sufficient to analyze data for the adopted children only. Another example is the hypothesis that intelligence, diligence, task orientation, and school marks are associated as a quadruplet, but only because the frequency in the cell "high intelligence, high diligence, high task orientation, and good marks" is relatively high compared with the frequency expected under the assumption of, say, no correlation between the variables under study.

Table 5.2

A Classification of Hypotheses in Structure
Identification

Goal of hypothesis testing	Type of hypothesis	
	General	Local
Rejection of hypothesis	I	II
Model fitting	III	IV

Hypotheses of Types III and IV can be compared with one another in the same way as hypotheses of the first two types. They differ from one another mainly in terms of the proportion of variables involved in a given analysis. A hypothesis of Type IV differs from one of Type II in a specific way: Model fitting seldom is done with the most specific hypotheses possible, that is, with hypotheses referring to only one cell in a contingency table. Hence the structural assumptions regarding the quadruplet mentioned above can be tested only with respect to the associations.

2. THE PROCESS OF STRUCTURE IDENTIFICATION

In Figure 5.3 the process of structure identification is summarized (see Klir, 1979; Vansteenkiste, Spriet, & Bens, 1979). Obviously, the process of structure identification has to begin with the selection of the purpose of the study, that is, with the set of questions that are intended to be addressed by an empirical investigation. The purpose of an investigation usually determines the object of investigation; for example, in developmental psychology, one studies persons at different stages of the life span; in learning psychology, one studies persons at different points in the learning process. All these decisions have to be compatible with constraints that are specific to social science research; for example, availability of subjects, replicability of data collection, financial arrangements, ethical issues, and reliability of repeated measures.

After these basic decisions are made, one must determine the method of structure identification. In "uncertain environments" — that is, when the structural characteristics cannot be predicted from theoretical or prior empirical knowledge — one of the procedures for structure search can be applied. If the number of variables is not too large, the computation of all possible relations should be considered.

In many cases, however, it is possible to define a structure before data analysis and to either test it as a whole or test each relation separately. For this purpose, it first must be decided which subsets of persons, occasions, and variables are necessary in a specific model. To compare, for instance, the professional careers of people from different social groups, reliable assign-

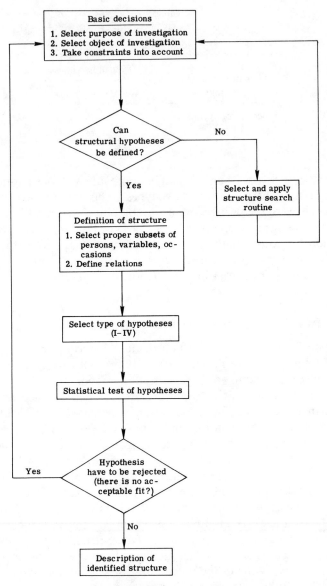

Figure 5.3 Structure identification.

ment to the grouping variable is crucial. Similarly, to investigate the effect
of therapeutic interventions, the choice of occasions of measurement is
critical. The second important step in the definition of a structure concerns
the relations, or types of structures, themselves. As was pointed out in
Section II, consideration of higher-order relations excludes most parametric

procedures from being applied to empirical data sets. In addition to the restriction to first- (and second-) order relations, most parametric models restrict the researcher to linear relations. In the study of development and change, however, pure linear relations can be trivially assumed a priori only in the case of one repeated measurement. When measuring on more than two occasions, nonlinear relations can be assumed, too, as, for instance, in learning processes where negatively accelerated curves or curves with one inflection point (ogive) are modal.

The next step in the structure identification process is the choice of the type of hypotheses to be tested. This step is closely connected with the previous one. When the structural hypotheses do not exclude any of the subjects, variables, or occasions, hypotheses of Types I and III are predetermined. When hypotheses are stated which concern single cells of a contingency table, certain model-fitting procedures cannot be applied, and so on. These examples show that, in most cases, both the generality of hypotheses and the goal of hypothesis testing depend upon the way in which hypotheses are formulated.

The statistical test of hypotheses is the decisive step in the structure identification process. When the overall fit is good, the subsequent decision to accept the hypotheses is easy. Vansteenkiste and associates (1979) point out that a well-chosen structure provides but few suggestions for further structure definitions. Only for poor correspondences between data and hypotheses does the search begin again. The results of one test can be used as evidence for further hypothesis formulations; these cannot be tested, however, until new data are gathered. The reason that new data are required after rejection of the hypothesis is the well-known fact that the α error in hypothesis testing is no longer controlled when subsequent testing is done with the same data.

IV. Application to the Study of Development and Change

In this section, to demonstrate more concretely the value of the concept of higher-order interactions and associations for the study of development and change, an empirical data set will be discussed (see Storath, 1982). The data reflect the teachers' verbal descriptions of the pupils' classroom-related behavior at the end of the school year. These descriptions were collected after the second, fourth, sixth, and eight year — that is, at the end of a teacher's contact with a class in an elementary school (*Grund-* and *Hauptschule*) in West Germany. The goal of this investigation was to determine the stability of independent teachers' ratings over eight years in elementary school for girls and boys in all rating categories. In addition, possible relations between the teachers' ratings and the sex of the pupils were investigated.

The rating categories C were (1) disciplined versus undisciplined, (2) modesty versus ambition, (3) degree of intellectual activity, (4) degree of nonconformity, and (5) sensitiveness versus indifference. In order to generate detailed information concerning the change process that is reflected by variations of the ratings, a specific transformation of the ratings was adopted: The transitions between each pair of ratings were scaled by determining which value combination in a preceding class was followed by which value combination in the succeeding class. This means that not only were the positions of each individual in each category in each occasion scaled but also the pathways from year to year. The first step in this pathway is the transition from a given position in the second year to a position in the fourth year. The last step in the pathway is the transition from the sixth to the eighth year. Hence, in addition to the frequency distribution in each year, a transition variable, indicating the structure of change, was also scored. This scoring procedure led to three variables that replaced the variable "years," namely, "preceding ratings" (P, 3 levels), "succeeding ratings" (S, 3 levels), and "transitions" (T, 3 levels). Altogether, structural analysis as applied to a 3 (preceding ratings: second, fourth, and sixth year) $\times$ 3 (transitions: second to fourth, fourth to sixth, and sixth to eighth year) $\times$ 3 (succeeding ratings: fourth, sixth, and eighth year) $\times$ 2 (gender: female, male; symbolized by G) $\times$ 5 (rating categories; symbolized by C) contingency table. Omitting the descriptive parameters of single variables, $\binom{5}{2}$ bivariate reltions, $2 \cdot \binom{5}{3}$ relations in variable triplets, $2 \cdot \binom{5}{4}$ relations in variable quadruplets, and 2 relations in the quintuplet, or $t = 42$ undirected relations can be computed.

Because this number was not so large that one became hopelessly lost in parameters, a full structural analysis—without restriction to only a few relations, and not a structure search program—was computed. Because of the possible wide overlap of the three variables that represent the number of years in school, and in order to detect easily any spurious relations among these variables, application of information theory measures seemed to be appropriate; thus, a suitable program was applied (PARTITI by Krippendorff, 1978). Instead of describing all relations exhaustively, some details will be enumerated that illustrate the characteristics of the analytical procedures that have been discussed.

With regard to the ten bivariate relations, generally expected results were obtained. The ratings given by the teachers were stable (preceding $\times$ succeeding ratings were highly associated) but the variation within the ratings increased with the age of the children [$r(PT) > r(ST)$ and $r(PC) > r(SC)$]. There was no bivariate association at all between gender and categories. The trivariate associations show that 96.08% of the variation between P, S, and T can be described by the bivariate relations because the interaction covers only 3.92% of the variation. Similarly, the interaction in the triplet P, S, and G explains only 1.07% of the variation. In both cases the associations themselves are significant.

In the triplets P, T, and C and S, T, and C, the interactions explain much more of the variation in the significant associations. In the former, 14.13% of the variation is due to the interaction, whereas in the latter it is 15.71%. The interpretation may proceed as follows. The predictability of the teachers' ratings from one rating situation to the following one — that is what is explained by T — is high. Since, for the transmission, $r(PTC) > r(STC)$ holds true, the increasing variation mentioned above can be seen again. In addition, the high positive interactions signify that the predictability of the teachers' ratings does not apply in the same way to all categories of the pupils' behavior. Indeed, a look at the average scores of the pupils in the rating categories over all observation points leads to an explanation. In category one (disciplined versus undisciplined) there was a constant trend toward the "disciplined" pole, and in category three a U-shaped curve indicated that the perceived intellectual activity of the pupils had its highest values at the beginning and at the end of the observed time interval. The changes in the average ratings in the remaining three categories are very small: there is nearly no trend and the variation remains constant.

One negative interaction, namely $i(PSC)$, in the set of 10 triplets indicates that there can be dependencies in the sense of spurious associations. The negative portion covered 5.79% of the respective association. If one holds constant the remaining third variable in the bivariate associations $r(PS)$, $r(PC)$, and $r(SC)$, one does not obtain a reduction of any of these associatons to a nonsignificant value. Therefore, this negative portion will be neglected in the interpretation.

The role of the sex of the pupils may be explained by the quadruplets. The third-order association $r(PTGC)$ is significant. Its interaction explained only 2.53% of this relation. This indicates that only this small percentage of the variation within P, T, S, and C is covered in addition to that covered by lower-order interactions. The $\binom{4}{3}$ triplets that can be built with these variables account for almost the same portion of the variation within this quadruplet. The comparison of $r(PTGC)$ with $r(STGC)$ illustrates the impact of sex. Again, the relation $r(PTGC) > r(STGC)$ holds true, but unlike the quadruplet $PTGC$, the interaction portion in $r(STGC)$ covered 6.43% of the variation. Referring to the discussion of the triplets P, T, and C and S, T, and C, this result may be interpreted as a sex effect that becomes apparent only in the later observation points. The reason for this interpretation is that the portion of variation accounted for by the sex variable increases in the later ratings and transitions. This increase signifies that in later school years more knowledge of the pupils' sex is needed in order to be able to predict the pupils' pathway in the teachers' ratings. This result is not modified by incorporation of the fifth variable. The interaction in the quintuplet covers only 3.15% of this variation and will therefore be neglected.

There are two reasons why significance testing was done in only a few cases. First, it was not decided a priori how many relations were to be included in the interpretation, hence $\alpha^* = \alpha/42$ was the appropriate significance level. The second reason seems more important. In χ^2 analysis as well as in information theory it is possible to interpret results in terms of portions of variation covered. This seems to be appropriate in cases where the independence of successive significance tests cannot be demonstrated.

To summarize, a two-step strategy was applied to a set of five variables in order to analyze its structure. First, all possible undirected relations were computed. In the interpretation of successively higher-order relations the value of composing larger groups from the variables was estimated by the portion of variation covered specifically by the new group. The role of the time variable was underscored by subdividing the points in time into three subvariables which emerged as highly associated. However, they did not control each other, because holding one of them constant did not diminish the association between the remaining two. Substantively, the analysis revealed that the overall stability of teachers' ratings of the pupils' classroom-related behavior is high. However, this overall stability decreases within the observed period of 8 years. The analysis of first- and second-order relations among the variables in question provided no indicator that could be used for an explanation of this decease. Only the third-order interactions in which the sex variable was involved revealed that teachers tend towards sex-oriented differential ratings when pupils grow older. This result was used to explain the change in the lower-order relations.

V. Summary

The general purpose of this paper was to show which structural properties of empirical data sets can be dealt with using nonparametric procedures. In the first section the term "structure" was defined. This term refers to two sets of properties: (1) the set of elements in the structure and (2) the relations between these elements. Structural research usually focuses on relations.

The general discussion of relations was concentrated on interactions, associations, and the order of relations. A definition of interaction, in which this kind of relationship was considered as independent of associations (i.e., nonparametric correlations), was given. The extension to higher-order associations and interactions was the most important part of the analysis of these structural properties that cannot be dealt with by application of parametric correlation-related procedures. Such procedures are restricted to the analysis of relations not higher than second order.   It should be noted that this characteristic of *nonparametric* structural modeling is a purely computational one.   It has nothing to do with assumptions about theoretical distributions that should fit the empirical ones or with requirements regarding the quality of the data.   Therefore, the desirable properties of nonparametric methods have not been stressed; they were implicitly considered as a welcome by-product.

As a consequence of the rather small significance given to the specific statistical properties of nonparametric methods in the present chapter, the description of statistical procedures designed to deal with relations of any order was restricted to some formal characteristics.   The connections between the definitions of relations and two statistical procedures, namely, χ^2 and information theory-based decomposition, were outlined in terms of these formal characteristics.   It was shown that associations and interactions are independent of each other only in part.

Although χ^2 and information theory decomposition procedures are formally equivalent, it was shown that they do not describe the same kind of relations.   In the information theory approach an assessment is made not only of how clear-cut the assignment of an individual to a single cell in the data matrix is but also of how much variation has been covered by each variable in question.   Hence, the variation shared by d variables can be large only if each of these variables covers large portions of the overall variation.   In the χ^2 approach only the first characteristic is assessed.

The final third of this chapter dealt with the detection of structures.   Two search strategies were outlined; namely, hypothesis-free and hypothesis-directed search.   In principle, in the former all logically and semantically meaningful relations must be computed.   This can lead to a tremendous number of relationships that must be interpreted, especially when all directed relations are taken into account.   Automatic search procedures or restriction to only one level of relations reduced this problem.   The hypothesis-free search process is chosen when hypotheses can be stated only atheoretically or when important structural characteristics must not be overlooked.   In the second approach hypotheses are stated in a general form, involving all elements of the empirical data matrix, or as local hypotheses, in which subsets of persons, variables, or occasions are concerned, before data analysis.   In both cases the goal can either be to reject the hypotheses or fit the a priori-specified model.

One application of the characteristics of nonparametric models to the analysis of development and change was outlined in Section IV.   An empirical example, describing the time-related change of teachers' ratings of pupils' classroom-related behavior, was given.   Information theory-based analyses revealed that teachers' ratings are stable.   However, taking the number of years in school into account, a decrease in the stability in the later years could be observed. Only after third-order relations were computed could one determinant of this decrease in stability of ratings be identified: Generally, as pupils grow older, a sex difference tends to appear in teachers' ratings of the pupils' attributes.

In addition to its substantive value, there is a methodological significance to this example that is reflected in two characteristics. First, it is clear that a considerably higher percentage of the variation can be exhausted if higher-order relations are taken into account. Second, there can be structural characteristics that are not indicated at all by pairwise relations.

Acknowledgments

I wish to thank Roger A. Dixon for his very helpful comments and for his support in many "structural" and semantic problems. I am also indebted to Walter Lehmacher, Gustav A. Lienert, and John R. Nesselroade for their helpful comments on earlier drafts of this chapter.

References

Attneave, F. *Applications of information theory to psychology.* New York: Holt, 1959.
Bishop, Y. M. M., Fienberg, S. E., & Holland, P. W. *Discrete multivariate analysis: Theory and practice.* Cambridge: MIT Press, 1975.
Broekstra, G. Constraint analysis and structure identification. *Annals of Systems Research,* 1976, *5,* 67–80.
Broekstra, G. Structure modelling: A constraint (information) analytic approach. In G. J. Klir (Ed.), *Applied general systems research: Recent developments and trends.* New York: Plenum Press, 1977. (a)
Broekstra, G. Constraint analysis and structure identification II. *Annals of Systems Research,* 1977, *6,* 1–20. (b)
Broekstra, G. Probabilistic constraint analysis for structure identification: An overview and some social science applications. In B. P. Zeigler, M. S. Elzas, G. J. Klir, & T. J. Ören (Eds.), *Methodology in systems modelling and simulation.* Amsterdam: North–Holland, 1979.
Cavallo, R. E. *The role of systems methodology in social science research.* Boston: Nijhoff, 1979.
Eddington, A. S. The theory of groups. In J. R. Newman (Ed.), *The world of mathematics.* New York: Simon & Schuster, 1956.
Froman, T., & Hubert, L. J. Application of prediction analysis to developmental priority. *Psychological Bulletin,* 1980, *87,* 156–166.
Gaines, B. R. General system identification: Fundamentals and results. In G. J. Klir (Ed.), *Applied general systems research.* New York: Plenum Press, 1978.
Gokhale, D. V., & Kullback, S. *The information in contingency tables.* New York: Dekker, 1978.

Hildebrand, D. K., Laing, J. D., & Rosenthal, H. *Prediction analysis of cross classifications.* New York: Wiley, 1977.

Jöreskog, K. Statistical estimation of structural models in longitudinal developmental investigations. In J. R. Nesselroade & P. B. Baltes (Eds.). *Longitudinal research in the study of behavior and development.* New York: Academic Press, 1979.

Klaus, G., & Liebscher, H. (Eds.). *Wörterbuch der Kybernetik* (Vol. 1). Frankfurt: Fischer, 1979. (a)

Klaus, G., & Liebscher, H. (Eds.). *Wörterbuch der Kybernetik* (Vol. 2). Frankfurt: Fischer, 1979. (b)

Klir, G. J. General systems problem solving methodology. In B. P. Zeigler, M. S. Elzas, G. J. Klir, & T. J. Ören (Eds.), *Methodology in systems modelling and simulation.* Amsterdam: North–Holland, 1979.

Klix, F. *Information and Verhalten.* Berlin: VEB Deutscher Verlag der Wissenschaften, 1971.

Krauth, J. Ein Vergleich der KFA mit der Methode der log-linearen Modelle. *Zeitschrift für Sozialpsychologie, 1980, 11,* 233–247.

Krauth, J., & Lienert, G. A. *KFA: Die Konfigurationsfrequenzanalyse.* Freiburg: Alber, 1973.

Krippendorff, K. A spectral analysis of relations—Further developments. *Proceedings of the 4th European Meeting on Cybernetics and Systems Research* (Vol. 4), Linz, March 1978, 69–83.

Krippendorff, K. An algorithm for identifying structural models of multivariate data. *International Journal of General Systems, 1981, 7,* 63–79.

Kullback, S. *Information theory and statistics.* New York: Dover, 1968.

Lancester, H. O. *The chi-squared distribution.* New York: Wiley, 1969.

Lehmacher, W. A more powerful simultaneous test procedure in configural frequency analysis. *Biometrical Journal, 1981, 23,* 429–436.

Lienert, G. A. *Verteilungsfreie Methoden in der Biostatistik* (Vol. 1). Meisenheim am Glan: Hain, 1973.

Lienert, G. A. *Verteilungsfreie Methoden in der Biostatistik* (Vol. 2). Meisenheim am Glan: Hain, 1978.

Lienert, G. A. Second-order correlation in repeated measurement designs. *Biometrical Journal, 1981, 23,* 217–223.

Lienert, G. A., & Wolfrum, C. Simplified formulas for three-way chi-squared testing. *Biometrical Journal, 1980, 22,* 159–167.

Lindner, K. *Zur Problematik der α-Adjustierung bei der Konfigurationsfrequenzanalyse.* Paper presented at the 24th Tagung experimentell arbeitender Psychologen, University of Trier, 1982.

Mittenecker, E., & Raab, E. *Informationstheorie für Psychologen.* Göttingen: Hogrefe, 1973.

Mooijaart, A. Latent structure analysis for categorical variables. In K. G. Jöreskog & H. Wold (Eds.), *Systems under indirect observation: Causality-structure-prediction, Part I.* Amsterdam: North–Holland, 1982.

Müller, N. Functions of life-trees for explaining social phenomena. *PAIS, 1980, 4,* 317–330.

Siegel, S. *Nonparametric statistics for the behavioral sciences.* New York: McGraw–Hill, 1956.

Storath, R. *Zur Problematik verbaler Schülerbeurteilungen.* Unpublished master's thesis, Universität Erlangen, 1982.

Vansteenkiste, G. C., Spriet, J., & Bens, J. Structure characterization for system modelling in uncertain environments. In B. P. Zeigler, M. S. Elzas, G. J. Klir, & T. J. Ören (Eds.), *Methodology in systems modelling and simulation.* Amsterdam: North–Holland, 1979.

Victor, N., Lehmacher, W., & Van Eimeren, W. (Eds.). *Explorative Datenanalyse.* Berlin: Springer, 1980.

Vogel, F. *Probleme und Verfahren der automatischen Klassifikation.* Göttingen: Vanden-
hoeck & Ruprecht, 1975.

von Eye, A. Die Assoziationsstrukturanalyse auf informationstheoretischer Basis. *Zeitschrift
für Klinische Psychologie und Psychotherapie,* 1981, *29,* 216–227. (a)

von Eye, A. *Methodologische Argumente in der psychologischen Ähnlichkeitsmessung.* Paper
presented at the "Habilitationskolloquium," University of Trier, 1981. (b)

von Eye, A. On the equivalence of the information theoretic transmission-measure to the
common χ^2 statistic. *Biometrical Journal,* 1982, *24,* 391–398.

von Eye, A., & Brandtstädter, J. Lebensbäume als entwicklungspsychologische Modelle: An-
sätze zur Analyse von Lebensereignissequenzen. *Trierer Psychologische Berichte,* 1981,
8(2), 1–22.

Wermuth, N. Model search among multiplicative models. *Biometrics,* 1976, *32,* 253–263.

Zalecka-Melamed, A. J., & Zeigler, B. P. Structure identification of discrete time systems. In
G. J. Klir (Ed.), *Applied general systems research: Recent developments and trends.* New
York: Plenum Press, 1977.

6

Individual and Context in Developmental Psychology: Conceptual and Theoretical Issues*

RICHARD M. LERNER

I. Introduction

In the United States, the 1970s were marked by a rediscovery by psychologists of the importance of the context and ecology of human development (Bronfenbrenner, 1977, 1979; Jenkins, 1974; Lerner, Hultsch, & Dixon, 1983; Mischel, 1977; Petrinovich, 1979; Sarbin, 1977; see also Naumann & Hüfner, Chapter 3, this volume). For instance, interest emerged in bidirectional relations between developing people and the multilevel, interrelated settings within which they live their lives (e.g., the family, the community, the physical environment, and the culture, including its system of symbols and values). In addition, the philosophical work of Stephen Pepper (1942), which discussed the use of a contextual world view for science, began to appear on the reference lists of developmental psychology publications; and

* My work on this paper was supported in part by grants from the John D. and Catherine T. MacArthur Foundation and from the William T. Grant Foundation.

perspectives about human development that emerged and became crystallized during this period were depicted as resting on contextual and/or dialectic philosophical foundations (Baltes, 1979; Hultsch & Hickey, 1978; Lerner, Skinner, & Sorell, 1980; Meacham, 1981; Riegel, 1976).

The essential conceptual feature of this contextual zeitgeist was the view that the characteristics of intraindividual development could not be explained without reference to changes in the context of development. Such reference was required because intraindividual development was believed to be reciprocally and causally linked to ("embedded in") changes in the context. That is, part of the very fabric of individual development was woven of variables derived from the context. This context was conceptualized as being made up of multiple, embedded levels (of being), with variables associated with each level changing as a consequence of the influences of variables at other contextual levels *and* as a consequence of the actions of the developing person on the context (Lerner & Busch-Rossnagel, 1981).

To illustrate with an example to be returned to again, the implications of a child's temperamental individuality for his or her personality development have been argued not to lie in any organismic association between particular features of temperament (e.g., high activity level or low regularity or rhythmicity of biological functions) and specific aspects of personality (e.g., adjustment). Instead, what temperament implies for personality development has been suggested to lie in the level of congruence, match, or "goodness of fit" (Lerner & Lerner, 1983) between a particular aspect of temperament and the demands or presses of the psychosocial and physical context. For instance, some parents may desire or demand highly regular eating, sleeping, and toileting behaviors of their children, while for other parents such biological rhythmicity may be irrelevant (see Super & Harkness, 1981). A child who was biologically arrhythmic would not match the former type of demand and, as such, the import of this feature of his or her temperament might be to promote poor parent–child relations; a consequence of a history of such relations might be poor adjustment.

Three features of this illustration are important to note here: First, the import of the person's organismic characteristics for his or her development is explained by reference to the *relation* between the organismic characteristics and the characteristics of the context. Second, therefore, the presses and demands of the organism's context must be understood to be part of the explanation of individual development, and it should be emphasized that such demands vary across societies, cultures, and history (Lerner & Lerner, 1983; Super & Harkness, 1981). Thus, the multilevel influences on development — the person, the immediate context, and the broader societal, cultural, and historical settings — are apparent. Finally, despite the importance of the context, it is the organism's characteristics — in providing a fit or a lack thereof—which establish the adaptive, maladaptive, or neutral link between organism and setting. Thus, any contextual–*developmental* theory, in attempting to understand the possibilities for change provided by the context (R. M. Lerner, 1984), must not ignore the structural and functional nature and characteristics of the organism. As will be stressed later, this point has been emphasized by theorists forwarding "probabilistic epigenetic organismic" ideas of development (e.g., Gottlieb, 1970, 1976; R. M. Lerner, 1976, 1978, 1979, 1980, 1982, 1984; Schneirla, 1957), ideas which have been recently labeled by Overton (1984) as organismic–contextual ones.

In short, several developmental psychologists have maintained that, as a consequence of person–context interdependency, a potential for plasticity exists across the life span; if intraindividual development is a synthesis of intraorganism and contextual variables, and if the context does and/or can be made to change, then the person's developmental trajectory can, at least in part, be altered. It follows that constraints on development—for example those imposed by genes or early experience—are not as great as advocates of noncontextual orientations have previously argued (Brim & Kagan, 1980; R. M. Lerner, 1984).

Views emphasizing contextual influences on development are controversial in at least two respects. First, some developmental psychologists see the ideas of reciprocal person–context relations and of plasticity across life as representing serious challenges to a concept of development which stresses ideas such as normative progression, universality, irreversibility, and final end state. Indeed, some of these critics (e.g., Kaplan, 1983) argue that attempting to incorporate the influence of contextual changes into intraindividual organism progressions leads to the loss of any useful concept of development. Basically, this first arena of controversy derives from the long-standing belief that development is an idealized process, a conceptual "metric" against which intraindividual changes are compared in order to judge whether they represent development. While it *is* the case that one first needs a concept of development in order to adequately study development, this criticism is that no useful or adequate concept of development exists in extant attempts to integrate contextual with intraindividual change (Kaplan, 1983). In short, this criticism is that only change, not development, is being assessed by contextually derived empirical research represented, for example, by the corpus of data associated with the life-span view of human development (Baltes, Reese, & Lipsitt, 1980; Lerner & Busch-Rossnagel, 1981).

The second arena of controversy generated by the contextual perspective involves the point that *all* theories of development do believe that the context, or some locus of influence rather obviously related to "context" (e.g., environment or experience), is related intimately to development. For instance, in psychodynamically oriented organismic theories (e.g., Erikson, 1959; Freud, 1954), experience has the potential either to facilitate or inhibit stage progression (see Emmerich, 1968). In mechanistically oriented behavioristic theories (e.g., Bijou, 1976; Bijou & Baer, 1961) the crucial role of the "reinforcing environment" in behavior acquisition is stressed. Thus, one may criticize contextually oriented developmentalists for (1) either presenting ideas merely derivative of those found in other approaches or (2) believing that they are presenting an alternative approach to developmental theory and research when, in fact, their ideas may be reduced to already well-known, rather simplistic, principles of conditioning (see, e.g., Bijou, 1976).

Some of the developmentalists involved in these controversies and most of the psychologists who have commented about these and other issues dividing contextual from other perspectives about human development have recognized that the basic issues producing these arguments revolve around metatheoretical, or paradigm, differences (e.g., Kuhn, 1978; R. M. Lerner, 1980, 1984; Looft, 1973; Overton, 1973, 1978, 1983; Overton & Reese, 1973, 1981; Reese & Overton, 1970). Simply put, the range of perspectives in current developmental psychology about the use of a contextual perspective and/or the role of contextual variation in intraindividual development can be understood by reference to the differences in the ways organismically, mechanistically, and contextually oriented developmentalists conceptualize: (1) what it is that develops in a human's development and (2) what mechanisms or processes provide the bases of such development. Thus, by considering prototypic organismic, mechanistic, and contextual treatments of these two issues it will be possible to address what I see as a central mission of this chapter: an evaluation of the usefulness of conceptualizing reciprocal individual and context relations as central in theoretical and empirical endeavors aimed at describing, explaining, and optimizing human development.

II. Key Questions of Human Development

The most fundamental issues in the study of human development pertain to the nature–nurture controversy (Lerner, 1976, 1978; Overton, 1973); that is, an inquiry into where the souce of development lies. There is a clear relationship between a theorist's stance on these issues and his or her response to questions such as "what is development?" and "what are the processes by which development occurs?" Historically, there have been instances wherein theorists have emphasized the independent, isolated action of either hereditary mechanisms (e.g., Sheldon, 1940, 1942) or environmental mechanisms (e.g., Skinner, 1938; Watson, 1913, 1918) for some selected subset of an organism's behavioral repertoire (see Gould, 1981). However, due to the impact of essays by Anastasi (1958), Lehrman (1953), and Schneirla (1956, 1957), today most developmentalists acknowledge that processes or variables from both nature and nurture sources contribute to development. Thus, questions are raised about modes of contribution among variables derived from each of these sources. Significant issues concerning the meaning and constitution of the contributing sources also exist. Finally, the concept of "interaction" is invoked, in that many theorists believe that variables from the two sources act in other than additive ways to bring about development. However, the concept of interaction itself proves to be highly controversial.

A. WHAT DEVELOPS? WHAT ARE THE PROCESSES OF DEVELOPMENT?

The key features of organismic, mechanistic, and contextual developmental paradigms have been described in several essays (e.g., Lerner, 1976, 1978; Looft, 1973; Overton & Reese, 1973, 1981; Reese & Overton, 1970). These features will only be summarized here.

1. THE ORGANISMIC PARADIGM

From the organismic perspective, development of a given process (e.g., cognition) is an idealized, normative, intraorganismic phenomenon. Qualitative change — for example, as represented by emergent structural reorganization (e.g., Piaget, 1970) or focal reorientation in the mode of dealing with the world or with gratifying one's emotions (e.g., Erikson, 1959; Freud, 1954) — is seen as the key feature of development. Thus, the organismic approach is a holistic one, one wherein formal cause and, in its "purest" philosophical formulation, also final cause (Nagel, 1957; Pepper, 1942) provide the basis of developmental explanation. However, given this explanatory orientation, especially when it is cast within an idealized view of developmental progression, material and efficient causative agents — for instance, as derived from the context enveloping the organism — are seen as irrelevant to the sequence of development and as such to the form the organism takes at any point in this sequence. The context can inhibit or facilitate, that is, speed up or slow down, developmental progression, but it cannot alter the quality of the process or its sequential universality. If a contextual variable does alter the quality or sequence of an organism's progression, then by definition that feature of functioning was not a component of development.

Gottlieb (1970) has labeled this version of organicism *predetermined epigenesis.* Victor Hamburger's organismic position epitomizes this view: "The architecture of the nervous system and the concomitant behavior patterns result from self-generating growth and maturation processes that are determined entirely by inherited, intrinsic factors, to the exclusion of functional adjustment, exercise, or anything else akin to learning" (1957, p. 56).

2. THE MECHANISTIC PARADIGM

From a mechanistic, behavioristic perspective organisms differ across their life span only in the quantitative presence of qualitatively identical behavioral units, that is, elements of the behavioral repertoire acquired by the causally efficient laws of conditiong (e.g., Bijou, 1976; Bijou & Baer, 1961). Here the organism is seen as a host (Baer, 1976) of these elements, and even the most complex human behavior is believed reducible to these identically constituted units (Bijou, 1976). The only constraint on behavior change in a "consequent" period of life is imposed by past (i.e., antecedent) reinforcement history; the repertoire of behaviors present in the organism at any point in time may moderate the efficiency by which current stimuli can extinguish or otherwise modify any particular behavior in the repertoire. As will be explained later, however, the meaning of "past reinforcement history" is such as to preclude any strong view of the potential for change in the portions of life beyond the earliest periods.

Indeed, from the mechanistic, behavioral perspective no strong, or idealized, view of development is present. Instead, the concept of development is reduced to a concept of change in the elements of the behavior repertoire; change is therefore brought about by the processes of addition to or subtraction from the behavioral repertoire via conditioning. Consequently, change at any point in life becomes largely a technological matter, always done with regard to past reinforcement history and pertaining to such issues as management of stimulus contingencies and of reinforcement schedules (e.g., in regard to building up, reducing, or rearranging a behavioral chain).

However, given the belief in the continuous and exclusive applicability of, and only of, functional (read: efficient, and in some cases material; Skinner, 1966) stimulus–behavior relations, only the most simplistic view of the context is found in this perspective (e.g., Bijou, 1976). I do not use the term "simplistic" in any pejorative sense; rather, the term serves to indicate that in the behavioristic tradition one can use only those features of the context—

that is, the stimulus environment, in the terms of this perspective—that can be translated into stimulus–response units. Features of the context which cannot be translated (i.e., reduced) into such units are invisible in this approach. For instance, sociopolitical historical events or qualitative, emergent changes in social structures must either be reduced to elementaristic, behavioral terms or ignored.

Moreover, because of a necessarily unequivocal commitment to reducing behavior to efficiently causal antecedents, the mechanistic behavioral (or functional analysis; Baer, 1982) position must be committed to the views (1) that early (indeed the earliest) stimulus–response experience is prepotent in shaping the rest of life and (2) that therefore there can be no true novelty or qualitative change in life (Lerner & Kauffman, 1984). That is, taken literally, the belief that any current behavior or event can be explained by, or reduced to, an antecedent efficient cause—or a stimulus, in behavioral terms—means that all of life must ultimately be explainable by the earliest experience of such antecedent–consequent relations, and so any portion of "later" life must be explained by efficiently causal prior events. Thus, nothing new or qualitatively distinct can in actuality emerge subsequent to these initial events. Zukav (1979) explains this feature of mechanistic thinking (in regard to Newtonian physics) by noting that

> if the laws of nature determine the future of an event, then, given enough information, we could have predicted our present at some time in the past. That time in the past also could have been predicted at a time still earlier. In short, if we are to accept the mechanistic determination of Newtonian physics—if the universe really is a great machine—then from the moment that the universe was created and set in motion, everything that was to happen in it already was determined.
>
> According to this philosophy, we may seem to have a will of our own and the ability to alter the course of events in our lives, but we do not. Everything, from the beginning of time has been predetermined, including our illusion of having a free will. The universe is a prerecorded tape playing itself out in the only way that it can. (p. 26)

The mechanistic behavioral position represents a "translation" into psychological theory of this natural science, efficiently casual philosophy that Zukav describes in regard to Newtonian physics; that is, the first physical antecedent–consequent relation is transformed into the first, or at least a quite early, stimulus–response connection. And, although it is not emphasized in many current discussions of mechanistic behavioral, or functional analysis, perspectives (e.g., Baer, 1982; Reese, 1982), the early proponents of this view were quite clear in their belief that early experience was prepotent in shaping all of life (see Kagan, 1983). For instance, John Watson (1928) argued that, "At three years of age the child's whole emotional life plan has been laid down, his emotional disposition set" (p. 45). Similarly, Edward Thorndike (1905, pp. 330–331) contended that:

> Though we seem to forget what we learn, each mental acquisition really leaves its mark and makes future judgment more sagacious . . . nothing of good or evil is ever lost; we may forget and forgive, but the neurones never forget or forgive. . . . It is certain that every worthy deed represents a modification of the neurones of which nothing can ever rob us. Every event of a man's mental life is written indelibly in the brain's archives, to be counted for or against him.

The consistency between these statements and the position of John Locke, writing almost two centuries earlier, is striking. Locke (cited in Mandelbaum, 1971, p. 151) asserted that:

> The little or almost insensible, impressions on our tender infancies, have very important and lasting consequences: and there it is, as in the fountains of some rivers, where a gentle application of the hand turns the flexible waters into channels, that make them quite contrary courses; and by this little direction, given them at first, in the source, they receive different tendencies, and arrive at last at very remote and distant places. I imagine the minds of children as easily turned, this or that way, as water itself.

In sum, as a consequence of such views, there is a belief among mechanistic behavioral psychologists that the potential changes able to be induced in the person by later experience are quite limited; consequently, there exists the view that the potential for plasticity in later childhood, adolescence, or in adulthood and aged years is constrained.

3. THE CONTEXTUAL PARADIGM

From a contextual perspective the "organism in relation" (Looft, 1973) or the "organism in transaction" (Dewey & Bentley, 1949; Pervin, 1968; Sameroff, 1975) with its context is the focus of developmental analysis. Although final cause is explicitly excluded in contextualism (Dixon, Hultsch, & Lerner, in preparation), all other forms of cause are seen as applicable. Indeed, only in contextualism is there an appreciation of incidental cause (Reese, 1979), as instanced by the interest among life-span developmentalists in the role in intraindividual change of non-normative life and historical events (e.g., see Hultsch & Plemons, 1979).

Although it must be emphasized that the transaction or "dynamic interaction" (Lerner, 1978, 1979, 1980) between organism and context is what develops in development, it is important to note that because of its admittance of multiple causative "agents" (formal, efficient, material, and incidental) into developmental explanation, contextually derived perspectives do not exclude features of theories associated with organismic developmental theories. A major example is the use made by contextually oriented theorists (e.g., Lerner & Busch-Rossnagel, 1981) of the orthogenetic principle (Werner, 1957) to describe the nature of change in the relations between individuals and their contexts. In fact, this principle has been used in even broader contextually related analyses, namely, those pertinent to the relations among large scale systems in the universe (Prigogine, 1978, 1980).

In short, a contextual perspective need not, should not, and typically does not (R. M. Lerner, 1984) avoid the use of universalistic and thus constantly applicable principles of development. Instead, as stressed earlier in this chapter, the emphasis in such approaches is on the *relation* between the structural and functional characteristics of the organism and the features (e.g., the demands or presses) of the organism's context. Indeed, particular attention is paid to the mutual constraints and opportunities provided by both elements in the relation, by both organism and context (R. M. Lerner, 1984). Thus, rather than see ideas (such as "orthogenesis") that have traditionally been used primarily to depict intraorganism development in reference to the individual–psychological level of analysis alone, the use of such ideas is made in reference to a "unit of analysis," the "organism in transaction." These units differ from those found in many (i.e., predetermined epigenetic) organismic formulations (e.g., Kaplan, 1983).

Moreover, another point of contrast with some organismic formulations arises (e.g., see Nagel, 1957) because the contextual perspective excludes any notion of final cause and thus leads to a belief in the potential plasticity of the organism across life. That is, as was also noted earlier in this chapter, contextual–developmental formulations do not emphasize the intrinsically preformed or inevitable time tables and outcomes of development; instead, such formulations stress that the influence of the changing context on development is to make the trajectory of development less certain in respect to the applicability of norms to the individual (Gottlieb, 1970). Thus, contextual–developmental conceptions emphasize the probabilistic character of development and in so doing admit of more plasticity in development than do predetermined epigenetic conceptions. In other words, the contextual view of development stressed by the present writer (R. M. Lerner, 1976, 1978, 1979, 1980, 1982, 1983, 1984) and by other contributors to the life-span developmental psychology literature (e.g., Baltes, 1979, 1983; Brim & Kagan, 1980) is one labeled as "probabilistic epigenetic organismic" by Gottlieb (1970) and developed by him (Gottlieb, 1976) and earlier by Schneirla (1956, 1957) and Tobach and Schneirla (1968). Overton (1984) has labeled this conception as organismic–contextual.

The term *probabilistic epigenesis* was used by Gottlieb (1970) "to designate the view that the behavioral development of individuals within a species does not follow an invariant or inevitable course, and, more specifically, that the sequence or outcome of individual behavioral development is probable (with respect to norms) rather than certain" (p. 123). Moreover, he explains that this probable, and not certain, character of individual development arises because probabilistic epigenesis necessitates a bidirectional structure–function hypothesis. The conventional version of the structure–function hypothesis is unidirectional in the sense that structure is supposed to determine function in an essentially nonreciprocal relationship. The unidirectionality of the structure–function relationship is one of the main assumptions of predetermined epigenesis. The bidirectional version of the structure–function relationship is a logical consequence of the view that the course and outcome of behavioral epigenesis is probabilistic: it entails the assumption of reciprocal effects in the relationship between structure and function whereby function (exposure to stimulation and/or movement of musculoskeletal activity) can significantly modify the development of the peripheral and central structures that are involved in these events. (p. 123)

More recently, Gollin (1981) has taken a similar stance, one which emphasizes that while epigenesis may be probabilistic, as Gottlieb argues, it is not dispersive or chaotic. That is, a purely contextual approach sees the components of life as completely dispersive (Pepper, 1942). Indeed, Pepper believes that it is the dispersive character of contextualism which is the key idea making it a world view distinct from the organismic one, a world view in turn marked by integration. If the term *development* is to have meaning beyond that of mere change, it must imply, at the very least, that the changes in an organism (or system) are systematic, successive ones (Lerner & Kauffman, 1984). Thus, a world view which stressed only the dispersive, chaotic, and disorganized character of life would not readily lend itself to the derivation of a theory of development.

Thus, Gollin (1981) explains that probabilistic developmental change is not dispersive because the living system — the organism — has organization and internal coherence, and these features constrain the potentials of the *developmental context* to affect the system. He says that

the determination of the successive qualities of living systems, given the web of relationships involved, is probabilistic. This is so because the number of factors operating conjointly in living systems is very great. Additionally, each factor and subsystem is capable of a greater or lesser degree of variability. Hence, the influence subsystems have upon each other, and upon the system as a whole, varies as a function of the varying states of the several concurrently operating subsystems. Thus, the very nature of living systems, both individual and collective, and of environments, assures the presumptive character of organic change.

Living systems are organized systems with internal coherence. The properties of the parts are essentially dependent on relations between the parts and the whole (Waddington, 1957). The quality of the organization provides opportunities for change as well as constraints upon the extent and direction of change. Thus, while the determination of change is probabilistic, it is not chaotic. (p. 232)

Gollin's position illustrates that one needs to understand that development occurs in a multilevel context and that the nature of the changes in this context lead to the probabilistic character of development; but one needs to appreciate too that the organism shapes the context as much as the context shapes it.

Recent essays by Scarr and her associates (Scarr, 1982; Scarr & McCartney, 1983) make similar points. Scarr (1982) notes that

> two big questions have occupied developmental theorists from antiquity to the present day. . . . First, is the course of human development directed primarily by structures in the environment that are external to the person, or is development guided principally by the genetic program within? Second, is development primarily continuous or discontinuous? (p. 852)

Answering the first question bears on the idea of probabilistic epigenesis; answering the second relates to the concept of plasticity. In regard to the first issue, Scarr explains that

> answers to the first question have shifted in recent years from the . . . empiricist position to the . . . nativist view. Neonativist arguments, however, do not assume the extreme preformism of the early century. Development does not merely emerge from the precoded information in the genes. Rather, development is a *probabilistic* result of indeterminate combinations of genes and environments. Development is genetically guided but variable and probabilistic because influential events in the life of every person can be neither predicted nor explained by general laws. Development, in this view, is guided primarily by the genetic program through its multilevel transactions with environments that range from cellular to social. The genetic program for the human species has both its overwhelming commonalities and its individual variability because each of us is both human and uniquely human. (pp. 852–853)

In regard to the second question, Scarr suggests that, as a consequence of an organism's biological contributions *and* the probabilistic transactions this biology has with its multilevel context, neither complete consistency nor complete change characterize the human condition. Instead:

> Human beings are neither of glass that breaks in the slightest ill wind nor of steel that stands defiantly in the face of devastating hurricanes. Rather, in this view, humans are made of the newer plastics—they bend with environmental pressures, resume their shapes when the pressures are relieved, and are unlikely to be permanently misshapen by transient experiences. When bad environments are improved, people's adaptations improve. Human beings are resilient and responsive to the advantages their environments provide. Even adults are capable of improved adaptations through learning, although any individual's improvement depends on that person's responsiveness to learning opportunities. (p. 853)

In other words, there exists

> a *probabilistic* connection between a person and the environment. It is more likely that people with certain genotypes will receive certain kinds of parenting, evoke certain responses from others, and select certain aspects from the available environments; but nothing is rigidly determined. The idea of genetic differences, on the other hand, has seemed to imply to many that the person's developmental fate was preordained without regard to experience. This is absurd. By involving the idea of genotype → environment effects, we hope to emphasize a probabilistic connection between genotypes and their environments. (Scarr & McCartney, 1983, p. 428)

Similarly, Gollin (1981) notes that

> the relationships between organisms and environments are not interactionist, as inter-action implies that organism and environment are separate entities that come together at an interface. Organism and environment constitute a single life process. . . . For analytic convenience, we may treat various aspects of a living system and various external environmental and biological features as independently definable proper-ties. Analytical excursions are an essential aspect of scientific inquiry, but they are hazardous if they are primarily reductive. An account of the *collective behavior* of the parts as an organized entity is a necessary complement to a reductive analytic pro-gram, and serves to restore the information content lost in the course of the reductive excursion. . . . In any event, the relationships that contain the sources of change are those between organized systems and environments, not between heredity and envi-ronment. (pp. 231–232)

A final point about the contextual probabilistic epigenetic view needs to be highlighted. Although, as was noted earlier in the chapter, both contextual and mechanistic behavioral perspectives make use of the context enveloping an organism in attempts to explain development, it is clear that they do so in distinctly different ways. Contextually oriented theorists to not adopt a reflexively reductionistic approach to conceptualizing the impact of the context. Instead, because of a focus on organism–context transactions, and thus a commitment to using an interlevel, or relational, unit of analysis (Lerner et al., 1980), the context may be conceptualized as composed of multiple, qualitatively different levels: for example, the inner–biological, the individual–psychological, the outer–physical, and the sociocultural (Riegel, 1975, 1976). Moreover, although both the mechanistic and the contextual perspectives hold that changes in the context become part of the organism's intraindividually changing constitution, the concept of "orga-nism" found in the two perspectives is also quite distinct. The organism in contextualism is not merely the host of the elements of a simplistic environ-ment. Instead, the organism is itself a qualitatively distinct level within the multiple, dynamically interacting levels forming the context of life. As such, as emphasized earlier in this chapter, the organism has a distinct influence on the multilevel context that is influencing the organism. As a consequence the organism is, in short, not a host but an active contributor to its own development (Lerner, 1982; Lerner & Busch-Rossnagel, 1981).

B. THE ROLE OF THE CONCEPT OF "INTERACTION"

A contextual perspective captures the complexity of a multilevel context (1) without ignoring the active role of the organism in shaping, as well as being shaped by, that context and (2) without sacrificing commitment to useful prescriptive, universal principles of developmental change. These two foci are integrated within the contextual orientation at the level of the presumed *relation* between organismic and contextual processes. The contextual perspective differs substantially from those of the organismic and mechanistic perspectives. Indeed, perhaps the key distinction between these three paradigms is in their respective conceptualization of how nature- and nurture-related processes interact. To summarize and expand the distinctions I made earlier concerning the way the concept of "interaction" is used within each of the three perspectives, let me return, first, to the mechanistic behavioral view. Psychologists such as Bijou (1976) argue that a person's development derives from an interaction between past reinforcement history and the current reinforcement context. But, since the organism is the "host" (Baer, 1976) or locus of the past reinforcement history, Bijou construes his concept of interaction as pertaining to *organism–environment* relations. Nevertheless, Bijou's view is that the organism is a largely passive component in the swirl of past and present reinforcements surrounding it. The organism plays no primary role in shaping the context that influences it. Since the entities that interact (past and present stimulus contingencies) are not qualitatively distinct, and because of the restricted role delegated to the organism in this form of organism–environment interaction, some reviewers (Lerner, 1976, 1978; Overton, 1973) have characterized the type of interaction illustrated by Bijou's position as a *weak* interaction.

As is the case with the mechanistic–behavioristic tradition, the type of interaction found in organismic developmental stage theory may be characterized as being of the weak variety. This is somewhat ironic because organismic developmental theory has been termed a strong developmental position (Overton & Reese, 1973; Reese & Overton, 1970). Here, although variables associated with both organism and context are said to be involved in the interactions associated with developmental (i.e., stage) progression, I have noted that contextual variables are only seen to facilitate or inhibit primarily intrinsic trajectories (Emmerich, 1968); contextual variables cannot alter the direction, sequence, or quality of developmental change. However, something of a paradox exists here, as I will indicate in Section III in discussing the concept of "critical" period in organismic theory, for in some organismic theories (e.g., Erikson, 1959; Freud, 1954) contextual variables can contribute to altering the import of developmental changes for adaptive functioning.

Moreover, in the organismic developmental perspective the nature of developmental progression is controlled by a maturational timetable (Erikson, 1959) or other biological phenomena (Freud, 1954) that are taken to be impervious to environmental influence insofar as their impact on the quality of development is concerned. The organism is no more an influence on such biological variables than it is a determinant of the array of genes it receives at its conception. Thus, although the prime locus of developmental change lies within the organism, the organism is no more an active agent in the interaction of this internal basis of development with the external environment than it is in mechanistic, behavioral theories such as those of Bijou (1976; Bijou & Baer, 1961).

For reasons of intellectual completeness, it may be noted that another concept of interaction is found in the developmental literature, and may be labeled *moderate* (Lerner & Spanier, 1978, 1980). Here both organism and environment are seen as equally weighted conceptually as influences on developmental outcomes. But, the nature of these sources' relationship while interacting may be conceptualized as analogous to the interaction term in the analysis of variance. Although organism-associated and environment-associated variables combine (in an additive manner describable by the general linear model) to influence developmental outcomes, both are construed to exist independent of (uninfluenced by) the other before (and presumably after) they interact, and both are unchanged by the other during their interaction.[1]

The concept of moderate interaction is not typically articulated as a feature of a particular theory of human development. Instead, it is found in the perspective to studying behavior that Gollin (1965) labeled the "child psychology" approach. This perspective is characterized by an ahistorical Subjects × Tasks approach to the analysis of behavior and is contrasted by Gollin (1965) with the historical subjects × Tasks – Levels approach characteristic of what he terms the "child development" perspective. In the child psychology approach, the goal is to determine the empirical contribution of organism-related variables (often vaguely represented by using age or sex as a factor) and environment-related variables (typically represented operationally by a specific task or manipulation), separately and in additive combination (i.e., "interactively"), to variation in a dependent variable. In other words, the concept of moderate interaction is typically expressed as a methodological component of what is also termed the experimental child psychology approach (Reese & Lipsitt, 1970) and involves the treatment of subject

[1] Nesselroade (personal communication, June, 1982) points out that "moderate" interaction is the most "comfortable" conception from the standpoint of continuity of influences. It is because the organism-associated and environment-associated influences are unaffected by each other that one can have an interactive relationship in the ANOVA sense. Alternatively, one may have "interdependent transformational" systems, with the interactive effects on development defined in terms of the systems, and not by particular variables or system states; this latter, systems-type interaction conception is associated with the notion of "strong" interaction which is discussed later in the chapter.

and task, or organism and environment (or heredity and environment, in the analogous analysis of variance approach to determining heritability), as necessarily separate, independent factors whose interaction effect or contribution is a linear, additive one. The interaction effect itself may combine two sources in a nonlinear, multiplicative way. That effect, however, adds linearly to the total variability.

Finally, a *strong* concept of organism – environment interaction (Lerner & Spanier, 1978, 1980; Overton, 1973), transaction (Sameroff, 1975), or dynamic interaction (Lerner, 1978, 1979) is associated with a contextual perspective. As was noted in the preceding discussion of probabilistic epigenesis, this concept stresses that organism and context are always embedded each in the other (Lerner, Hultsch, & Dixon, 1983); that the context is composed of multiple levels of being, with variables associated with each level changing interdependently across time (i.e., historically); and that because organisms influence the context that influences them, they are efficacious in playing an active role in their own development (Lerner & Busch-Rossnagel, 1981).

Moreover, because of the mutual embeddedness of organism and context, a given organismic attribute will have different implications for developmental outcomes in the milieu of different contextual conditions. As was illustrated in the earlier example of the role of contextual demands in influencing the significance of a given temperamental attribute for adjustment, this is the case because the organism attribute is only given its functional meaning by virtue of its relation to a specific context. If the context changes, as it may over time, then the same organism attribute will have a different import for development. In turn, the same contextual condition will lead to alternative developments in that different organisms interact with it. To state this position in other and somewhat stronger terms, a given organismic attribute only has meaning for psychological development by virtue of its timing of interaction, that is, its relation to a particular set of time-bound contextual conditions. In turn, the import of any set of contextual conditions for psychosocial behavior and development can only be understood by specifying the context's relations to the specific, developmental features of the organisms within it. This central role for the timing of organism – context interactions in the determination of the nature and outcomes of development is, of course, the probabilistic component of probabilistic epigenesis (Gottlieb, 1970; Scarr, 1982; Scarr & McCartney, 1983).

In sum, organismic, mechanistic, and contextual approaches to development adopt contrasting concepts of interaction. A distinctive feature of the contextual approach is in its treatment of the concepts of time and timing, a treatment which contrasts with that found in the other two approaches. In my view, issues associated with the contextual treatment of the concepts of time and timing both give the perspective its potential for opening up new avenues of developmental theory, research, and intervention and at the same time impose serious, largely methodological constraints on the current use of a contextual perspective for these endeavors.

III. The Concepts of Time and Timing in the Contextual Perspective

Development is a time-related concept, and conceptions of development derived from any paradigm will necessarily deal with the concept. However, the concept is a difficult one to define precisely, despite the fact that many people acquiesce to a general statement about time being a linear, universal, and absolute metric for ordering events in terms of an antecedent–consequent sequence (but not, of course, a necessarily causal one in this sense).

In actuality, there are two time-related concepts used in developmental psychology. First, developmentalists talk of the time spent at (the duration of) a particular ontogenetic epoch. Simply, this use of time involves the notion of *rate of development.* For example, the sensorimotor stage lasts from birth to about 2 years of age (Piaget, 1970), and the anal stage lasts from about the end of the first year to about the end of the second (Freud, 1954). A similar use of time occurs when describing the time spent at acquiring a particular behavior; this use is often operationalized as the number of trials needed to reach some criterion of performance. Organismic theorists treat interindividual differences in time, or rate of development (Hertzog & Lerner, in press), as one of the two ways in which organisms can differ; final level of development is the other (Emmerich, 1968; Lerner, 1976). However, such individual differences are of little theoretical or empirical interest to organismic developmentalists. In contrast, however, mechanistic and contextual developmentalists share an interest in the bases of interindividual differences in rate of development (Baer, 1970; Wohlwill, 1973; Lerner & Ryff, 1978) and seek the explanatory bases of such duration differences.

Of course, the nature of the searches for differences in rate of development derives from a given researcher's paradigmatically based theory of development. In practice this search becomes one of trying to identify how the variables thought to influence behavioral development are presumed to interrelate to influence rate of development. Moreover, this identification involves the concept of timing.

A second time-related concept used by developmentalists is *timing.* This concept refers to the co-occurrence of two or more variables presumed to influence behavior at a particular point of time in a person's development. In other words, some representation of the standard, linear, universalistic time metric (e.g., chronological age) is used as a reference axis on which to specify a baseline point when two or more variables of interest coexist.

A. THE ORGANISMIC POSITION

The role of timing is conceptualized by organismic, mechanistic, and contextual theorists quite differently, but the differences are strongly related to their respective concepts of interaction. In organismic theory the timing of nature–nurture interaction is crucial for adaptive organismic development. Nurture variables, however, are constrained in their import for adaptation by the prepotent influence of the idealized, normative, developmental sequence, a sequence often conceptualized as being maturationally based (e.g., Gesell, 1946, 1954) and/or governed by a maturational "ground plan" (Erikson, 1959). This view is, of course, a statement of the critical period hypothesis; this hypothesis amounts to an assertion that a universal sequence of development, uninfluenced in its quality by the context, prescribes chronological limits within which the context must act in order for the sequence to continue optimally. In other words, the view of timing in organismically derived theory is one wherein across normal development there is a prescribed normative co-occurrence of the variables providing the basis of development. The organismic sequence not only prescribes when particular experiences should co-occur but, as such, circumscribes the effects of experiences on development.

B. THE MECHANISTIC POSITION

Timing has not been an issue of major interest to mechanistically oriented behavioral developmentalists. Of course, there is concern with how reinforcement regimens involving fixed or variable interval schedules influence behavior acquisition. There is not, however, a large body of research concerned with how best to temporally interrelate some current reinforcement situation with a given organism's past reinforcement history in order to produce some target acquisition at some "optimal rate," a set of relations that would be an analogue to the timing issue in organismic and contextual approaches.

C. THE CONTEXTUAL POSITION

I have indicated in the preceding discussion that from a contextual–developmental (i.e., a probabilistic epigenetic) perspective, timing is central in influencing the nature and outcomes of development. That is, due to continual changes in the multiple levels of the context that affect the organism, neither the specific features of the organism that are formed as a consequence of contextual transaction nor the timing of these organism – context transactions can be meaningfully said to exist invariantly across organisms. Thus, there is little use for a concept which prescribes normative co-occurrences of variables. Instead, the qualitative and quantitative changes composing an organism's development derive from variables which co-occur in a probabilistic manner.

An Example of a Contextual View. Elsewhere (R. M. Lerner, 1978, 1979, 1980, 1984) I have described how the timing of dynamic organism – environment interactions provides the basis of probabilistic epigenetic change. Figure 6.1, taken from one of these earlier papers (Lerner, 1979), illustrates the central role of timing in these interactions among nature and nurture variables, interactions that provide the bases of development in this contextually derived conception.

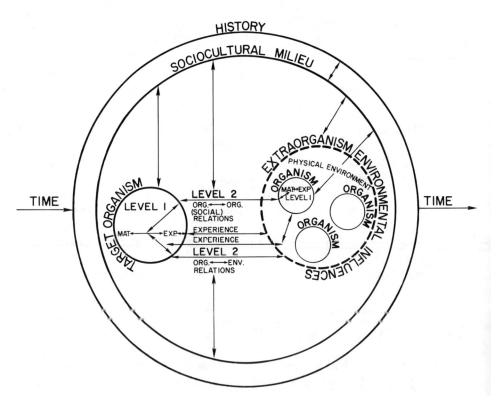

Figure 6.1   A dynamic interactional model of development.   Source: Lerner, 1979, p. 277.

Employing Schneirla's terms (1957), "maturation" is used in Figure 6.1 to represent endogenous organism changes and "experience" is used to denote all stimulative influences acting on the organism over the course of its life span. A conception of interaction levels is represented in the figure. The organism's individual developmental history of maturation – experience interactions (what I term Level 1 development — a term analogous to Riegel's, 1975, inner – biological developmental level) provides a basis of differential organism – environment interactions; in turn, differential experiences accruing from the individual developmental history of organism – environment interactions, or Level 2 development (a term analogous to Riegel's individual – psychological developmental level), provide a further basis of Level 1 developmental individuality.

As is illustrated in the figure, endogenous maturation – experience interactions are not discontinuous with exogenous organism – environment interactions. As a consequence of the timing of the interactions among the specific variables involved in an organism's maturation – experience interactions, a basis of an organism's individual distinctiveness is provided. This organism concomitantly interacts differently with its environment as a consequence of this individuality. In turn, these new interactions are a component of the organism's further experience, and thus serve to further promote its individuality. Endogenous maturation – experience relations provide a basis of organism individuality, and, as a consequence, differential organism — environment (exogenous) relations develop.

In essence, then, the target organism in the figure is unique because of the quality and timing of endogenous Level 1 maturation – experience interactions; but the experiences that provide a basis of Level 1 development are not discontinuous with other, extraorganism experiences influencing the target individual. The target interacts with environmental influences composed of other organisms (themselves having intraindividual, Level 1 developmental distinctiveness) and physical variables which also show individual change over time. Indeed, all tiers of Level 2 — the extraorganism (social), the physical environmental, the sociocultural, and the historical — have variables which all change over time. Not only does the timing of interactions among variables within and across all tiers provide a distinct experiential context affecting the developing organism, but this distinctiveness is itself shaped by the individually different organism.

Two sets of implications arise as a consequence of the reciprocity between changes at Levels 1 and 2. The first set of implications emphasizes individual development. Level 2 interchanges will show interindividual differences because of Level 1 intraindividual distinctiveness; the feedback received as a consequence of these differential interactions will be different among individuals and will promote further Level 1 and Level 2 individuality. This process provides the basis of a circular function (Schneirla, 1957) between an individual and its environment, a function which allows the organism to be an active agent in its own development and allows one to characterize the individual's developmental trajectory as potentially plastic in character.

The second set of implications emphasizes social change. From the model represented in Figure 6.1 it is clear that there is a systematic connection between individual development and at least some social changes; this connection—already implied in the immediately preceding discussion—becomes evident if one recognizes that the set of individually different and differentially developing organisms living at any one time constitute a key portion of an individual's social context and, in part, social change. In other words, if each organism may be characterized at any one point in time as possessing both Level 1 and Level 2 individuality, if these characteristics of individuality change systematically as a consequence of each organism's being embedded reciprocally in a context with other individually different organisms, and if the set of all organisms surrounding a given target organism represents elements of that organism's social world, *then* this set defines a feature of the social context, changes in which constitute a portion of social change.

This analysis gives both the social context and social change two important features. First, it gives them both an inherent developmental quality; this arises as a consequence of the social context being in part comprised of developing organisms. Second, this analysis again underscores the contributions of the individual organism, first in that the organism affects other organisms (i.e., the interpersonal component of the social context), and hence elicits feedback to itself, and second in that the organism itself is—with respect to any other target organism—a key element of the social context.

Finally, this analysis provides a rationale for integrating the study of contextual variables marked by concepts such as cohort effects, normative, history-graded influences, and non-normative events into a comprehensive view of developmental processes. The concepts of "cohort effects" and "history-graded influences" are similar in their concern with effects on development other than those prototypical of contributions made by individual organisms; they are part of the "extraorganism environmental influences" (including the "physical environment") depicted in Figure 6.1. They attempt to mark contextual events which provide commonality across organisms and shape the experiences of groups of individuals living at particular historical moments. In terms of the present conceptualization, the contextual experiences marked by these terms constitute an important component of Level 2 stimulative influences: they are components of Level 2 interaction that serve to make organisms living in a context at a given time systematically alike. As such, these components of Level 2 are part of the systematic influences both on individual development and on shaping the social context with which organisms transact.

IV. Limits and Problems of a Contextual Perspective

The concepts of organism, context, and the relations between the two found in a probabilistic epigenetic, developmental – contextual perspective are, as a set, quite distinct from those associated with organismic and mechanistic conceptions. As I have argued, such a contextual perspective leads to a multilevel, change-oriented concept of development, one in which the focus of inquiry is the organism – environment transaction. Further, such a contextual orientation places an emphasis on the potential for adaptive intraindividual change in structure and function — the potential for plasticity — across the life span. Yet, several conceptual and derivative methodological problems must be confronted in order to move such a contextual orientation from merely being a "perspective" to being a useful theory (Baltes, 1979) and, in turn, to use contextualism as a framework with which to study individual – context transactions.

First, substantively, we must recognize that despite the great amount of evidence that exists for human plasticity (R. M. Lerner, 1984), we still cannot answer several fundamental questions about the contextual, dynamically interactive parameters of plasticity. Are different levels of analysis and/or different targets within levels differentially plastic? For example, it may be the case that selected features of our genotype (e.g., the number of chromosomes we possess) cannot be altered (without, at least, severely damaging our organismic integrity) no matter what the nature of organism – context relations may be. At the same time, more molar, behavioral features of functioning may not be subject to such restrictions. For instance, are there limits to the number of languages a person can learn to speak or the number of names of people a person may know? No current evidence indicates that such limits exist.

In addition to not knowing fully the limits of plasticity that may currently characterize levels of analysis, we do not know what further substantive and technological advances may imply for the future character of these limits. If we take the idea of probabilistic epigenesis seriously, and if we recognize that science and technology represent natural parts of the human ecology, then we cannot anticipate where future scientific advances may lead. Thus, current limits of plasticity are not necessarily future ones. These limits are themselves plastic and will likely change in an ever-broadening direction in ways that, for some of us, are beyond our imagination.

But recognition that the limits of plasticity can change over time raises a developmental issue. The actualization of plasticity necessarily involves change and change can only be identified over time. Numerous questions exist about the rates of change of plastic processes at the several levels of analysis that transact to provide the bases of behavior. For one thing, it is clear that there is a "nonequivalent temporal metric" across the various levels of analysis (Lerner et al., 1980) involved in person–context transactions. That is, as illustrated in Figure 6.1, variables associated with all levels of the context change over time, but time may not have an identical meaning at all levels. One way to understand this is to note that the smallest meaningful division of time required for detecting change differs among levels. If time is one's "X axis," with the "Y axis" reflecting levels of one's target process, then sensible X-axis divisions used in detecting infant neuromuscular changes may be as small as weeks. However, the smallest sensible division used in detecting social institutional change may be a year. In addition, even within a given level time may not have an equivalent meaning at different points in development. For example, on the level of the individual, a 1-year separation between birthdays may seem to a five-year-old to be a vast length of time; to someone experiencing his or her thirty-ninth brithday, the 1-year period until the fortieth birthday may seem quite short; and to an eighty-five-year-old, having to wait for 1 year for some important event may again seem quite long.

The import of the nonequivalent temporal metric is that it may be difficult to detect the influence of changes promoted on one level at another one; for example, a change on the biological level (e.g., as promoted through better nutritional programs for children) may be difficult to detect at the societal level. Indeed, if an attempt is made to verify the existence of such an influence, it may be that a long-term, perhaps intergenerational, perspective need be taken; or in a within-cohort analysis, it may be that only interindividual differences in intraindividual change, and not intraindividual change itself, can be assessed.

Complicating this issue is this consideration, that even though the effects on society of a biological intervention may take a long time to detect, there is not necessarily symmetry of influence. That is, "upper-level" societal alteration and social change may affect quite visibly and relatively rapidly "lower-level" individual and biological processes. For example, changes in federal government funding for such things as school lunch programs for the poor, aid to dependent mothers, and medicare and medicaid for the elderly can have a relatively quick impact on health, cognitive, and familial functioning variables associated with an individual.

The issues of the nonequivalent temporal metric and of the asymmetry of interlevel influences can be seen to lead to other ones. Given different levels' rates of change one needs to know how processes at different levels connect to one another: How do interlevel influences occur? One answer to this question that my colleagues and I have followed is to explore the use of a "goodness of fit" model of person–context relations (e.g., Lerner & Lerner, 1983); here individual behavioral characteristics that are congruent with pertinent behavioral presses are studied for their import for adaptive person–immediate–social context (e.g., peer group) exchanges.

To again refer to the illustration employed earlier in this chapter, let me note how my associates and I use this model to study temperament. We use the term *temperament* to describe the *style* of behavior; not what a person does, but how he or she does whatever is done (Thomas & Chess, 1977). Our contextually derived goodness of fit model stresses that temperament only has meaning for the person as a consequence of the impact it has on the physical and social context.

Our view is that just as a person brings his or her characteristics of temperamental individuality to a particular social setting, so there are demands placed on the person by virtue of the social and physical components of the setting. These demands may take the form of (1) attitudes, values, or stereotypes held by others regarding the person's attributes; (2) the attributes (usually behavioral) of others with whom the person must coordinate, or fit, for adaptive interactions to exist; or (3) the physical characteristics of a setting (e.g., the presence or absence of access ramps for the motor-handicapped) which require the person to possess certain attributes (again, usually behavioral) for the occurrence of efficient interaction.

The person's temperamental individuality in differentially meeting these demands provides a basis for the feedback he or she gets from the socializing environment. For example, considering the second type of contextual demands that exist — those that arise as a consequence of the behavioral characteristics of others in the setting — problems of fit might occur when a child who is highly irregular in his biological functions (e.g., eating, sleep–wake cycles, toileting behaviors) interacts in a family setting composed of highly regular and behaviorally scheduled parents and siblings.

My colleagues and I (Lerner & Lerner, 1983; Thomas & Chess, 1977) believe that adaptive psychological and social functioning do not derive directly from either the nature of the person's characteristics of temperamental individuality per se or the nature of the demands of the contexts within which the person functions. Rather, if a person's characteristics of individuality match (or "fit") the demands of a particular setting, adaptive outcomes in that setting will accrue. Those people whose characteristics match most of the settings within which they exist should receive supportive or positive feedback from the contexts and should show evidence of the most adaptive behavioral development. In turn, of course, mismatched people, whose characteristics are incongruent with one or most settings, should show alternative developmental outcomes.

Several studies in our laboratory have assessed the use of the goodness of fit model among samples in the late-childhood to early-adolescent age range. In the first study completed in our laboratory, J. V. Lerner (1983) measured eighth-graders' temperaments. She also assessed the demands for behavioral style in the classroom maintained by each subject's classroom teacher and peer group. Those subjects whose temperaments best matched each set of demands had more favorable teacher ratings of adjustment and ability, better grades, more positive peer relations, fewer negative peer relations, and more positive self-esteem than did subjects whose temperaments were less well matched with either teacher and/or peer demands. Moreover, fit in one context predicted fit in the other context and, as such, temperamental fit with teacher (or peer) demands not only predicted teacher-related outcome measures but also the outcome measures derived from the other independent context, the peer (or teacher) context.

Further support for the use of the goodness of fit model is derived from a study by Lerner, Lerner, and Zabski (in press). This study also provides evidence that temperament – context fit also covaries with actual academic abilities. That is, the J. V. Lerner (1983) study demonstrated a relation between peer and teacher ratings and between teacher-assigned grades and goodness of fit. However, no relation between actual academic abilities and degree of fit was assessed. However, such a relation was found by Lerner and associates (in press). That is, for several temperament dimensions, fourth-grade students whose self-rated temperament provided the best fit to teacher demands not only had better teacher ratings of ability and adjustment but also scored better on two standardized achievement tests — the Stanford Achievement Test for Reading and the Comprehensive Test of Basic Skills — than did children showing a poorer fit to teacher demands.

In another study completed in our laboratory, Palermo (1982) assessed fifth-graders' ratings of their own temperaments, the fifth-graders' mothers' ratings of their children's temperaments, and the demands for behavioral style held by the teachers and mothers of the fifth-graders. Outcome measures included teacher ratings of classroom ability and adjustment, classroom peers' sociometric appraisals of each subject's positive and negative peer relations, and mother's reports of problem behaviors shown at home. Again, children whose temperaments provided a better fit to teachers' demands had more favorable scores on teacher-, peer-, and mother-derived outcome measures than did children for whom the fit was not as close. Most interestingly, the best predictors of *all* outcome measures — that is, of outcome measures derived from teacher, peer, and mother ratings — were the scores measuring fit between mother-rated temperament and teacher demands. In other words, we have in Palermo's (1982) data the best indication that temperament is not a within-the-person phenomenon; discrepancy scores derived from temperament rated by one source (mother) and demands derived from another independent source (teacher) not only were the best predictors of adaptation within the mother- and teacher-rated contexts but also within a third, and independent (peer), context.

The Palermo (1982) study extended our research beyond the school context to the home setting. Kacerguis (1983) continued with this emphasis, and focused on pre- versus postpubescent daughter–mother dyads. Steinberg and Hill (1978) found that parental responses to their children differed in relation to the child's pubertal status; for example, more problematic parent–child relations existed in parent–child dyads having a postpubescent child. Such findings led Kacerguis to speculate that the source of parent–child conflict differed between pre- and postpubescent daughter–mother dyads. That is, Kacerguis speculated that parents of prepubescents expect different behaviors of their children than do parents of postpubescents and as a consequence predicted that, to the extent that temperamental differences were involved in these different behavioral expectations, temperament should be differentially linked to parent–child conflict in the two puberty groups.

Studying a group of 53 prepubescent daughter–mother dyads and a group of 42 postpubescent daughter–mother dyads, Kacerguis obtained ratings by the mothers of the level of conflict in the parent–child relationship. In turn, all adolescents rated their own temperaments. Kacerguis's predictions were supported. Among the prepubescent daughter–mother dyads, higher scores on three temperament attributes (activity, rhythmicity, and reactivity) were significantly related to higher levels of conflict and higher scores on two other attributes (attention and adaptability) were significantly related to lower levels on conflict. In turn, the relations between temperament and parent–child conflict were markedly different among the postpubescent daughter–mother dyads. First, two significant reversals in direction of relationship occurred: higher activity level and rhythmicity scores were associated in this group with lower conflict scores. Second, no significant relations between either attention, adaptability, or reactivity and parent–child conflict were found, and all three of these relations differed significantly from the corresponding ones among the prepubescent daughter–mother dyads.

Finally, in regard to a last study completed to date in our laboratory, Windle and Lerner (1984) studied 153 young adult dating dyads (i.e., college students engaged in exclusive dating relationships). Each dyad member's temperament and demands–expectations for partner's temperament were measured. Within-dyad temperament–temperament and demand–demand correlations for each of five temperament attributes or corresponding demands were calculated. These correlations were compared to those which existed within 98 randomly formed dyads (i.e., dyads formed by randomly pairing 98 nondating college males with 98 nondating college females). Within the dating dyads, three of five temperament–temperament correlations (for adaptability, rhythmicity, and reactivity) and five of five demand–demand correlations were significant. In the "random dyads" only one of five temperament–temperament correlations (for rhythmicity) and none of the demand–demand correlations was significant. Moreover, the magnitude of six of the eight significant correlations in the dating dyads was significantly greater than the corresponding correlation in the "random dyads." Thus, in this study, temperament–temperament fit and demand–demand fit seem to mark the relation between a person and a significant other in his or her social context. That such congruence is not a feature of people not engaged in exclusive dating or intimate relationships — a type of social relationship central to adequate psychosocial functioning during the young adult portion of life (Erikson, 1959) — suggests the importance of a goodness of fit between the person and his or her significant interpersonal context in healthy, adaptive functioning in this portion of the life span.

Of course, the goodness of fit model is not the only conception of person–context relations that may be derived from a contextual orientation. Indeed, there perhaps are an infinity of possible interlevel relations that may occur and potentially a similarly large array of ways to model them. At this writing, we simply have not devoted enough thought and empirical energies to their investigation.

A. ISSUES FOR INTERVENTION

A contextual view of person–context relations and of plasticity raises several issues pertinent to intervention. First, the issue of asymmetry of interlevel influences raises largely unaddressed concerns about efficiency and about cost–benefit ratios. To reach a target at the cognitive–behavioral level of individuals — for example, the target of academic achievement — is it more efficient to institute a "bottom–up" strategy (e.g., to intervene at the biological level), a "parallel–level" strategy (e.g., to intervene by cognitive–behavioral means), or a "top–down" strategy (to intervene by instituting or changing social programs)? Which strategy leads to the greatest benefit relative to economic, social, and personal costs? We simply do not know the answers to these questions for very many of the potential targets of intervention.

Second, a decision about the level of analysis on which to focus one's intervention efforts is complicated by the fact that all levels of analysis are developing over time. While this feature of the human condition makes both concurrent and historical interventions possible, it again raises questions of efficiency and cost–benefit ratios. For example, when is it best to intervene during the left span to optimize a particular target process (and, of course, on what level is it best to focus one's efforts)? Are periods of developmental transition (e.g., puberty and retirement) or periods of *relatively* more stability better times within which to focus one's efforts? Moreover, do some intervention goals, such as the elimination of Fetal Alcohol Syndrome or FAS (Streissguth, Landesman-Dwyer, Martin, & Smith, 1980) require an intergenerational–developmental rather than an ontogenetic–developmental approach? In the case of FAS, for instance, may it not be of more benefit to intervene with women, who are " at risk" for becoming mothers who use excessive alcohol, before they become pregnant? Again, developmental intervention issues such as these have remained relatively unaddressed for most potential targets.

A final, relatively unaddressed issue that is worth raising here relates to direct and indirect intervention effects and to planned and unplanned effects. If an individual's plasticity both derives from and contributes to the other levels of analysis within which the individual transacts, then one must anticipate that actualizing the potential for plasticity at any one level of analysis will influence changes among other variables, both at that level and at other levels. From this perspective, one should always expect that any direct and/or intended effect of one's intervention will have indirect, and often unintended, consequences (Willems, 1973).

Such a recognition leads to two points. First, interventions should not be initiated without some conceptual or theoretical analysis of the potential indirect and unintended consequences. For instance, changing a spouse's assertiveness may be the direct, intended effect of a cognitive-behavior therapist's efforts. However, the changed assertiveness might lead to a diminution of marital quality and divorce. Such indirect effects may be unintended by the therapist and undesired by either therapist or client. Thus, my view is that one must think quite seriously about the broader contextual effects of one's intervention efforts. Clearly, a contextual, life span perspective like the one I have been using would be of use in this regard. It would sensitize one to the general possibility of, and perhaps some specific instances of, indirect effects of one's intervention efforts. Such reflection will be useful in several ways, a major consideration being that undesirable indirect effects may be anticipated; if so, then outcomes pertinent to the issue of cost–benefit ratios can be estimated before intervention begins.

Second, the fact that undesired effects may arise from one's intervention efforts raises the point that plasticity is a "double-edged sword": a system open to enhancement is open also to deterioration. That is, plasticity permits interventions to be planned in order to improve the human condition, but indirect effects may also cause either a target person's life condition and/or that of his or her context to deteriorate. Moreover, this problem is complicated by the recognition that as a consequence of people being transactionally related to their multilevel context, the failure to intervene and alter the context of life is itself an intervention (i.e., it keeps the context on a trajectory from which it might have been deflected if one had acted). Thus, one must assess the cost–benefit ratio not only of one's actions but also of one's failures to act.

V. Conclusions

Concepts of individual and context exist in organismic, mechanistic, and contextual views of development. In this chapter I have reviewed key issues involved in understanding how each perspective treats these concepts and have argued that only the probabilistic epigenetic–contextual perspective is suited for studying the relation between the active, developing organism and its context. Moreover, I have stressed that the transactional, or dynamic interactional, conception of this relation leads to a multilevel and hence multidisciplinary approach to human development, to a focus on the potential for plasticity across life, and to an appreciation of the role of the individual as an active producer of his or her own development.

In addition, however, I have pointed to some of the key conceptual and methodological issues that remain to be resolved if a contextual perspective is to be successfully used not only to study individual–context relations but to intervene to enhance such relations. Pessimism because of the presence of these problems is not warranted, however. Every approach to human development has limitations, as I hope I have made clear in this chapter. That there are problems to be resolved in regard to developmental contextualism does not single it out from other developmental paradigms.

Indeed, given that it was no earlier than the 1970s that this view of contextualism came to the fore, the clearness with which the problems have been articulated, the methodological advances that have already been made (e.g., see Nesselroade & Baltes, 1979), and the several data sets that speak to the empirical use of this contextual perspective (Baltes et al., 1980; Brim & Kagan, 1980) are reasons for great optimism for the future. This contextual view represents a "different drummer" for developmental psychology. Although as yet still playing relatively softly, the beat is steady, growing in intensity, and compelling. The 1980s may see more and more scientists begin to try to dance to the music.

Acknowledgments

I thank Athena S. Droogas, Patricia L. East, Nancy L. Galambos, Christopher K. Hertzog, David F. Hultsch, Karen Hooker, Marjorie B. Kaufman, Jacqueline V. Lerner, John R. Nesselroade, M. Bernadette Riedy, and Michael Windle for critical readings of an earlier draft of this paper. I am grateful also to Willis F. Overton for providing several stimulating comments which served to clarify my ideas and my presentation.

References

Anastasi, A. Heredity, environment, and the question "how?" *Psychological Review,* 1958, *65*, 197–208.

Baer, D. M. An age-irrelevant concept of development. *Merrill-Palmer Quarterly of Behavior and Development,* 1970, *16*, 238–246.

Baer, D. M. The organism as host. *Human Development,* 1976, *19*, 87–98.

Baer, D. M. Behavior analysis and developmental psychology: Discussant comments. *Human Development,* 1982, *25*, 357–361.

Baltes, P. B. On the potential and limits of child development: Life-span developmental perspectives. *Newsletter of the Society for Research in Child Development,* Summer 1979, pp. 1–4.

Baltes, P. B. Life-span developmental psychology: Observations on history and theory revisited. In R. M. Lerner (Ed.), *Developmental psychology: Historical and philosophical perspectives.* Hillsdale, N.J.: Erlbaum, 1983.

Baltes, P. B., Reese, H. W., & Lipsitt, L. P. Life-span developmental psychology. *Annual Review of Psychology,* 1980, *31*, 65–110.

Bijou, S. W. *Child development: The basic stage of early childhood.* Englewood Cliffs, N.J.: Prentice–Hall, 1976.

Bijou, S. W., & Baer, D. M. *Child development: A systematic and empirical theory* (Vol. 1). New York: Appleton–Century–Crofts, 1961.

Brim, O. G., Jr., & Kagan, J. Constancy and change: A view of the issues. In O. G. Brim, Jr., & J. Kagan (Eds.), *Constancy and change in human development.* Cambridge, Mass.: Harvard University Press, 1980.

Bronfenbrenner, U. Toward an experimental ecology of human development. *American Psychologist,* 1977, *32*, 513–531.

Bronfenbrenner, U. *The ecology of human development.* Cambridge, Mass.: Harvard University Press, 1979.

Dewey, J., & Bentley, A. F. *Knowing and the known.* Boston: Beacon, 1949.

Dixon, R. A., Hultsch, D. F., & Lerner, R. M. Dialectical and contextual models for the study of individual development and behavior: A critical comparison. Manuscript in preparation, 1984.

Emmerich, W. Personality development and concepts of structure. *Child Development,* 1968, *39*, 671–690.

Erikson, E. H. Identity and the life cycle. *Psychological Issues,* 1959, *1*, 18–164.

Freud, S. *Collected works* (Standard edition). London: Holgarth Press, 1954.

Gesell, A. L. The ontogenesis of infant behavior. In L. Carmichael (Ed.), *Manual of child psychology.* New York: Wiley, 1946.

Gesell, A. L. The ontogenesis of infant behavior. In L. Carmichael (Ed.), *Manual of child psychology* (2nd ed.). New York: Wiley, 1954.

184   RICHARD M. LERNER

Gollin, E. S. A developmental approach to learning and cognition. In L. P. Lipsitt & C. C. Spiker (Eds.), *Advances in child development and behavior* (Vol. 2). New York: Academic Press, 1965.

Gollin, E. S. Development and plasticity. In E. S. Gollin (Ed.), *Developmental plasticity: Behavioral and biological aspects of variations in development.* New York: Academic Press, 1981.

Gottlieb, G. Concepts of prenatal behavior. In L. R. Aronson, E. Tobach, D. S. Lehrman, & J. S. Rosenblatt (Eds.), *Development and evolution of behavior: Essays in memory of T. C. Schneirla.* San Francisco: Freeman, 1970.

Gottlieb, G. Conceptions of prenatal development: Behavioral embryology. *Psychological Review,* 1976, *83*, 215–234.

Gould, S. J. *The mismeasure of man.* New York: Norton, 1981.

Hamburger, V. The concept of development in biology. In D. B. Harris (Ed.), *The concept of development.* Minneapolis: University of Minnesota Press, 1957.

Hertzog, C., & Lerner, R. M. Developmental rate. In T. Husen & T. N. Postlethwaite (Eds.), *International encyclopedia of education: Research and studies.* Oxford: Pergamon Press, in press.

Hultsch, D. F., & Hickey, T. External validity in the study of human development: Theoretical and methodological issues. *Human Development,* 1978, *21*, 76–91.

Hultsch, D. F., & Plemons, J. K. Life events and life-span development. In P. B. Baltes & O. G. Brim, Jr., (Ed.), *Life-span development and behavior* (Vol. 2). New York: Academic Press, 1979.

Jenkins, J. J. Remember that old theory of memory? Well forget it. *American Psychologist,* 1974, *29*, 785–795.

Kagan, J. Developmental categories and the premise of connectivity. In R. M. Lerner (Ed.), *Developmental psychology: Historical and philosophical perspectives.* Hillsdale, N.J.: Erlbaum, 1983.

Kacerguis, M. A. *Child–mother relations in early adolescence: The roles of pubertal status, timing of menarche, and temperament.* Unpublished doctoral dissertation, The Pennsylvania State University, 1983.

Kaplan, B. A trio of trials: The past as prologue, prelude and pretext: Some problems and issues for a theoretically-oriented life-span developmental psychology; Sweeny among the nightingales—A call to controversy. In R. M. Lerner (Ed.), *Developmental psychology: Historical and philosophical perspectives.* Hillsdale, N.J.: Erlbaum, 1983.

Kuhn, D. Mechanisms of cognitive and social development: One psychology or two? *Human Development,* 1978, *21*, 92–118.

Lehrman, D. S. A critique of Konrad Lorenz's theory of instinctive behavior. *Quarterly Review of Biology,* 1953, *28*, 337–363.

Lerner, J. V. The role of temperament in psychosocial adaptation in early adolescents: A test of a "goodness of fit" model. *Journal of Genetic Psychology,* 1983, *143*, 149–157.

Lerner, J. V., & Lerner, R. M. Temperament and adaptation across life: Theoretical and empirical issues. In P. B. Baltes & O. G. Brim, Jr., (Eds.), *Life-span development and behavior* (Vol. 5). New York: Academic Press, 1983.

Lerner, J. V., Lerner, R. M., & Zabski, S. Temperament and elementary school children's actual and rated academic performance: A test of a "goodness of fit" model. *Journal of Child Psychology and Psychiatry,* in press.

Lerner, R. M. *Concepts and theories of human development.* Reading, Mass.: Addison–Wesley, 1976.

Lerner, R. M. Nature, nurture, and dynamic interactionism. *Human Development,* 1978, *21*, 1–20.

Lerner, R. M. A dynamic interactional concept of individual and social relationship development. In R. L. Burgess & T. L. Huston (Eds.), *Social exchange in developing relationships,* New York: Academic Press, 1979.

Lerner, R. M. Concepts of epigenesis: Descriptive and explanatory issues: A critique of Kitchner's comments. *Human Development,* 1980, *23,* 63–72.

Lerner, R. M. Children and adolescents as producers of their own development. *Developmental Review,* 1982, *2,* 342–370.

Lerner, R. M. Some dynamic and subjective features of the history of developmental psychology. In R. M. Lerner (Ed.), *Developmental psychology: Historical and philosophical perspectives.* Hillsdale, N.J.: Erlbaum, 1983.

Lerner, R. M. *On the nature of human plasticity.* New York: Cambridge University Press, 1984.

Lerner, R. M., & Busch-Rossnagel, N. Individuals as producers of their development: Conceptual and empirical bases. In R. M. Lerner & N. A. Busch-Rossnagel (Eds.), *Individuals as producers of their development: A life-span perspective.* New York: Academic Press, 1981.

Lerner, R. M., Hultsch, D. F., & Dixon, R. A. Contextualism and the character of developmental psychology in the 1970s. *Annals of the New York Academy of Sciences,* 1983, *412,* 101–128.

Lerner, R. M., & Kauffman, M. B. The concept of development in contextualism. Manuscript in preparation, The Pennsylvania State University, 1984.

Lerner, R. M., & Ryff, C. Implementation of the life-span view of human development: The sample case of attachment. In P. B. Baltes (Ed.), *Life-span development and behavior* (Vol. 1). New York: Academic Press, 1978.

Lerner, R. M., Skinner, E. A., & Sorell, G. T. Methodological implications of contextual/dialectic theories of development. *Human Development,* 1980, *23,* 225–235.

Lerner, R. M., & Spanier, G. B. A dynamic interactional view of child and family development. In R. M. Lerner & G. B. Spanier (Eds.), *Child influences on marital and family interaction: A life-span perspective.* New York: Academic Press, 1978.

Lerner, R. M., & Spanier, G. B. *Adolescent development: A life-span perspective.* New York: McGraw–Hill, 1980.

Looft, W. R. Socialization and personality throughout the life-span: An examination of contemporary psychological approaches. In P. B. Baltes & K. W. Schaie (Eds.), *Life-span developmental psychology: Personality and socialization.* New York: Academic Press, 1973.

Mandelbaum, M. *History, man and reason.* Baltimore: The Johns Hopkins University Press, 1971.

Meacham, J. A. Political values, conceptual models, and research. In R. M. Lerner & N. A. Busch-Rossnagel (Eds.), *Individuals as producers of their development: A life-span perspective.* New York: Academic Press, 1981.

Mischel, W. On the future of personality measurement. *American Psychologist,* 1977, *32,* 246–254.

Nagel, E. Determinism in development. In D. B. Harris (Ed.), *The concept of development.* Minneapolis: University of Minnesota Press, 1957.

Nesselroade, J. R., & Baltes, P. B. (Eds.). *Longitudinal research in the study of behavioral development.* New York: Academic Press, 1979.

Overton, W. F. On the assumptive base of the nature–nurture controversy: Additive versus interactive conceptions. *Human Development,* 1973, *16,* 74–89.

Overton, W. F. Klaus Riegel: Theoretical contributions to concepts of stability and change. *Human Development,* 1978, *21,* 360–363.

Overton, W. F. World views and their influence on psychological theory and research: Kuhn

— Lakatos — Lauden. In H. W. Reese (Ed.), *Advances in child development and behavior.* New York: Academic Press, 1984.

Overton, W. F., & Reese, H. W. Models of development: Methodological implications. In J. R. Nesselroade & H. W. Reese (Eds.), *Life-span developmental psychology: Methodological issues.* New York: Academic Press, 1973.

Overton, W. F., & Reese, H. W. Conceptual prerequisites for an understanding of stability– change and continuity–discontinuity. *International Journal of Behavioral Development,* 1981, *4,* 99–123.

Palermo, M. E. *Child temperament and contextual demands: A test of the goodness-of-fit model.* Unpublished doctoral dissertation, The Pennsylvania State University, 1982.

Peppei, S. C. *World hypotheses: A study in evidence.* Berkeley: University of California Press, 1942.

Pervin, L. A. Performance and satisfaction as a function of individual–environment fit. *Psychological Bulletin,* 1968, *69,* 56–68.

Petrinovich, L. Probabilistic functionalism: A conception of research method. *American Psychologist,* 1979, *34,* 373–390.

Piaget, J. Piaget's theory. In P. H. Mussen (Ed.), *Carmichael's manual of child psychology* (Vol. 1). New York: Wiley, 1970.

Prigogine, I. Time, structure, and fluctuation. *Science,* 1978, *201,* 777–785.

Prigogine, I. *From being to becoming.* San Francisco: Freeman, 1980.

Reese, H. W. Discussion. In R. M. Lerner (Chair), Symposium on "Child Development in Life-Span Perspective." Presented at 1979 Biennial Meeting of the Society for Research in Child Development, San Francisco. March, 1979.

Reese, H. W. Behavior analysis and developmental psychology: Discussant comments. *Human Development,* 1982, *35,* 352–357.

Reese, H. W., & Lipsitt, L. P. (Eds.). *Experimental child psychology.* New York: Academic Press, 1970.

Reese, H. W., & Overton, W. F. Models of development and theories of development. In L. R. Goulet & P. B. Baltes (Eds.), *Life-span developmental psychology: Research and theory.* New York: Academic Press, 1970.

Riegel, K. F. Toward a dialectical theory of development. *Human Development,* 1975, *18,* 50–64.

Riegel, K. F. The dialectics of human development. *American Psychologist,* 1976, *31,* 689–700.

Sameroff, A. L. Transactional models in early social relations. *Human Development,* 1975, *18,* 65–79.

Sarbin, T. B. Contextualism: A world view for modern psychology. In J. K. Cole (Ed.), *Nebraska Symposium on Motivation* (Vol. 24). Lincoln: University of Nebraska Press, 1977.

Scarr, S. Development is internally guided, not determined. *Contemporary Psychology,* 1982, *27,* 852–853.

Scarr, S., & McCartney, K. How people make their own environments: A theory of genotype → environment effects. *Child Development,* 1983, *54,* 424–435.

Schneirla, T. C. Interrelationships of the "innate" and the "acquired" in instinctive behavior. In *L'instinct dans le comportement des animaux et de l'homme.* Paris: Masson & Cie, 1956.

Schneirla, T. C. The concept of development in comparative psychology. In D. B. Harris (Ed.), *The concept of development.* Minneapolis: University of Minnesota Press, 1957.

Sheldon, W. H. *The varieties of human physique.* New York: Harper, 1940.

Sheldon, W. H. *The varieties of temperament.* New York: Harper, 1942.

Skinner, B. F. *The behavior of organisms.* New York: Appleton, 1938.

Skinner, B. F. The phylogeny and ontogeny of behavior. *Science,* 1966, *153,* 1205–1213.

Steinberg, L. D., & Hill, J. P. Patterns of family interaction as a function of age, the onset of puberty, and formal thinking. *Developmental Psychology,* 1978, *14,* 683–684.

Streissguth, A. P., Landesman-Dwyer, S., Martin, J. C., & Smith, D. W. Teratogenic effects of alcohol in humans and laboratory animals. *Science,* 1980, *209,* 353–361.

Super, C. M., & Harkness, S. Figure, gound and gestalt: The cultural context of the active individual. In R. M. Lerner & N. A. Busch-Rossnagel (Eds.), *Individuals as producers of their development: A life-span perspective.* New York: Academic Press, 1981.

Thomas, A., & Chess, S. *Temperament and development.* New York: Bruner–Mazel, 1977.

Thorndike, E. L. *The elements of psychology.* New York: Seiler, 1905.

Tobach, E., & Schneirla, T. C. The biopsychology of social behavior of animals. In R. E. Cooke & S. Levin (Eds.), *Biologic basis of pediatric practice.* New York: McGraw–Hill, 1968.

Waddington, C. H. *The strategy of genes.* New York: Macmillan, 1957.

Watson, J. B. Psychology as the behaviorist views it. *Psychological Review,* 1913, *20,* 158–177.

Watson, J. B. *Psychology from the standpoint of a behaviorist.* Phildelphia: Lippincott, 1918.

Watson, J. B. *Psychological care of infant and child.* New York: Norton, 1928.

Werner, H. The concept of development from a comparative and organismic point of view. In D. B. Harris (Ed.), *The concept of development.* Minneapolis: University of Minnesota Press, 1957.

Willems, E. P. Behavioral ecology and experimental analysis: Courtship is not enough. In J. R. Nesselroade & H. W. Reese (Eds.), *Life-span developmental psychology: Methodological issues.* New York: Academic Press, 1973.

Windle, M., & Lerner, R. M. The role of temperament in dating relationships among young adults. *Merrill-Palmer Quarterly,* 1984, *30,* 163–175.

Wohlwill, J. F. *The study of behavioral development.* New York: Academic Press, 1973.

Zukav, G. *The dancing Wu Li masters.* New York: Bantam Books, 1979.

7

Age, Period, and Cohort
Analysis and the Study of
Individual Development
and Social Change

ERICH W. LABOUVIE
JOHN R. NESSELROADE

I. Introduction

One line of attack that social and behavioral scientists have taken to try to comprehend individual development and social change phenomena has involved the collection and analysis of observations characterized simultaneously by chronological age, birth cohort of the observed individual, and the time or period of measurement. Despite the current level of interest in these classification dimensions, however, only relatively recently in the history of developmental psychology have the concepts of age, period (time of measurement), and cohort received more than just cursory attention. In spite of a rather intensive discussion over the past decade concerning the way these concepts bear on the understanding of individual development and social change (see e.g., Riley, in press), issues of causality and more precise identification of sources of change remain unsettled, and generally acceptable procedures for the estimation of related effects remain to be proposed.

INDIVIDUAL DEVELOPMENT
AND SOCIAL CHANGE:
EXPLANATORY ANALYSIS

189

In this chapter we will attempt to coordinate the viewpoints and information offered in previous analyses of the concepts and issues. It is our hope that a careful exposition of the concepts of age, period, and cohort from the perspective of developmental psychology will help the reader to approach issues related to the study of individual development and historical and social change more wisely.

II. Historical Perspectives

A. PRECURSORS IN DEVELOPMENTAL PSYCHOLOGY

Although the historical beginnings of the study of intraindividual patterns of change and development are often associated with the "longitudinal" child biographies that appeared during the second half of the nineteenth century, a more careful review (e.g., Baltes, 1979; Reinert, 1976, 1979) reveals even earlier precursors that indicate both significant theoretical (Carus, 1808; Tetens, 1777) and methodological insights (Quetelet, 1842; Süssmilch, 1741).

It was Quetelet in particular who not only presented a considerable set of cross-sectional data for large segments of the human life span but, in the interpretation of his findings, anticipated and defined several major design issues. Quetelet's discussions included the possible effect of period-specific historical events, the potential modification of age development through the impact of social change, and the need for systematic replication of observations and data collections across historical periods.

The fact that these early contributions were essentially ignored until quite recently may be due to the rapid development of the natural sciences during the eighteenth and nineteenth centuries. It seeems that developmental psychologists for the most part readily embraced the *ahistorical* paradigm of the natural sciences by defining the concept of time only in terms of chronological age, not in terms of historical time (Baltes & Nesselroade, 1979).

B. SCHAIE'S GENERAL DEVELOPMENT MODEL

Greater concern for developmentally adequate methodologies (Bronfenbrenner, 1963; Harris, 1963; Zigler, 1963) and the observation of significant discrepancies in the findings of cross-sectional and longitudinal studies (Damon, 1965; Kuhlen, 1963) pointed to the need to reassess the validity of assumptions underlying both theoretical perspectives and their associated methodologies. Given the inherent inadequacies of conventional longitudinal and cross-sectional approaches, and in line with Kessen's (1960) suggestion that meaningful designs for developmental problems involve either the interaction of age and environmental changes or an analysis of age functions in special populations, Schaie (1965) proposed a general developmental model with three components: chronological age, time of measurement, and birth cohort. Kessen's (1960) proposal that a response may be seen as a function of age, special population, and environment was reformulated by Schaie (1965) by substituting the term "cohort" for "special population" and the concept of "time of measurement" for the term "environment." In this context "cohort" implies the total population of organisms born at the same point or during the same interval of historical time. Time of measurement is assumed to indicate or index the state of the environment or the total environmental impact at a given temporal point.

Realizing the intrinsic interdependence among the three variables of age, cohort, and time of measurement, Schaie (1965) formulated 3 two-factorial designs for the purposes of describing behavioral development more adequately and identifying sources of change and their characteristics. Accordingly, the *cohort-sequential* method decomposes behavioral variation in relation to age and cohort. Due to the inherent confounding of time of measurement, it is, at the same time, necessary to assume that behavioral variation is not related to variations of time of measurement. In comparison, the *time-sequential* method considers behavioral variation in relation to age and time of measurement, thereby confounding cohort. Finally, the *cross-sequential* method considers behavioral variation in relation to cohort and time of measurement while confounding age. According to Schaie (1965, 1970, 1973), systematic application of the three methods in appropriate combinations makes it possible to separate the components of age, cohort, and time of measurement as representing three different sources of developmental change.

C. BALTES'S REFORMULATION OF SCHAIE'S MODEL

Reiterating the fact that the components of age, cohort, and time of measurement are formally interdependent and mathematically confounded in a three-factorial conception, Baltes (1968) suggested that a classification of individuals into a set of categories defined as segments of one or more time continua is completely inadequate to identify behavioral change components in terms of their "causal" determinants or underlying processes and antecedents. Realizing that the causal–analytic task requires more than just the observation of behavior at several points in time, Baltes (1968) proposed that Schaie's general developmental model be used only for the purpose of description. With the Cohort × Age matrix serving as the most desirable guide for collecting data on individual change and development, Baltes (1968) introduced the distinction between longitudinal and cross-sectional sequences, depending upon the use of repeated or independent observations along the age variable. Thus, Baltes's objective is more modest than Schaie's. Although recognizing the possible importance of cohort variability in developmental change and the need for cohort-sequential strategies, he does not believe that Schaie's model leads to valid causal analysis of the changes and variability observed.

The discrepancies between the Schaie and Baltes positions motivated further efforts at clarification by other authors (e.g., Buss, 1973; Labouvie, 1975). Schaie and Baltes (1975) tried to bring some closure to these discussions by identifying both the similarities and differences between their respective points of view. Accordingly, they proposed that their perspectives be considered in conjunction with a distinction between the two tasks of *description* and *explanation*. Both agreed that the description of behavioral development is achieved most completely and adequately by using longitudinal or cross-sectional sequences within the framework of a Cohort × Age matrix. Their views, however, continue to differ as far as the explanatory use of sequential designs is concerned. While Schaie believes that the application of sequential designs can lead to the identification of sources of both individual and environmental change, Baltes prefers strategies that explicate the time continuum more directly in terms of processes and antecedents (e.g., Baltes & Goulet, 1971; Baltes, Reese, & Nesselroade, 1977; Nesselroade & Baltes, 1979).

D. CATTELL'S FORMULATION

In response to the initial analyses by Schaie (1965) and Baltes (1968), Cattell (1970) provided an alternative conceptual and methodological definition of the problem. In a sense, Cattell's formulation represents a compromise between, and combination of, the positions of Baltes and Schaie by considering simultaneously both descriptive and explanatory objectives. Adopting the framework of a Cohort × Age matrix for data collection, a multiple set of cohort-specific age curves is decomposed into (1) an abstract normative or *ecogenic* life curve that is common or typical for all cohorts that are being considered and (2) an *epogenic* component which represents those aspects of the set of life curves that are different for different cohorts. Both components are assumed to be related to genetic (endogenous) and environmental (exogenous) sources of change. While it is proposed that ecogenic and epogenic components can be separated through analyses of variance of the Cohort × Age matrix, the relative contribution of endogenous and exogenous sources of change to each of the two components is assessed by using methods that provide an estimate of nature–nurture ratios.

Taken as a whole, the efforts by Schaie, Baltes, and Cattell indicate a concern with two major tasks pertaining to the investigation of individual and social–historical changes. One involves the formulation of data collection strategies that provide an adequate basis for the description of ontogenetic behavioral changes and an assessment of the invariance of the observed change functions across different cohort populations. The other involves the explication of commonalities and differences that are found for some finite set of cohort-specific age curves in reference to antecedent sources of change.

The remainder of this chapter will be concerned with an exploration of the conceptual issues that have to be addressed in order to arrive at a resolution of the general problems associated with age, period (time of measurement), and cohort analysis. First, the concept of time will be analyzed with respect to its incorporation into the description and explanation of developmental phenomena. After considering alternative conceptual approaches, we will discuss implications and issues in the context of selected substantive findings.

III. Age, Period, and Cohort Effects

A. THE CONCEPT OF TIME

Developmental sciences focus on the study of temporal sequences of events. That focus requires an incorporation of the time concept and time dimension into both the description and explanation of the developmental phenomena of interest. In what form time is to be incorporated into scientific activities has, of course, long been the subject of debate among both natural and social scientists.[1] Previous analyses and discussions of the time concept have emphasized both the directionality and relativity of time (e.g., Riegel, 1972, 1977). What has been left rather implicit in those discussions, however, is the relativity of a zero point, that is, the choice or definition of $t = 0$ in the process of time measurement. Yet, the choice is clearly related

---

[1] In our opinion even so-called age-irrelevant conceptions of development do not completely discard the concept of age–time. They merely choose to treat time–age as an ordinal variable along which to order sequences of events (e.g., Baer, 1970).

to scientific purpose and, we will argue, is highly germane to the analysis of age, period, and cohort effects in developmental psychology.

In classical experimentation, with its emphasis on events and phenomena being replicable across time, different researchers generally describe their observations in reference to different zero points of time (usually defined in terms of the onset of one or more experimental manipulations). Although specified with precision, these zero points are essentially arbitrary and *unrelated* to each other. In contrast to experimental time t, with multiple zero points, consider the concept of historical time T. It is based on the assumption that all events and phenomena of interest are located along a common time dimension with one *single,* though still arbitrary, zero point, $T = 0$.

As far as the study of individual development is concerned, the distinction between experimental and historical time leads immediately to the question of whether to formulate age-related or history-related models and theories, or combinations thereof (e.g., Baltes, Reese, & Lipsitt, 1980). In other words, the traditional emphasis on age-developmental models reflects assumptions that also characterize the domain of classical experimentation.

To see the relevance of the distinction between experimental and historical time more clearly, it is helpful to formalize the preceding considerations more precisely. Individuals who represent the relevant observational and experimental units have a finite life span along the dimension of historical time T, and different groups or cohorts of individuals continuously enter and exit at different points in time. For a particular cohort of individuals born at time T_c we may express some behavior B and related intraindividual changes as:

$$B_{ci} = \begin{cases} 0 & \text{for} \quad T < T_{ci} \\ f_{ci}(T) & \text{for} \quad T_{ci} \le T \le T_{di} \\ 0 & \text{for} \quad T_{di} < T \end{cases} \qquad (1)$$

In this representation T_{ci} indicates the time of birth, T_{di} the time of death of individual i. It is assumed that the *description* of behavioral phenomena in reference to historical time T is more general and, therefore, more appropriate unless it can be shown empirically for some historical time interval $[T_a, T_b]$ that $f_{ci}(T) = g_i(T - T_c)$ for $T_a \le T_c \le T \le T_b$. $T - T_c$, of course, is the chronological age (CA) of the individual born at time T_c. Such a condition is satisfied, for instance, for $B_{ci} = a(T - T_c)^2 = a_i(CA)^2$, but not for more complex relationships such as $B_{ci} = a_i(T^2 - T_c^2)$. If this condition is fulfilled, the developmental phenomenon of interest is invariant across cohorts (at least those born and living between T_a and T_b), and age, $T - T_c$, is sufficient for an accurate description of the behavior and its change over time. The most straightforward empirical test of whether or not this assumption is tenable for a particular behavioral domain and some historical time interval is obtained by using Cohort × Age sequential designs (Baltes, 1968) and making a *descriptive* comparison of the cohort-specific, longitudinal age curves of the behaviors studied. Obviously, the results of such comparisons will indicate the extent to which experimental time–age, historical time, or both need to be incorporated into the description and explanation of individual behavioral development.

To this point the concept of time has been analyzed only in relation to the description of the target phenomenon, namely, intraindividual change in behavior over time (e.g., Baltes, Reese, & Nesselroade, 1977). The complexity of matters increases considerably when the concept of time is extended to the task of explanation in the form of antecedent–process–consequent relationships. The extension requires not only an assessment of B_{ci} as expressed in Equation 1, but also the conceptualization and measurement of two additional domains involving sets of antecedents A_{ci} and mediating processes P_{ci}. Ultimately, however, it is the systematic mapping of the B_{ci} and their temporal characteristics onto the A_{ci} and P_{ci} and their respective temporal characteristics that is at the heart of a developmental causal analysis.

Illustration: Individual Development from a Historical Perspective. To illustrate the complexity of the task of explanation more concretely, the following hypothetical example of a model is presented without an *a priori* inclusion of chronological age. Model assumptions are:

1. Over some historical time interval $[T_a, T_b]$ individual change in behavior B is influenced by two antecedents, $A_1(T)$ and $A_2(T)$ for all cohorts entering and exiting during $[T_a, T_b]$;
2. The processes that translate both antecedents into behavioral effects are *invariant* and the effects are *cumulative* and *permanent;*
3. The effect of $A_1(T)$ is positive (B increases); the effect of $A_2(T)$ is negative (B decreases); both effects are additive;
4. The temporal characteristics of the two antecedents are as follows: $A_{1i}(T) = a_{1i}$ = constant for a given i with mean (a_{1i}) = constant and $\text{Var}(a_{1i})$ = constant for $T_a \leq T \leq T_b$; and $A_{2i}(T) = 0$ for $T < T_p$ and $T > T_q$ for all i; otherwise, $A_{2i}(T) = a_{2i}$ = constant for a given i with mean (a_{2i}) = constant and $\text{Var}(a_{2i})$ = constant for $T_p \leq T \leq T_q$. In other words, $A_{2i}(T)$ is assumed to be present only during the time period $[T_p, T_q]$.

Based on these assumptions (and using integral calculus), the behavior of individual i born at T_c and measured at time T_m is given by

$$B_{ci}(T_m) = \int_{T_c}^{T_m} A_{1i}(T)\, dt - \int_{T_c}^{T_m} A_{2i}(T)\, dt; \qquad T_a \leq T_c \leq T_m \leq T_b$$

Table 7.1

Differences in Age Patterns as a Function of Variations in Time of Birth (T_c) and Time of Measurement (T_m)

Individual and cohort	Age pattern[a]
A. Born and living before T_p	$B_{ci}(T_m) = a_{1i}(T_m - T_c)$
B. Born and living after T_q	$B_{ci}(T_m) = a_{1i}(T_m - T_c)$
C. Born before T_p and living beyond T_q	
Observed before T_p	$B_{ci}(T_m) = a_{1i}(T_m - T_c)$
Observed between T_p and T_q	$B_{ci}(T_m) = a_{1i}(T_m - T_c) - a_{2i}(T_m - T_p)$
Observed after T_q	$B_{ci}(T_m) = a_{1i}(T_m - T_c) - a_{2i}(T_q - T_p)$
D. Born between T_p and T_q and living beyond T_q	
Observed before T_q	$B_{ci}(T_m) = a_{1i}(T_m - T_c) - a_{2i}(T_m - T_c)$
Observed after T_q	$B_{ci}(T_m) = a_{1i}(T_m - T_c) - a_{2i}(T_q - T_c)$

[a] Average cohort age patterns are obtained by replacing the coefficients a_{1i} and a_{2i} with their averages $a_1.$ and $a_2..$ $T_m - T_c$ represents chronological age.

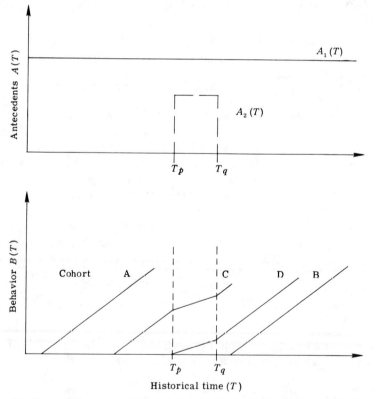

Figure 7.1   Temporal patterns of antecedents and behavior for four cohorts (see Table 7.1).

As shown in Table 7.1 and Figure 7.1, $A_{1i}(T)$ contributes an age-related increment of behavioral change that is replicable and invariant across successive cohorts. In contrast, $A_{2i}(T)$ generates changes that depend on the location of T_c and T_m relative to T_p and T_q.

Although the example model was chosen to simulate relatively simple conditions and processes, it clearly illustrates the basic problem that permeates discussions and analyses of the concepts of age, cohort, and period. Specifically, the example dramatizes the question of whether or not precise knowledge of B_{ci} for some specified historical time interval $[T_a, T_b]$ and a corresponding set of cohorts is sufficient to permit valid inferences with regard to antecedents A_{ci}, processes P_{ci}, and their respective temporal characteristics.

B. DESCRIPTION VERSUS EXPLANATION

Before proceeding any further in this discussion, it is necessary to comment at least briefly on our usage of the terms "description" and "explanation" in the context of studying temporal change phenomena (see also Baltes, Reese, & Nesselroade, 1977). As was suggested earlier, the distinction between the tasks of description and explanation are seen primarily in terms of a difference in emphasis. At one extreme, description involves a systematic recording of behavioral events or outcomes that are ordered within a Cohort × Age or a Cohort × Time matrix. At the other extreme, explanation is seen to require, in addition to these descriptive activities, the systematic observation of possible antecedents and the formulation of underlying processes in reference to the same Cohort × Age or Cohort × Time matrices. This view obviously suggests that time, regardless of whether it is used as experimental time – age or as historical time, is not given the status of an independent variable. Instead, it is seen to represent an inherent part of *both* dependent and independent variables, that is, of consequents, processes, and antecedents. In other words, this view represents a logical extension of Wohlwill's (1973) position.

A salient implication of removing time from independent variable status is that the question of how to use and incorporate the time variable cuts across both description and explanation tasks. An answer to the question, therefore, can be developed from two different directions. From an explanatory point of view, it seems desirable to begin with a specification of the temporal characteristics of antecedent and process functions in order to deduce or predict those of the behavioral consequents. From a descriptive point of view, it is often more practical to begin with an observation and specification of the temporal characteristics of the behavioral outcomes.

Regardless of the relative merit one may attribute to either approach, it is important to realize that the problems of how to (1) incorporate the time dimensions and (2) formally represent the temporal characteristics of the target variables and concepts remain to be considered in both cases. In other words, the problem of confounding the parameters of age, cohort, and time of measurement and the questions of whether or not and how to unconfound them are matters that need to be discussed to some extent as quite separate from the issue of description versus explanation.

C. REPRESENTATIONS OF THE TIME CONCEPT

According to Baltes, Reese, and Nesselroade (1977), developmental psychology is concerned with the study of intraindividual change and interindividual differences in intraindividual changes. More concretely, this definition implies that the relevant data consist of multiple sets of change curves. In the simplest case, they may represent behavioral change curves of individuals or certain groups of individuals. In other cases, the set of behavioral curves may be supplemented by a set of curves representing possible antecedents (see, for instance, Figure 7.1).

In the present context we are, of course, concerned with the fact that individuals and groups of individuals do not enter and exit their environment at the same point in historical time. In other words, behaviors, antecedents, and processes in reference to a specific individual or group of individuals "exist" (as defined in Equation 1) over a finite historical time interval with a certain time of onset (time of birth) and an "endpoint" at which some observation is made (time of measurement). Time of onset and time of endpoint automatically determine the duration of the time interval considered.

When considering the representation of a multiple set of change curves in relation to time, it is useful to distinguish explicitly between three different possibilities. They may be involved either singly or in combinations.

1. For a given historical time interval $[T_a, T_b]$, the temporal functions for processes, antecedents, and behaviors (i.e., P_{ci}, A_{ci}, and B_{ci}) are assumed to fulfill the following conditions: $P_{ci} = p_i(T - T_c)$, $A_{ci} = g_i(T - T_c)$, and $B_{ci} = f_i(T - T_c)$. In other words, all relevant processes, antecedents, and behaviors are assumed to be related to age, $T - T_c$, only according to functions that are invariant across different cohorts. This position emphasizes invariance of age-related phenomena, or *ahistorical continuity,* across historical time and, in that sense, is limited to the study of normative, age-graded changes in the three domains (Baltes, Cornelius, & Nesselroade, 1979; Baltes, et al., 1980).

2. For a given historical time interval $[T_a, T_b]$, the temporal functions are assumed to satisfy the following condition: $P_{ci} = p_i(T)$, $A_{ci} = g_i(T)$, and $B_{ci} = f_i(T)$. That is, the relevant processes, antecedents, and behaviors are assumed to be normative history-graded phenomena (Baltes et al., 1979, 1980). According to this position, various cohort-specific functions simply represent different segments of these history-graded functions and therefore do not have to exhibit identical levels and forms in relation to age, $T - T_c$, in order to satisfy this condition. In contrast to the first case, the second perspective obviously emphasizes the notion of *historical* continuity as quite different from that of ahistorical continuity.

3. For a given historical time interval $[T_a, T_b]$, the temporal functions are assumed to fulfill the following conditions:

$$P_{ci} = p_{1i}(T_c, T) = p_{2i}(T_c, T - T_c) = p_{3i}(T, T - T_c)$$

$$A_{ci} = g_{1c}(T_c, T) = g_{2i}(T_c, T - T_c) = g_{3i}(T, T - T_c)$$

$$B_{ci} = f_{1i}(T_c, T) = f_{2i}(T_c, T - T_c) = f_{3i}(T, T - T_c)$$

This perspective assumes that the relevant processes, antecedents, and behaviors are simultaneously age- and history-graded according to functions whose temporal representation is not reducible to one of the previous two cases. At the same time, however, the mathematical interdependence between time of birth, age, and time of measurement as expressed in the tautology $T = T_c + (T - T_c) = T_c + CA$ makes it possible to choose among three different, though formally equivalent, representations. For instance, consider again the temporal function $B_{ci} = a_i(T^2 - T_c^2)$. It is not reducible to a form containing only one time parameter. But two alternative, though equivalent, representations are, namely, $B_{ci} = a_i T_c \cdot CA + a_i \cdot CA^2$ and $B_{ci} = 2a_i T \cdot CA - a_i \cdot CA^2$. Furthermore, it is also obvious that the temporal representation of functions that are simultaneously age- and history-graded is always reducible to one containing only *two* time parameters.

In relation to the three cases just described, two additional points should be considered. First, in the same sense in which the three sets of conditions were specified in reference to a finite historical time interval, they may also be defined with differential applicability for different segments of the human life span. Second, the particular presentation of conditions chosen above should not be misinterpreted as stating that assumptions about processes, antecedents, and behavioral consequents need to reflect identical temporal characteristics. In fact, one of the important points demonstrated by our example model (see Figure 7.1) is that the observation of age-related behavioral changes does not at all imply that the underlying processes and antecedents are also age-related. It is most likely, however, that if processes and antecedents are only age-related (Case 1), the resulting behavioral changes will be age-related, too.

Finally, following the classical interpretation of time series models (Anderson, 1976), one may also attempt a decomposition of the two-parameter set of functions of Case 3 in terms of a functionally simple combination of the first two conditions. For instance, such models would typically assume that $B_c(T) = B_1(T - T_c) + B_2(T)$ or $B_c(T) = B_1(T - T_c) \times B_2(T)$.

D. SOLUTION STRATEGIES

When considering the relative merit of the various strategies that have been proposed in the past (e.g., Converse, 1976; Fienberg & Mason, 1979; Goldstein, 1979; Jackson, 1975; Mason, Mason, Winsborough, & Poole, 1973; Price, 1976; Schaie, 1965, 1970, 1973) to solve the problem of estimating the effects of age-, period-, and cohort-based influences, it is important to keep in mind exactly what it is that one is trying to find a solution for. From the previous discussion it is clear that one has to distinguish between two problems. The first involves the *specification of temporal relationships*. While a review of the psychological literature might give the impression that this problem is limited to the domain of behavioral change functions, we would like to emphasize that it is equally applicable to the domains of antecedents and process change functions. At the same time, however, it is possible that differences in the emphasis given to each domain are associated with differences in the choice of data collection strategies. For instance, since intraindividual behavioral change represents the ultimate target of their research, developmental psychologists may well prefer data sets that are gathered within the framework of a Cohort × Age matrix, although they may, and in fact do, accept Cohort × Time matrices as providing somewhat incomplete subsets of the former (Nesselroade & Baltes, in press). By contrast, sociologists who study historical changes in sociocultural conditions (which, from a psychological perspective, fall into the category of possible antecedents) may find the Cohort × Time or Age × Time matrices to represent more appropriate frameworks for their data gathering.

The second and more basic problem concerns the *identification of antecedents and the formulation of processes* that, in combination, lead to the observed behavioral change functions. Distinguishing between them is not meant to imply that the two problems should or can be treated separately. In fact, previous debates clearly suggest just the opposite. However, since the first problem represents only one aspect or part of the second, we agree with Baltes (1968) and Glenn (1976) that solutions to the specification problem do not represent solutions to the broader issue, especially if the former are only concerned with a representation of the temporal character-istics of the behavioral outcomes (see also Baltes, Cornelius, & Nesselroade, 1979).

Strategies that are purely mathematico-statistical in their orientation have failed to resolve the issues for two reasons. First, they have been motivated, by and large, by an exploratory rather than a confirmatory, hypothesis-test-ing stance. Second, it seems that the choice of a particular data collection matrix (Cohort × Age, Cohort × Time, Age × Time) has been assumed to dictate automatically the form of the analytical model used on the obtained data set.

The situation here is obviously quite similar to that of exploratory factor analysis. That is, while it is relatively simple to extract a factor structure from a set of empirical intercorrelations, it is quite a different matter to decide how to position the system of reference axes in the factorial space. Applied to the present context, it means that exploratory analyses of data sets gathered by any one of Schaie's three sequential methods cannot produce solutions to the representation problem that are uniquely determined. In other words, a given empirical data set can always be represented by many different, though mathematically and statistically equivalent, functions in-volving pairs of the three time parameters. It would certainly be misleading to assume that the choice of a data gathering matrix represents a solution to this uniqueness problem.

In view of these comments we would like to suggest that the use of mathe-matico-statistical solution strategies be placed within the context of a confir-matory, hypothesis-testing approach. For instance, one may ask whether a hypothesized structure of means based on a one-parameter, two-parameter, or three-parameter model fits a given data set. Of course, formulations of the hypothesized models would have to be based on some substantive theo-retical considerations. From a methodological point of view, such a confir-matory approach can be implemented in the case of quantitative data by using multivariate techniques developed by Sörbom and Jöreskog (1976). Discussion of fitting models to qualitative data has been presented by Clogg (1982), for example. Furthermore, once the switch from an exploratory to a confirmatory orientation is made, the specification problem as just defined becomes completely irrelevant.

IV. Interpretation of Effects

Although the logical status of historical time is not quite the same as that of chronological age — for instance, age can be replicated across historical time but the converse, by definition, is not possible — they are similar in that both lack the characteristics of full-fledged experimental variables (e.g., see Baer, 1970; Baltes, 1968; Baltes, Cornelius, & Nesselroade, 1979; Baltes & Goulet, 1971; Baltes, Reese, & Nesselroade, 1977; Wohlwill, 1973). Although we would argue that both concepts can never be completely irrelevant in a scientific context concerned with the phenomena of individual development and sociocultural change, either singly or together, it is nevertheless clear that the specific status of either one will depend on both their empirical use as design variables and their theoretical use in the formal description of the temporal characteristics of antecedents, processes, and behavioral consequents.

A. AGE AND HISTORICAL TIME AS ERROR OR DISTURBANCE

In the simplest case one may treat variability in relation to age or historical time as error variance due to disturbances; such variability is of little a priori theoretical interest.   For the developmental psychologist it is, of course, historical time which may be given that status (Baltes, Cornelius, & Nesselroade, 1979).   For sociologists and historians, on the other hand, it is more likely to be age (but see, e.g., Featherman, Chapter 8, this volume). Both approaches are alike in being based on one-parameter models, with the first one assuming ahistorical continuity of age-related phenomena and the second emphasizing continuity of historical trends regardless of age.   Thus, neither position permits the study of interrelationships between individual ontogenetic development and sociohistorical changes.

B. AGE AND HISTORICAL TIME AS FACETS OF GENERALIZABILITY

The most straightforward extension of either of the one-parameter positions just mentioned involves the systematic use of the second time parameter to formulate more adequate data gathering strategies and to provide more detailed descriptions of phenomena.   As pointed out before, the developmental psychologist studying interindividual differences in intraindividual changes will generally prefer to render historical time operational in the form of cohort (time of birth) and collect descriptive data within the framework of a Cohort × Age matrix.   On the other hand, sociologists interested in ongoing cultural changes may want to include age in order to describe cultural changes more completely within the context of a Time × Age matrix where historical time is made operational as time of measurement.[2] In the first case it is cohort, in the second, age, that is regarded as a dimension which has been "sampled" and is, therefore, the subject of concerns about generalization.   In either case, the goal is to assess the relative degree of stability or invariance of the phenomenon of interest (Baltes et al., 1979).

C. AGE AND HISTORICAL TIME AS PART OF ANTECEDENT, PROCESS, AND CONSEQUENT VARIABLES

When age and historical time are important components of theoretical formulations of human development, both time parameters may serve either as empirical indicators of not yet fully explicated theoretical constructs within a confirmatory, hypothesis-testing approach to the target change phenomenon or as inherent elements of the representation of a multiple system of antecedents, processes, and consequents as outlined above.   In either case it is necessary to consider how historical time is to be defined in the conceptualization of antecedent–process–consequent relations. Should it be incorporated as time of birth (cohort) or as time of measurement?   As we indicated earlier, the use of cohort or time of measurement as design variables for the purposes of data collection is quite independent of their use in the formal representation of changes in antecedents, processes, and consequents.   Therefore, the nature of hypothesized processes and mechanisms is likely to have a bearing on whether cohort or time of measurement represents a more appropriate index of historical time.

If the population of individuals as it exists at any given time is viewed as the unit of analysis and if one wishes to emphasize historical continuity of sociocultural changes, time of measurement is an optimal initial choice. Each single time of measurement represents merely one point in an ongoing series or sequence, and the fact that certain individuals are born and certain others die at any one of these points in time is irrelevant.   In contrast, as suggested by Baltes, Cornelius, and Nesselroade (1979), developmental psychology's focus on the individual as the unit of analysis favors cohort (time of birth) as an index of historical time.   Although each cohort population exists over an extended interval of historical time, time of birth is given a special conceptual status in the sense that it serves to define sequences of separate

---

[2] We prefer to view the Cohort × Time matrix as merely representing a subset of the more complete Cohort × Age matrix.   Since age can be systematically replicated across historical time in the form of either cohort or time of measurement, the Cohort × Age and the Age × Time matrices seem to be preferable as data collection strategies.

populations of individuals. In other words, the fact that certain individuals are born while certain others die at any given point in time is no longer irrelevant.

To illustrate the difference between both perspectives more concretely, consider the following descriptive example. Assume that during the historical time interval $[T_a, T_b]$ the behavioral change function $B(T)$ includes a recurring age-related trend and a superimposed historical trend. From a time-of-measurement perspective we may write

$$B(T) = B_{\text{age}} + B_{\text{time}}$$

with

$$B_{\text{age}} = a_0(T - T_c) \quad \text{and}$$

$$B_{\text{time}} = aT - bT^2 \quad \text{for} \quad T_a \leq T_c < T \leq T_b$$

From a time-of-birth (cohort) perspective the *same* function $B(T)$ can be represented for any given cohort born at T_c as

$$B_c(T) = B_{\text{age}}^* + B_{\text{cohort}}$$

with

$$B_{\text{age}}^* = (a_0 + a)(T - T_c) - b(T - T_c)^2 \quad \text{and}$$

$$B_{\text{cohort}} = (aT_c - bT_c^2) - 2bT_c(T - T_c)$$

Obviously, the use of conventional analysis of variance models in conjunction with a Cohort $\times$ Age matrix favors the second representation and makes it difficult to conceptualize models of ongoing, continuous historical trends as viewed by the first perspective. In that sense, it is easy to see that a preference for certain data collection strategies and certain analytical models will affect not only the description of the change phenomena of interest but will also implicitly bias the formulation of underlying processes and mechanisms.

If the concept of cohort is used to characterize significant aspects of antecedents and processes, the value of considering the term "period" only in the sense of *cohort periods* seems worth pursuing. In other words, a historical time interval $[T_a, T_b]$ can be subdivided into segments $[T_{ai}, T_{bi}]$, $(i = 1, 2, \ldots)$ such that individuals born within the same time segment represent a relatively homogeneous subpopulation. For instance, the generation of individuals born and raised during the Great Depression constitute a relatively homogeneous subpopulation with the Great Depression representing a normative antecedent having developmental impact (e.g., see Elder, 1974). Of course, it is open to debate how this homogeneity is to be defined. In general, developmental psychologists will tend to base it on the commonality of age-related trends in behaviors, processes, or antecedents either in reference to the total life span or some specified age segment thereof. Consequently, the same historical time interval may be subdivided into different sets of cohort periods depending on one's criterion of what constitutes a homogeneous subpopulation.

If historical time is conceptualized as time of measurement, a given historical time interval is viewed as a whole rather than as a succession of separate cohorts of individuals. The concept of cohort becomes irrelevant and reference to a specific individual or group of individuals is only made in terms of age. Thus, one may introduce the concept of *historical period* to demarcate certain time segments on the basis of the temporal characteristics of historical trends over the total time interval studied.[3] For instance, in our example of Table 7.1 the interval $[T_p, T_q]$ may be defined as a distinct historical period given the temporal characteristics of antecedent $A_2(T)$. As in the case of the cohort concept, the segmenting of the total time interval into sets of periods will depend on the choice of criteria. As before, they may be based on a consideration of antecedents, processes, or consequents and their particular temporal characteristics.

As stated before, we believe that preferences for a particular conceptualization of historical time ought to take account of one's perspectives on models, units of analysis, and hypothesized effects. Previous uses of data analytic models have failed to provide a more balanced approach and have unnecessarily contributed to the confusion surrounding the concept of historical time and its twofold use in the form of cohort and time of measurement.

V. A Substantive Illustration of Concepts

To provide some additional perspective on the treatment of age, period, and cohort effects in developmental psychology and to offer further substantive context for technical consideration of analysis models, we will take a brief look at selected outcomes of empirical research conducted to examine age, period, and cohort effects. Empirical investigations in developmental psychology that have been conducted within the general framework of age, time of measurement, and cohort as primary design components have, as a group, spanned a considerable portion of the life span. The major studies have tended to be basically descriptive in design and to focus on cognitive–intellectual performance and personality measures. Moreover, the outcomes have generally substantiated the effect on development of influences

---

[3] Continuity as used here does not imply mathematical continuity.

associated with the historical time dimension. The prevalence of cohort or generation and time of measurement effects on individual development has reinforced the need to recognize the influence of sociohistorical changes on individual development and to focus more sharply on the possible sources of such influence in developmental theorizing. In addition, from a methodological perspective the importance of introducing a variety of controls (e.g., for retest and selective attrition effects) into the design of developmental psychology studies has been strongly underscored by the results of studies designed to permit the assessment of such confounds (Labouvie, Bartsch, Nesselroade, & Baltes, 1974; Nesselroade & Baltes, 1974, in press).

Rather than present a summary of relevant outcomes from the developmental psychology literature, we will review a study of adolescent personality and ability change done by Nesselroade and Baltes (1974, 1984) that illustrates conception, design, measurement, and analysis issues pertinent to age-, period-, and cohort-defined analytic schemes. The reader interested in detailed accounts of various age-, period-, and cohort-based approaches to the examination of developmental change can consult reports of individual projects (e.g., Baltes, Baltes, & Reinert, 1970; Baltes & Reinert, 1969; Nesselroade, Schaie, & Baltes, 1972; Riegel, Riegel, & Meyer, 1967; Schaie, 1972; Schaie, Labouvie, & Buech, 1973; Schaie & Parham, 1977; Schaie & Strother, 1968a, 1968b; Woodruff & Birren, 1972) or reviews of several studies (e.g., Baltes, Cornelius, & Nesselroade, 1978, 1979).

Nesselroade and Baltes (1974, in press) conducted a 2-year sequential longitudinal study of personality and ability changes in 1800 male and female adolescents in West Virginia. The basic design, which was descriptive in nature, is presented in Table 7.2. Subjects in the longitudinal samples (Cohorts 1954, 1955, 1956, and 1957) were measured in 1970, 1971, and 1972. A random sample of retest controls was drawn and measured for the first time in 1972. An additional control group was made up of the students who, after participating as part of the core longitudinal group in the initial assessment in 1970, dropped out of the study.

The measurement battery consisted of the 14 scales of the High School Personality Questionnaire (HSPQ) (Cattell & Cattell, 1969), 20 scales of the Personality Research Form (PRF) (Jackson, 1968), and six subtests of the Primary Mental Abilities test battery (Thurstone & Thurstone, 1962). The 14 HSPQ and 20 PRF scales were collapsed to 10 general personality dimensions (e.g., extraversion, anxiety) for subsequent analysis (Nesselroade & Baltes, 1975).

Data analyses were performed to test for significance of main and interaction effects of age–cohort, sex, and time of measurement on 10 personality and 6 ability measures. Scores were correlated over the 1-year periods

Table 7.2

Nesselroade and Baltes's (1974) Longitudinal
Sequences Design[a]

		Time of measurement		
Cohort	Sex	1970	1971	1972
1954	M	16	17	18
	F	16	17	18
1955	M	15	16	17
	F	15	16	17
1956	M	14	15	16
	F	14	15	16
1957	M	13	14	15
	F	13	14	15

[a] Cell entries are age of subjects at particular times
of measurement. January 1 of each year was the
mean testing time ($=2$ months). Samples of randomly selected retest control subjects were drawn
from cohorts 1954–1957 and tested for the first time
in 1972. The core longitudinal sample and dropouts
were contrasted on 1970 scores to estimate dropout
effects.

(1970–71, 1971–72) and the 2-year period (1970–72) to assess stability.
Analyses for testing and selective dropout effects were made also.

The outcomes presented by Nesselroade and Baltes (1974, 1984) supported two key conclusions: (1) simple cross-sectional and longitudinal designs need to be augmented both by sequential strategies and by the inclusion
of control groups if developmental change is to be described accurately and
(2) developmental change is influenced greatly by the cultural movement
vis-à-vis age-based sequences. The latter conclusion, in turn, argues
strongly for the further refinement of concepts and analytical tools that are
appropriate for empirically decomposing general developmental phenomena into their constituent parts, some of which are attributable to social–
environmental antecedents. Thus, for example, the finding that there were
very clear changes and differences among groups on dimensions such as
independence, achievement, and conscientiousness but that patterns were
not closely tied to chronological age or birth cohort implicates social change
factors as an important influence on the personality differences found
among individuals.

VI. Conclusion

A. IMPLICATIONS AND FUTURE DIRECTIONS

The methodological issues and substantive research outcomes that have been identified here have several important implications for future work. Consider first what the substantive results suggest. The evidence that individual development is subject to influences which, at this time, can only be linked grossly to temporal dimensions requires that serious students of development work toward strengthening assessments of such effects and interrelationships by (1) refining concepts and developing more powerful methodologies and (2) formulating explicit theories and explanations to pinpoint the actual nature of the antecedent–consequent relationships now only implied by the observation of cohort, age, and time of measurement effects.

The discussion of methodological issues points to some avenues whereby concepts may be refined and methods strengthened to help advance the study of behavioral development. One area of activity needing sustained attention is the further definition and elaboration of criteria for determining appropriate representation of the dimension of historical time. Clearly there is no necessity to formulate a priori substantive problems in relation to all three dimensions. But there is a need for developmentalists to consider explicitly on theoretical grounds which particular representation (one involving one, two, or three dimensions) is likely to be the most fruitful one to explore.

In a related vein, the assumption of a confirmatory, hypothesis-testing posture provides one route to the resolution of identification problems. Assuming such a posture requires more than a conscious decision, however, if it is to amount to other than a heady exercise in the use of high-powered algebra and mathematical statistics. Testable causal networks must be articulated but they must represent serious attempts at theorizing and not simply ad hoc or a posteriori ideas reflecting the characteristics of "at hand" data. Systematically articulated and tested, however, theory-derived hypotheses can lead to a better understanding of the relationships between individual development and sociohistorical change phenomena (Nesselroade & Baltes, 1984).

B. SUMMARY

1. The course of developmental psychology has been strongly influenced by the concepts and approaches borrowed from other disciplines. The *ahistorical* paradigm of the natural sciences resulted in a slavish reliance on

chronological age as the only time parameter of importance and confused and retarded the scientific progress of developmental psychology.

2. Attempts to formulate more productive developmental models include the general developmental model of Schaie which explicitly included age, period, and cohort as distinct sources of effects, Baltes's reformulation of Schaie's model into a bifactorial one emphasizing both the pertinence for developmentalists of the Age × Cohort configuration as well as the risks involved in the use of Schaie's model for causal–analytic investigation, and Cattell's formulation of epogenic and ecogenic components of the life curve for describing and exploring developmental change.

3. Articulating conceptions of time and incorporating them into the description and explanation of developmental phenomena are among the most critical matters to be resolved. How the dimensions of historical and experimental time are to be made operational on theoretical or conceptual grounds determines the nature of the resolution of identification problems in age-, period-, and cohort-based formulations of development. There is no ubiquitous confounding of the three time parameters.

4. The importance of recognizing different temporal dimensions and understanding their differences applies to the study of antecedent conditions and processes as well as to behavior change functions in conceptions of development.

5. In developing solutions to so-called age, period, and cohort design and analysis problems, two matters must be dealt with. One is the specification of temporal relationships and the other is the identification of antecedents and the formulation of processes that account for observed behavioral change functions. The use of confirmatory, hypothesis-testing approaches will aid in resolving some of the uniqueness problems associated with the testing of developmental change models.

References

Anderson, O. D. The interpretation of Box-Jenkins time series models. *The Statistician,* 1976, *26,* 127–145.

Baer, D. M. An age-irrelevant concept of development. *Merrill–Palmer Quarterly,* 1970, *16,* 238–246.

Baltes, P. B. Longitudinal and cross-sectional sequences in the study of age and generation effects. *Human Development,* 1968, *11,* 145–171.

Baltes, P. B. Life-span developmental psychology: Some converging observations on history and theory. In P. B. Baltes & O. B. Brim, Jr. (Eds.), *Life-span development and behavior* (Vol. 2). New York: Academic Press, 1979.

Baltes, P. B., Baltes, M. M., & Reinert, G. The relationship between time of measurement and age in cognitive development of children: An application of cross-sectional sequences. *Human Development,* 1970, *13,* 258–268.

Baltes, P. B., Cornelius, S. W., & Nesselroade, J. R. Cohort effects in behavioral development: Theoretical and methodological perspectives. In W. A. Collins (Ed.), *Minnesota Symposia on Child Psychology* (Vol. 11). Hillsdale, N.J.: Erlbaum, 1978.

Baltes, P. B., Cornelius, S. W., & Nesselroade, J. R. Cohort effects in developmental psychology. In J. R. Nesselroade & P. B. Baltes (Eds.), *Longitudinal research in the study of behavior and development.* New York: Academic Press, 1979.

Baltes, P. B., & Goulet, L. R. Exploration of developmental variables by manipulation and stimulation of age differences in behavior. *Human Development,* 1971, *14,* 149–170.

Baltes, P. B., & Nesselroade, J. R. History and rationale of longitudinal research. In J. R. Nesselroade & P. B. Baltes (Eds.), *Longitudinal research in the study of behavior and development.* New York: Academic Press, 1979.

Baltes, P. B., Reese, H. W., & Lipsitt, L. P. Life-span developmental psychology. *Annual Review of Psychology,* 1980, *31,* 65–100.

Baltes, P. B., Reese, H. W., & Nesselroade, J. R. *Life-span developmental psychology: Introduction to research methods.* Monterey, Calif.: Brooks–Cole, 1977.

Baltes, P. B., & Reinert, G. Cohort effects in cognitive development of children as revealed by cross-sectional sequences. *Developmental Psychology,* 1969, *1,* 169–177.

Bronfenbrenner, U. Developmental theory in transition. In H. W. Stevenson (Ed.), *Child psychology.* Chicago: University of Chicago Press, 1963.

Buss, A. R. An extension of developmental models that separate ontogenetic change and cohort differences. *Psychological Bulletin,* 1973, *80,* 466–479.

Carus, F. A. *Psychologie zweiter Theil: Specialpsychologie.* Leipzig: Barth, 1808.

Cattell, R. B. Separating endogenous, exogenous, ecogenic, and epogenic component curves in developmental data. *Developmental Psychology,* 1970, *3,* 151–162.

Cattell, R. B., & Cattell, M. D. L. *Handbook for the Jr.–Sr. High School Personality Questionnaire "HSPQ".* Champaign, Ill.: Institute for Personality and Ability Testing, 1969.

Clogg, C. C. Cohort analysis of recent trends in labor force participation. *Demography,* 1982, *19,* 459–479.

Converse, P. E. *Cohort-analyzing party identification.* Unpublished manuscript, University of Michigan, 1976.

Damon, A. Discrepancies between findings of longitudinal and cross-sectional studies in adult life: Physique and physiology. *Human Development,* 1965, *8,* 16–22.

Elder, G. *Children of the Great Depression.* Chicago: University of Chicago Press, 1974.

Fienberg, S. E., & Mason, W. M. Identification and estimation of age–period–cohort models in the analysis of discrete archival data. In K. Shuessler (Ed.), *Sociological methodology 1979.* San Francisco: Jossey–Bass, 1979.

Glenn, N. D. Cohort analysts' futile quest: Statistical attempts to separate age, period, and cohort effects. *American Sociological Review,* 1976, *41,* 900–904.

Goldstein, H. Age, period and cohort effects—A confounded confusion. *BIAS,* 1979, *6,* 1–24.

Harris, C. W. (Ed.). *Problems in measuring change.* Madison: University of Wisconsin Press, 1963.

Jackson, D. J. *A reformulation of Schaie's model of developmental change.* Paper presented at the meeting of the Gerontological Society, Louisville, Kentucky, October, 1975.

Jackson, D. N. *Personality research form.* Goshen, N.Y.: Research Psychologists Press, 1968.

Kessen, W. Research design in the study of developmental problems. In P. H. Mussen (Ed.), *Handbook of research methods in child development.* New York: Wiley, 1960.

Kuhlen, R. G. Age and intelligence: The significance of culture change in longitudinal versus cross-sectional findings. *Vita Humana,* 1963, *6,* 113–124.

Labouvie, E. W. An extension of developmental models: Reply to Buss. *Psychological Bulletin,* 1975, *82,* 165–169.

Labouvie, E. W., Bartsch, T. W., Nesselroade, J. R., & Baltes, P. B. On the internal and external validity of simple longitudinal designs. *Child Development*, 1974, *45*, 282–290.

Mason, K. C., Mason, W. M., Winsborough, H. H., & Poole, W. K. Some methodological issues in cohort analysis of archival data. *American Sociological Review*, 1973, *38*, 242–258.

Nesselroade, J. R., & Baltes, P. B. Adolescent personality development and historical change: 1970–1972. *Monographs of the Society for Research in Child Development*, 1974, *39* (1, Serial No. 154).

Nesselroade, J. R., & Baltes, P. B. Higher order convergence of two distinct systems of personality: Cattell's HSPQ and Jackson's PRF. *Multivariate Behavioral Research*, 1975, *10*, 387–408.

Nesselroade, J. R., & Baltes, P. B. (Eds.). *Longitudinal research in the study of behavior and development*. New York: Academic Press, 1979.

Nesselroade, J. R., & Baltes, P. B. Sequential strategies and the role of cohort effects in behavioral development: Adolescent personality (1970–1972) as a sample case. In S. A. Mednick & M. Harway (Eds.), *Longitudinal research in the United States*. Boston: Nijhoff, in press.

Nesselroade, J. R., & Baltes, P. B. From traditional factor analysis to structural–causal modeling in developmental research. In V. Sarris & A. Parducci (Eds.), *Experimental psychology in the future*. Hillsdale, N.J.: Erlbaum, 1984.

Nesselroade, J. R., Schaie, K. W., & Baltes, P. B. Ontogenetic and generational components of structural and quantitative change in adult behavior. *Journal of Gerontology*, 1972, *27*, 222–228.

Price, D. O. *A respecification of variables in cohort analysis*. Unpublished manuscript, Univ. of Texas at Austin, 1976.

Quetelet, A. *A treatise on man and the development of his faculties*. Edinburg: William & Robert Chambers, 1842.

Reinert, G. Grundzüge einer Geschichte der Human-Entwicklungspsychologie. In H. Balmer (Ed.), *Die Europäische Tradition: Tendenzen, Schulen, Entwicklungslinien. Die Psychologie des 20. Jahrhunderts, Vol. 1*. Zürich: Kindler, 1976.

Reinert, G. Prolegomena to a history of life-span developmental psychology. In P. B. Baltes & O. G. Brim, Jr. (Eds.), *Life-span development and behavior* (Vol. 2). New York: Academic Press, 1979.

Riegel, K. F. Time and change in the development of the individual and society. In H. W. Reese (Ed.), *Advances in child development and behavior* (Vol. 7). New York: Academic Press, 1972.

Riegel, K. F. The dialectics of time. In N. Datan & H. W. Reese (Eds.), *Life-span developmental psychology: Dialectical perspectives on experimental research*. New York: Academic Press, 1977.

Riegel, K. F., Riegel, R. M., & Meyer, G. Sociopsychological factors of aging: A cohort sequential analysis. *Human Development*, 1967, *10*, 27–56.

Riley, M. W. Age strata in social systems. In R. H. Binstock & E. Shanas (Eds.), *Handbook on aging and the social sciences* (2nd ed.). New York: Van Nostrand Reinhold, in press.

Schaie, K. W. A general model for the study of development problems. *Psychological Bulletin*, 1965, *64*, 92–107.

Schaie, K. W. A reinterpretation of age-related changes in cognitive structure and functioning. In L. R. Goulet & P. B. Baltes (Eds.), *Life-span developmental psychology: Research and theory*. New York: Academic Press, 1970.

Schaie, K. W. Limitations on the generalizability of growth curves of intelligence: A reanalysis of some data from the Harvard Growth Study. *Human Development*, 1972, *15*, 141–152.

Schaie, K. W. Methodological problems in descriptive developmental research on adulthood and aging. In J. R. Nesselroade & H. W. Reese (Eds.), *Life-span developmental psychology: Methodological issues.* New York: Academic Press, 1973.

Schaie, K. W., & Baltes, P. B. On sequential strategies in developmental research and the Schaie-Baltes controversy: Description or explanation? *Human Development,* 1975, *18,* 384–390.

Schaie, K. W., Labouvie, G. V., & Buech, B. V. Generational and cohort-specific differences in adult cognitive functioning: A fourteen-year study of independent samples. *Developmental Psychology,* 1973, *9,* 151–166.

Schaie, K. W., & Parham, I. A. Cohort-sequential analyses of adult intellectual development. *Developmental Psychology,* 1977, *13,* 649–653.

Schaie, K. W., & Strother, C. R. A cross-sequential study of age changes in cognitive behavior. *Psychological Bulletin,* 1968, *70,* 671–680. (a)

Schaie, K. W., & Strother, C. R. The effects of time and cohort differences on the interpretation of age changes in cognitive behavior. *Multivariate Behavioral Research,* 1968, *3,* 259–294. (b)

Sörbom, D., & Jöreskog, K. G. *Confirmatory factor analysis with model modification.* Chicago: International Educational Services, 1976.

Süssmilch, J. P. *Die göttliche Ordnung in den Veränderungen des menschlichen Geschlechtes, aus der Geburt, dem Tod und der Fortpflanzung desselben erwiesen.* Berlin: Realschulbuchhandlung, 1741.

Tetens, J. N. *Philosophische Versuche über die menschliche Natur und ihre Entwicklung.* Leipzig: Weidmanns Erben und Reich, 1777.

Thurstone, L. L., & Thurstone, T. G. *SRA Primary Mental Abilities.* Chicago: Science Research Associates, 1962.

Wohlwill, J. F. *The study of behavioral development.* New York: Academic Press, 1973.

Woodruff, D. S., & Birren, J. E. Age changes and cohort differences in personality. *Developmental Psychology,* 1972, *6,* 252–259.

Zigler, E. Metatheoretical issues in developmental psychology. In M. H. Marx (Ed.), *Theories in contemporary psychology.* New York: Macmillan, 1963.

8

Individual Development and Aging as a Population Process

DAVID L. FEATHERMAN

I. Introduction

Metatheoretical statements often reorient scientific thinking about a phenomenon and have redirective implications for conventional methodology. Such is the character of this chapter, for its goals are to encourage both more creative thought about individual development and aging and a methodological approach to the study of these phenomena which is consistent with the thesis that development and aging are synonymous processes occurring within societal populations. My metatheory invites sociologists, population biologists, and other students of macrolevel processes to reconceptualize intraindividual change over the organism's life span as reflecting more than endogenously driven organismic development. It encourages collaboration with life-span psychologists who, from a contextualistic–organismic metatheoretical position, view individual development as both contextually determined and context determining (e.g., Gollin, 1981; Lerner & Busch-Rossnagel, 1981; Schneirla, 1957). At the same time it emphasizes potentially unique intellectual contributions from nonpsychological, nonpersonological conceptions of individual development and from the disci-

INDIVIDUAL DEVELOPMENT
AND SOCIAL CHANGE:
EXPLANATORY ANALYSIS

plines concerned with population genetics and the institutional features of collective life. One outcome of this intellectual dialectic among the disciplinary perspectives is an opportunity to think synthetically about the concepts of aging and development. Another is a chance to explore new methodology.[1]

II. Statement of the Thesis

Put simply, the central idea of my thesis is that individual development is the outcome of a continuing evolutionary process in which *Homo sapiens* is adapting to its changing environment. That individuals develop or change systematically after birth (and perhaps over the entire course of life) is the result of a historical or evolutionary process expressed at the level of the species and realized as a consequence of *Homo'* adaptive ascendancy within its niche through cooperative communal organization. Human social organization, itself a part of the individual's environment, is a fundamental and proximate cause of neonatal development and other age-related changes over the life span. Within this framework, processes commonly denoted as development and aging, and indeed even longevity itself, are cast as social products to be understood within the particular features of a specific societal and historical context. Among the latter are the causal bases of age stratification within social systems that lead to some level of age-graded events for a collectivity at a particular historical moment and to broad similarities in individual life courses or psychological biographies during that period.

The foregoing characterization of development emphasizes its properties as a *population process* rather than as an intraindividual process. Any given individual may develop or age in a highly unique way.[2] But such idiographic biography of rich individuality is set within limits of interindividual commonality of nomothetic change across the life span. It is only from these nomothetic patterns that developmental or age-related change can be discerned, an assertion that is defended subsequently. It is these common-

---

[1] As with all metatheoretical arguments, the organizing thesis of this chapter ultimately is not subject to disconfirmation. Only those more specific hypotheses, derived from metatheory, are. Perforce, this chapter risks sounding argumentative or too loosely provocative as it contrasts its thesis with contending contextualistic and other metatheories. It is hoped that its value to science is not diminished by these limitations but rather will encourage more carefully articulated viewpoints and derivative hypotheses.

[2] See Lerner (1983) for an excellent statement of how the individual develops through his or her passage through successive environmental contexts which are both chosen and affected by the person's presence. This process he terms *probabilistic epigenesis* to denote the stochastic nature of both individual and contextual change and their organic interrelatedness.

alities that arise from (or are caused by) the properties of the human genome, on the one hand, and of the operation of human social systems, on the other. Both the genome and the social system are intellectual abstractions that refer to interrelated products of the species' evolutionary history—so called coevolution (e.g., Lumsden & Wilson, 1981). Both are features of human population genetics and social relationships within societal or community contexts.

Thus, I have called my methatheory a *population perspective* on development and aging. It argues that individuals may manifest development, but that a causal understanding of why individuals develop or tend to manifest only certain ranges and patterns of age-related change must be based on a population level of analysis.[3]

Before I put forward the rationale for this population perspective it is advisable to define what I mean by development, for this key term differentiates my orientation from kindred contextualistic life-span metatheories (e.g., Baltes, Reese, & Lipsitt, 1980; Lerner, 1983). *Development* is one form of time-dependent change of the organism's state. This change can be quantitative, as in moving from one level of a continuous variable to another over some interval of observation; it may also be qualitative. The special feature which discriminates development from such generic quantitative and qualitative change in time is *duration dependence,* a characteristic of the rate of change. If the rate of leaving (or entering) a state is a function of the time spent in that state, then change is dependent upon duration. In other words, if I am more likely than you to move from one state of intellectual functioning or from one behavioral state to another because I have been in the current state for a longer interval, then changes in our "mini-society" of two with respect to the intellectual functions and behaviors in question are developmental. If we both are at equal risk of leaving the current state (or entering another) irrespective of our individual times in the current state, change in our two-person system is nondevelopmental.

Two implications of this definition of development are important to note at the outset. First, developmental change is equivalent to aging. Duration dependence implies that the rate of change is a function of the person's age in

---

[3] A similar point of view was stated by Melvin Marx: "It may be suggested that more attention be paid to nomothetic problems involving intra-organismic development and organization. Principles of this nature are necessarily based on similarities among individuals discovered as a result of intensive study of a number of individual subjects" (1956, p. 20). I am indebted to John Nesselroade for this citation. My position goes beyond Marx's by suggesting that causal explanations for the question, Why developmental rather than nondevelopmental change over some interval of life time?, reside in the operation of human societies, communities, and institutions, on the one hand, and in the genome of the species and other genetic subpopulations, on the other.

some reference state — his or her time spent in that state. As will be articulated below, some developmental changes are graded by birth age, while others are marked by age in state without reference to birth age per se. In this usage of development and aging as synonymous terms, a processual life-span definition is advanced rather than one based on the form, structure, or content of change. For example, development is not equated with orthogenetic principles of hierarchical differentiation and integration (e.g., Kaplan, 1983; Lerner, 1983; Werner, 1957); neither is aging equated with senescent decline and/or loss of differentiation through selective optimization of functioning (e.g., Baltes & Baltes, 1980; Strehler, 1977).

A second implication is more methodological. My approach identifies developmental and nondevelopmental changes over time from comparisons across persons — from a population of individuals constituting a given collectivity during a particular historical interval. As will be noted subsequently, it is not possible to detect which changes over some time interval are duration dependent (and therefore developmental by definition) from the analysis of the life of a single individual. Further, given the causal attributions for development that one would wish to elaborate within a population metatheory, it makes little sense to study the biography of only a single person. The latter personological approach allows one to describe intraindividual change over time; it does not permit one to say that any such change is developmental (without further assumptions about the structure or form of change — e.g., that it conforms to orthogenetic principles) or to analyze why development has or has not occurred.[4]

The rationale for my thesis is both substantive and methodological. I shall begin with the former by stating the basis for claiming that both development and aging, as commonly understood, are evolutionary products of population processes — social products, if you will. For this discussion only, development will refer to the sequential growth, differentiation, and hierarchical integration of the organism over a long postnatal period, even across the life span. It assumes individual development will manifest plasticity, or the potential for intrapersonal change (e.g., Baltes & Baltes, 1980; Lerner, 1984). Aging will refer, as with convention, to senescence of func-

---

[4] Paul Baltes put me in mind of an analogy that is of some use in differentiating the relative merits of a psychological, personological approach to development from those of the population perspective. Darwin, in constructing a theory of evolution, did not have Mendel's theory of genetic transmission of characteristics. Still, Darwin could elaborate a theory of evolution and prompt a line of empirical research. As with evolutionary research, a psychology of individual development can emerge without a full explanation of why development occurs. But just as today evolutionary biology would be heavily handicapped without the tools of modern genetics, a contextualistic developmental psychology without a science of population biology and of sociology is similarly handicapped.

tioning. The objective of this first rationale is to show that population and societal levels of analysis are appropriate to building explanations for why we develop and age.

III. Evolution, Development, and Aging: A Synergistic Relationship in Human Society

A number of behavioral and natural scientists (e.g., Gould, 1977; Lerner, 1984; Lumsden & Wilson, 1981; Washburn, 1981) recently have reevaluated evolutionary arguments about the "coevolution" of human social organization and psychological development. The upshot of this interpretation is that cooperative human communities evolved in a synergistic manner with the putatively unique cognitive capacities of *Homo sapiens;* and products of this synergistic coevolution are the specific patterns of longevity and age-related changes that demarcate human development.

The details of this coevolutionary argument can be summarized succinctly. According to the hunting hypothesis (Wilson, 1975), early *Homo* possessed several preadaptive advantages for the emergence of high cognitive capacities within its ecological niche: bipedal locomotion; prehensile, free hands for tool making; relatively high initial intelligence; and a partially carnivorous diet with access to hooved animals in the African savannah. Smallish in stature, early *Homo'* adaptive success probably was enhanced by tool making and by cooperating in the hunt. Hunting for game and avoidance of predation were rendered more successful through coordination of cooperating individuals, for which the specific capacities for language, symbolization, and "reification" (Lumsden & Wilson, 1981, p. 381) would have had high instrumental value.

These evolutionary ecological circumstances of early *Homo* are thought to have given impetus to radical changes in psychological development and longevity. One change affected the timing of maturation in the central nervous system of the neonate. Neoteny, a form of heterochronic evolutionary change (Gould, 1977), refers to the extended neonatal period of growth and maturaton that set *Homo* apart from its primate ancestors. Evolutionary research tends to link the neotenous pattern of development, especially in the cerebral cortex and in the functions it regulates, to the rather "sudden" anatomical expansion of the homonid brain. Whether the anatomical and neural changes were antecedents or consequences of a protracted neonatal developmental period within the context of an elaborating social organizaton (i.e., sexual division of labor, communal habitats, and child rearing) is unclear (e.g., see Lovejoy, 1981; Fisher, 1982). It is likely that these developments were "autocatalyzing" or mutually reinforcing in their impacts for the selective adaptaton of *Homo.*

One can argue that neoteny and the longer maintenance of juvenile physical characteristics (paedomorphism) are products of *Homo'* historical adaptation to its new niche through the mechanism of human social organization. Therefore, development, narrowly denoting processes of growth and maturation in childhood, is a product of the sociological history of human populations. The distinctively long developmental period of childhood in humans — a period of extended plasticity prior to canalization of genetic potential and a heritage of neotenous ontogeny — is linked causally to humankind's social ecology over the broad spectrum of evolutionary time (see Lerner, 1983, for an elaboration of this idea).[5]

This point of view applies with equal force to the longevity of modern *Homo,* for whom an extended postreproductive period of middle and old age has become common over the last two centuries. In an evolutionary framework, this is a sudden change. Again, the mechanism is based in human social organization — namely, technological innovations and adoption of public health practices that have extended longevity through the control of acute diseases and the postponement of chronic ones (Fries, 1980). One might say that increasingly more optimal environments for the survival of older humans enable the species to realize its full genetic potential for longevity, much in the manner that many primates in controlled zoological environments tend to survive to older average ages than their contemporaries in natural settings (Washburn, 1981).

The uniquely long preparatory and postreproductive periods of the human life course undoubtedly are connected. One could say that the

---

[5] Humankind's coevolution of genetic heritage, intellectual capacities, and social organization seems to reflect a synergistic interdependency — a complex of mutually reinforcing adaptations leading from *Homo habilis* to *Homo sapiens* in a relatively short interval of evolutionary time (see Lumsden & Wilson, 1983, pp. 154–163). Accordingly, any effort to identify cause and effect is difficult, especially given the heavily speculative interpretations of highly incomplete evolutionary evidence. My emphasis on the necessary but not sufficient role of social organization is both heuristic and consistent with at least some readings of the available evidence. For example, Lumsden and Wilson, in attempting to account for the rapidly emergent dominance of *Homo sapiens* and its advanced cognitive capacity (including the reorganization of the existing brain-to-body-mass ratio in which the cerebral cortex became a much weightier component), comment: "The combination of an already sizable brain, a primate social organization, and free hands overcame the resistance to advanced cognitive evolution that had shackled the living world during the previous two billion years" (1983, p. 163). Accepting Lumsden and Wilson's conclusion that coevolution's "products and its instruments are one and the same" (1983, p. 163), I wish to make one point — namely, that without the adaptive advantages that social organization apparently provided, it seems unlikely that psychological development in contemporary humankind would manifest plasticity over a significant portion of the life span.

explosion of material and symbolic culture, mastered throughout an extended socialization, has, this side of nuclear holocaust, provided for the extension of the life span. Some (e.g., Lerner, 1984; Baltes & Baltes, 1980) go further to suggest that the features of neotenous development that are so apparent in childhood also manifest themselves in the variability and plasticity of aging processes in late adulthood and old age (e.g., Greenough & Green, 1981). For example, intervention studies of cognitive and intellectual functioning in contemporary American elderly suggest that normally untapped reserves, or latent biogenetic capacities, can be activated so that mental performance shows less or no decline under optimal rather than typical environmental settings (e.g., Baltes & Willis, 1982). Such life-span studies of cognitive performance stress the apparently great volume of behavioral plasticity across the age spectrum — that is, a continual potential for intraindividual change and for the expression of large interindividual differences in such changes that characterizes human development. By implication, a major limitation of plasticity and variability are the features of communal life and societal process at each historical moment.[6]

[6] Neurobiological evidence (e.g., Greenough & Green, 1981) that plasticity of functioning pervades the life span also suggests that such potential may decline in advanced old age. Among current cohorts of aged humans, life experiences of restricted range, richness, and challenge might be associated with such declines. In addition, the relative recentness in evolutionary time of advanced old age is not likely to be consistent with the emergence of a direct genetic mechanism of selection for senescence (see Strehler, 1977, Chapter 10, for a review of contending hypotheses). Still, if senescence is an indirect product of selective pressure for reproductive vigor in youth (via pleiotropic action promoting senescence by the very genes which earlier promoted vigor), one might link these declines in plasticity with a genetic program for aging. However, the role of social organization in the life cycle pattern of plasticity is not obviated by this interpretation. The pleiotropic genetic pattern underlying life cycle variation probably has been reinforced by the natural history of the roles and statuses allocated to age groups.

Contentious relationships among age categories, especially over the timing and rights of accession by the younger into the more privileged statuses of the older (e.g., Foner & Kertzer, 1978; Nydegger, 1983), have been a pervasive if not dominant tone of "generational relationships" in all known societies. Oldest members of societies have rarely occupied a dominant place in community life and been provided with broad range in their environments. Whether such an arrangement of age stratification, which favors the younger and middle-aged adults (relative to a given society's pattern of longevity), has had greater adaptive value for *Homo sapiens* is open to debate. Some have argued that the relatively greater vigor, challenging and experimental behavior, and correlated neurobiological plasticity in youth, coupled with the reflective cultural "wisdom" and traditional *Verstehen* of older adults, is an evolved arrangement of human social organization that provides for optimal adaptive advantage in a changing, unpredictable environment or broad ecological range. It gives the *collectivity* of interrelated age groups a better chance to survive by increasing the reproductive success of the childbearing and rearing individuals. (See Clayton and Birren, 1980, and Baltes and Dittmann-Kohni, 1982, for speculative discussions of the development and advantages of "wisdom" in human societal functioning.)

Finally, an extension of life into advanced chronological years through human intervention has exposed *Homo sapiens* to death owing to senescence. Our forebears died from accidents and acute diseases during or shortly after the reproductive period of the life cycle. Aging as senescence always may have been latent within the genetic composition of *Homo sapiens* (see footnote 6), but its revelation over the past few hundred years is an outcome of modern culture and human social organizaton. In this fundamental sense, humans are collectively responsible for their own aging and death from senescence.[7]

IV. Individual Development: A Critique of Personological Thinking

While it is recognized by child psychologists that differences in development can reflect variability in social and cultural contexts, it is less common to recognize the converse: commonalities in behavioral change may mirror age-graded features of social systems rather than endogenous orthogenesis (e.g., Flavell, 1970). By contrast, life-span psychologists and sociologists do stress the limitation of variability by social factors (e.g., Baltes et al., 1980; Rosenmayr, 1982), so that the relative prevalence of age-graded events and social roles in childhood and their absence in old age, relative to non-normative events, help to explain the apparent patterns of increasing variability in development over the lifespan.[8] By such an argument, one might say that children "develop" while adults do not, meaning that there are more sequential, typical changes in behavior and capacity during childhood than at any other point in the lifetime of contemporary cohorts.

From a population perspective, neither the narrow definition of development nor the broader life-span conception goes far enough. The narrow denotation recognizes development as consisting of only those qualitative or quantitative changes within the individual that are sequential, irreversible,

---

[7] Cutler (1981) illustrates how choices of life-styles may influence individual variation in morbidity and mortality around the (historical) mean of longevity (viz., mean age of death for a cohort). These data reaffirm the connection between human agency and aging.

[8] For Baltes and associates (1980) and a variety of life-span developmentalists, ontogenesis, expressed as intrapersonal change from birth to death, is an embedded or contextual phenomenon. Individual development is thought to reflect three major sets of influences: (1) age-graded influences of specific biogenetic origin or sociocultural mores; (2) history-graded influences of exogenous source, acting to create existentially similar cohorts by birth or relatively contemporaneous experience; and (3) non-normative, idiosyncratic influences of an intra- and extrapersonal source that increase the heterogeneity of age- or time-related commonalities within a birth cohort as it ages.

universal, and moving toward some defnite end state. The Piagetian model of cognitive maturation in children through the mid-teen years follows such a metatheoretical, biopsychological conception of development. Taking cognitive changes as a point of reference, sociologists can only agree with life-span psychologists that biological metatheories of development are unable to embrace the longitudinal data for the intellective performances of individuals and successive birth cohorts (see Featherman, in press, and Baltes, Dittmann-Kohli, & Dixon, in press, for summaries). The life-span denotation, recognizing age-graded, history-graded, and non-normative influences on development, still phrases development as something that happens to the person or through personal agency across his or her entire lifetime (see Lerner, Chapter 6, this volume). In this contextualistic view, developmental functions can be discontinuous, reversible, and variable across subpopulations. The life-span denotation is tantamount to the view of development as any change that is a function of time, whether the latter be chronological age or some socioculture designation. However, a population perspective that incorporates the sociohistorical, evolutionary interpretations summarized above sees individual development in both the narrow and broad senses as incomplete.

By focusing on the individual, proponents of both the broad and narrow definitions of development miss what apparently are the most important bases of the distinctions that differentiate child developmental metatheories from life-span developmental models: namely, whether there are lifelong potentials for plasticity and variability in capacity and performance. Neither the theoretical systems of child development nor those of life-span psychology seem to ask the right questions or account for empirical observations within their personological metatheories. Child developmentalists, with their biologistic metatheory of physical growth and differentiation, disregard individual variability as measurement error or as nondevelopmental change. The causal source of developmental change is common biopsychological and perhaps psychosocial factors. What they do not make problematic is the source of what is common and what is variable — that is, the basis of what differentiates developmental (in their terms) from nondevelopmental change. Life-span conceptions of development suggest that the basis of differentiation might consist of age-graded, history-graded, and non-normative influences. These are expressed with differential impact across the course of life. But life-span psychological theories cannot explain why age-graded factors may dominate the childhood years or why age-grading exists, so that the ensuing developmental functions tend to take the form of sequentiality, irreversibility, and universality during these years. Nor can they account either for the irregular impact of history-graded (cohort-forming) events or the apparently greater force of non-normative events which multiply and amplify individual differences in development during mid-life and in the elder years.

In short, neither child nor life-span developmental theories of individual change seem able to explain why some time-dependent change functions are developmental and others are not (in the case of the narow definitions) or why some developmental functions (e.g., the sequential, irreversible, universal ones) are more typical of some ages than others (in the case of the broad definition). To my thinking, *development* is a term that has descriptive or definitional significance at the psychological or individual level. It has only limited analytical significance, since apparently its presence or absence at different times or in different manifestations in the human life cycle cannot be explained by individual-level processes.

To make sense out of individual development, to account for it in terms of its degrees of manifest plasticity and variability in individuals' capacities and behaviors across the life span, one must construct a new metatheory. In such a conception, individual or psychological development is a population phenomenon that reflects an outcome of societal or communal adaptations to changing environmental conditions (allowing the latter to include active agency on the environment). Development is a product of person–setting interactions within the constraints and contingencies imposed on these interactions both by aspects of collective life and the biogenetic heritage of the species. It is the latter two sets of factors which form the antecedent proximate or causal conditions in population analysis, and it is these factors that one would use to explain plasticity and variability as variables in the behaviors and capacities of individuals across their lives and of successive birth cohorts. Development is not something that a person evinces as she or he ages and that is mediated by life events and biological changes. Rather, psychological development is itself the product of societal and biogenetic population processes that create the conditions (causation) for more or less individual variability and intraindividual malleability (plasticity) across the life span and for either continuity or change in both variability and plasticity across the developmental histories of successive birth cohorts.

Lerner (1983; Chapter 6, this volume) offers a similar, contextualistic definition of development. What develops is indeed not the individual but the transactional relationship between the organism and its context, where the latter can be either external or internal (see also Dewey & Bentley, 1949; Looft, 1973; Pervin, 1968; Sameroff, 1976). Such an approach accepts the variety of age-graded, cohort-specific, and idiosyncratic non-normative agents of change to which the life-span developmentalists call attention. It is the changing composition and temporal coincidence of these major classes of influences that appear to be the driving forces for development or the markers for developmental change in the transactional framework. But if such changes are development, then the why and how of development become questions for which psychological or individual-level explanations provide few illuminating answers.

The problem is that even Lerner's transactional conception begs the question of development as a special kind of change.[9] If development is sequential and (in the population) typical age-related change, including changes in transactions, then the transactional approach, like other psychological conceptions, must seek explanations for development in the basis of this sequentiality and statistical normativity. The distinction of developmental change from other change functions, even in the transactional framework, calls for explanations at sociological and/or biological population levels, since sequential and normative (including typically non-normative) change is likely to be manifestations of evolutionary ecological processes at the population biological and societal levels.

V. A Conceptual Schema of Development as a Population Process

Figure 8.1 makes the idea of human development as a social and biological population process more concrete. One can conceive of at least three levels

---

[9] In fairness to Lerner, his contextualistic, probabilistic – epigenetic concept of development is not without a definition of development. He accepts Werner's (1948, 1957) orthogenetic principle which asserts that all developmental change proceeds from "a state of globality, or lack of differentiation, to a state of differentiation, integration, and hierarchic organization. . . . Thus, it is not the level of analysis that is crucial for determining if development has occurred. Rather, it is the features of the changes that take place that determine this" (Lerner, 1983, pp. 39–40). Allusions to conceptions of "self-organizing systems" (e.g., Prigogine, 1978, 1980) often buttress the claim that tendencies to hierarchical differentiation are part of the natural operation of the universe and all its component "systems." Such claims are intriguing but highly speculative.

Lerner's definition of development is neither more nor less arbitrary than mine, but it leads to different elaborations of a contextualistic model of individual change. Lerner's is a bi-directional model in which the person and his or her context are bound together in an organic interplay of cause and effect which defies analysis (when everything is at one and the same time a cause and a consequence of everything else and levels of analysis are disallowed; Lerner, 1983, Figure 2). Further, the hierarchical character of development seems unnecessarily restrictive. Would it not rule out developmental change for large segments of the life spans of some subpopulations, including many elderly, for whom "selective optimization" or "selective preservation" may be features of de-differentiation?

My own preference is to define development without reference to the content of change, allowing content to be a variable to be explained across persons and/or time. Development itself will refer to a specific time dependency of change—duration dependence—in which hierarchical and nonhierarchical changes both are permissible. In this manner both conventional definitions of development, qua hierarchical change, and aging, qua de-differentiating senescence, can be incorporated under a common rubric of either "developmental" change or "aging."

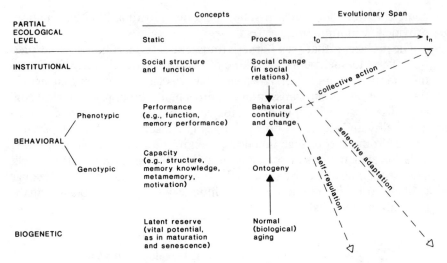

Figure 8.1 Conceptual scheme of human development and aging.

of concepts that commonly are distinguished in developmental research: the biogentic, the behavioral, and the institutional. Within the behavioral, one might subdivide the level into a "genotypic" or latent part and a "phenotypic" or manifest part. Sociologists typically focus on institutional levels; psychologists, on the behavioral; and biologists, on the biogenetic. Associated with each level are both static and process concepts. Institutional concepts refer to social structure and function at some moment in the life of a social system. Analogously, the behavioral concerns of psychologists often distinguish between the manifest performances or behavioral functions (e.g., memory performance, intellective performance, motivation) and the underlying latent capacities or structures (e.g., memory knowledge, motive, cognitive schema). At the biogenetic level, one might call attention to the vital potentials within and among cellular, molecular, and organ systems that define a latent reserve; that is, organic conditions for both capacities and performances.

In addition to static concepts there are ideas about processes at each level, processes that create the conditions for what behavioral scientists mean by development; these processes are themselves interrelated. Beginning at the biogenetic level, processes of normal aging across the components of latent reserve set biological conditions for the ontogeny of psychological capacities. Similarly, at the institutional level, changes in social relations—social change broadly construed—set conditions for ontogenetic processes at the phenotypic behavioral level that are expressed as either continuity or change in performances.

In this framework, behavioral continuity and change are products of the interplay among the three levels, although in an ultimate causal sense not all levels may play an equally important role. The hypothesis of causal import that underlies my schema of human development is that both ontogeny of capacities and continuity or change in behavior originate from patterns of social change and normal aging. Put another way, the hypothesis put forward is that behaviors and capacities are potentially likely to change (develop), and either do so or not as a function of changing (evolving) potentials in the biogenetic substrate and/or changing parameters in the societal or institutional superstrate. And at any moment, persons will develop along more versus less similar trajectories of qualitative and quantitative change according to the variabilities permitted by the social and biological changes.

For example, if a birth cohort experiences a high degree of age-graded differentiation in the developmental tasks that it is expected to master prior to adulthood, as might be illustrated in age-graded hierarchically organized school curricula in modern societies, individuals sampled from the cohort would appear to develop along (relatively) universal, sequential, unidirectional trajectories. It is interesting to note that child developmental psychology as a systematic research specialization in the United States emerged around the turn of the century, more or less coincident with the widespread establishment of age-graded school enrollment patterns in North America (Smelser & Halpern, 1978). Pedagogical thinking about the intellectual abilities of quite young children (especially under age 5) vacillated substantially up to that point, often reflecting theological or parent-centered interests (Kaestle & Vinovskis, 1978). One can only wonder how (child) development might be described within a hypothetical social context of less pervasive age-graded school enrollment and curricula. Would developmental texts differentiate child development from psychological and behavioral changes in adults? Would child development be any less variable in its individual manifestations than adult development?

Figure 8.1 also suggests that individuals' behaviors can affect their own and others' development. The mechanisms are several, and they differ with respect to the scope of time over which an effect is traced (see evolutionary span in Figure 8.1). One can distinguish mechanisms of personal self-regulation that alter one's levels of vital potential and either change the speed or direction of normal biological aging, or both. Life-style expressions in the consumption of alcohol, tobacco, and animal fats are examples of such self-regulations that affect one's ontogeny and behavioral development through the process of biological aging (e.g., Cutler, 1981). Individuals' actions in concert, or collective action, can affect development through the alteration of institutional contexts. For example, public policies or administrative decisions that establish and enforce bureaucratic organizations in schools and firms create career trajectories and life-course timetables that can affect large segments of populations and birth cohorts (e.g., Grandjean, 1981; Mayer & Muller, 1982; Meyer, in preparation). Such examples of collective action are a major basis of social change, and they affect development by altering the environmental constraints on behavioral constancy and change. Unlike individual self-regulation, collective actions exert their influences over a longer span of time and may not affect the development of individuals in the cohorts whose aggregated individual actions were the basis of the social change. Finally, social change itself can affect ontogeny and behavioral development through its impact on normal aging, although again over a longer evolutionary span. Forms of adaptation of institutions to changing physical settings (e.g., nutritional regimens during droughts or economic depressions; post nuclear settlements), sociopolitical contexts (e.g., military conscription of youth), and informational environments (e.g., longevity increases after Pasteur) can have selective implications for species survival and for culling of subpopulations. Insofar as collective actions are the major basis of social change, individuals can influence their own development through social change (via collective action) and through changes in normal aging (via aggregated self-regulation and over successive cohorts via collective action, social change, and selective adaptation).

The metatheory of development implied by Figure 8.1 is explicitly that of a biological and sociological population process working itself out in an evolutionary or historical time perspective. What one means by individual or psychological development (i.e., age-related or time-related changes in children versus changes in adults) and what developmental functions one can describe for a given birth cohort (i.e., the substance of developmental change as in plasticity, hierarchical sequentiality, and/or interpersonal variability in any content dimension of change) are not naturally given constructs. They are evolutionary products in which the contingencies and constraints of population processes and life in collectivities continue to play a preeminent role. Children develop postnatally to significant degrees because of the adaptative significance of human communities and cooperative social organizaton. Plasticity as a feature of developmental potential throughout the life span apparently follows from the same evolutionary history. Variability in developmental trajectories between children and adults and among both children and adults seems to reflect differential patterns of age-graded social institutions and their sequential alignment for substantial segments of each successive generation and birth cohort (e.g., Featherman, 1980; Kohli, 1982). Thus, individual development can neither be completely defined nor explained without reference to properties of collectivities and historical populations.[10]

VI. Developmental Change Functions in Historical Populations

Defining human development in an evolutionary ecological framework is not novel. For example, Schneirla (1957, p. 86) generalizes across all species to argue that development is the product of biological maturation (including

[10] Sociologists and other population-level analysts of aging or development are wont to focus on interindividual commonalities in time-related phenomena, whereas psychologists and other person-level analysts tend to emphasize and focus upon intraindividual phenomena. The former orientation is essentially normative; the latter, ipsative, in construing constancy and change. In principle, each approach complements the other. On the one hand, the population or normative approach is useful in identifying life-course patterns which are common clusters of time-related phenomena — the "common variance" — in a population of statistical observations of age-related phenomena. In that framework, "unique variance" at the level of the single individual or small numbers of unsystematically related individuals (lacking common variance) might be regarded as error variation or without substantive interpretation. On the other hand, an ipsative analysis of the individual as his or her own control might reveal important time-related outcomes, as is illustrated by clinical cast studies in developmental research.

The point of view taken by my population metatheory is that the normative approach is the means of discovering and analyzing life-course patterns in a societal (total variance) framework. It is variation among *and* within these patterns that constitutes the problematic data in a population analysis. Thus, total population variance, differentiated subpopulation variance, and individual variance around these subpopulation "norms" all are of substantive import. The extent of subpopulation and individual variation at any point in time (and trend over time) is in fact one of the most important features of a society to be explained within a population orientation.

In addition, the population metatheory views the ipsative, intraindividual approach as complementary only to the extent of helping to describe a case's status within the framework either of a preestablished or of a strong a priori definition of development (aging). It argues that interindividual variation must be analyzed in order to establish where and for whom "development" occurs and to interpret single-case studies. Alternatively, one must have a template or a strong a priori definition (e.g., Werner's concept of orthogenesis, or the similarly teleonomic biological growth model underlying conventional child developmental research) that frees one to study a single individual's person – context interaction out of the collective context of history and society. In a sense, the latter view freezes history and society (in adopting a strong prescriptive definition of development) except for the immediate "microsystem" (Bronfenbrenner, 1977) of the person. Lerner's (1983) probabilistic – epigenetic approach and emphasis of the highly individualized pattern of psychological and social development over the life span in many (but not all) respects falls into this approach. From the metatheoretical point of view of my thesis, such person-centered analysis is unnecessary and inappropriate, despite its emphasis of synergistic person – context causation and its value within the scope of another metatheoretical paradigm.

growth and differentiation) as guided and prompted by experience over the typical life history of all species. From insects to humans, general developmental progressions, such as physiological and behavioral rhythms, often are discovered to be driven by exogenous or environmental conditions rather than endogenous factors (1957, pp. 90–91). Among social animals, especially humankind's complex "euculture" (Lumsden & Wilson, 1981) and social organization, development takes on a more complicated construction as "experience" assumes a larger, more individually varied, more historically (temporally) variable role in development. Lerner's (1983; Chapter 6, this volume) conception of individual development as an embedded, transactional process is consistent with this view.

However, the sociological argument I have sought to expound extends the logic of evolutionary contextualism. It suggests that *human development (aging) is a sociohistorical variable to be explained by population processes at the biological and societal levels.* It proposes that human development is a special form of time-dependent process that can vary across people and history. Because it can vary as a characteristic of historical populations, different age groups, social classes, or other socially defined subpopulations may manifest differential degrees of development. To the extent that social categories capture the fullness of individual variability, these categories suggest important causal factors in developmental "experience." And developmental change can be greater or lesser in its variability across individuals (groups) and in its differentiation from nondevelopmental change in one historical moment as contrasted with another. In this conceptual framework, some humans may develop while others do not; some age categories may manifest developmental changes, but not necessarily all; adults may develop in some societies or in some epochs but not in others; developmental change may be hierarchical and sequential or it may not. These variations across people, time, and change functions become explicable only in a population framework in which they are the dependent variables—where age- or time-related changes are the dependent variables (see Wohlwill, 1973, Chapter 2, for a somewhat similar suggestion).

Behavioral, psychological, or individual development is defined or described by intraindividual change over time. A developmental function (after Wohlwill, 1973, pp. 32–35) is a prototypical or normative trajectory of change, expressed as a function of time, for a specific population of individuals in which the vagaries of idiosyncratic situational factors (e.g., illness) are sorted out in order to reveal the common diachronic pattern of intraindividual change. But precisely because the analyst is rarely able to determine before the fact which interpersonal situational factors are common causes and which are errors of measurement or other extraneous individual conditions, developmental functions can only be discerned from a population of individuals. Thus, the explanation of developmental change — accounting for normative sequences of states and/or trajectories of quantitative fluctuation in time — directs the analyst toward those factors that create developmental sequences (viz., normative or prototypical time-related changes) rather than nondevelopmental change (i.e., randomly related to time and/or highly individualistic change patterns with aging).[11] Such explanations, by definition, lead to sociological and population biological causes rather than individualistic, person-centered ones. It is only when development is taken out of its historical context that it becomes a matter of individual development rather than one of a population process. In an ahistorical framework, development is a constant, or a mode around which interindividual variability is "noise" in an otherwise personological explanation of intraindividual change.

VII. Strategies for Analyzing Human Development as a Population Process

The second rationale for the population perspective on aging (development) is methodological. In the subsequent sections of this chapter I define development more precisely, offer three important conceptual instances of developmental change as cases of age- or time-in-state-dependent phenomena, and allude to statistical strategies for the empirical study of development as aging (see Featherman, in preparation, for an extended treatment of the statistical methods and applications).

In view of metatheoretical arguments that human development is best conceived as a transactional product or evolutionary outcome of autocatalytic systems' properties in historical human populations (i.e., self-organization; Jantsch, 1980), it seems desirable to redefine the empirical study of development. The reorientation is simply to sample and record the time paths of behaviors or capacities of entities (persons) from a population (e.g., birth cohorts or series of cohorts over the historical interval that encompasses their collective lives) and to analyze these life histories for evidence of statistical commonalities in time-related change. Operationally, develop-

---

[11] This is not the same as a "non-normative event" in the sense of Baltes and associates (1980). Non-normative events can trigger quite normative time-related consequences (e.g., the 7-day common cold), even though the onset of the event itself is not typically related to age; see below. By contrast, non-normative change is simply random change in time across a population of individuals, where events or entrance into states has only individualistic consequences.

mental change is studied as an analysis of variation across population elements within some historical interval. What is identified empirically as developmental change is common variance in time dependencies of some attribute of an element.[12] Developmental change is explained by searching for those putatively causal factors that underlie the interentity commonality in time dependency. In a population framework, individual development is not studied as intraindividual change and interindividual differences in such change (e.g., Baltes & Nesselroade, 1979); it is studied via interindividual commonalities in time-dependent change.[13]

Explanations of normative, age-graded changes lie at the heart of such analytical schemes, but so do understandings of events whose manifestations create a rather uniform timetable for those who undergo them irrespective of their times ("ages") at onset. It is the organization of such events and event sequences in terms of subpopulations defined by the "age" of the process (chronological or social) that constitutes the analytical agenda and causal question for developmental research. But the primitive theoretical elements of a population conception of human development are its definitions. I shall identify and illustrate three instances of time-dependent change — age-graded transitions, event transitions, and duration dependence — and then postulate a hierarchical logical relationship among them. Elsewhere (Featherman, in preparation) I speculate about their theoretical status in building a population explanation of human development.

---

[12] Elements can be persons, other organisms, or other units of social organization. It is best not to begin by aspiring to construct a general developmental paradigm for all types of elements, including a definition of what constitutes development, since humans, animals, and institutions differ along important dimensions that figure into their relationships to their respective environments (e.g., Hannan & Freeman, 1977).

[13] The individual change paradigm of developmental psychology appears to assume a prototypical developmental function as a benchmark when it asserts that the study of development begins with the study of the individual over time (e.g., Wohlwill, 1973, p. 33; see also footnote 9). The assumption seems to be that there are species-level, largely biogenetic mechanisms that make the unfolding of one person's life history a sufficient universe for the definition and causal analysis of development. Such a point of view recognizes both interindividual commonalities and differences, but it does not make these population characteristics part of the desiderata of development. In this psychological view, individual variations generally are conceived as deviations from the "structural" basis of ontogeny (e.g., Werner, 1948, 1957). This view does not find greater or lesser population variance to be problematic for the identification or definition of developmental change. Rather, interpersonal variation is explained as exogenous or context-induced deviation from the "true" ontogenetic function. Whenever these perturbations arising from the context become pervasive, as when "non-normative" and "history-graded" influences on development dominate age-graded influences in middle and old age (Baltes et al., 1980; Baltes & Nesselroade, 1979, pp. 15–20), developmental change becomes difficult to detect and developmental psychologists differ over its existence.

A. DURATION DEPENDENCE

By definition, all change in some entity's state occurs over some temporal interval and is a function of time. The longer the interval of observation, the more likely one is to observe a state-to-state transition, or event, which can either be a qualitative or quantitative shift from the state occupied at t. To distinguish development or aging from this generic dynamic of events — from change in general — one requires a further specification, and in my metatheory the concept of duration dependence denotes that special kind of time-dependent change.

Duration dependence is a condition of the rate of change in a set of events for a societal population or some biological or social subpopulation. Just as one can characterize the speed of an automobile from its acceleration or change (increase) in speed, so one can ask if the rate of change is stationary or not. When the rate of change in the population of interest is nonconstant (nonstationary), aging or development is occurring; when the rate is constant (stationary) for all entities in the population, the observed change is not developmental change or aging.

If the rate of change is duration dependent, then persons in some developmental state (viz., in the process of leaving the state) are developing at different rates as a function of their "ages" or time spent in that state. By contrast, if the rate is stationary, all elements of the population experience the same likelihood or pace of leaving the original state at any given moment without regard to their durations or waiting times in that state. A system, or societal subpopulation, in which the rate of change is stationary is not without change. For example, in a stationary population process which also is at equilibrium, one can observe individual entities moving from state to state. However, the distribution of individual cases across the state space remains the same, or in equilibrium, despite change at the individual level. In such an example, individual change is taking place in the absence of aging or development and is a property of the *collectivity* of individuals in the subpopulation.

The definition of developmental change as a function of the rate of change, namely nonstationary or nonconstant rates of change, has two important implications. First, it allows a truly life-span approach to the study of development. The definition is freed of any specific functional form of change, a longstanding problem in reconciling developmental research on adults with that on children (e.g., Baltes, 1979, Baltes et al., 1980). It permits the synthesis of life-span research on development with life-span research on aging (e.g., Riley, 1979, forthcoming; Riley & Abeles, 1982) by making aging and development synonymous with a process whose dynamic depends on entities' "ages in state." Second, the definition explicitly calls for a comparative method of analysis within a population framework. The characteristic of being or not being stationary in the rate of change cannot be determined from the analysis of a single entity or individual. Indeed, as mentioned in the preceding paragraph, an individual can manifest change over time, even though the likelihood of his or her experiencing some event (state transition) at a given instant is neither greater nor less than another person's (that is, the likelihood is not tied to their relative "ages").

B. AGE-GRADED TRANSITIONS

The essence of development (aging) is duration dependence in the rate of interindividual change. Age-graded transitions from state to state are the most obvious and familiar instances. Consider the individual as potentially being in one and only one state at any instant. If in a population of such persons their respective likelihoods of leaving one psychological or behavioral state for another is a function of their birth ages, the event of transition is age graded. Age-graded events are characterized by common, or statistically normative, ages. The classical case of child development readily comes to mind, in which age-graded events (marked since the time of birth) are prototypically qualitative, quantitative, hierarchically unidirectional, and normative.

However, age-graded transitions need not be hierarchically unidirectional, irreversible, or correspond to calendar or birth age in the literal sense. For example, certain biological periodicities like the circadian rhythms that have approximately a 24-hour cycle (Moore-Ede, Sulzman, & Fuller, 1982) also can manifest age grading as I have used this term. Circadian rhythms conform to the definition of age-graded change because they typically are entrained to the dirunal timekeeper *(Zeitgeber)* of the day–night celestial cycle. That is, the cycle's state or "age" is chronologically common or normative in a population of persons because it is tied to specific organic responses to a commonly experienced state of the *Zeitgeber*. In this periodic or cyclical process, dawn would be equivalent to date of birth in the more commonly understood linear aging process. Yet all age-graded transitions, whether periodic or unidirectional, imply a common (normative) sequence of states by which the developmental status of the person is gauged relative to a known order among the states. Developmental change is measured by state-to-stage transitions according to a timetable that is chronological (e.g., age-specific changes or day–night periods of being asleep or awake) in that it is inherently marked by the simple ordinal relationships of before and after.[14]

The age grades consist of states or state clusters, sets of capacities, and/or performance functions that differentiate grades from each other. Since by definition time of onset (i.e., birth) does not vary across persons, what is problematic in the study of age-graded transitions is the composition of states that constitute a grade and the trajectory or sequence of grades. The mechanisms that initiate, maintain, and alter age-graded transitions are subjects for one kind of causal analysis of development within a population framework.

C. EVENT TRANSITIONS

Age-graded institutions involve duration dependence in the rates of change measured since time of birth; that is, the risk of change starts at birth. They imply a set of states which have relatively common profiles of (birth) age incumbency attached to them for a given society or subpopulation. But not all duration-dependent changes, not all development or aging, is confined to events that are experienced as a function of time since birth.

Event transitions are those where exposure to the risk of change starts with some non-age-graded event. The onset of an influenza infection, wounds from an accident, a spell of unemployment usually are not age-graded (although in historical perspective they may or may not tend to be so in the population). Still, the temporal course of the flu, the healing of a wound, and the search for a job typically are duration dependent (i.e., they have nonstationary rates of change). To the extent that they and other durations within a state are nonstationary, such states and the events that define their onset contain important developmental information.

Recognizing that such event transitions may have developmental (duration-related) consequences but yet lack an age-specific chronological onset should give one pause in thinking about adult development. Many developmentalists now describe the adult years as composed of fewer age-graded transitions and more non-normative ones (e.g., Baltes et al., 1980). The implication is either that adults do not develop, because the change trajec-

---

[14] Age grades, as states with nearly constant times of onset in the population, divide chronological time into periods of risk to one or more state-defining events. Chronological time can be marked by birth-dated ages or by other regular units of time, whether periodic or serial. Thus, age grades might best be designated as chronological grades and age-graded transitions as chronological transitions between states as measured against a universal scale of regular time units.

tories of adults become highly heterogeneous, or that they fail to manifest change functions that parallel those of children. Yet neither of these conclusions need be valid insofar as the "non-normative" events of adulthood have a normative time-dependent course among those undergoing these transitions. The distinction is crucial and illustrates the difference between event transitions and age-graded transitions. Neither is fundamentally nor inherently more developmental than the other; neither may entail more intrapersonal change over a given unit of time nor greater interindividual differences in those changes *among those exposed to the risks* of such change.

In the case of age-graded transitions, the onset of exposure (to risk) is more chronologically constant (beginning at birth) and a greater proportion of the total population is at risk than with event transitions. But in the *subpopulation* defined by the "non-normative" event, developmental changes may proceed at least hypothetically in the same fashion as characterizes age-graded transitions in the *total* population. This is important, for it implies that adult development may not be different from child development if one analyzes time-dependent changes in terms of populations exposed to events that have developmental consequences. This is to say that the characterization of the duration-dependent consequences of entry into a state should be distinguished from the developmental trajectories of persons of different ages.

This separation then allows the analyst to study development as duration-dependent transitions *within* states and also to study the duration-dependent transitions *among* states. The former are event transitions; the latter, age-graded transitions. The study of event transitions is nested within the study of age-graded transitions, since there is a logical hierarchical and temporal relationship between them. Age-graded transitions are complexes of event transitions in which the chronological times of onset are normative in the population; that is, rate of change is the same for members of a birth cohort, but it differs across cohorts (or ages of persons at any moment of observation). By studying persons according to their ages (or the same group of persons over chronological time), one tends to cast development as age-graded changes. Alternatively, by studying the subpopulation exposed to events with duration-dependent consequences, one casts development in broader conceptual and empirical terms, and one may find that the fundamental nature of development takes on the features of the temporal relationships among the events (e.g., whether they are age-graded, whether they are hierarchically sequential, whether event sequences and complexes demand compatible or conflicting behaviors and capacities, whether exposure is confined to specific subpopulations).

This distinction returns the discussion to the fundamental importance of a population frame of reference for the analysis or explanation of develop-

ment. In that perspective one attempts to answer illustrative questions such
as, Why is the onset of an event relatively constant across elements in the
population?; What is the causal basis for the serial pattern of event transitions?; Why do we observe historical variations in the age grading of events,
the seriation among events, and the population distributions of age grading
and event trajectories? Referring back to the argument underlying Figure
8.1, I suggest that answers lie in the ongoing evolutionary relationships
between biogenetic processes and in social system changes within populations and subpopulations.

With these three types of time-dependent changes in mind, what does it
mean to say that developmental behaviors are those that change over time
(e.g., Wohlwill, 1973)? What are their implications for the study of human
development as a population process? To sum up, duration dependence is a
condition that establishes that changes in state are related to aging; its presence signals that aging or development is taking place within a population.
If changes are occurring — that is, individuals are moving from state to state,
but in the *population* such changes are not dependent upon the ages (time in
state) of elements — then the system is stationary and development (aging) is
not taking place in the population. In this sense, not all changes over time at
the individual level reflect developmental changes in the population. But if
changes are dependent upon time — upon the onset and duration of exposure of each population element — then the analyst must search for those
events which mark the start of periods of risk to certain subsequent events.

This point of view is an important specification of the notion that development is a time-dependent process. It distinguishes the study of development
from the general analysis of change by linking changes that occur subsequent
to the onset of some state-defining event to the duration of time in that state
for the subpopulation which has experienced the event. Chronological age
per se (against the benchmark of birth) is not the index of time but, rather,
"age" since the onset of the state-defining event. And, in the population
framework, it is this special type of change (aging qua duration dependence)
which is the phenomenon to be explained, that is, the dependent variable.
Thus, the first step in the analysis of developmental change within a population perspective is the determination of duration dependence and its causal
explanation as a special type of change.

The second step in analyzing developmental change is the description and
explanation of time-dependent processes as event transitions which are duration dependent. To repeat for clarification: Behaviors which change over
time depend on time — are time dependent — almost by definition; but they
are not developing, in the view taken here, unless they show duration dependence for the relevant subpopulation. Event transitions are instances of
duration-dependent change in which the waiting time to leave the state —

the period of risk to change — is not correlated with birth age. Therefore, duration dependence is nested logically within event transitions, and the task of the analyst is to explain why some events do and others do not entail developmental change in the subpopulation exposed to them.

Finally, the study of developmental change must attempt to explain why some event transitions are age graded. Age-graded transitions are by definition duration dependent, because in the population the time since birth predicts who will be in each grade. On the other hand, not all event transitions are age graded, since time of onset may not be duration dependent (i.e., be tied to chronological age). One interesting logical case for analysis involves age-graded event transitions which are time dependent but in which change is not duration dependent. In this instance, time of onset of the status-defining event is duration dependent, but the changes within the state are not. In this hypothetical example, age-graded transitions cannot be perfectly serial — one following immediately upon another, as illustrated by age – set societal transitions — for in that case both age-grading and event transitions must be duration dependent since duration between and within events accounts for the full extent of time since birth.[15]

VIII. Conclusion

This chapter has been written with the aim of both specifying and broadening the understanding of human development and aging. Its central argument — that development and aging are lifelong processes of historical populations — is related to a variety of contextualistic, ecological metatheories (e.g., Bronfenbrenner, 1977; Lerner, Chapter 6, this volume; Riley, forthcoming) that encompass multiple and two-way influences between societal change and individual change over the life span. Its independent contribution is through a synthesis of a "strong" population view of developmental change with a methodological approach to the study of development through dynamic models.

The chapter takes the strong stand that development is but one form of time-related change which is transformed into duration-dependent change through evolutionary processes linking population biology with (social) institutional processes in these populations. In this framework, developmental or aging patterns by age or cohort can only be explained against the background of (1) nondevelopmental change and (2) the formation of age-

---

[15] In prototypical age – set societies, time since birth is divided into an exhaustive set of successive age grades across which a birth cohort passes as a corporate entity toward death. Empirically, such perfect cases are never observed (e.g., Foner & Kertzer, 1978).

related behavioral functions under the influence of cohort-forming events and age-graded transitions in societies over historical time. The dynamic models are the most appropriate tools for the study of how time-dependent change and development (aging) emerge as historically variable processes or differentiate the experiences of individuals across subpopulations and various sociopolitical systems. They seem to accomplish the long-sought goal of developmentalists (and gerontologists) for a way to make change (aging) the dependent variable (e.g., Wohlwill, 1973) and for integrating the study of ontogenetic change with that of institutional change.

It is at least hypothetically plausible that controversies about the presence or absence of development in adulthood and old age and the view that most changes in the latter half of life reflect idiosyncratic or non-normative events are both grounded on a misidentification and misspecification of developmental change. This chapter has offered a quite different view according to which change in time is the raw datum in which an analyst searches for developmental or duration-dependent change as a special case. By conceptually differentiating developmental changes which are age-graded in their onset from those which are simple event transitions, it has freed the concept of normative change to represent the extent of population commonality in a particular time-dependent function. Operationally, it is likely that dynamic models of change (e.g., event analysis) are more appropriate for the study of aging and development than conventional methods for cross-sectional and panel studies (Featherman, in preparation; Singer & Spilerman, 1979). Using these models, taken together with the richness of continuous event histories of state-to-state changes, one can analyze processes of change and identify the features of duration dependence, event transitions, and age-graded shifts.

My population metatheory is truly a life-span perspective. In this perspective of a population in process, development and aging are synonyms for change over the lifetime in reference to other lifetimes. By contrast, development and aging conventionally are defined so as to refer to different functional forms of change, as is implied by equating one with growth and hierarchical differentiation and the other with senescent decline. My alternative view is that this practice is needless and unwise; it assumes too much about the historical ineluctability and universality of growth and decline and leads to potentially false a priori assumptions in research on specific age subpopulations.

The population approach to development and aging that I have taken underscores the causal primacy of biogenetic and societal sources of developmental change and deemphasizes the personological or psychological ones (even while recognizing reciprocality of effects among levels). This has not been motivated by disciplinary chauvinism but rather by the logic, laid out in

Figure 8.1, that the major conditioning factors for behavioral change are either biogenetic or social structural: they are the constraints and opportunities either of individual capacities or of institutional features of collective life. While not ignoring the truism that it is human action that realizes capacity and creates social institutions, the population position insists that it does so only within the context of communities and collectivities with a historical and evolutionary legacy. That legacy is most important, both philosophically and conceptually, for the population argument. Human choice and agency, and the putatively unique neonatal development and cognitive abilities that underlie them, are themselves the products of evolutionary history in which the conditions of human social organization were a central causal element.

In the population perspective, development and aging are synonymous phenomena to be explained in terms of historical principles and the appreciation for diversity. The historical principles are those of population and evolutionary biology, which focus on biogenetic processes in the species (and subspeciation). Correspondingly, the principles for the study of historical change and process at the institutional, societal, and cultural levels also are important for understanding the evolving open social system. Psychological processes also are important, yet I view them as evolutionary products of the interplay between biogenetic and sociocultural processes in the population.

Diversity (individual differences and interindividual variation in aging), in this view, arises from evolutionary variation in the genome and in the capacities of social systems to create and tolerate individual differences, including differences in the abilities to innovate and imagine. Diversity manifests itself in historical and individual differences in life cycle patterns of constancy and change in behavior and capacity. This leads to the idea that individual development is a variable to be explained and not just described.

Out of some amalgam of biogenetic potential, humans in social interaction, faced by the conditions of their niche in the biosphere, have created communities in which the division of labor and the rewards from it are sometimes more, sometimes less, tied to age. Sometimes the link is specific to a portion of the lifetime; other times the linkage is pervasive. Sometimes some classes of persons are more visibly aging, in the sense of progressing along a society's timeline, than others. If one studies development or aging by starting with the individual, one must become lost. If one tries to explain it by starting with intraindividual change and then moving to interpersonal differences in this change, one lacks the set of observations by which explanation of change is possible. Aging, or development, is a population process.

References

Baltes, P. B. On the potential and limits of child development: Life-span developmental perspectives. *Newsletter of the Society for Research in Child Development,* 1979 (Summer), 1–4.

Baltes, P. B., & Baltes, M. M. Plasticity and variability in psychological aging: Methodological and theoretical issues. In G. E. Gurski (Ed.), *Determining the effects of aging on the central nervous system.* Berlin: Schering AG, 1980.

Baltes, P. B., & Dittmann-Kohli, F. Einige einfuhrende Uberlegungen zur Intelligenz im Erwachsenenalter. *Neue Sammlung,* 1981, *22,* 261–278.

Baltes, P. B., Dittmann-Kohli, F., & Dixon, R. A. New perspectives on the development of intelligence in adulthood: Toward a dual-process conception and a model of selective optimization with compensation. In P. B. Baltes & O. G. Brim, Jr. (Eds.), *Life-span development and behavior* (Vol. 6). New York: Academic Press, in press.

Baltes, P. B., & Nesselroade, J. History and rationale of longitudinal research. In J. R. Nesselroade & P. B. Baltes (Eds.), *Longitudinal research in the study of behavior and development.* New York: Academic Press, 1979.

Baltes, P. B., Reese, H. W., & Lipsitt, L. P. Life-span developmental psychology. *Annual Review of Psychology,* 1980, *31,* 65–110.

Baltes, P. B., & Willis, S. Plasticity and enhancement of intellectual functioning in old age: Penn State's Adult Development and Enrichment Project (ADEPT). In F. I. M. Craik & S. E. Trehub (Eds.), *Aging and cognitive processes.* New York: Plenum Press, 1982.

Bronfenbrenner, U. Toward an experimental ecology of human development. *American Psychologist,* 1977, *32,* 513–531.

Clayton, V., & Birren, J. The development of wisdom across the life span: A reexamination of an ancient topic. In P. B. Baltes & O. G. Brim, Jr. (Eds.), *Life-span development and behavior* (Vol. 3). New York: Academic Press, 1980.

Cutler, R. G. Life-span extension. In J. L. McGaugh & S. B. Kiesler (Eds.), *Aging: Biology and behavior.* New York: Academic Press, 1981.

Dewey, J., & Bentley, A. F. *Knowing and the known.* Boston: Beacon, 1949.

Featherman, D. L. Schooling and occupational careers: Constancy and change in worldly success. In O. G. Brim, Jr. & J. Kagan (Eds.), *Constancy and change in human development.* Cambridge, Mass.: Harvard University Press, 1980.

Featherman, D. L. The life-span perspective in social science research. In P. B. Baltes & O. G. Brim, Jr. (Eds.), *Life-span development and behavior* (Vol. 5). New York: Academic Press, in press.

Featherman, D. L. Biography, society and history: Individual development as a population process. In A. B. Sørensen, F. Weinert, and L. Sherrod (Eds.), *Human development: Interdisciplinary perspectives.* Manuscript in preparation.

Fisher, H. E. Of human bonding. *The Science,* 1982, *22,* 18–23; 31.

Flavell, J. H. Cognitive changes in adulthood. In L. R. Goulet & P. B. Baltes (Eds.), *Life-span developmental psychology: Research and theory.* New York: Academic Press, 1970.

Foner, A., & Kertzer, D. I. Transitions over the life course: Lessons from age-set societies. *American Journal of Sociology,* 1978, *83*(5), 1081–1104.

Fries, J. Aging, natural death, and the compression of morbidity. *New England Journal of Medicine,* 1980, *303,* 130–135.

Gollin, E. S. Development and plasticity. In E. S. Gollin (Ed.), *Developmental plasticity: Behavioral and biological aspects of variations in development.* New York: Academic Press, 1981.

Gould, S. J. *Ontogeny and phylogeny.* Cambridge, Mass.: Belknap Press, 1977.

Grandjean, B. D. History and career in a bureaucratic labor market. *American Journal of Sociology,* 1981, *86*(5), 1057–1092.

Greenough, W. T., & Green, E. J. Experience and the changing brain. In J. L. McGaugh, J. G. March, & S. B. Kiesler (Eds.), *Aging: Biology and behavior.* New York: Academic Press, 1981.

Hannan, M. T., & Freeman, J. The population ecology of organizations. *American Journal of Sociology,* 1977, *82*(5), 929–964.

Jantsch, E. *The self-organizing universe: Scientific and human implications of the emerging paradigm of evolution.* Oxford: Pergamon Press, 1980.

Kaestle, C. F., & Vinovskis, M. A. From apron strings to ABCs: Parents, children, and schooling in nineteenth-century Massachusetts. In J. Demos & S. S. Boocock (Eds.), *Turning points: Historical and sociological essays on the family.* Chicago: University of Chicago Press, 1978.

Kaplan, B. A trio of trials. In R. M. Lerner (Ed.), *Developmental psychology: Historical and philosophical perspectives.* Hillsdale, N.J.: Erlbaum, 1983.

Kohli, M. *Social organization and subjective construction of the life course.* Paper presented at the International Conference on Life-Course Research on Human Development. Max-Planck Institut fur Bildungsforschung, Berlin, 1982.

Lerner, R. M. *The plasticity of individual–social context relations across life: A dynamic interactional model.* Paper presented at the American Sociological Association meeting in Detroit, Mich., 1983.

Lerner, R. M. *On the nature of human plasticity.* New York: Cambridge University Press, 1984.

Lerner, R. M., & Busch-Rossnagel, N. A. Individuals as producers of their development: Conceptual and empirical bases. In R. M. Lerner & N. A. Busch-Rossnagel (Eds.), *Individuals as producers of their development: A life-span perspective.* New York: Academic Press, 1981.

Looft, W. R. Socialization and personality throughout the life-span: An examination of contemporary psychological approaches. In P. B. Baltes & K. W. Schaie (Eds.), *Life-span developmental psychology: Personality and socialization.* New York: Academic Press, 1973.

Lovejoy, C. O. The origin of man. *Science,* 1981, *221,* 341–350.

Lumsden, C. J., & Wilson, E. O. *Genes, mind, and culture.* Cambridge, Mass.: Harvard University Press, 1981.

Lumsden, C. J., & Wilson, E. O. *Promethean fire: Reflections on the origin of the mind.* Cambridge, Mass.: Harvard University Press, 1983.

Marx, M. H. Sources of confusion in attitudes toward clinical theory. *Journal of General Psychology,* 1956, *55,* 19–30.

Mayer, K. U., & Müller, W. *The development of the state and the structure of the life course.* Paper presented at the International Conference of Life-Course Research on Human Development. Max-Planck Institut fur Bildungsforschung, Berlin, 1982.

Meyer, J. The institutionalization of the life course and the effect on the self. In A. B. Sørensen, F. Weinert, and L. Sherrod (Eds.), *Human development: Interdisciplinary perspectives.* Manuscript in preparation.

Moore-Ede, M. C., Sulzman, F. M., & Fuller, C. A. *The clocks that time us: Physiology of the circadian timing system.* Cambridge, Mass.: Harvard University Press, 1982.

Nydegger, C. Family ties of the aged in cross-cultural perspective. *The Gerontologist,* 1983, *23*(1), 26–32.

Pervin, L. A.   Performance and satisfaction as a function of individual–environment fit. *Psychological Bulletin,* 1968, *69,* 56–68.

Prigogine, I.   Time, structure, and fluctuation.   *Science,* 1978, *201,* 777–785.

Prigogine, I.   *From being to becoming.*   San Francisco: Freeman, 1980.

Riley, M. W.   Introduction: Life-course perspectives.   In M. W. Riley (Ed.), *Aging from birth to death.*   Washington, D.C.: American Association for the Advancement of Science, 1979.

Riley, M. W.   Age strata in social systems.   In R. Binstock & E. Shanas (Eds.), *Handbook of aging and the social sciences* (2nd ed.).   New York: Van Nostrand, forthcoming.

Riley, M. W., & Abeles, R.   Introduction: Life-course perspectives.   In M. W. Riley, R. P. Abeles, and M. S. Teitelbaum (Eds.), *Aging from birth to death* (Vol. 2).   Boulder, Colo.: Westview Press, 1982.

Rosenmayr, L.   Biography and identity.   In T. Hareven & K. J. Adams (Eds.), *Aging and life-course transitions: An interdisciplinary perspective.*   New York: Guilford Press, 1982.

Sameroff, A. L.   Transactional models in human development.   *American Psychologist,* 1976, *31,* 689–700.

Schneirla, T. C.   The concept of development in comparative psychology.   In D. B. Harris (Ed.), *The concept of development.*   Minneapolis: University of Minnesota Press, 1957.

Singer, B., & Spilerman, S.   Mathematical representations of developmental theories.   In J. R. Nesselroade & P. B. Baltes (Eds.), *Longitudinal research in the study of behavior and development.*   New York: Academic Press, 1979.

Smelser, N. J., & Halpern, S.   The historical triangulation of family, economy, and education.   In J. Demos & S. S. Boocock (Eds.), *Turning points: Historical and sociological essays on the family.*   Chicago: University of Chicago Press, 1978.

Strehler, B. L.   *Time, cells, and aging* (2nd ed.).   New York: Academic Press, 1977.

Washburn, S. L.   Longevity in primates.   In J. L. McGaugh, J. G. March, & S. B. Kiesler (Eds.), *Aging: Biology and behavior.*   New York: Academic Press, 1981.

Werner, H.   *Comparative psychology of mental development.*   New York: International Universities Press, 1948.

Werner, H.   The concept of development from a comparative and organismic point of view.   In D. B. Harris (Ed.), *The concept of development.*   Minneapolis: University of Minnesota Press, 1957.

Wilson, E. O.   *Sociobiology: The new synthesis.*   Cambridge, Mass.: Harvard University Press, 1975.

Wohlwill, J. F.   *The study of behavioral development.*   New York: Academic Press, 1973.

9

Individual Development in Social Action Contexts: Problems of Explanation

JOCHEN BRANDTSTÄDTER

I. Introduction

Developmental psychology is about to rediscover the active role of the individual in shaping his or her own development. Growing emphasis is placed on the view that human development can be comprehensively explained only by analyzing the social and cultural action contexts which instigate and regulate it (Lerner & Busch-Rossnagel, 1981; Brandtstädter, in press). Of course such an "actionist" conceptualization of development cannot claim originality. It has precursors in the social – philosophical writings of Vico and Hegel and can be traced back further to ancient Greek philosophy (see Bunge, 1979). Today, however, there is more empirical evidence than ever before to substantiate the view that human development, even in its basic biological aspects, is to a large extent a modifiable process and a cultural product.

In postulating an "action" approach to human development we are faced with serious epistemological and methodological problems which need to be more thoroughly investigated. Some of these problems are intrinsically related to the concept of action, with its aspects of goal-relatedness, rule orientation, reflexivity, freedom of choice, and self-determination. I will elaborate this point in later sections. We may get a first glimpse of these problems from Plato's paradigm of developmental construction: the metaphor of an artist fashioning a sculpture. The initial stage of the artistic process comprises of certain material and ideational elements: for example, the tools, the uncut raw material, the professional knowledge of the artist. During the executive phase the artistic object goes through series of cognitively controlled, mechanically mediated transformations, which may be conceptualized—in modern terminology—as a sequence of TOTE (test–operate–test–exit) cycles. The final product is distinct from the uncut piece of work not only in outer appearance; it is the more or less successful realization of an action plan. As such, it is—like any other cultural product—a carrier of meaning. Historians of subsequent ages might undertake hermeneutic efforts to reconstruct this meaning.

As a metaphor for human development, Plato's paradigm admittedly has shortcomings. One may take offense at thinking of humans as the "material" for modification. The individual as producer or coproducer of his own development is, of course, both the subject and object of action. Furthermore, human development is not a monothematic process. Rather, it must be conceptualized as "multidirectional" and "multicontextual"; that is, functionally different trajectories and different regulative levels of development can be distinguished. It could also be argued that the making of an instrument which serves some extrinsic purpose might be a more appropriate metaphor for guided human development than the paradigm of artistic production. Nevertheless, let me contemplate the given paradigm a little further.

Obviously, there are different approaches to the problem of explaining or reconstructing the formation of an artistic product. From a natural science perspective one might perhaps be interested in the mechanical, biochemical, or neurophysiological processes involved in the production. From a cultural science perspective, however, it seems more appropriate to reconstruct the reasons, motives, and constraints of the artist's constructive work: to analyze his action situation with regard to guiding aesthetic ideals, technical knowledge, expressive intentions, and so on—factors which in turn may be related to belief systems, value patterns, and action potentials constituting the historical and cultural background of action.

Clearly such an approach provides only partial explanation, but it focuses on just those aspects that are relevant for understanding the work as a cultural product. It seems that "why" questions in the context of social and cultural sciences differ in basic respects from those raised in the context of natural sciences.

Like artificial construction, human development is more than a multidimensional time-related change process: It is an actively regulated and culturally constructed process. This seriously limits the generalization of developmental patterns beyond the actual cultural context with its constituent development-related belief structures, value patterns, and modification potentials (Gergen, 1980). Can the conception of a "nomothetic" developmental psychology aimed at universal laws of development be maintained under such conditions, or does developmental psychology have to be reconceptualized instead as a "science of individuality" (Shotter, 1980)? Is there a basic methodological gap between the natural and social or cultural sciences passing across developmental psychology, or can these branches of research be integrated into a common methodological framework? These are the key questions with which we will deal in the remainder of the chapter. Considering the newly invigorated metatheoretic discussions about "explanation and understanding" in the human and social sciences (see Apel, Manninen, & Tuomela, 1978; Riedel, 1978), these questions seem to have considerable programmatic importance.

II. Laws and Quasi Laws, Plasticity and Universality of Development

Unimpressed by ongoing discussions about the possibility of strictly universal laws in the social sciences (see Krimerman, 1969), many, if not most, psychologists favor a nomological interpretation of their discipline (e.g., Herrmann, 1979). This favored interpretation, however, sometimes involves a sloppy use of the concept of scientific law. The bulk of generalizations in psychological research and theorizing can hardly be interpreted in a strictly nomological sense.

Consider for example the "inventory of scientific findings" in psychology collected by Berelson and Steiner (1964). What we find is a rather heterogeneous mixture of plain empirical generalizations (e.g., "The earlier the socialization, the stronger the guilt feelings," p. 71; "Most people do not recall all their dreams in the morning," p. 175), of contingencies which are obviously specific to certain historical and cultural contexts (e.g., "The higher the class, the later the age at marriage and the greater the number of unmarried women," p. 482; "Lower class children get less encouragement from their families to continue their education," p. 470), and of lawlike propositions, which on a closer look hardly differ from definitions or tautological statements (e.g., "The farther the distance between classes, the less movement between them," p. 471; "Stimulation and contact — physical, mental, social — are necessary for normal human development," p. 64). Very few if any of the general propositions in this comprehensive collection can claim universal validity in the nomological sense.

Considering the notoriously limited "generalizability" of psychological findings, the realization of a nomological program in psychology seems to face great difficulties. Actually, alleged law formulations in psychology usually refer to contingent regularities, which hold only under specific and by no means invariant social, cultural, and historical context conditions. Uniformities of this kind have to be distinguished from laws that in the nomological sense contain neither individual constants nor spatiotemporal limitations; at best, such uniformities may be designated as "quasi-laws" (see Albert, 1966). For purposes of explanation or prediction in psychology, we certainly cannot dispense with quasi-laws. By eliminating them, we would reduce the body of accumulated psychological knowledge to scanty fragments (see Lenk, 1979a). It is the unjustified nomological generalization of quasi-laws, rather than the use of hypothetical quasi-laws, that needs to be criticized in psychology. Premature nomological interpretations tend to block further inquiry into the formative and sustaining conditions of quasi-lawful regularities. Only through such research, however, can progress toward the ideal of universal theories be achieved.

If human development is a plastic, culturally regulated process, it might seem utopian to expect more from developmental psychology than just local generalizations of the quasi-law type. As mentioned above, a host of research findings document the cultural and historical relativity and ecological variability of developmental patterns. Examples include Age $\times$ Cohort interactions for developmental functions in the personality and ability domain, transcultural variations in socialization patterns for gender identity and occupational roles, as well as historical changes in development-related beliefs or values (Baltes & Baltes, 1980; Baltes, Reese, & Lipsitt, 1980). Human development is placed in a regulative framework of interacting and conflicting resources, potentials, goals, and demands on the individual and the social level—factors that are, in turn, subject to evolutionary and sociocultural changes. Thus, should we not prepare to revise developmental psychology continuously for each successive period and generation (Montada, 1979)? Should we not meet any nomological claims in developmental psychology with skepticism (Gergen, 1980)?

Such critical questions are frequently countered by the argument that there is a "basic stock of universal competencies" in human development (Kagan, 1979). Indeed, cross-cultural comparisons of developmental patterns are often impressive more because of the universality than because of the specificity of findings. Neonates of different cultures or ethnic groups have a similar reflex repertoire; there are highly invariant basic patterns in early affective and cognitive development (e.g., in the manifestation of separation anxiety, in the development of epistemic motivations, in the formation of the object concept in the Piagetian sense); there are universal structural–linguistic aspects of language and language development (for further discussion, see Dasén, 1977; Kagan, 1979; Warren, 1980).

How can these seemingly contradictory positions be reconciled? In my opinion, controversies about the plasticity–universality issue in developmental psychology often suffer from certain methodological flaws. First and foremost, it is a mistake to believe that the dispute about the possibility of universal law formulations in developmental psychology can be settled by pointing to empirical results from cross-cultural or transgenerational generalizability studies. There is, of course, much to recommend the methodological rule: to avoid the mistake of nomologically universalizing local quasi-laws, the relationship in question should be tested under varied sociocultural circumstances (Gadenne, 1978). This recommendation holds at least as long as one does not bother about the notorious problems of methodological falsificationism (Stegmüller, 1980). But low generalizability or high contextual specificity of developmental finding does not by any means exclude the possibility of reducing the observed variation to invariant basic processes. Contextual invariance of a developmental pattern, in turn, is not sufficient to substantiate nomological universality because the observed stability may only be due to the fact that critical contextual conditions (e.g., intervention motives, modification potentials, relevant ecological conditions) have not been changed or have even been actively stabilized within the cultural or historical range studied. Generalization studies can only span a limited empirical range, so they are themselves subject to a generalization problem. Since generalizations cannot be defended on a purely inductive basis, successful transcontextual replication is not sufficient to justify any universality claims. It might be added parenthetically that this is the weak point of the original Campbell–Stanley theory of external validity (Gadenne, 1976). How then can universality claims be substantiated? Although there is as yet no generally accepted explication of the scientific law concept, there is nevertheless a fairly general agreement that lawful relations in the strict sense differ from mere contingent uniformities in being not only general but also inevitable (Hanson, 1958; Kamlah & Lorenzen, 1967). Universal validity in this strict sense cannot be conclusively substantiated by empirical evidence alone; it has to be substantiated on a stronger deductive basis. We will elaborate this viewpoint in the following section.

The universality–plasticity controversy in developmental psychology suffers not only from an insufficient distinction between laws and empirical generalizations but also from a related confusion of different epistemological levels in research and theorizing. More specifically, there is often no clear distinction between developmental patterns and the processes which generate such patterns. Elsewhere I have sketched an epistemological model that may help to bridge the gap between "universalistic" and "relativistic" viewpoints. In the proposed model the following epistemological levels for research on human development are recognized (Brandtstädter, in press):

1. *Modeling of data systems:* Descriptive – statistical systematizations such as contingency tables, correlation matrices, time series, and so on;
2. *Modeling of generative developmental systems:* Construction of models that help to explain, understand, or reconstruct the formation of empirical patterns on Level 1.

To account for higher-level developmental changes that involve generative developmental systems (e.g., evolutionary or sociocultural system changes), we have to proceed to a third epistemological level (and eventually to further ones):

3. *Modeling of generative metasystems of development:* Construction of models which help to explain, understand, or reconstruct the formation and change of generative systems modeled on Level 2.

The model allows for different levels of generality. Through epistemological transitions from lower to higher levels the empirical variability of developmental data patterns and context-specific quasi-laws can be successively reduced to more general developmental principles. The reconstruction of empirical correlation systems through causal models or systems of structural equations (e.g., Rogosa, 1979) represents a typical example of such reduction. However, we should note that many causal models in developmental psychology obviously involve antecedent – consequent relationships of a quasi-law type and thus call for further explanatory analyses. At this juncture, we again touch upon the question of whether a nomological, or causal – analytic, scheme is appropriate to explain or reconstruct the formation of developmental patterns in a cultural action context. We will address this question later and now turn to another methodological problem which is intimately related to the issues discussed thus far.

III. Structural Implications and "Pseudoempirical" Research in Developmental Psychology

In the previous section I argued that the universal necessity of a lawful relationship can be conclusively ascertained only — if at all — on an a priori basis, namely, by demonstrating that the relation can be derived from necessarily true propositions or structural implications. At this juncture, it seems

worthwhile to take a closer look at the distinction between structural implications and contingent empirical relationships and at the consequences of
confusing empirical and structural relations in developmental psychological
research (see also Brandtstädter, 1982).

A. DISTINGUISHING BETWEEN STRUCTURAL IMPLICATIONS AND EMPIRICAL HYPOTHESES

For a first rough approximation we will characterize structural implications as relationships that are implied by the formal or semantic structure of
a concept and which, therefore, do not have to be empirically tested but can
be derived by appropriate conceptual analysis. Thus, structural implications correspond to a priori propositions in the traditional Kantian sense (for
a more refined explication of a priori or nonempirical truth see Lorenzen,
1969). Common examples of a priori true propositions are: "$2 + 4 = 6$";
"In a Spanish opening in chess, White opens *Pawn e4* and Black answers
Pawn e5"; "Events which have not yet occurred cannot be remembered." Of
course, an understanding of such sentences presupposes certain structural
learning experiences. But certainly one who understands the sentences will
not attempt empirical investigations in order to test them. The validity of
the sentences can be shown by reference to the accepted meaning or to the
construction rules of the terms involved.

Unfortunately, the nonempirical character of certain propositions is not
always as obvious as in the given examples. In the social sciences and
especially in psychology it is often not evident whether a proposition is to be
considered a definition or meaning postulate or an empirical research hypothesis; statements like "Aggression implies frustration," "Social shyness is
a correlate of introversion," or "A positive self-concept is a necessary condition for mental health" may be considered to be examples of such equivocal
propositions. There are also cases in which some methodological sophistication is needed to unmask the nonempirical character of a proposition.
For example, there is empirical evidence that in a sociogram in which each
subject has at least one vote, the resulting structure implies weak cliques;
however, graph-theoretical analysis shows that this is not an empirical law
but a necessary structural relationship resulting from the fact that it is impossible to connect k nodes by k or more directed arrows without producing a
cyclic substructure (Lenk, 1975a). Likewise, it is a recurrent finding that if
all individuals with a certain fixed sum score are selected from an n-variate
distribution, the intercorrelations of the n variables within this subsample
are attenuated, a finding which again is not an empirical law but an inevitable consequence of the linear restriction imposed by selection. The exam-

ples considered show that structural implications, although without empirical content, are not necessarily trivial or uninstructive. The examples highlight the fact that only on the basis of explicit semantic or formal structure
analyses can we differentiate between structural implications and empirical
hypotheses; the distinction is not an absolute, but a relative one.

B. THE FUSION OF ANALYTICAL AND EMPIRICAL ELEMENTS IN THE DEFINITION OF THEORETICAL TERMS

For theoretical concepts, we can roughly distinguish two aspects of meaning (Stegmüller, 1970): (1) empirical meaning, which is given to the theoretical term by connecting it, via correspondence rules, to observational or,
more generally, pretheoretical terms; (2) structural meaning, which results
from the contextual relationship of the theoretical term to other concepts
within the conceptual net of a theory. If we further stipulate that theoretical
networks should be open for elaboration, differentiation, and partial revision of their conceptual structure, it must be recognized that, contrary to
early neopositivist or operationalist positions, the meaning of theoretical
terms cannot be exhausted by a finite set of empirical reduction postulates,
and even less so by single operational definitions (see also Cook & Campbell,
1979). Intelligence, of course, is not only what the intelligence test measures
but something which has to be sufficiently determined on the conceptual
level before we can attempt to measure it (for a more detailed critique of the
operationalist approach see Lenk, 1975b).

If we propose a list of reduction statements in order to give a partial
interpretation of theoretical terms, the list will usually contain sufficient
reduction statements (of the general format: For all individuals p, if p under
testing conditions T_i shows the behavior B_i, then p has the disposition D) as
well as necessary reduction statements (for all p, if p has D, it shows B_j under
T_j). Such a list of reduction statements has some interesting and seemingly
paradoxical features. On the one hand, it implies empirical hypotheses.
From the conjunction of a necessary with a sufficient reduction statement
we can deduce an empirical relationship of the general form: For all p, if p
shows B_i under T_i, the p shows B_j under T_j. It follows that an interpretative
system containing necessary and sufficient reduction statements is not a
purely definitional or analytic construction. On the other hand, the system
cannot be considered purely empirical. Although some reduction postulates might be eliminated from the list in light of contradictory evidence,
others are so central to the meaning of the theoretical term in question that
they cannot be eliminated.

Let us consider as an example the explication of the term "want" (see also Brandt & Kim, 1963). The following reduction statements could be proposed (where *P* stands for "person," *O* for "object," and *PwO* for "*P* wants *O*"): (1) For all *P*, if *PwO*, the *P* shows a pupillary dilation when he or she perceives *O*. (2) For all *P*, if *P* enjoys the occurrence of *O*, then *PwO*. Obviously, in light of empirical evidence reduction statement 1 could be more easily dropped from the list of reduction statements than reduction statement 2. Whoever argued against the second reduction statement could be suspected of not knowing what "want" means.

We see that systems of meaning postulates or reduction statements are a strange amalgamation of analytical and empirical elements. Stegmüller (1969) characterizes them as "quasianalytical" systems. In a similar vein, Lenk (1975b, p. 180) states that, contrary to operationalist conceptions, "conceptual and empirical elements . . . are inextricably linked" in the definition of theoretical terms. The above considerations suggest that we distinguish between a structural core and a marginal "core extension" of theoretical concepts (Herrmann, 1976); the demarcation between the core and the margin of a concept, however, may be fuzzy.

C. THE CONFUSION OF STRUCTURAL IMPLICATIONS AND EMPIRICAL RELATIONS IN DEVELOPMENTAL RESEARCH

For developmental psychology, an interesting consequence of the preceding considerations is that conceptual structures may imply developmental sequences. If, for example, a developmental task or state B conceptually implies another developmental task or structure A, then A is a conceptually necessary condition for B and B cannot be attained prior to A. As was mentioned before, the derivation of such structurally implied developmental sequences presupposes conceptual–analytic efforts. It seems that the importance of such analytic efforts, which provide the very basis of meaningful research, is seriously underrated in developmental psychology. As a consequence, structural implications are often confused with research hypotheses and "empirically tested." Two examples of such confusion taken from developmental psychological research will be considered more closely.

The first example comes from moral development research. Central to the "cognitive developmental approach" to moral judgment (e.g., Kohlberg, 1976) is the proposition that certain social–cognitive competencies of "role taking," "perspective taking," and so on, which obviously are involved in the interpretation or understanding of actions in social contexts, are necessary (but not sufficient) conditions of competent moral judgment. Numerous investigations have been conducted in order to test this proposition empirically (see Selman, 1976). Nevertheless, it seems possible to derive this assumption as a structural implication from a conceptual analysis of moral judgment. Competent moral judgment obviously requires the competent use of moral predicates such as "guilty," "responsible," and so on. According to accepted rules of moral language it is, for example, not only unjust but also conceptually inappropriate to hold an individual responsible for a behavioral event that is known or perceived to be out of the individual's control. Thus, a critical prerequisite of competent moral judgment is the distinction between involuntary or forced (non-actional) behavior and controlled action. Furthermore, to the extent that a given behavior can be reconstructed as a controlled action, the moral evaluation of the action presupposes an analysis of the action situation with respect to the actor's goals, expectations, perceived behavioral freedom, and so on; such analyses may form the basis of exculpatory explanations (see Baier, 1970). Hence competent moral judgment, in presupposing the competent use of moral language, implies just those action-interpretative or hermeneutic processes to which concepts such as "role taking" or "perspective taking" refer. This implication, however, is not an empirical but a conceptual relation. Attempts to empirically test this relation seem questionable because the relation is one of the conceptual criteria to which we must refer when constructing a valid measure of competent moral judgment (this problem is comparable to the "theoreticity" of measurements in physics; Stegmüller, 1980).

The second example of confusing structural implications and empirical relations comes from research on semantic memory and language acquisition. Here a basic assumption is that the meaning of words is embedded in structural networks consisting of interrelated semantic components. Hence, it should be possible to derive developmental sequences in language acquisition from an analysis of these semantic interrelations. Using the semantic memory model of Norman and Rumelhart (1975) as a frame of reference, Gentner (1975) has in this manner derived a sequence of acquisition for possession verbs. She first performed a conceptual dependency analysis showing, for example, that the semantic structure of the verb "trade" entails the semantic structures of "give" and "take." From these semantic analyses several developmental hypotheses were derived, such as the proposition that the acquisition of "trade" presupposes the acquisition of "give" and "take." These hypotheses were then empirically substantiated by age-comparative experiments. It should be noted, however, that the conceptual dependency analyses from which the developmental propositions were derived evidently do not aim at a mere description of factual language patterns but rather at a reconstruction of competent language use.

Hence, the derived acquisition sequences should be considered as structural implications rather than as empirical hypotheses. Indeed, the act of trading entails the acts of giving and taking not empirically but conceptually; these acts are constituent parts of the action scheme of trading. If the word "trade" is used by a subject in a way that does not conform to these stipulations, this does not falsify an empirical hypothesis but violates a conceptual rule. In the socialization context of a verbal community such rule violations are followed by regulative actions to bring about "correct" language behavior. This fosters the convergence of factual developmental patterns with idealized conceptual structures. Conceptually implied and culturally constructed developmental sequences of this type, however, cannot be equated with natural process laws.

Research-guiding conceptual core structures cannot be considered to be causal structures as long as we retain the Humean concept of causality which postulates the logical independence of causes and effects. Rather, these core structures should be considered as idealized or prototypical constructions. This is not to say that they are or should be immune from revision. It cannot be the task of empirical research to "falsify" such ideal-type constructions; research efforts of this kind could indeed be characterized as "pseudoempirical" (Smedslund, 1979). Empirical research may describe the extent to which these ideal-type constructions are factually realized, analyze the conditions relevant to their realization, and check whether a given empirical representation or interpretation of conceptual core elements yields a successful organization of experience.

IV. Developmental Psychology as a Natural and Cultural Science: Problems of Integration

We have argued that in most cases empirical uniformities in developmental psychology cannot be nomologically generalized. A developmental trajectory is not in itself "variable" or "stable" to a greater or lesser extent; its apparent stability or variability is rooted in a given cultural action context with certain interests and potentials of developmental modification. Even physiological and somatic maturation patterns must, to a large degree, be relativized to a given cultural situation which provides and controls certain critical developmental conditions (Garn, 1980). If development is considered a joint product of hereditary and environmental conditions, then environment clearly must be conceived of as a cultural environment, that is, as an artificial developmental ecology which has been arranged to meet certain interests and (developmental) values and, as Gehlen (1971) put it, has become the "second nature" of man. Hence, in contrast to a strict causal–

nomological position stipulating invariant cause – effect relations (if A, then B follows invariably), a voluntaristic stance often seems more appropriate for systematizing experience in developmental psychology: if A, then B, as long as the relevant social context has neither the interest nor the pertinent knowledge to change this relationship (Watkins, 1957).

A comprehensive understanding of human development thus seems to imply two different tasks: first, the explanation of natural (biochemical, biophysical, biogenetic, etc.) mechanisms on which human development in its physical aspects depends, and second, the reconstruction of the human action and decision contexts which constitute the historical and cultural basis of development. Developmental psychologists agree that both perspectives should be considered. The question is how to integrate them into a common methodological framework. This question is highly controversial and perhaps should not be approached with the expectation that it can be resolved in a definitive and clear-cut manner.

A.   REFLEXIVITY PROBLEMS

The occurrence of reflexive predictions in social science has been a much debated issue in discussions concerning the methodological unity of natural and cultural sciences (Honolka, 1976). Gewirth (1954) formulates the argument as follows:

> In dealing with social phenomena, social science deals largely if not entirely with things which impinge directly on men's values. . . . The aim of social science may be to attain knowledge of the laws of these matters. . . . Since, however, man as conscious voluntary agent is in large part both the knower and the subject-matter of these laws, his knowledge of their impact on his values may lead him to react on the laws reflexively in order to change them. Consequently, the laws of the social sciences cannot have the same fixity of permanence as the laws of the natural sciences. (p. 230)

In developmental psychology, reflexive processes may occur whenever development-related information (descriptions, explanations, or predictions) is used in planning development-oriented actions. Examples can be found both in the realm of professionally applied developmental psychology and on the level of developmental interventions in everyday contexts such as education of dyadic interaction. Professional as well as "naive" interventions are based on more or less sophisticated or stereotyped assumptions about development. Assumptions and stereotyped beliefs about development manifest themselves not only in overt actions but also in the cultural and institutional products and settings of such actions, which constitute an "institutionalized operativity" (Warren, 1980). The institutional structures of our educational systems may be taken as an example. The differentiation of educational systems is backed by assumptions about structure and development in the ability and personality domain. The integration and internal permeability of the course system depend on hypotheses about the intraindividual variability and long-term predictability of achievement-related dispositions. Educational resources also are placed along the life span according to beliefs or stereotypes about intraindividual variability and plasticity of development at different age levels. If individual development is embedded in cultural and historical change processes (Baltes and Nesselroade, 1979), then historical change as an "ecogenesis through actions" (Rudolph & Tschohl, 1977, p. 183) must, in turn, be related to changes in action-relevant knowledge and belief systems. Thus, developmental psychology seems to be trapped in a reflexive loop: the developmental patterns and quasi-laws it attempts to describe and analyze already are deeply influenced by information about development. In a pointed manner we may say that developmental psychology is itself part of the antecedent conditions of the processes it tries to investigate.

At first glance, the occurrence of reflexive dynamics seems seriously to restrict the application of the covering law model (Hempel & Oppenheim, 1948) for uses of explanation and prediction in the social sciences. The area of preventive developmental intervention (see Brandtstädter & von Eye, 1982) is especially suited for illustrating these problems.

As a central characteristic, prevention involves self-destroying prophecies: the prediction of negatively valued developmental outcomes activates preventive efforts, which aim at the falsification of the prediction. In less fortunate circumstances, preventive predictions may also become self-fulfilling prophecies, for instance as a result of labeling effects (Jones, 1977). Can preventive prediction, in spite of such reflexivity problems, be modeled after the covering law scheme? According to the covering law model, an event is explained by deriving the statement which describes the event (the *explanandum*) from a system of premises (the *explanans*) comprising (a) statements which describe antecedent conditions and (b) deterministic law formulas that relate the antecedent conditions to the explanandum event. Many authors, including Hempel and Oppenheim themselves, have considered the covering law scheme to be an appropriate model not only for explanation but also for scientific prediction. According to this view, scientific explanation and prediction differ merely in pragmatic respects (see also Popper, 1961): in the case of explanation we ask for the laws and antecedent conditions to explain the given event, whereas in the case of prediction we ask for the consequences which can be derived from given antecedent conditions and law formulas (for a discussion of the assumption of structural equivalence of explanation and prediction, see Lenk, 1975b). If we conceptualize preventive prediction according to the covering law scheme, how can we, vis à vis the self-destructive potential of preventive predictions, maintain the validity of the law formulation on which we have based our predictions? It might be argued that the derived prediction has failed because the intervention has introduced a change in the antecedent conditions or because the intervention context in other respects deviates from the idealized conditions necessary for a stringent falsification of the law statement (Opp, 1970). But these arguments only seem to conceal the basic problem: antecedent – consequent relations which can be voluntarily interrupted may at best be considered as quasi-laws but not as nomological relations in the strict sense.

On closer analysis, however, the occurrence of reflexive predictions does not seem to exclude a nomological conception of social science or to be irreconcilable with a monistic methodological position integrating natural and social or cultural sciences. It has to be noted that reflexive predictions (or structurally analogous phenomena) also occur in the physical or technical domain, for example, in self-regulating technical systems (Grünbaum, 1963). If we remember the distinction between quasi-laws and the generative processes which produce relationships of the quasi-law type, we cannot rule out the possibility of a reductive "nomologization" of self-reflexive processes.

At this level of analysis, it becomes evident that the basic problem is not the occurrence of reflexive descriptions, explanations, or predictions in developmental psychology. Rather, the question is whether or not the nomological model can be used to explain human *actions* which (in the social context) bring about reflexive dynamics.

B.   PROBLEMS OF ACTION EXPLANATION

The quest for an appropriate model of action explanations presupposes a closer analysis of the action concept. Although philosophical, psychological, and sociological action theories yield partially different explications, some points of conceptual convergence can be noted (Lenk, 1978a).

Actions are commonly characterized as behavioral processes which at least to some degree are under the individual's control. This criterion distinguishes actions from behavioral occurrences that just happen to, or are passively experienced by, the individual. Standard examples of such behavioral occurrences include blushing, growing, sweating, fainting, and stumbling. The individual may of course be capable of intentionally bringing about such behavioral events, but then the act of bringing about the event rather than the behavioral event itself constitutes an action (Brennenstuhl, 1975; Thalberg, 1977).

Closely connected to the definitional criterion of control competence is the conceptualization of action situations as choice situations. Accordingly, a behavior is an action only insofar as the individual has the choice or is free to engage in another course of action (if "he could have done otherwise"; see Chisholm, 1966; Danto, 1973). As we have already mentioned, a given behavior, for conceptual reasons, cannot be morally evaluated unless it can be interpreted as an act which was, within certain limits, free and under the individual's control. This is a reference point of strategies for excuse and exculpation in moral or legal discourses (Austin, 1956; Brennenstuhl, 1975; Riedel, 1978).

Central to the action concept is the concept of rule. Actions are subject to rules in a twofold sense: rules or cultural regulations (formal or informal norms, customs, laws) *restrict* as well as *constitute* actions (the distinction between regulative and constitutive rules was originally proposed by Kant; see also Searle, 1968). If we consider actions such as greeting, formulating an excuse, playing chess, and dancing, it becomes evident that behavioral patterns of this type can be understood and interpreted as meaningful actions only in a context of rules. As rule-conforming and rule-constituted behavior, actions are intimately connected to social and cultural institutions; to understand actions, one has to be acquainted with this institutional background (Winch, 1958; Mischel, 1968; Toulmin, 1974).

The above structural elements of the action concept can also be found in psychological research programs, often, however, framed as empirical hypotheses. For example, research on attribution processes, self-perception, and social cognition has related aspects of action such as perceived behavioral freedom and control to the attribution of intentionality and responsibility and the development of self-efficacy beliefs (Bandura, 1977; Bem, 1972; Harvey, 1976; Ross, 1981). Such relationships obviously conform to the given conceptual explications of the action concept.

It follows from the considerations above that actions cannot be reduced to corporeal or physical events or event patterns. Action is not just behavior but behavior which is subsumed under an act type on the basis of certain interpretations and reconstructions (accordingly, Lenk, 1978a, conceives of actions as "interpretational constructs"). A certain behavior is interpreted as an action by imputing certain attributes such as control, freedom of choice, and intentionality. The informational base for such interpretational attributions is provided not only by the overt behavior pattern; equally important is information about the behavioral context (about the institutional setting of the behavior, about the subject's competencies and previous experiences, about normative restrictions, and so on). The process of action interpretation, of course, is regulated and constituted by cultural rules (especially by rules of language).

If action situations are conceptualized as choice situations, an appropriate explanation of action has to give the reasons for the individual's action preferences. Action explanations in ordinary language generally refer to the goals and intentions of the actor. To systematize such teleological explanations, von Wright (1971) has proposed the scheme of "practical syllogism": "A intends to bring about p; A believes that he can bring about p only by doing a; therefore A prepares to do a." Conclusions of this type obviously can fail in predicting the factual behavior; for example, if A is incapable of or prevented from doing a, if A's intentions have changed, or if the act of doing a is inconsistent with other of A's intentions that have not been included in the explanation scheme. The scheme can be refined, however, to take such restrictions into account (von Wright, 1971). Again we should note that the basic idea of explaining actions by relating them to cognitive and evaluative premises also constitutes a core assumption in psychological action models, particularly in models of the expectancy $\times$ value type (Heckhausen, 1980).

Recent debates about the nomological interpretation of action and about the related issue of the methodological unity of the natural and social sciences have centered around the logical status of practical syllogisms. Along with other "intentionalists," von Wright (1971) rejects a causal interpretation of the scheme. He argues that the relation between intentions, beliefs, and actions is not a causal but a conceptual one, so that assumptions about intentions, beliefs, and actions cannot be independently tested. Hence, intentions and beliefs should not be considered as causal antecedents of action (in the Humean sense) but as structural implicates or conceptual components of the action concept. For the developmental sciences, it seems to follow that an "actionist" perspective, which considers development as a process controlled and regulated to a large extent by human actions, is hardly compatible with a (causal –) nomological conception of development.

We shall not go into details here of the controversies between logical intentionalists (G. H. von Wright, G. E. M. Anscombe, A. I. Melden, F. Stoutland, R. Taylor, T. Mischel, and others) and causalists (A. I. Goldman, D. Davidson, C. G. Hempel, R. Tuomela, and others; for further discussion see contributions in Brand & Walton, 1976; Lenk, 1978b, 1979b). We will, however, briefly consider just two objections which have been raised against the logical relation argument. Werbik (in press) recently argued that the action orientations of a subject can already be determined in the phase of action planning, without methodological reference to factual actions, by asking the subjects about their intentions and beliefs. The author, however, adds the reservation that this procedure presupposes certain methodological precautions to establish a valid or authentic (trustful, sincere) communication. But then, evidently, the problem arises as to how it can be ascertained that such an "ideal" dialogue situation has been realized without comparing verbal reports and factual actions. Furthermore, we may hypothesize that the individual himself uses certain conceptual rules in the self-ascription of intentions and beliefs (Brandtstädter, 1979). Similar difficulties arise if we conceptualize action explanations as dispositional explanations. Obviously, practical syllogisms implicitly assume a rational agent. Hence, the following explanation may be suggested (Hempel, 1968):

Premise 1: P was a rational agent;
Premise 2: P was in a situation of type S (characterized by certain intentions, beliefs, perceptions, etc.);
Law statement: In a situation of type S a rational agent will do the act A;
Conclusions: Therefore, P did A.

The structure of this explanatory argument conforms to the covering law model. But how can the rationality disposition of the subject (Premise 1) be assessed? If we stipulate that an individual is a rational agent if and only if he chooses those actions which he believes to be necessary to reach his goals — that is, if he acts according to the practical syllogism — we are obviously again trapped in a vicious circle. It seems that rationality is a constitutive element of the action concept (Schwemmer, 1976).

The last problems strongly resemble the problems of distinguishing between structural implications and empirical hypotheses (see Section III.A) discussed earlier. Thus it seems that the core problem of the intentionalist–causalist controversy is not restricted to the context of action theory but crops up generally in theoretical explanations.

Hence, if we try to interpret empirically the basic constituents of the action concept (e.g., by proposing measurement models or reduction postulates for the determination of "intentions" or "beliefs"), we may expect that the resulting system of relations will be neither purely empirical nor purely analytic or definitional, but quasi-analytical in the sense explicated above. Even then, however, a strict causalist interpretation which presupposes the logical or conceptual independence of beliefs, values, and actions remains a position that is difficult to defend.

After all, it may be that action explanations should be conceptualized not as nomological deductions but more appropriately as rational reconstructions. From this perspective, action is explained as a result not of causal antecedents but of rational arguments which relate actions to the actor's system of goals and maxims. Rationality, then, is considered not as an empirical disposition but as an ideal-typical construction which we use as a methodological device in the explanatory reconstruction of action. It seems that such an explanatory approach preserves the discussed meaning facets of the action concept (for an elaboration of this explanatory model see Schwemmer, 1976).

It should be noted that a methodological conception which conceives of actions as generated and, within limits, modifiable through argumentation offers a conceptual framework for a critical reconstruction of development-oriented actions and action-related developmental processes. As scientists, we can argue critically not against laws of nature but against actions and cultural processes which are based on arguments. We may question the validity of action-guiding cognitions, goal orientations, and so on. For an applied developmental psychology, this position offers the perspective of a methodologically founded concept of developmental counseling as a profes-sional contribution to the solution of orientation problems and conflicts which may arise in developmental planning on the individual, institutional, and political levels (for further discussion, see Brandtstädter, in press).

V. Conclusion

How can we answer the initial question concerning the methodological integration of natural and cultural science perspectives in developmental psychology? To attempt a final answer would certainly be premature. A causal – nomological framework in the traditional sense seems to be inappro-priate for the integration of both perspectives. It may, however, turn out that the methodological gap can be bridged or even closed by a more sophis-ticated nomological research concept that takes into account the problem of quasi-analytical statements and the constitutive function of nonempirical core elements in research and theorizing. In a recent formulation, von Wright (1979) seems to come to a similar conclusion:

> Only after considerable toil philosophical thinking has reached the insight that causal antecedents and deductive reasons are fundamentally different. European rational-ism of the eighteenth century did not really know this difference; not Descartes, certainly not Spinoza, not even Leibniz. We usually say . . . that through David Hume philosophers reached this insight for the first time. And we may add that since Hume, philosophical thinking is captured within the cause – reason dichotomy. To grasp the problems of the action concept we first of all have to overcome this dichot-omy. (p. 426)

Acknowledgments

I am grateful to Nancy Galambos and Amy J. Michele for their valuable assistance in the English translation of this chapter.

References

Albert, H. Theorie und Prognose in den Sozialwissenschaften. In E. Topitsch (Ed.), *Logik der Sozialwissenschaften.* Köln: Kiepenheuer & Witsch, 1966.

Apel, K. D., Manninen, J., & Tuomela, R. *Neue Versuche über Erklären und Verstehen.* Frankfurt a.M.: Suhrkamp, 1978.

Austin, J. L. A plea for excuses. *Proceedings of the Aristotelian Society,* 1956, *57,* 1–30.

Baier, K. Responsibility and action. In M. Brand (Ed.), *The nature of human action.* Glenview, Ill.: Scott, Foresman, 1970.

Baltes, P. B., & Baltes, M. M. Plasticity and variability in psychological aging: Methodological and theoretical issues. In G. Gurski (Ed.), *The effects of aging on the central nervous system.* Berlin: Schering, 1980.

Baltes, P. B., & Nesselroade, J. R. History and rationale of longitudinal research. In J. R. Nesselroade & P. B. Baltes (Eds.), *Longitudinal research in the study of behavior and development.* New York: Academic Press, 1979.

Baltes, P. B., Reese, H. W., & Lipsitt, L. P. Life-span developmental psychology. *Annual Review of Psychology,* 1980, *31,* 65–110.

Bandura, A. Self-efficacy: Toward a unifying theory of behavioral change. *Psychological Review,* 1977, *84,* 191–215.

Bem, D. Self-perception theory. *Advances in Experimental Social Psychology,* 1972, *6,* 1–62.

Berelson, B., & Steiner, G. A. *Human behavior: An inventory of scientific findings.* New York: Harcourt, Brace, & World, 1964.

Brand, M., & Walton, D. (Eds.). *The nature of human action.* Dordrecht: Reidel, 1976.

Brandt, R., & Kim, J. Wants as explanations of action. *Journal of Philosophy,* 1963, *60,* 425–435.

Brandtstädter, J. Bedürfnisse, Werte und das Problem optimaler Entwicklung. In A. Klages & P. Kmieciak (Eds.), *Wertwandel und gesellschaftlicher Wandel.* Frankfurt a.M.: Campus, 1979.

Brandtstädter, J. Begriffliche Voraussetzungen der Moralpsychologie. In W. Kempf & G. Aschenbach (Eds.), *Konflikt und Konfliktbewältigung.* Bern: Huber, 1981.

Brandtstädter, J. Apriorische Elemente in psychologischen Forschungsprogrammen. *Zeitschrift für Sozialpsychologie,* 1982, *13,* 267–277.

Brandtstädter, J. Entwicklung in Handlungskontexten: Aussichten für die entwicklungspsychologische Forschung und Theorienbildung. In H. Lenk (Ed.), *Handlungstheorien—interdisziplinär* (Vol. III, 2). München: Fink, in press.

Brandtstädter, J., & von Eye, A. *Psychologische Prävention: Grundlagen, Programme, Methoden.* Bern: Huber, 1982.

Brennenstuhl, W. *Handlungstheorie und Handlungslogik.* Kronberg: Scriptor, 1975.

Bunge, M. *Causality and modern science* (3rd ed.). New York: Dover, 1979.

Chisholm, R. M. Freedom and action. In K. Lehrer (Ed.), *Freedom and determinism.* New York: Random House, 1966.

Cook, T. D., & Campbell, D. T. Causal inference and the language of experimentation. In T. D. Cook & D. T. Campbell (Eds.), *Quasi-experimentation: Design & analysis issues for field settings.* Chicago: Rand McNally, 1979.

Danto, A. C. *Analytical philosophy of action.* Cambridge: Cambridge University Press, 1973.

Dasén, P. R. Are cognitive processes universal? In N. Warren (Ed.), *Studies in cross-cultural psychology* (Vol. 1). New York: Academic Press, 1977.

Gadenne, V. *Die Gültigkeit psychologischer Untersuchungen.* Stuttgart: Kohlhammer, 1976.

Gadenne, V. Ableitung und Prüfung psychologischer Theorien. *Zeitschrift für Sozialpsychologie,* 1978, *9,* 66–77.

Garn, S. M.   Continuities and change in maturational timing.   In O. G. Brim, Jr. & J. Kagan (Eds.), *Constancy and change in human development.*   Cambridge, Mass.: Harvard University Press, 1980.

Gehlen, A.   *Der Mensch: Seine Natur und seine Stellung in der Welt* (9th ed.).   Bonn: Bouvier, 1971.

Gentner, D.   Evidence for the psychological relation of semantic components: The verbs of possession.   In D. A. Norman & D. E. Rumelhart, *Explorations in cognition.*   San Francisco: Freeman, 1975.

Gergen, L. J.   The emerging crisis in life-span developmental theory.   In P. B. Baltes & O. G. Brim, Jr. (Eds.), *Life-span development and behavior* (Vol. 3).   New York: Academic Press, 1980.

Gewirth, A.   Can men change laws of social science?   *Philosophy of Science,* 1954, *21,* 229–241.

Grünbaum, A.   Comments on Professor Roger Buck's paper "Reflexive Predictions."   *Philosophy of Science,* 1963, *30,* 370–372.   Reprinted in L. I. Krimerman (Ed.), The nature and scope of social science: A critical anthology.   New York: Appleton–Century–Crofts, 1969.

Hanson, N.   *Patterns of discovery.*   London: Cambridge University Press, 1958.

Harvey, J. H.   Attribution of freedom.   In J. H. Harvey, W. J. Ickes, & R. F. Kidd (Eds.), *New directions in attribution research* (Vol. 1.).   Hillsdale, N.J.: Erlbaum, 1976.

Heckhausen, H.   *Motivation und Handeln.*   Berlin: Springer, 1980.

Hempel, C. G.   Rational action.   In N. S. Care & C. Landesman (Eds.), *Readings in the theory of action.*   Bloomington: Indiana University Press, 1968.

Hempel, C. G., & Oppenheim, P.   Studies on the logic of explanation.   *Philosophy of Science,* 1948, *15,* 135–146; 152–157; 172–174.

Herrmann, T.   *Die Psychologie und ihre Forschungsprogramme.*   Göttingen: Hogrefe, 1976.

Herrmann, T.   *Psychologie als Problem: Herausforderungen der psychologischen Wissenschaft.*   Stuttgart: Klett–Cotta, 1979.

Honolka, H.   *Die Eigendynamik sozialwissenschaftlicher Aussagen: Zur Theorie der self-fulfilling prophecy.*   Frankfurt a.M.: Campus, 1976.

Jones, R. A.   *Self-fulfilling prophecies: Social, psychological, and physiological effects of expectancies.*   Hillsdale, N.J.: Erlbaum, 1977.

Kagan, J.   Universalien menschlicher Entwicklung.   In L. Montada (Ed.), *Brennpunkte der Entwicklungspsychologie.*   Stuttgart: Kohlhammer, 1979.

Kamlah, W., & Lorenzen, P.   *Logische Propädeutik: Vorschule des vernünftigen Redens.*   Mannheim: Bibliographisches Institut, 1967.

Kohlberg, L.   Moral stages and moralization: The cognitive developmental approach.   In T. Lickona (Ed.), *Moral development and behavior: Theory, research and social issues.*   New York: Holt, Rinehart & Winston, 1976.

Krimerman, L. I. (Ed.).   *The nature and scope of social science: A critical anthology.*   New York: Appleton–Century–Crofts, 1969.

Lenk, H.   Über strukturelle Implikationen.   *Zeitschrift für Soziologie,* 1975, *4,* 350–358. (a)

Lenk, H.   *Pragmatische Philosophie: Plädoyers und Beispiele für eine praxisnahe Philosophie und Wissenschaftstheorie.*   Hamburg: Hoffmann & Campe, 1975. (b)

Lenk, H.   Handlung als Interpretationskonstrukt: Entwurf einer konstituenten- und beschreibungstheoretischen Handlungsphilosophie.   In H. Lenk (Ed.), *Handlungstheorien— interdisziplinär* (Vol. II, 1).   München: Fink, 1978. (a)

Lenk, H. (Ed.).   *Handlungstheorien— interdisziplinär* (Vol. II, 1).   München: Fink, 1978. (b)

Lenk, H. (Ed.).   *Handlungstheorien— interdisziplinär* (Vol. II, 2).   München: Fink, 1979. (a)

Lenk, H. *Pragmatische Vernunft: Philosophie zwischen Wissenschaft und Praxis.* Stuttgart: Reclam, 1979. (b)

Lerner, R. M. & Busch-Rossnagel, N. A. (Eds.). *Individuals as producers of their own development.* New York: Academic Press, 1981.

Lorenzen, P. *Normative logic and ethics.* Mannheim: Bibliographisches Institut, 1969.

Mischel, T. Epilogue. In T. Mischel (Ed.), *Human action: Conceptual and empirical issues.* New York: Academic Press, 1968.

Montada, L. Entwicklungspsychologie auf der Suche nach einer Identität. In L. Montada (Ed.), *Brennpunkte der Entwicklungspsychologie.* Stuttgart: Kohlhammer, 1979.

Norman, D. A., & Rumelhart, D. E. Explorations in cognition. San Francisco: Freeman, 1975.

Opp, K. -D. *Methodologie der Sozialwissenschaften.* Reinbek: Rowohlt, 1970.

Popper, K. M. *The poverty of historicism.* London: Routledge & Kegan Paul, 1961.

Riedel, M. *Verstehen oder Erklären? Zur Theorie und Geschichte der hermeneutischen Wissenschaften.* Stuttgart: Klett–Cotta, 1978.

Rogosa, D. Causal models in longitudinal research: Rationale, formulation, and interpretation. In J. R. Nesselroade & P. B. Baltes (Eds.), *Longitudinal research in the study of behavior and development.* New York: Academic Press, 1979.

Ross, M. Self-centered biases in attributions of responsibility: Antecedents and consequences. In T. Higgins, C. P. Herrmann & M. P. Zanna (Eds.), *Social cognition: The Ontario Symposium* (Vol. 1.). Hillsdale, N.J.: Erlbaum, 1981.

Rudolph, W., & Tschohl, P. *Systematische Anthropologie.* München: Fink, 1977.

Schwemmer, O. *Theorie der rationalen Erklärung: Zu den methodischen Grundlagen der Kulturwissenschaft.* München: Beck, 1976.

Searle, J. R. *Speech acts.* London: Cambridge University Press, 1968.

Selman, R. L. Social–cognitive understanding: A guide to educational and clinical practice. In T. Lickona (Ed.), *Moral development and behavior: Theory, research and social issues.* New York: Holt, Rinehart, & Winston, 1976.

Shotter, J. *Towards a science of individuality: Intentionality and the ecology of everyday social life.* Paper prepared for the conference on Discovery Strategies in the Psychology of Action, Bad Homburg, January 20–23, 1981 (Prepublication draft, 1980).

Smedslund, J. Between the analytic and the arbitrary: A case study of psychological research. *Scandinavian Journal of Psychology,* 1979, *20,* 129–140.

Stegmüller, W. *Probleme und Resultate der Wissenschaftstheorie und Analytischen Philosophie* (Vol. 1). Berlin: Springer, 1969.

Stegmüller, W. *Probleme und Resultate der Wissenschaftstheorie und Analytischen Philosophie* (Vol. 2). Berlin: Springer, 1970.

Stegmüller, W. *Neue Wege der Wissenschaftsphilosophie.* Berlin: Springer, 1980.

Thalberg, J. *Perception, emotion and action: A component approach.* Oxford: Blackwell, 1977.

Toulmin, S. E. Rules and their relevance for understanding human behavior. In T. Mischel (Ed.), *Understanding other persons.* Oxford: Blackwell, 1974.

von Wright, G. H. *Explanation and understanding.* Ithaca, N.Y.: Cornell University Press, 1971.

von Wright, G. H. Das menschliche Handeln im Lichte seiner Ursachen und Gründe. In H. Lenk (Ed.), *Handlungstheorien—interdisziplinär* (Vol. II, 2). München: Fink, 1979.

Warren, N. Universality and plasticity, ontogeny and phylogeny: The resonance between culture and cognitive development. In J. Sants (Ed.), *Developmental psychology and society.* London: Macmillan, 1980.

Watkins, J. W. N.   Historical explanation in the social sciences.   *British Journal for the Philosophy of Science*, 1957, *8*, 104–117.   Reprinted in L. I. Krimerman (Ed.), *The nature and scope of social science: A critical anthology*.   New York, Appleton–Century–Crofts, 1969.

Werbik, H.   Über die nomologische Auslegung von Handlungstheorien.   In H. Lenk (Ed.), *Handlungstheorien—interdisziplinär* (Vol. III, 2).   München: Fink, in press.

Winch, P.   *The idea of a social science and its relation to philosophy.*   London: Routledge & Kegan Paul, 1958.

10

Multifaceted Systems Modeling: Structure and Behavior at a Multiplicity of Levels

BERNARD P. ZEIGLER

MARIETTA L. BABA

I. Introduction

Culture, viewed as a uniquely human adaptive mechanism, extends and enhances, but is also limited by, the biological substrate on which it is founded. Cultural evolution is preconditioned by the potentials of its individual carriers to forge and transmit its advances. Conversely, the expression of human potential is tempered by the cultural context in which it unfolds. This mutuality of constraint in individual and cultural evolution must be understood on at least two levels: the sociocultural group and the individual. Conventional approaches, whether reductionistic or holistic, must necessarily fail to address the essence of this problem of linking of levels, the former because it seeks to model the individual component apart from its cultural milieu (hoping eventually to synthesize group behavior from these components) and the latter because of its exclusive focus on group properties.

INDIVIDUAL DEVELOPMENT
AND SOCIAL CHANGE:
EXPLANATORY ANALYSIS

265

Multifaceted systems modeling methodology has been advocated as an approach to the disciplined examination of system properties from many viewpoints and levels (Zeigler, 1978, 1979, 1984). It recognizes that achieving an in-depth understanding of the many aspects into which reality partially decomposes requires the phrasing of questions, advancement of hypotheses, construction of models, and gathering of data at many levels of aggregation and under many restrictive experimental regimens. More than this, it proposes concepts for the integration of the partial models that result from such limitations in scope.

The objective of this chapter is to apply the multifaceted methodology to the mutuality of constraint between sociocultural group and individual dynamics. While preliminary in nature, we hold the results to be indicative of the possibilities for a disciplined attach on the problem at the multiplicity of levels it requires. More generally, we believe that the results justify the serious extension of the multifaceted approach to other interrelations between social systems and their individual elements.

The organization of this chapter is as follows: In Section II the multifaceted systems approach and its concepts for the integrated organization of models around the questions that give rise to them are reviewed. To illustrate the approach, in Section III three categories of mutuality of constraint are identified and several models are formulated (based partly on existing ones) that clarify, refine, and could answer some of the questions raised in each of the categories. Finally, some conclusions are drawn concerning the benefits of multifaceted systems modeling for addressing the correlation between dynamics at the individual level and those at higher levels of organization that are exemplified by cultural and other systems, abstractions of interest to social science.

II. A Brief Review of Multifaceted Systems Modeling

We first will present an informal review of the basic concepts of model construction and multifaceted systems theory that set the framework for our subsequent discussion. The reader wanting more exposition is referred to Zeigler (1976, 1979, 1984).

A. MODELS

A model is constructed by linking a set of *components* (which are themselves models) so that they interact. Components have *inputs* and *outputs* through which the interaction is mediated. A *coupling* scheme specifies how the outputs of one component are fed to the inputs of another. As illustrated in Figure 10.1, a component has an internal mechanism which determines how inputs are processed and what outputs are produced. Models are *dynamic;* that is, they exist over some interval of a time axis. The *state* of a component at any time instant is a summary of its past history up to that instant. When a component processes inputs, the internal effect is a change in its state. Components may be characterized as *passive* or *active*. A passive component can undergo state transitions and generate outputs only in response to the immediate presence of inputs. An active component can, in addition, execute state transitions and generate outputs in the absence of inputs. Inputs, states, and outputs are represented concretely by sets of input, state, and output *variables,* respectively. Variables correspond to measurements that are conceivably performed on the real system. The current state of technology may or may not permit these measurements to be realized in reality.

Usually, one considers a component to be an instance of a *model class.* All instances of such a class have the same internal mechanism. Any two such instances are interchangeable at any time in any context provided that they are in the same state. In a *parameterized* model class, a set of parameters is associated with each instance. The particular values assigned to the parameters of a component determine the nature of its internal mechanism. Thus any two instances are interchangeble at any time in any context provided that they have the same parameter values and are in the same state.

Depending on the questions being asked, especially on the lengths of the time periods of interest, variables of a real world entity may be represented by model counterparts as either state variables or parameters. Over relatively short periods such variables may be considered constants with values determined when the component came into existence. In this case, their

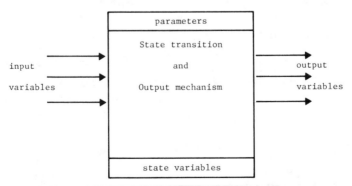

Figure 10.1   General structure of a model component.

model counterparts are treated as parameters. Over relatively long periods, if these variables are subject to change, they may be treated as state variables. In this case, of course, the internal mechanism of the component must dictate how the changes are brought about. To control the complexity of a component, its variables may be stratified into *structural levels*. The variables at a given level act as parameters for all lower levels and as state variables for all higher levels. Thus variables at the lowest level are state variables, while those at the highest level are parameters. Such stratification should be correlated with volatility and time scale: The greater the frequency with which a variable is likely to change, the lower the level that it should occupy in the stratification.

Example: Adaptive Simulation Model of Agricultural Development. A model for explaining the transition of a sociocultural group from a subsistence strategy based on natural plants to a strategy based on incipient agriculture along the lines of Reynolds (1981) will be used for illustration. The model is noteworthy in that it accounts for empirical archaeological data that give evidence of this transition solely on the basis of autonomous transformation of the group's resource management strategies. By contrast, other explanations postulate that the importing of innovations from other cultures was critical in inducing the transition from hunter–gatherer to agricultural organizations. We present a simplified facsimile of Reynolds's model for purposes of exposition.

The components of the group are individual humans, while the environment consists of components representing types of edible plants. In this model, the individual humans are active components, while the plant components are passive. As illustrated in Figure 10.2, the individuals are capable of carrying out a set of primitive activities of two kinds: resource collection and incipient agricultural activity. A resource collection activity is characterized by a designated plant type and a time at which plants of this type are scheduled to be sampled. Since the period during which plants bear fruit is short, and what is not immediately collected is lost, selection and scheduling of collecting activities is a nontrivial problem. Incipient agricultural activities are similarly characterized by a designated plant type and a time of scheduled planting. As repeated experience in planting may increase the plant's productivity, there is an adaptive pressure to shift from emphasis on resource collection to incipient agricultural activities.

At any given time an individual is characterized by a *strategy* that determines the nature and mix of the collection and cultivation activities. The model is run over yearly periods and the performance of each strategy is evaluated in terms of the amount and nutritional value of the resources collected relative to the needs of the group. The climatic conditions affect-

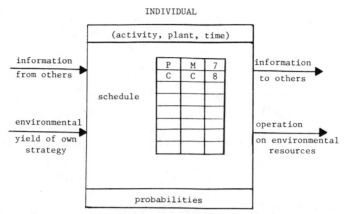

Figure 10.2 Example of a model component based on Reynolds's (1981) model. Each individual is an active component controlled by a schedule, that is, a sequence of triples (activity, plant, time), each triple designating a resource activity to be performed on a plant type for a certain time duration.

ing plant growth are determined by rainfall level probabilities. More successful strategies are made to propagate among the individuals and are subjected to random modifications via processes analogous to genetic replication and mutation. In the simplest version, the mechanisms for propagation and modification are invariant. Thus this model exemplifies the following stratification of variables:

1. State variables
   a. individual: schedule of activities remaining to be performed; types and values of collected resources so far
   b. environment: types and values of currently available resources
2. Next level variables
   a. strategies (constant over yearly periods)
   b. plant productivities
3. Parameters
   a. propagation and modification probabilities
   b. probabilities of rainfall levels

Note that the above state variables, next level variables, and parameters are variables whose values are subject to decreasing frequency of change, as required in our concept of stratification.

A second version of the model incorporates a decision-making component which alters the propagation and modification probabilities based on a long term assessment of the performance of the strategies they generate. In this version, the latter probabilities are thus no longer parameters but are variables subject to adaptation.

The primary measure employed in judging the technological level of a modeled group is the number of incipient agricultural activities incorporated into the current strategy mix of its individuals. Different versions of the model display different patterns of increase in this measure over simulated runs of 500-year durations. For example, in an environment of invariant climatic characteristics, an equilibrium is reached in which the agricultural level exceeds that reached in an environment subject to long-term fluctuations in rainfall probabilities. The model was validated by comparing its yearly distributions of collected plants with archaeological evidence of chronological shifts in plant frequencies.

B. LINKAGE TYPES AND INTERACTIVE COMPLEXITY

To recapitulate: a model consists of a set of components and a coupling scheme. Such a scheme is a set of pairs or *links* of the form:

$$<\text{output variable}>_i \rightarrow <\text{input variable}>_j$$

indicating that a particular output variable of component i is to be fed to a particular input variable of component j. One can visualize the scheme in terms of a digraph (directed graph) whose points are labeled by the components and where an arrow runs from point i to point j if there is a corresponding link involving i and j in the coupling scheme.

Various *types of linkage* can be identified; for example, control, communication, and transfer of material or energy. Accordingly, the coupling scheme can be put together as a union of coupling schemes for each type of linkage existing in the model. Each *subcoupling scheme* may be represented by a separate digraph, these subdigraphs may be unified into a single digraph in which the arrows are labeled by the type of linkage. This approach makes it possible to use properties of digraphs and measures of their complexity to characterize the nature and complexity of component interaction.

Figure 10.3 illustrates two general kinds of coupling applicable to cultural models. In Figure 10.3a, each individual component interacts directly with the environment and shares this information directly with all other individuals. This complete interaction is possible for a group of small size. By contrast, individuals in Figure 10.3b share information directly only with a limited subset of individuals, as is appropriate for a group of large size. This subset may consist of family relatives and/or physically adjacent neighbors. The propagation of information from an individual to all others must necessarily take more time in the second case and would be less reliably communicated in the event of transmission errors (cf. the game of transmitting whis-

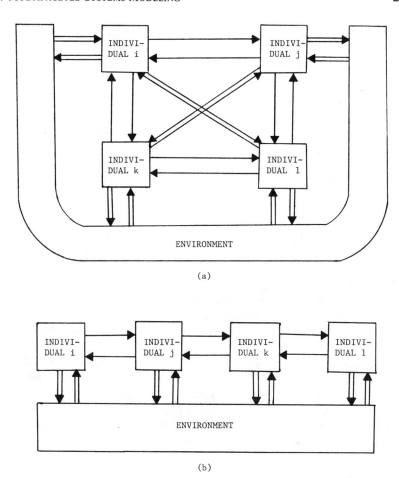

Figure 10.3 Coupling scheme examples: (a) total sharing of information among a small number of individuals; (b) limited sharing among large number of individuals. Single-shaft arrow represents information; double-shaft arrow operation/yield.

pers down a long line). An implication of such information flow considerations might be that adaptive progress would be much slower for a large group than for a small one unless hierarchical or other structures exist to coordinate the assimilation of information (Reynolds & Zeigler, 1979).

Just as with the volatility of variables, it is possible for a coupling scheme to remain in force during some period and then change to a different form. In this case, a mechanism must be provided for determining the change in structure. Although advocated for some time as important for social system modeling (Oren, 1979), this time-varying approach to model structure is still not well exemplified in the literature nor well understood.   However, it would seem to be the appropriate concept for modeling the evolution of sociocultural group organizational structure, as we suggest in Section III.A.

Examples of interactions and linkage types at various levels are:

1. Interactions between individuals: commands, communication, material transfer, mating
2. Interaction between sociocultural group and its environment: exploitation of various resource types
3. Interaction between sociocultural groups: trade–plunder, warfare, cross-fertilization

C. COUPLING RESULTANTS

A model constructed by linking component models may itself be employed as a component in a higher-level model.   To do so requires that its input, state, and output variables be identified.   This process is straightforward.   Any component input variable that has not been linked by the coupling to an output is an input variable of the model; in the same way, any output variable of a component that has not been linked to an input variable is an output variable of the model.   The state variable set of the model is the union of the state variable sets of each of the components.   Hierarchical model construction results when this process of employing already-constructed models as components in higher-level models is repeated some finite number of times.

D. MODELING OBJECTIVES: SYSTEM ENTITY STRUCTURE

Models are built to answer questions about reality.   The kinds of components and interactions that are represented in them should reflect the questions that motivated their construction.   These objectives orient the model-building process by determining such factors as the *system boundaries,* the model components of relevance, and the *level of resolution* at which they will be represented.   "System boundaries" refers to the delimiting of a part of reality as a focus of attention.   The effect of the rest of the real world on the enclosed portion is represented by the choice of input variables.   Having chosen the system boundaries, we are in a position to undertake a *decomposition* of the system enclosed by them into a set of *component systems.*   Each of these component systems may also be decomposed, and so on, until some level of resolution is reached that is believed to be satisfactory for answering the motivating questions.

A "trace" of this decomposition process is represented in the *system entity structure*. The entity structure is based on a treelike graph embodying the system boundaries and decompositions which have been conceived for the system; an example to be discussed later is shown in Figure 10.4. An *entity* signifies a conceptual part of the system which has been identified as a component in one or more decompositions. Several ways of decomposing the same entity may be represented, each one being called an *aspect*. Actually, both entities and aspects are better thought of as types of components and decompositions, respectively, since (subject to some constraints) they may appear more than once in the structure. In fact, anywhere it is placed an entity or aspect carries with it the same decomposition substructure. This means that new refinements of decompositions may be specified by reapplying existing ones. A second important role of the entity structure is to organize the variables which have been proposed for the system. This will become clear after the next concept is introduced.

E. EXPERIMENTAL FRAMES

The concept of *experimental frame* is intended to characterize modeling objectives by specifying the form of the experimentation that is required to obtain answers to the questions of interest. At a minimum, an experimental frame specifies the input and output variables that are of interest. *Input* variables are variables that are supposed not to be under the control of the model, or counterpart real, system. Therefore, their behavior over time must be specified as input time series or *segments*. *Output* variables are variables to which a model should be able to assign values over time in response to input segments. Thus, for an experimental frame, data may be collected as ordered pairs of input and associated output time segments. It is by examining, aggregating, and processing such data that answers to the motivating questions may be obtained. *Performance measures* are such aggregations of primary input – output data that are intended to help evaluate the capability of a system to carry out certain goals of interest.

The concept of performance measure borrowed from systems engineering (Wymore, 1976) is applicable to sociocultural systems if one takes the view that such systems may be characterized by potentially conflicting, because simultaneously unrealizable, goals: that of benefiting each member on the one hand, and surviving as a group on the other. Thus, possible performance measures are:

1. Individual oriented
   a. uniformity of distribution of (material, energy, knowledge, information) to individuals (quality of life)
   b. degree of realization of individual genetically determined potentials (low infant mortality, high longevity, high diversity and sophistication in trades and arts and crafts)
2. Group oriented
   a. cultural autopoiesis: ability to replicate template of cultural organization from generation to generation
   b. ability of group to withstand and adapt to shocks in the environment

We stress that such performance criteria are measures of achievement of objectives that may or may not characterize the system being modeled. A performance measure is useful to the extent that it helps correlate the behavior of a model to that of the system it is intended to represent. Such would be the case, for example, when a model contains mechanisms for optimizing two performance measures that conflict and the behavior of the model, as observed through the trajectories of these variables, matches that of the real system. If no such correlation can be made, it may be concluded that these particular measures, and the underlying objectives that they imply, do not characterize the system under study.

In addition to the specification of the input–output interface, an experimental frame may specify *run control* variables and admissible segments. This portion of a frame is responsible for initializing experiments and terminating them when trajectories exhibited by the model variables do not belong to the specified class of admissible control segments.

F. ENTITY STRUCTURE ORGANIZATION OF MODELS AND FRAMES

One of the main roles of the entity structure is to organize models and experimental frames. The basic idea is to associate models and frames with the entities they concern. Each entity thus represents a component of the real system and therefore ought to be linked to the experimental frames that embody questions about it (the component) and to the models developed to answer such questions. Attached to each entity in the entity structure are the variables that may be employed to construct models and frames for the entity. Since each entity is actually a type of component, these attached variables are also transported with the entity wherever it occurs.

G. ENTITY STRUCTURE AND HIERARCHICAL MODEL CONSTRUCTION

Choice of system boundaries and decomposition of the system within the boundaries are mirrored in the entity structure by a process in which the structure is pruned so as to represent the decomposition of a particular model. The pruning process begins with the selection of an entity (representing the choice of system boundaries enclosing a system of interest). It proceeds down the structure, selecting an aspect of the entity (representing a decomposition). The process proceeds recursively, applying itself to each of the entities of the aspect (representing the highest-level components of the model for the entity). The process stops when entities are reached that are to be regarded as *atomic;* no aspect is selected for such entities.

Model construction now takes place in the reverse direction. Variables are selected for the atomic components and categorized as input, state, or output, and an internal mechanism for effecting the model dynamic behavior is specified. A coupling scheme is specified for each lowest-level aspect and the resultant under this scheme becomes the next level component. This construction process continues upward until the initially selected entity is reached. The result is a hierarchically constructed model for the initially selected entity.

III. Multifaceted Model Framework for Issues in Mutuality of Constraint

Evolutionary anthropology views culture as an adaptive mechanism, unique to humans, that is designed to capture, harness, and distribute environmental energy and resources for the survival and well-being of its carriers (Stewart, 1955). We shall adopt this postulation of cultural system function as fruitful for the development of models, subject to the caveat expressed previously concerning validity of presumed performance measures (Section II.E). It follows that major components of all cultural systems include: (1) a techno-economic base that captures materials and energy from its environment, (2) a social structure that organizes individuals to carry out energy production, environmental exploitation, and resource distribution activities, and (3) an ideology which constitutes a set of ideas and values that rationalize and motivate social behavior and the relations of production (White, 1959). At least one more component should be added to this classical view: (4) an information – knowledge-handling base that acquires information about the world, formulates it as knowledge, and transmits it from individual to individual and from generation to generation (Flannery, 1973). The structures and activities that characterize a sociocultural group at any time must be consistent with those that are realizable within the biological constraints of its individuals. Conversely, these structures and activities impose constraints on the actualization of individual characteristics that are biologically feasible.

Three kinds of issues are raised concerning mutuality of constraint between individual and sociocultural group characteristics: (1) individual capabilities and alternative mechanisms of cultural evolution, (2) individual development correlations with cultural evolution, and (3) individual and systemic impediments to cultural advance. In Type 1 issues, we postulate certain primitive (in the sense of fixed and preexisting) capabilities of individuals and ask about mechanisms which might bring about advances in the sociocultural organization of these individuals. Thus we are concerned with effects of individual properties on the evolution of group properties with the former taken as invariant (at the level of the primitives). Type 2 emphasizes a greater symmetry between group and individual as it concerns the coevolution of properties at both levels. Finally, Type 3 assumes that certain sociocultural group structures have evolved and questions the relative importance of both the systemic constraints imposed by such group structures and those imposed by individual traits on further progress of the group.

In formulating such issues within the multifaceted model framework, we necessarily must be modest in our scope. We shall choose only some of the representative issues in each category and provide only sketches of the various elements that would be involved in the construction of a meaningful family of models. We hope that upon concluding, the essence will have been conveyed and the reader stimulated to pursue the approach in more depth.

An entity structure for the questions to be considered is shown in Figure 10.4. A sociocultural group coupled to its environment is represented by the entity (SC/Env) pair. Such sociocultural groups may be coupled together to constitute a network of (SC/Env) pairs, which is the highest-level entity to be considered. (Three parallel lines connecting an entity with one below it signify that zero, one, or more of the lower-level entities constitute the higher-level one.) There are two aspects considered for a sociocultural group. It may be decomposed into individuals as expressed in the elemental aspect or into sectors as expressed in the sociotechnological aspect. An individual may be further represented as an interaction of activities or as a progression of life cycle phases. Each such phase may be further associated with activities that are carried out in the phase. This is expressed by hanging the activities aspect from the phase entity as well as from the individual entity.

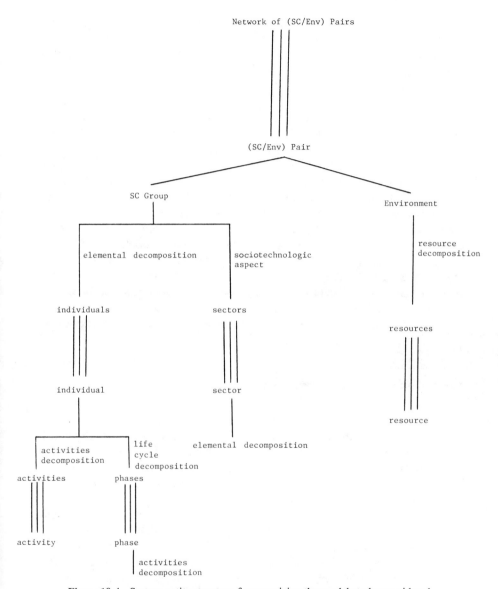

Figure 10.4   System entity structure for organizing the models to be considered.

Note that since the elemental aspect has been attached to the sector entity, each sociotechnological sector can be further decomposed into the individuals that constitute this sector at any time. Moreover, all further substructuring of an individual also applies to individuals of a given sector. This formally permits an individual's life cycle or activity properties to depend on the sector to which he or she belongs. It also sets up a framework for the construction and correlation of models of sociocultural groups on both the micro and macro levels (Section III.B).

In general, models and experimental frames may be considered for any entity in the entity structure. They may be constructed at any degree of resolution permitted by the substructure hanging below the entity in the entity structure. Thus the most comprehensive model consistent with the entity structure is that in which a network of sociocultural groups is represented down to the level in which each of the groups is the resultant of a coupling of sociotechnologic sectors. In turn, each sector is explicitly modeled as an interaction of individuals that are represented as sequences of life cycle phases. Finally, each of the latter phases is a chaining of activities. While within the realm of conceptual contemplation, it would not be computationally feasible to construct and simulate such a model. Various simplifications that restrict the depth of resolution or the system boundaries contemplated are therefore employed. The modeling of sociotechnical structures (Section III.A) illustrates this idea. The advantage of the multifaceted approach, however, is that the simplifications are considered in the context of an inclusive structure and can therefore contribute to a coherent picture of the system as a whole.

A. ALTERNATIVE MECHANISMS FOR CULTURAL EVOLUTION

The first set of questions to be raised for illustrating the multifaceted systems approach concerns alternative mechanisms of cultural evolution. We shall restrict our formulation of these questions to consideration of the evolution of resource utilization strategies as they might be involved in the transition from hunter–gathering to agriculture.

A *gradualist* mechanism formulates cultural advance as an incremental process in which innovations are gradually disseminated, refined, and assimilated into the cultural heritage of a group. The incorporation of an innovation is *autonomous* if it is synthesized from primitives available within the group culture itself and *externally induced* if the innovation is incident from a source external to the cultural group.

An alternative mechanism for cultural evolution suggested by Baba and Zeigler (see Chapter 1, this volume) borrows its conception from that of the *punctuated equilibria* paradigm suggested for genetic evolution (Gould & Eldredge, 1977). Recognizing the conservatism of large sociocultural groups, Baba and Zeigler postulate that cultural innovations are nurtured within smaller subgroups that to some extent are isolated from the main one. Such cultural experiments normally are submerged within the dominant regime, but may get a chance to expand in influence during stressful circumstances such as might be induced by a radical change in environmental characteristics. If an innovation confers special ability to cope with the new circumstances, the subgroup adopting it may be the only one to emerge intact and flourish thereafter. In this view, noticeable cultural change may be a relatively rare occurrence that, once triggered, rapidly takes hold.

The following experimental frames and models presume the existence of primitive activity components in individuals capable of being synthesized to realize group capabilities that are not yet manifest.[1] A progression involves: (1) an isolated group in a constant environment; (2) the same group in a dynamic, stressed environment; (3) a network of groups in the constant environment; and (4) a network of groups in the stressed environment. The punctuated equilibria hypothesis is formulated at the last level of complexity.

Frames EF1 and EF2 and Model M1 relate to an isolated sociocultural group in interaction with its environment. The pruned entity structure on which these objects are based is shown in Figure 10.5. Frames EF1 and EF2 are outlined in Figure 10.6; Model M1 (patterned after Reynolds's model, Section II.A) is outlined in Figure 10.7. In Frame EF1, the environment is considered to be a source of resources with constant characteristics and the frame is concerned with studying cultural evolution under these circumstances. That significant evolution is possible in this case is suggested by Reynolds's model. General questions concern whether or not models of form M1 can reach the specified levels of performance in the specified time available while remaining stable. Stability refers to the existence of the group as an entity as distinct from its individual elements; the group may be judged unstable if it falls below a certain size or if the amount of interaction among individuals falls below a certain level. The expectation of the punctuated equilibria hypothesis is that an equilibrium between group and environment would be reached before the specified level of performance is reached.

In Frame EF2 the constancy of the environment is removed and the group is subjected to environmental stress and shock. Stress variables are formulated as input variables affecting levels of resource abundance. For example, a change in climatic conditions may drastically reduce the availability of

---

[1] Such components are comparable to the culturgens of Lumsden and Wilson (1981), who advance a theory of genetic control of culturgen combinatorics. However, our models do not involve resolution down to the genetic level; they are neutral with respect to possible mechanisms for mediating synthesis via recombination of primitive activity elements.

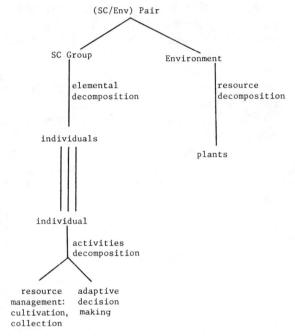

Figure 10.5   Pruned entity structure for mechanisms of cultural evolution.

certain plants.   Input segments formalize the occurrence of stress over time: shocks may be modeled as events that occur either once or in some cyclical or randomized repeated pattern.

In experimental Frames EF3 and EF4 and Model M2 (see Figures 10.8 and 10.9), situations relevant to the punctuated equilibria hypothesis are represented.   Model M2 decomposes a sociocultural group into subgroups, each of which is considered to be an SC group modeled by M1.   Heterogeneity in the component groups is necessary in order to formulate the punctuated equilibria hypothesis.   This may be effectuated ab initio by differences in the assignment of values to parameters of the copies of M1 or their initialization in different states.   Alternatively, the variation could develop in time as a difference in state caused either by irregularities in the coupling scheme digraph linking the SC groups or by exposure of the groups to different environmental characteristics.   Studies from biological counterparts (Zeigler, 1978) suggest that the behavior of a network of groups may be radically different from that of an individual group when intergroup linkages are much less intense than intragroup ones.

```
EF1: Autonomous Evolution of Isolated SC Group in Constant
              Environment

  input variables: none (invariance of environment is
                                   assumed)

  output variables: measures of organizational complexity
                     measures of performance

  run control variables: measures of organizational
                                         complexity
                           measures of stability
                           measures of equilibrium
  initialization conditions: model is set into desired
                             initial level of organizational
                             complexity
  termination conditions: run until desired level of
                           organizational complexity
                           is reached
                        or equilibrium is attained
                        or instability sets in
                        or observation time period
                           is exceeded



EF2: Stressed Evolution of Isolated S-C Group

  input variables: environmental stresses

  input segments:

     * single shocks causing low levels of resources
     * repeated randomized or periodic shocks or other
       oscillations of resource levels

  (otherwise same as EF1)
```

Figure 10.6 Experimental Frames (EF1 and EF2) for evolution of a of sociocultural group.

Note that such a formulation allows for testing the effectiveness of a network of sociocultural groups, but it does not provide an account of how such a network could originate. One such account would have the network evolve via the formation of subgroups and their spinning off from the main body (see Baba and Zeigler, Chapter 1, this volume). An expanded model capable of exhibiting such evolution would naturally be formulated with a time varying structure as suggested in Section II.B. Mechanisms for bringing about such structural change would specify how a subgroup forms and is separated from the main body. Establishment of the linkages that arise between the two groups and the evolution of this coupling would also have to be dynamically specified. Also important would be the inclusion of mechanisms for the destruction of a subgroup or its reincorporation into the main

```
Model M1:

  components:

   individuals:

     input: evaluations of performance of own activities
            reports of performance of others' activities

          output: execution of activities on environment
                  sending of performance reports to others

          state: schedule of activities remaining to be executed

                     resource management strategy
                        (adaptively modified)

    environment:

      input: execution of group activities

      output: evaluation of performance of activities

      state: availability and productivity of resource types

  coupling scheme:

      linkage types: communication of performance reports
                       (individual-individual)
                     evaluation of performance
                       (environment-individual)
```

Figure 10.7   Model for evolution of a sociocultural group.

body under conditions in which the former becomes unstable or unviable in relation to the main, or other, groups. Although the details can be expected to differ radically, analogies in the domain of cellular biology may be suggestive for modeling the origin of a subgroup and its spin-off from a main

```
  EF3: Autonomous Evolution of Network of SC Groups

      Definition is similar to that of EF1 except that:

    * specification is made concerning the nonhomogeneity in
      initial performance levels of the groups

    * measures of performance, complexity, and stability
      are summaries of individual SC group measures


  EF4: Stressed Evolution of Network of SC Groups

      (same as EF2 with same modification as in EF3)
```

Figure 10.8   Experimental Frames (EF3 and EF4) for evolution of a network of sociocultural groups.

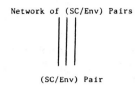

Network of (SC/Env) Pairs

(SC/Env) Pair

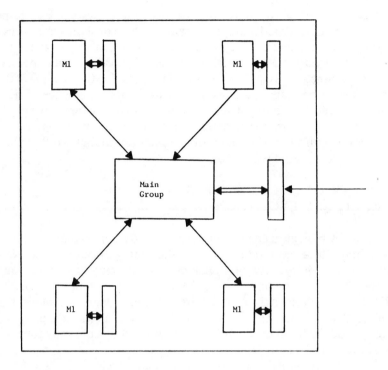

Model M2:

components: SC Group-Environment Pairs
(each is a copy of model M1)

coupling scheme:

linkage types:

intermigration of individuals

interchange of activities performance information

mechanism for structural change:

formation of subgroup of main group

spin-off and coupling to main group and environment

destruction or reincorporation back into main group

Figure 10.9 Pruned entity structure and model for evolution of a network of sociocultural groups.

sociocultural group. In particular, the framework of autopoiesis (Zeleny, 1981) suggests that the development of a topological boundary and a self-sufficiency of reproductive processes within that boundary are among the important conditions for the identification of a subset of the main group as a (semi-) autonomous sociocultural group.

Frames EF3 and EF4 are the counterparts of Frames EF1 and EF2, respectively. They subject Model M2 to the same tests of constant versus stressed environmental behavior. One main difference is that performance measures of the network are summaries of the set of individual group measures. In a test of a punctuated equilibrium mechanism, taking the maxima of these measures is appropriate, since one is looking for the emergence of significantly advanced subgroups. On the other hand, averages are appropriate if the objective is the comparison of the performance of a single homogeneous organization with the performance of an organization that is differentiated into somewhat isolated subgroups.

B. INDIVIDUAL DEVELOPMENT AND CULTURAL EVOLUTION

Several key biological changes have characterized the evolution of hominids; among these are modifications in the timing of ontogenetic events. Longer infancy, delayed maturation, increased retention of juvenile characteristics past maturity, and increased longevity are examples (Campbell, 1972; Harrison, Weiner, Tanner, & Barnicot, 1964; Napier & Napier, 1967; Schultz, 1960; Tanner, 1978). Such ontogenetic changes have provided a longer period for brain development and for learning culturally transmittable knowledge.

Evidence of remarkable plasticity in human development (see Lerner, Chapter 6, this volume) suggests that social and cultural mechanisms may also be important regulators of life cycle timings. In particular, the nature of the techno-economic base of a cultural system may constrain and be constrained by life cycle parameters. Thus cultures at different levels of techno-economic productivity may exhibit different timings of life cycle events consistent with labor force, educational, and other requirements.

Our illustrative formulation of such an individual development–cultural evolution correlation focuses on the replicative aspects of a sociocultural organization, that is, on its ability to preserve the templates that define its culture despite the ever-changing generations of individuals. In this context, the tasks of an individual include biological self-reproduction, learning the group's environmental knowledge and behavioral conventions, and transmitting this knowledge to offspring. Assuming biologically fixed reproductive and information processing capacities, the increased duration of life cycle phases may be expected to enhance reproductive, learning, and transmission capabilities. On the other hand, such prolongation may be counterproductive from an adaptive standpoint (reduced ability to respond to rapid environmental shifts) as well as from an energetic one (reduced efficiency of group skewed to older ages). Thus one might expect that optimum timings exist for different levels of group complexity and environmental variability.

Based on the pruned entity structure of Figure 10.10, Models M3 and M4 are formulated to investigate the correlation of life cycle parameters with techno-economic organization (Figure 10.11).

Model M3 is a refinement of a model of type M1 whose parameters have been set so that the SC group is in equilibrium with its environment. The model is simplified by dropping the adaptive decision-making component and extended so that each individual possesses a life cycle. The resource management activities are (parametrically) distributed in this cycle, with most falling in the maturity phase. In addition, biological reproduction,

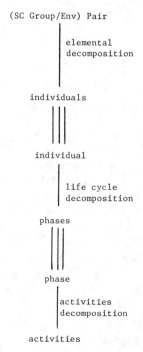

Figure 10.10 Pruned entity structure for individual development and cultural evolution.

```
Model M3:

components:

    individuals:

        input: receipt of instruction units for
                                management activities
               signals for reproduction initiation
               evaluations of performance of self activities

        output: execution of resource management activities
                creation of offspring
                sending of instruction units for
                                management activities

        state: schedule of activities remaining to be
                                executed
               levels of activity instruction units
               age and phase in life cycle

    environment: (same as M1)

coupling scheme:

    linkage types: transmission of instruction units
                   communication of reproduction signals
                       (individual-individual)
                   evaluation of performance
                       (environment-individual)


Model M4 (composition of M3 with decision component of M1)
```

Figure 10.11   Models for life cycle phase parameter optimization.

learning, and teaching activities are distributed in the life cycle. Learning proceeds in units and a new individual is unable to carry out a given resource utilization activity until a given (parametric) number of units for it have been accumulated. Primitive activities have relatively low unit requirements, while composite strategies have correspondingly high unit requirements. The effectiveness of an activity is age dependent, with decline setting in after some (parametric) age. The durations of life cycle phases are parameters and determine the maximum number of activities that can be performed.

In experiments within Frame EF1, the effect of adding the extra overhead costs of knowledge transmission to an SC group in equilibrium with its environment is examined. The deterioration in resource management performance and in organizational complexity level are observed as life cycle phase parameters are altered. Optimum assignments in which the deterioration is minimized are sought.

Model M4 extends M3 by reincorporating the adaptive decision-making components. The question now being asked in Frame EF1 is whether, with the optimal life cycle parameters previously found, the SC group can evolve in organizational complexity so that its optimum performance is actually attained. Then, in Frame EF2, the effect of a changing environment is assessed, with the expectation that the larger the environmental variability, the larger the deterioration in level of achieved performance. A new search for optimal life cycle parameters would be expected to reveal that a reduction in phase durations would achieve better performance under such circumstances.

C. MACRO- AND MICROLEVEL IMPEDIMENTS TO CULTURAL ADVANCE

Despite the lack of sophisticated tools, the diagnosis of current socioeconomic problems and the formulation of prescriptions for solving them is of concern to social science (Tornatzky, 1982).

The issues we shall formulate here concern the analysis of SC groups which are "in trouble," that is, whose progress measured by performance or organizational complexity has stagnated or is in decline. Inability to adapt to a changing environment may be one cause. However, we shall assume a prevailing stable environment that could be better exploited were the group to employ improved resource exploitation methods. One factor holding up the development and application of new methods might be a lack of investment in knowledge generation (science) and transmission (education). We consider this budgeting process to be a systemic constraint imposed by the organization of the group. However, constraints due to human limitations, such as conservatism and inability to assimilate new concepts, might just as well be operating.

Such dilemmas may well be exemplified in modern technological societies. On the one hand, governmental policies may impede growth in industrial productivity by placing low priorities on mathematics and science education and on basic science research. On the other hand, the advanced technological nature of the modern workplace may already be more intellectually challenging than a good portion of the worker population can handle (resistance to automation may stem less from the fear of being displaced than from the fear of not being able to cope). Viewed in this light, the task becomes one of identifying the primary bottleneck and then formulating corrective measures accordingly.

The methodology for diagnosing the key causative factors for a particular SC group would involve construction of a model and identification of the parameter values that calibrate its behavior to the observed historical record and/or response to intentionally designed inputs. A sensitivity analysis would then be performed on the model to predict which changes in structure and parameter settings result in the largest improvement in performance. Were this stage to be reached, the next would be one of social systems engineering: how to bring about the recommended modifications.

As an example, consider Model M5, which is based on a sociotechnological decomposition into knowledge generation (KG), knowledge transmission (KT), knowledge application (KA), and executive (EX) components (see Figures 10.12 and 10.13). Each component could be further decom-

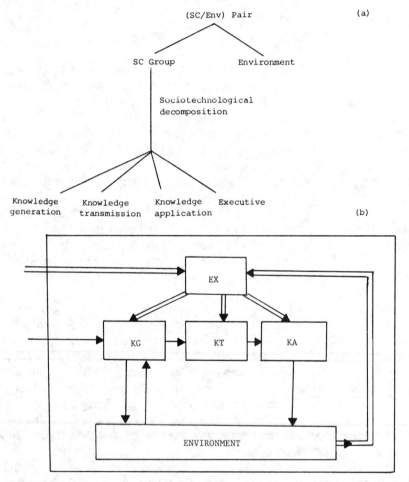

Figure 10.12 Pruned entity structure (a) and model (b) for sociotechnological constraints on cultural advance.

Model M5:

components:

KG: input: budget income
             reports of strategy performance
             infusion of strategies and tools

    output: tested strategies

    state: stock of strategies, size, surplus income

    parameters: knowledge generation rate constant
                 effectiveness characteristics

KT: input: budget income
             tested strategies
             infusion of tools

    output: transformed strategies

    state: stock of strategies, size, surplus income

    parameters: transmission delay and degradation
                effectiveness characteristics

KA: input: budget income
             transformed strategies

    output: mix of applied strategies

    state: size, surplus income

    parameters: conservatism ratio

EX: input: environmental yield
           information about other components

    output: allocation of budgeted income

    state: size, surplus income, memory of past yields

    parameters: distribution ratios

Environment: input: mix of applied strategies

             output: yield

             parameters: strategy yields

Experimental Frames

EF5: Probes for Model Structure Identification

input: infusion of new resource exploitation strategies
       infusion of tools for knowledge generation and transmission
       augmentation of income

output: stock of strategies belonging to KG
        mix of strategies employed by KA
        size, income, surplus of each component

Figure 10.13   Model description for Figure 10.12 and associated experimental frames (EF5) for sociotechnological system diagnosis.

posed into its participating individuals, as we shall soon show. Here, however, the model employs higher-level abstractions which are intended to validly represent aggregate characteristics of the individual properties. The model provides KG with a space of possible environmental exploitation strategies to explore. At any given time, some of these have been evaluated and the better ones maintained in a knowledge base. The task of KT is to convert this knowledge to a form understandable to KA. Constraints in human abilities involved in this process are represented by delay and degradation in the flow of strategies along the path KG → KT → KA. Conservatism in the uptake of available strategies by KA is represented by its incorporating only a fraction into its mix of applied strategies. Delay, degradation, and the fractional update are parameters representing human constraints.

EX executes a budgeting process in which the resource yield of the KA component is distributed among the components. Various models of the process can be postulated, the simplest being a fixed proportion (parametric) allocation. The size, income, and accumulated surplus of each component determine the effectiveness with which it carries out its function (effectiveness may be expected to increase and then decline as size, income, and surplus are increased).

In line with the emphasis on the identification of model structure, experimental Frame EF5 (Figure 10.13) envisions the application of probe inputs and the observation of their effects, common in many applications of modeling. Intentional probes are possible only for an existing SC, but historical records of events such as knowledge infusion from another culture might also be available. Thus Frame EF5 has input variables for introducing new knowledge and tools for new knowledge generation and transmission. It also has input variables for inserting positive or negative increments of income into the budgeting process. Its output variables permit us to observe the effects of the above probes, such as the delay and degradation in uptake of introduced or generated knowledge, the allocation of extra income, and changes in effectiveness with increased income.

One can conceive of constructing an elaborated version of M5 that decomposes each component into its participant individuals. This presumes, of course, that the individuals of the SC group are specialized in occupation. In the elaborated version, M6 (not shown), the nonsystemic constraints, such as conservatism, are incorporated into the models of the individuals and an explicit link made between aggregations of these models and the abstractions employed in M5.

The concept of valid model simplification can be employed to establish relations between the micro and macro models. Model M5 is said to be a valid simplification of M6 within experimental Frame E5 if the two models are behaviorally equivalent when viewed within this frame. With the proper formulation, such behavioral equivalence may be established by demonstrating the existence of an appropriate structure preserving morphism to relate the two models (i.e., a correspondence of the state sets of the models that preserves their transition and output structures). Since both models are in fact parametric, such a morphism actually sets up a parameter value correspondence that matches up assignments of parameter values to the respective models that result in their equivalence within the desired frame. It is such a parameter correspondence that enables the correlation of properties at the microlevel represented by M6 with those at the macrolevel M5. This concept is discussed in greater detail by Zeigler (1976, 1978, 1979, 1982).

IV. Conclusions

Mutuality of constraint in the evolution of a sociocultural group and the development of its individual members has been examined within three categories: (1) assuming fixed individual capabilities, a category embracing the kinds of mechanisms that bring about reorganization to more advanced sociocultural levels; (2) a category embracing individual life cycle parameter correlations with techno-economic complexity; and (3) a category that includes impediments to cultural advance arising from both systemic and individual constraints. This mutuality of constraint can be addressed at many levels and with respect to a multiplicity of organizational and individual properties. In this chapter a first attempt was made to lay out the kinds of questions that can be asked from this perspective, the kinds of models that might be used to address them, and the kinds of data that might be gathered to support these models. Our approach derived from two sources, multifaceted systems modeling, which is a methodology for mapping real world systems to computerized forms and organizing such models within a coherent framework, and cultural anthropology, which involves the empirical investigation of sociocultural organizations.

Conventional reductionistic and holistic approaches that restrict themselves to inquiry at a single level (local and global, respectively) cannot do justice to the multilevel issues involved in the mutuality of constraint problems that we have raised. In applying the multifaceted methodology, we have demonstrated that it is possible simultaneously to formulate hypotheses and construct models at a number of levels of aggregation in a disciplined and integrated manner. This integration operationalizes what modern philosophers of science point out, that science progresses by seeking to weave a consistent fabric out of the diverse facts and theories it generates. The greater the power of the tools at our disposal for performing this consistency testing, the greater the progress we are likely to make toward a comprehensive understanding of our world.

The application of multifaceted systems methodology to questions of evolutionary anthropology has granted us a glimpse of the opportunities for understanding in greater depth the mutuality of constraint in individual and cultural evolution. However, the state of the art in either discipline is not up to more than tempting us with these possibilities. The future may be different.

References

Campbell, B. *Human evolution.* Chicago, Aldine, 1972.

Cooke, R., & Renfew, K. L. (Eds.). *Transformations: Mathematical approaches to cultural change.* New York: Academic Press, 1979.

Flannery, K. Origins of agriculture. *Annual Review of Anthropology,* 1973, *2,* 271–310.

Gould, S. J., & Eldredge, N. Punctuated equilibria: The tempo and mode of evolution reconsidered. *Paleobiology,* 1977, *3*(2), 115–151.

Harrison, G. A., Weiner, J. S., Tanner, J. M., & Barnicot, N. A. *Human biology.* New York: Oxford University Press, 1964.

Lumsden, C. J., & Wilson, E. O. *Genes, mind, and culture: The coevolutionary process.* Cambridge, Mass.: Harvard University Press, 1981

Oren, T. I. Concepts for computer-aided modelling. In B. P. Zeigler, M. S. Elzas, G. J. Klir, & T. I. Oren (Eds.), *Methodology in systems modelling and simulation.* Amsterdam: North Holland, 1979.

Napier, J. R., & Napier, P. H. *A handbook of living primates.* London, Academic Press, 1967.

Reynolds, R. An adaptive computer simulation model of the acquisition of incipient agriculture in prehistoric Oaxaca, Mexico. *Proceedings of the Congress of the International Union of Prehistoric Scientists,* 1981, 202–216.

Reynolds, R., & Zeigler, B. P. A formal mathematical model for the operation of consensus-based hunting–gathering groups. In R. Cooke & K. L. Renfew (Eds.), *Transformations: mathematical approaches to cultural change.* New York: Academic Press, 1979.

Schultz, A. H. Age changes in primates and their modification in man. In *Human growth.* London: Pergamon Press, 1960.

Stewart, J. H. *Theory of cultural change: The methodology of multilinear education.* Urbana: University of Illinois Press, 1955.

Tanner, T. M. Focus into man: Physical growth from conception to maturity. Cambridge, Mass.: Harvard University Press, 1978.

Tornatzky, L. G., Eveland, J. D., Boylan, M. G., Hetzner, W. A., Johnson, E. C., Roithman, D., & Schneider, J. *The Process of innovation: Analyzing the literature.* Washington, D.C.: National Science Foundation, 1982.

Wymore, W. *Systems engineering methodology for interdisciplinary teams.* New York: Wiley, 1976.

White, L. A. *The concept of evolution in cultural anthropology.* Washington, D.C.: Anthropological Society of Washington, DC, 1959.

Zeigler, B. P. *Theory of modelling and simulation.* New York: Wiley, 1976.

Zeigler, B. P. Multilevel, multiformalism modelling: An ecosystem example. In E. Halfon (Ed.), *Theoretical ecological systems.* New York: Academic Press, 1978.

Zeigler, B. P. Structuring principles for multifaceted system modelling. In B. P. Zeigler, M. S. Elzas, G. J. Klir, & T. I. Oren (Eds.), *Methodology in systems modelling and simulation.* Amsterdam: North Holland, 1979.

Zeigler, B. P. *Multifaceted modelling and discrete event simulation.* London: Academic Press, 1984.

Zeleny, M. What is Autopoiesis? In M. Zeleny (Ed.), *Autopoiesis: A theory of living organization.* New York: North Holland, 1981.

11

Analysis of Qualitative Data in Developmental Psychology

H. JÖRG HENNING
GEORG RUDINGER

I. In Search of Appropriate Methods within the Framework of Qualitative Developmental Theories and Models

A. DATA, MODELS, AND THEORIES

In this chapter we will consider some methods that may be used to analyze qualitative data in developmental psychology. To talk about data at the beginning of the chapter or, for that matter, at the initiation of a research process seems like taking the second or third step before the first, because "data" in the Coombsian sense, and also as we use the term, are created by transforming and interpreting observations. The selection of situations and aspects of behavior, the kind or mode of observation, the sampling of times, events, and individuals — all these decisions are already guided by the theoretical and practical interest of the researcher. Date are in no way identical with observations; they already express in some way one's theory of behavior. The group of statistical models for data analysis that the researcher selects depends on these interpretations of "reality" and on the inferences that are intended to be drawn from the data. The level of measurement does not necessarily imply a certain type of statistical procedure. Reaction-time measurements, for example, since physical time is taken, seem self-evidently to be on the ratio-scale level. If, however, the cognitive structure or process theory on which data are based is "qualitative," these highly precise measures are not used, and every statistical model that is "appropriate" for this scale level has a surplus not covered by the theory.

To take another example, consider the assumption that there is a sharp rise of intelligence up to adulthood and, afterwards, a slight but steady decline. In order to prove this "theory," one has to test hypotheses about ratios of differences; in this case it is necessary to have interval-scaled data and to apply statistical models drawn from the family of general linear models.

Given the view that development is the structural rather than the continuous change of the psychic system by processes such as differentiation and hierarchization (development versus growth; see Overton & Reese, 1973; Wohlwill, 1973), hypotheses to be tested have to be formulated in qualitative instead of quantitative terms. Variables have to be defined as discrete instead of continuous, and inferences will refer to statements about order instead of differences. The adequacy of the tools for data analysis has to be evaluated with regard to these decisions in the scientific research process (see also von Eye, Chapter 5, this volume).

It is easy to see that the appropriateness of a statistical technique is primarily not an empirical question. It does not make much sense to maintain that the linear model is not suitable for detecting, describing, or explaining developmental changes per se, or that approaches derived from systems theory are the better ones, or that the qualitative models we would like to present are the best ones. These statements may seem trivial, because for many readers this message is widely accepted and well known. However, we have the impression that a gap continues to exist between this statement (attitude) and actual research (behavior). In the majority of empirical investigations this critical reasoning is lacking, as is the appropriate translation of ideas of theoretical and methodological progress into practical research.

B. STRUCTURE AND SEQUENCES

The term *development* implies two central components: (1) ". . . the notion of a system, possessing a definite structure and a definite set of preexisting capacities"; and (2) "the notion of a set of sequential changes in the system, yielding relatively permanent but novel increments not only in its structures but in its modes of operation as well" (Nagel, 1957, p. 17). Hoppe-Graff (1982), following these assumptions, defined a developmental sequence as an ontogenetic series of states of the psychic system which occur with a theoretically predicted regularity in all observed individuals (i.e., with interindividual uniformity; see Featherman, Chapter 8, this volume). Regularity is assumed if there is a high probability that the states are concatenated with each other in the theoretically postulated order. It is difficult, even in the case of simple, unitary sequences, to demonstrate such a "high" probability. It is even more difficult in the case of divergent, multiple sequences.

Hoppe-Graff raises another important point by distinguishing, in line with our arguments, between sequential theories (or, as we call them, qualitative theories), developmental sequences, and ordinal developmental scales. There exists, however, an inclusive relationship between these sequential – qualitative theories, developmental sequences, and ordinal scales. Every sequential theory implies the assumption of at least one developmental sequence, and the existence of a developmental sequence implies the existence of an ordinal scale, but not vice versa. Sequential theories (e.g., those of Piaget, Erikson, Freud, Kohlberg, Flavell) postulate certain order relations between their theoretical core concepts such as hierarchy or structure and/or sequences. They also describe, construct, and explain the regularity of the ontogenetic ordering of developmental states, stages, phases, periods, and so on. So, for example, the Piagetian global phases of cognitive development are described by means of formal logic, and the individual's progression through these stages is explained by basic developmental mechanisms such as equilibration or the principle of organization. In this chapter we will limit our discussion to the kinds of theories mentioned above. Instead of giving additional definitions of terms such as *sequence, structure,* and *qualitative,* we will simply refer back to the programmatic approaches of authors like Bentler (1971), van den Daele (1969), Wohlwill (1973), Riegel (1976), Overton and Reese (1973), Aebli (1978), Fischer (1980), and Coombs and Smith (1973), who tried to derive from qualitative – sequential developmental theories testable models depicting developmental sequences.

C. MODELS FOR QUALITATIVE DATA

A widespread and growing number of methodologists share the conviction that most psychological theories are qualitative in the sense that upon a closer look, the majority of hypotheses derived from them express ordinal relations between variables rather than quantitative ones. However, most hypotheses are formulated and tested within a framework of metric interval-

or higher-level scales. There exist different points of view regarding the propriety of this situation. On the one hand, according to Young (1981), "the omnipresence of qualitative data" is considered to be one of the main impediments to rapid progress in psychology. The implication is that one should be interested in the quantification of qualitative data. On the other hand—and this is our opinion, too—the omnipresence of qualitative data reflects realistically the state of theory building in the social and behavioral sciences. Therefore, one should look for and adapt for use statistical techniques capable of handling qualitative data. Such qualitative theories have their own merit and should not be considered necessarily inferior to quantitative ones. This insight may be one reason why recent methodological literature in the social and behavioral sciences has introduced a number of new inference procedures appropriate to the analysis of nominal and ordinal data. Unfortunately there is no agreed-upon taxonomy of methods for the analysis of qualitative data and, because of the relative newness of the statistical methods involved, only a few authors have offered concise, well-documented presentations of these methods, methods that we believe are most relevant for the analysis of developmental data (Bentler, 1980; Henning, 1981; Hoppe, Schmid-Schönbein, & Seiler, 1977).

Small wonder, then, that the application of qualitative analysis methods or techniques to real data from developmental psychology is very rare. To many applied scientists, these techniques are novel, and to many statisticians and theoreticians who might otherwise foster their use, applied work does not seem worthwhile. Yet many problems that arise in applied work indicate the need for further methodological considerations, as the reader will learn in Section II. In that section some tests of assumptions from the theories of Piaget and Erikson and from the work on disengagement will be presented. The fact that our decision concerning the particular methods that seem appropriate for our purposes leads to an extremely selective sample of techniques may be demonstrated by referring to Bentler's (1980) taxonomy of qualitative data (Table 11.1). Bentler's article offers an excellent survey of these methods, including some reasonable suggestions and valuable perspectives for their application.

D. TYPES OF CHANGE AND INTERINDIVIDUAL DIFFERENCES

Independent of the choice of particular statistical models, qualitative approaches face design problems that are similar to those of the psychometric paradigm in measuring change. Developmental researchers have been made fully aware of these problems through in-depth treatments both in the

Table 11.1

Taxonomy of Models for Qualitative Data[a]

Model	Source
I. Latent attribute models	
1. Latent structure models	Lazarsfeld & Henry (1968)
Latent class model	Goodman (1974)
Latent class with response error	Dayton & MacReady (1980)
2. Scalability models	
Scalogram analysis	Guttman (1950)
Probabilistic scale analysis	Proctor (1970)
Multiple scale analysis	Mokken (1971)
Bi- and multiform scales	Goodman (1975a, 1975b)
Probabilistic validation	Dayton & MacReady (1976)
Order analysis	Krus (1976)
Scaling of order hypothesis	Davison (1979, 1980)
Probabilistic unfolding	Coombs & Smith (1973)
Quasi-independence model	Goodman (1975)
3. Latent trait models	
Rasch model	Rasch (1966); Fischer (1976)
Normal ogive model	Lord & Novick (1968)
Three parameter logistic model	Birnbaum (1968)
Logistic change model	Fischer (1976)
4. Factor analysis models	
FA for dichotomous variables	Muthen (1978); Christoffersson (1975)
Monotonicity analysis	Bentler (1970)
II. Prediction models	
1. Dichotomous regression model	
Logit model	Grizzle, Starmer, & Koch (1969)
2. Structural equation models	
LISREL	Jöreskog & Sörbom (1981)
Partial Least Squares (PLS)	Wold (1979)
3. Cross-classification with errors models	
Prediction analysis	Hildebrand et al. (1977)
Fitting cross-classification	Thomas (1977)
Matching model	Hubert (1979)
4. Multidimensional contingency table with	
Partial Least Squares	Wold & Bertholet (1983)
III. Multinomial response models	
1. Log-linear model	Goodman (1972); Bishop, Fienberg, & Holland (1975); Haberman (1979)
2. Analysis of correspondence	Benzécri (1973); Linder & Berchtold (1982)
3. Dual scaling for categorical data	Nishisato (1980)

[a] This taxonomy of models was initiated by Bentler (1980) and has been expanded by the present authors.

field of methodology and design of developmental studies (Baltes, Reese, & Lipsitt, 1980; Nesselroade & Baltes, 1979) and in the area of cognitive developmental studies (Keats, Collins, & Halford, 1978; Kluwe & Spada, 1980; Rauh, 1978). For example, in the qualitative paradigm, from a cross-sectional design it is possible only to *infer* change (i.e., a developmental sequence). From aggregated data of many individuals gathered at one measurement occasion, the inference of change is drawn from the configuration of variables in relation to a developmental process. This procedure leads to acceptable results only under the additional assumption that the underlying developmental process is cumulative in character (see Hoppe et al., 1977). In a longitudinal design the sequence (change) can be "directly" observed, loosely speaking. And only in a longitudinal design is the researcher in a position to compare, analogously with the psychometric approach, different types of changes such as intraindividual change, interindividual differences in intraindividual changes, and so on.

In our opinion, it is currently the interindividual differences in intraindividual changes aspect that especially attracts the attention of many researchers. For a long time the assumption of universal, invariant sequences that were generalizable over people, time, cultures, social classes, and so forth, was of special theoretical interest. However, empirical research failed to establish this type of developmental sequence as the predominantly valid developmental pattern. Empirical and some critical theoretical analyses (e.g., Gergen, 1977; Phillips & Kelly, 1975) of hierarchical theories of development (e.g., the Piagetian invariance approach) led to the conclusion that the development of cognitive structures is not accurately represented by strict sequences in the structure of concrete operations (e.g., quantity → weight → volume; Sheppard, 1978). As a result, in our own research we formulated the hypothesis that cognitive structure is more differentiated and more complex than a "Guttman-like" simple order. Developmental sequences and structures can be designated either in the "logical Piagetian structure" of a unidimensional hierarchy or as multiple – multidimensional patterns of partial orders, tree-structure, or bi- or multiform scales, the forms of which are illustrated in Figure 11.1.

Each structure in Figure 11.1 is based on four items with two response categories, zero and one. The well-known Guttman structure forms a sequence of simple ordinal character (Figure 11.1a). This scale was termed by Goodman (1978) a "uniform scale." It is assumed that most of the subjects can be classified; that is, scaled by the "true score pattern" of that scale form. Figure 11.1b illustrates the branching into a "biform scale." These scale types may be the result of different substantial strategies being used to reach a definite pattern of behavior, developmental stage, or task. For instance, on the one hand a biform scale can be the representation of a

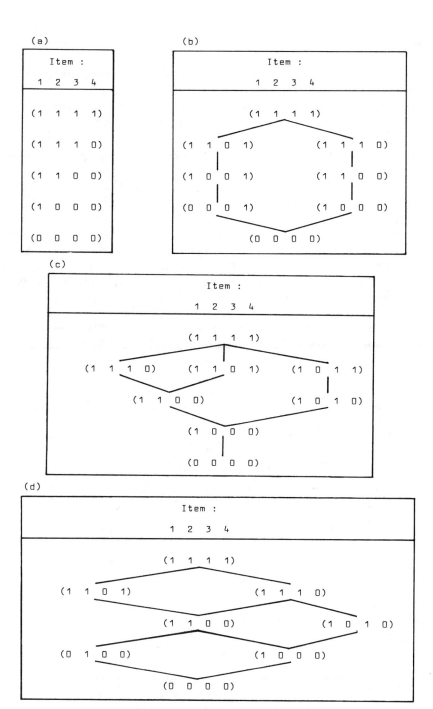

Figure 11.1 Examples of uniform (a) biform (b), and multiform (c, d) scales.

cognitive process reaching the highest level by two alternative ways. On the other hand, however, a biform scale gives evidence of the existence of two different classes of subjects in the population of interest. Each of these classes fits a uniform scale, but they differ from each other in one or more response patterns. The combined uniform scales constitute the biform scale. These scale types, which accommodate stage skipping or regression processes to an earlier level of development, give an alternative representation of unilineal progressions to that presented in the dynamic change models of Singer and Spilerman (1979, p. 166).

Figures 11.1c and 11.1d illustrate some forms of "multiform scales" representing far more complex structures. For example, a divergent or convergent progression (sensu van den Daele, 1969) can be represented by these scale types. The most complex structure is given by the "symmetric and asymmetric diamonds" represented by Figure 11.2. Also termed "partial order configurations," they result from a systematic and differentiated branching process of a *complete* scalogram in two dimensions. This structure offers some new possibilities in theory building. For example, as indicated by Shye (1978, p. 225), the joint direction of the diamond structure

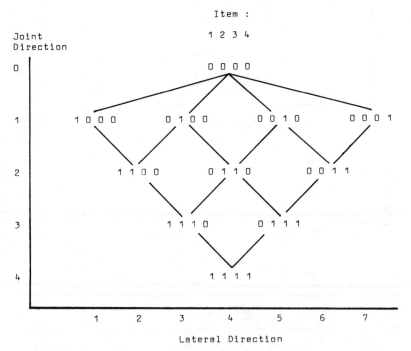

Figure 11.2   Example of a symmetric diamond structure (see Shye, 1978, p. 274).

"would indicate the speed or intensity of process" taking place in some cognitive, temporal, or any other space. The "lateral direction would give an idea of how advanced the process is" according to the type of space assumed. These scale forms, response patterns, and complex structures need to be recognized as the essential parts of developmental theories transformed in a partial order hierarchy of "true score response patterns."

From the qualitative schemes described above it is possible to assess change or stability of a hypothetical structure under several options:

1. *Differential developmental sequences.* A structure changes its simple (or complex) branching pattern either to more complexity (or to more simplicity) with ongoing time (age). That change pattern can be observed by means of a *longitudinal* design within a selected cohort.

2. *Discriminating developmental sequences.* A structure is explored or confirmed in, for instance, a cross-sectional design involving samples differing in some relevant variables of interest (e.g., school types; types of developmental tasks; different situations; different courses of critical life events). Discriminating sequences can be used in educational and diagnostic fields.

3. *Quasi-differential developmental sequences.* As in items 1 or 2, complex branching structures are assumed. In both, however, the complexity is interpreted as an attribute of substantive meaning of the analyzed tasks, items, or situations, that is, of the field of content. Here complexity is considered to be an attribute of the analyzed sample (population). If it is possible to separate a sample into two (or more) parts, with each subsample generating a simple Guttman-like structure that differs from the structure of the other subsamples, the combined result will be a bi- (or multi-) form scale.

We will now consider the crucial point of mapping the observed response pattern to models representing individual development and/or social change. Table 11.2 should both clarify the arrangement of observations into individual response patterns and show how hypothetical structures are made operational in a priori patterns. There is no unique solution to the problem of how to conceptualize different change processes within persons, between persons, in a situation, over several situations, or over time. It is a matter of interpreting the fit of an observed response data matrix to an a priori pattern or expected response matrix.

The first step in probabilistic statistical data analysis is to aggregate the individual observed response patterns into a data matrix by determining the frequencies of the several patterns. Next, this matrix of aggregated data must be compared with the expected response patterns matrix. Statistical evaluation is done according to some probabilistic model with specified

Table 11.2

Mapping Observations into Response Patterns and A Priori Patterns Defining Structural
Hypothesis of Individual–Social Change

	Possible observations of subjects to 4 items—already coded		
Subject	Observations, Time 1	Observations, Time 2	Change patterns, Time $(2-1)^a$
1	0000	1000	1000
2	1000	1100	0100
3	1000	0100	1100
4	1100	1110	0010
5	1010	1110	0100
6	1110	1111	0001
.	....	....	....

‖   ⇑
Mapping to the model   Fit of the model
⇓   ‖

	A priori patterns for a uniform scale type		Expected change matrix
Frequency			
.	0000	1000	1000
.	1000	1100	0100
.	1100	1110	0010
.	1110	1111	0001
.	1111	1111	0000

^{a} A "1" indicates a change in observation over time.

"recruitment probabilities" (see Figure 11.9). These evaluations are possible only for patterns at Time 1, and independently for patterns at Time 2. Now, the following questions arise: Is the structure the same at both times? Does Structure 2 differ from Structure 1? What are the "critical" a priori patterns in which they differ? Could or should they differ? These questions can be answered by the probabilistic models described and used subsequently in this chapter.

It is also possible to construct patterns for a *change matrix* by coding any change in patterns at Time 1 and Time 2 as "1" and no change as "0." The frequencies of these "change patterns" can be fitted to an expected change matrix that represents a particular kind of developmental change.

Several aspects of social change can be studied. For example, people from different social environments may form different a priori (and observed) patterns at one point of measurement. Scaling methods are examples of appropriate tools for identifying these different groups. Some social phenomena occur between points of observation and change the response structure in a characteristic direction. Thus, different, identifiable subpopulations of respondents behaving in a homogeneous manner result in more or less mutually exclusive a priori (and observed) change patterns. We can only point to the general possibility here due to the fact that a sufficient discussion of mapping procedures for individual and/or social change cannot be given without concrete operational knowledge of some developmental or social change theory of interest.

Several groups of models listed in Table 11.1 can be used to construct and test simple, unidimensional structures and sequences. Some of these models are also suitable for assessing complex structures, trees, and sequences. The log-linear model and the Dayton and MacReady model are especially useful in developmental and qualitative structure studies.

For the group of latent attribute models — including models for scalability of response patterns — Clogg and Sawyer (1981) and Henning (1981) have given empirical examples involving the comparison of alternative methods (including the Mokken scale analysis, Krus's order analysis, the Dayton and MacReady model, Goodman's quasi-independence model, the Guttman scalogram analysis, and Proctor's probability scale model). Other latent attribute models and techniques are discussed by Dayton and MacReady (1980); Gliner (1982); Hubert, Golledge, Costanzo, and Richardson (1981); Plewis (1981); Davison (1980); Goldstein (1979, 1980); Goodman (1981); Singer and Spilerman (1979); and Krauth and Lienert (1981).

An alternative technique for analyzing contingency table data to assess change, development, and prediction success was developed by Hildebrand, Laing, and Rosenthal (1977). Froman and Hubert (1980) applied this technique to the study of developmental priority and Hoppe-Graff (1982) to developmental sequences of class inclusion. Henning (1979) presented several applications from different areas of psychology.

The gist of the methodological observations presented thus far may be summarized in the following programmatic way. With these statistical techniques it is possible to test a large variety of developmental models, such as synchronous progression, horizontal decalage, vertical decalage, and reciprocal interaction. Similarly, it is possible to represent and validate divergent or convergent progressions with these techniques (see van den Daele, 1969). Symmetric and asymmetric diamond or partial-order configurations also can be defined or postulated theoretically as a priori structures and empirically tested.

The psychometric approach in perhaps its most advanced form (the LISREL approach by Jöreskog & Sörbom, 1981) distinguishes different levels of change. There can be change in (1) the number of latent variables; (2) the factor loadings; (3) the errors of observed variables; (4) the covariances between the latent variables; and last but not least, (5) the means of the latent variables. Of course, one can imagine simultaneous combinations of these change features; for example, number of latent variables constant, factor loadings changing, factor intercorrelations constant, and so forth. In our opinion there are some parallels between these quantitative–structural concerns and aspects of qualitative–structural analysis. Analogous to the quantitative structural changes just listed are changes in the levels of hierarchies, speed, spacing, loops, relation, and concatenation between the qualitative features of developmental processes. These relations can be disjunctive, conjunctive, or compensatory. However, it is important to take into consideration that without substantial developmental theory, neither qualitative nor psychometric approaches can provide a general rule for defining change. The researcher has to determine explicitly his or her concrete conception of change — which levels, aspects, and facets are involved — on a case-by-case basis, just as we will do in the examples of Section II. For many developmental conceptions, methodological solutions can be offered. In the way a psychometrically oriented researcher investigates differences between and within persons, so the "qualitative" researcher can investigate multiple and cumulative sequences. Perhaps the qualitatively oriented researcher is in a better position than the psychometrically oriented one in studying relations between the elements, variables, or features of a developmental process as mentioned above.

Some problems remain unsolved, however. Even in the psychometric approach a methodologically satisfying answer to the question of how to establish relations between nested systems of different levels of aggregation does not exist. Multilevel analysis from sociology may offer some promise but, in general, the state of affairs is as disappointing for the methodologist as for the substantive researcher interested in cause–effect, interaction, and reciprocity relations between different levels of aggregation in individual and social unit information.

Hierarchically ordered systems of increasing abstraction are well known in ecologically oriented developmental research as macro-, meso-, microsystems. Also, the individual is regarded as a system of a special kind. Changes in the macrosystem include, for example, change from an industrial society with steadily accelerated economic growth to a state of zero growth or change in a society from liberal social attitudes to more conservative ones. Examples of mesosystem changes are changes in the school system from planned curricula to student's choice, the changing proportion of female and male teachers (e.g., increased feminization of the teacher role), and the initiation or removal of TV shows such as Sesame Street. Changes in the microsystem include the loss of a spouse, the birth of a child, and the changed style of communication between parents and children. Although it may be possible to compare (quasi-) differential or discriminating sequences combined with different facets of the superordinate system, we do not yet see how the superordinate changes of systems can be incorporated into developmental sequences; that is, how to relate them directly to individual changes.

II. Illustrations from Different Fields of Developmental Psychology

Our selection of examples from different fields of research in developmental psychology is geared toward demonstrating how the techniques and procedures actually work; our aim is not just to supply additional elaboration and summary of the kinds of methods that are available. The philosophy underlying the following procedures is a very simple one. The form of developmental scale, response pattern, or complex structure needs to be derived from an explicitly stated developmental structure. With such guidance the number of possible sequential patterns of items (e.g., 2^n for n dichotomous items) usually shrinks to a much smaller number of logically and/or theoretically admissible patterns.

Assessing the structure, evaluating changes, and looking for the complexity of patterns can be done in an exploratory or confirmatory way. For these purposes special probabilistic models exist which include definitions of error (e.g., inadmissible patterns) and the fitting of data to hypothetical a priori structures that represent particular models of development.

Most of the illustrations that follow are limited to empirical applications of methods beyond Guttman scaling (see Figures 11.1 and 11.2), the method most often used to demonstrate the ordinal character of developmental tasks and structures. With the more elaborated statistical models that were mentioned earlier, one is able to test alternative formulations of the theoretical components by model comparison procedures (χ^2 and likelihood ratio tests) and to answer questions about the nature of change in a methodologically and statistically satisfying manner (see Section III.C and Figure 11.11).

A. EXAMPLE 1: DETECTING COGNITIVE STRUCTURES IN PIAGETIAN INVARIANCE TASKS

Preliminary Remarks. Piagetian theory concerning invariance of tasks and the concept of conservation assumes a closed system of, for example, concrete operations of thinking.[1] The period of development of these

---

[1] We are grateful to Hellgard Rauh, Free University of Berlin, for the use of her theories and data in examples 1 and 2.1.

intellectual operations is approximately ages 4 to 10. Piaget asserts an irreversible, hierarchical sequence of development, one that is not changed by situational influences. This assumption, however, is only valid for the sequence from the stage of sensorimotoric development to the final stage of formal operations. There are no clear hypotheses about the process of development within a specific stage (e.g., concrete operations). Piagetian theory does not explain how or in what order children systematize their operations of thinking, nor by which fields of experiences they are influenced. Different interpretations of the nature of regularity of the developmental process of the child's knowledge structures allow the sources of influence on development to range from individual to social change. Different developmental structures may have their causes in educational and cultural differences, the divergent experiences of children, and dependence on the research material (i.e., on the types of invariance tasks) or in combinations of these (see, e.g., Lerner, Chapter 6, and Featherman, Chapter 8, this volume).

But additional criticism can be raised against the rigidity of the hierarchical order of stages that denies dynamic processes of developmental change. Some children can perform tasks from higher-level stages before they solve the tasks of the "preordered" lower stages. Aebli (1978) modified the Piagetian approach by distinguishing two types of sequences. The first type includes irreversible structures and sequences and accords development an implicational order (see Brandtstädter, Chapter 9, this volume). The second type of sequence is based on differences in complexity, and therefore may be influenced by educational and environmental situations. Thus, it may happen that a proposed "Piagetian sequence" is broken by children with special individual experiences (e.g., training) or by groups of children living in unusual social surroundings. Further critical notes on a strong hierarchical theory are given by Gergen (1977), Lerner (Chapter 6, this volume), Phillips and Kelly (1975), and Sheppard (1978). A critical evaluation of Piagetian theory in perceptual development is given by Gigerenzer (1982).

These preliminary remarks set the stage for the following empirical example and demonstration based on a strict hierarchical theory, the purpose of which is to evaluate Guttman-like a priori response patterns and uniform scale types. There is a great deal of empirical (and theoretical) evidence that cognitive development in the field of concrete operations is more complex than is assumed when fitting a strict hierarchical model (e.g., see Henning, 1981; Rauh, 1972). Such considerations lead to hypotheses about higher branching structures of response patterns (see Figure 11.3).

It is not our purpose here to provide systematic statistical support for alternative or modified theories of cognitive development, although this empirical demonstration would be valuable to someone intending to de-

(a)

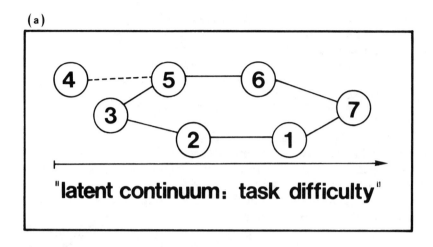

(b)

```
Sample 2.1:  N = 45 children primary school age 5.8 - 7.1
Sample 2.2:  N = 45     "         "       "    age 15 months later
Sample 2.3:  N = 45     "         "       "    age 3rd grade
Sample 2.4:  N = 45     "         "       "    age 4th grade
Sample 3  :  N = 34 children "Montessori school" 3rd grade
Sample 4  :  N = 203 (116 + 87) children age 4 - 7 (Table 11.3)
```

Figure 11.3 Model of a cognitive two-way-process (a) and investigated samples for invariance task groups (b). The hypothetical task structure for the 7 task groups is based on Samples 2.1–2.4 and 3, derived from empirical results with Mokken scaling, Dayton and MacReady analysis, and Krus order analysis.

velop alternatives.   Rather, in this chapter we are primarily concerned with applying novel methods of scaling and structure search and validation to real empirical data.   Although this example offers some methodology and applications for different approaches to the study of individual development and social change, the solution of remaining theoretical questions is left to others.

Prior Empirical Knowledge and Structural Characteristics.   Reexamination of data sets from Piagetian invariance tasks (Rauh, 1979) with multiple scale analysis (Mokken, 1971), order analysis (Krus, 1976), and the Dayton and MacReady model (1976a) provided initial evidence that the previously assumed simple hierarchical Guttman-like structure of that material was not at all valid. Twenty-nine invariance items were investigated and combined in seven task groups:

1. Item group of numbers–quantities (chips)
2. Item group of numbers–quantities (puppets)

3. Item group of numbers – quantities (trains)
4. Item group of Müller – Lyer illusions
5. Item group of Piagetian lengths
6. Item group of continuous quantities (volume)
7. Item group of continuous quantities (juice – water)

These item groups constitute the empirical material on which most of the statistical computations and fits of models that follow are based.

Piagetian theory implicitly assumes a simple ordered hierarchy of the seven listed invariance task groups. Earlier reanalyses of similar material, however, resulted in the hypothesis that task group structure is characterizable as a cognitive, two-way process (see Figure 11.3a). Starting with items of Group 3, the most difficult items of Task Group 7 are reached by one of two possible ways. Either children "prefer" the string of "discrete quantities" (Task 3 – 2 – 1 – 7) or they prefer the string of "continuous quantities" (Task 3 – 5 – 6 – 7). As in earlier investigations, Task Group 4 (Müller – Lyer items) was identified in every new sample case (see Table 11.3) as containing "nonscalable" items. This analysis was done using the Mokken model. Parenthetically, younger children were more able than older ones to solve the items of Group 4 (a result quite independent of correct solutions to other invariance items). As noted by Rauh (1972, p. 176), this result contradicts findings by Gruen (1968).

The prior empirical knowledge concerning those relationships was obtained mainly by application of Mokken's scale analysis. But this technique is not suitable for assessing all multiple strings of a hypothetical structure of developmental tasks taken as a whole, that is, in their full complexity and generality. According to the Mokken scale analysis findings, however, we could state the research hypothesis that cognitive structure in the development of concrete operations is mapped by some biform two-way process (see Figure 11.3). If this hypothesis were to hold, developmental sequences and structures could be designed as a multiple and multidimensional pattern of partial order, tree structure, biform scale, or possibly higher multiform scales.

Results. First, the unidimensionality of all seven task groups was checked. By the Mokken model Item Groups 4 and 7 were identified as nonscale items rather than as items building a different, second scale. The other five item groups were interpreted as a strong scale in a probabilistic sense (Loevinger's scalability coefficient $H = .57$). For comparison purposes, a Guttman scale of hierarchical order has to reach a coefficient of approximately 1. This outcome leads to several salient questions. Should we have accepted this probabilistic uniform scale solution? Is there a way to get further evidence on the nature of this scale? What would happen to this

Table 11.3

Results of Mokken Scale Analysis for the Seven
Task Groups[a]

Item number	Item coefficient H	Item δ^*
Testing scalability, Loevinger's coefficient H		
H = 0.5663	$\delta^* = 14.1204$	
3	0.6504	10.1716
2	0.6205	10.2767
5	0.4799	7.9484
1	0.5892	9.4945
6	0.4887	6.8623
Final Scale 1; 5 items		
Excluded items		
7	0.2369	4.0128
No Scale 2		
Nonscale items 4 and 7		

[a] Sample size is 203 (Sample 4).

scale if the responses were analyzed with stronger goodness of fit models, such as the Proctor or the Dayton and MacReady models?

To answer these questions, we prepared three different *item orders* and crossed them with four different a priori response pattern structures (see Table 11.4). The three item inputs were: (1) order of presentation according to their assumed logical structure as defined by Piaget $(1-2-3-5-6)$; (2) order of the corresponding sample difficulties of items $(6-2-1-3-5)$; and (3) order of item homogeneity as analyzed by the Mokken model $(2-3-1-5-6)$ (see Table 11.3). Only the first item order is hypothesis directed, whereas the other input orders are more speculative and experimental in character.

The four *a priori structures* are shown in Figure 11.4. We selected, for purposes of demonstration (1) a concept attainment structure, according to which children are able to solve problems in an all-or-nothing fashion; (2) a Guttman-like structure which should correspond to the above-mentioned findings of Mokken scaling; (3) a two-way biform structure reduced by the Item Groups 4 and 7 that is directed by the stated hypothesis; and (4) a diamond structure which could have explained most of the variance in the data by the great number of a priori response patterns. Results with the Dayton and MacReady model were somewhat surprising. All tests of goodness of fit were highly significant in every combination of input order of items with an assumed a priori structure: no hypothesized structure fit the data. The results under the proposed Guttman structure were opposed to the findings by Mokken scaling. One would have expected similar results in

Table 11.4

Results Obtained with the Dayton & MacReady model[a]

	Order of presentation			Difficulties			Homogeneity		
	χ^2	df	p	χ^2	df	p	χ^2	df	p
Concept attainment	64.95	28	<.005	64.95	28	<.005	64.96	28	<.005
Guttman structure	62.34	24	<.005	43.49	24	<.01	63.67	24	<.005
Reduced two-way biform	61.04	23	<.005	46.04	23	<.005	62.61	23	<.005
Diamond structure	No convergence and no estimation possible								

[a] Sample size is 203 (Sample 4).

comparing a probabilistic Guttman scale evaluated with Proctor's model and the relatively strong probabilistic scale computed with Mokken's model.

What is the structure of these five invariance task groups? To continue developing an answer to that question, we next decided to apply the log-linear model to explore possible hidden dependencies and structures in the data that had not yet been validated. Note that no a priori structure was given when we started these exploratory analyses. Rather, several model hypotheses starting with the independence of all item groups were tested in a hierarchical order; that is, by initially assuming only main effects, then adding two-way interactions, then adding three-way interactions, and so on.[2] Note that a sequence of each two items is interpreted as a two-way interaction, a sequence of three items is grasped by a three-way interaction (including the two-way interactions), and so on. Task Group 4 was excluded from the analyses because of its special character noted above. The test of "independence," hypothesis H_1, led to a significant solution ($\chi^2 = 405.19$; $df = 57$; $p < .005$). The assumption of an overall independence of all relationships between the six task groups did not hold. Next, model hypotheses given by the stepwise integration of more and more interaction effects into the hierarchy character of several log-linear models were tested and all showed significant results. Only model hypothesis H_2, which allowed for *all* two-way interactions between the task groups, led to a nonsignificant result ($\chi^2 = 45.76$; $df = 42$; $p = .32$). This model, which gave a fairly good description of the structure, indicated that the data for this multicontingency table can be

---

[2] However, there are some statistical problems connected with this strategy of selecting the "best" model from other possible models that also fit the data. A χ^2 goodness of fit test only allows us to test a particular model. The test statistics are not statistically independent, so the corresponding significance levels cannot be interpreted in the usual way. Fienberg (1977) and Haberman (1979) discussed some solutions to this problem, but "there is no all-purpose, best method of model selection" (Fienberg, 1977, p. 47).

	Item:	3	2	1	5	6
Concept Attainment		0	0	0	0	0
Model		1	1	1	1	1
Guttman Structure		0	0	0	0	0
		1	0	0	0	0
		1	1	0	0	0
		1	1	1	0	0
		1	1	1	1	0
		1	1	1	1	1
Reduced Two-Way Biform		0	0	0	0	0
Model		1	0	0	0	0
		1	1	0	0	0
		1	1	1	0	0
		1	0	0	1	0
		1	0	0	1	1
		1	1	1	1	1
Diamond Structure		0	0	0	0	0
Model		1	0	0	0	0
		0	1	0	0	0
		1	1	0	0	0
		0	0	1	0	0
		0	1	1	0	0
		1	1	1	0	0
		0	0	0	1	0
		0	0	1	1	0
		0	1	1	1	0
		1	1	1	1	0
		0	0	0	0	1
		0	0	0	1	1
		0	0	1	1	1
		0	1	1	1	1
		1	1	1	1	1

Figure 11.4   Analyzed model structures for Sample 4 ($N = 203$).

reconstructed by the main effects and all interactions of first order.   But the only interactions of interest for a two-way process as depicted in Figure 11.3a would have been $(3-2)$, $(2-1)$, $(1-7)$ and $(3-5)$, $(5-6)$, $(6-7)$.   This model hypothesis (H_4) failed ($\chi^2 = 122.24$; $df = 51$; $p < .005$) to explain the variance and structure in the data.   Thus, there exists no plausible interpretation of the solution H_2.   Accepting all possible two-way interactions (i.e., all bivariate relationships between items) would be of neither theoretical nor empirical value.

In relation to the process of structure identification (see Figure 5.3 in von Eye, Chapter 5, this volume) all steps were considered: (1) The object of investigation was determined; (2) structural characteristics were predicted from theoretical and empirical prior knowledge, which seemed to be sufficient; (3) several different statistical tests and scaling models were selected; and (4) the confirmation and exploration of structure was tried. To sum up: Neither the hypothesis of reduced cognitive two-way process (see Figures 11.3a and 11.4) nor the other speculative exploratory hypotheses (see Figure 11.4) could be confirmed satisfactorily by any of the models applied. Hence, a reasonable structure to characterize the present data is missing.

Before search for structure can begin again, new data should be gathered. Before doing this, however, some reflections on the extremely "disappointing" outcomes in structure identification may be useful. Consider the age range of the subjects. Sampling 4 – 7 year-old children was justified given the intention to investigate the process of concrete operations in the sense of Piaget. At this age there is a transition from the stage of preoperational thoughts to the stage of concrete operations. But was this really the "proper" age subset of children to draw from in light of possible cultural, environmental, educational, and experimental factors that might influence development? Perhaps many single "small group" structures existed in the data. Analyzed simultaneously, all systematic structural variance could have overlapped and produced, as a whole, a random pattern without any detectable characteristics.

A special option of the Mokken model allows for deeper analysis by identifying subsets of subjects that are homogeneous in relation to the items under investigation. When adequate variables to characterize the sample are present, this improvement of proper, homogeneous subsets of subjects should be attempted. To demonstrate this final step of structural analysis, we used the two sample variables on which we had scores—"sex" and "social class." Mokken analysis was then applied to all 29 items which formed the seven task groups. The results obtained with this analysis are summarized in Table 11.5.

The overall analysis indicated two scales. Scale I contained 22 items and Scale II contained all items of Task Group 7 (juice items). These scales were fixed and tested in the above subsamples for homogeneity. In three of the four cases significant departures from scale homogeneity were observed; that is, different subsamples produced different scales and in consequence of this we concluded that possibly different structures are involved. Further item analysis showed that items of Task Group 3 (train items) differentiate between male and female subsamples and that Items 1 and 2 (chips items) differentiate between the social class subsamples. Researchers conducting a new study and a new hypothesis-directed structure identification process should try to be broadly aware of empirical findings, of which the ones presented here are only an example.

Table 11.5

Sample and Item Analysis via Mokken Model[a]

Subsample classification	N	Fixed scale I (22 items)			Fixed scale II (7 volume items)		
		H_i	H_m	T	H_i	H_m	T
Social class							
Low	56	.40 ⎤			.26 ⎤		
Medium	50	.52 ⎬	.55	4.98	.56 ⎬	.50	16.10
High	97	.60 ⎦			.61 ⎦		
Sex							
Male	80	.42 ⎤			.43 ⎤		
Female	37	.63 ⎦	.55	4.34	.44 ⎦	.43	.00

[a] H_i is homogeneity for fixed scales in subsamples; H_m is homogeneity for fixed scales in total sample; and T is significance statistic—distributed approximative t-values. Sample size is 203.

B. EXAMPLE 2: ASSESSING COGNITIVE DEVELOPMENT IN LONGITUDINAL DATA

The models presented in the chapter can be used for both cross-sectional and longitudinal data. Which kind of analysis is chosen depends mainly on the form of research design and on the theoretical meaning or interpretation to be given to empirical observations. The sort of methodology and the construction of research designs for analyzing longitudinal data is linked with the problems and assumptions underlying developmental sequences and stages (e.g., Campbell & Richie, 1983; Pascual-Leone, 1980). In the following, two examples are presented to illustrate how to handle longitudinal data. This approach will be elaborated by Henning, Rudinger, Chaselon, and Zimmermann (1985).

1. EXAMPLE 2.1: LONGITUDINAL SAMPLE FOR PIAGETIAN INVARIANCE

A sample of 45 children were presented with the seven task groups during each of the first four school years (see Figure 11.5). Here we will focus on the problem of specifying general change from first to fourth grade in answering the invariance questions. Hypothesis H_1 specified a Guttman structure corresponding to the item difficulties. Change was expected to occur in the values of item difficulties but not in the latent Guttman structure reflecting the developmental process. But no Guttman structure was identified. Rather, what was found was that only the general item difficulties de-

```
No. of possible patterns: 64
No. of observed patterns: 12
```

Guttman Structure	Item: 1 2 3 5 6 7
	0 0 0 0 0 0
	0 0 1 0 0 0
	0 0 1 1 0 0
	0 1 1 1 0 0
	0 1 1 1 1 0
	1 1 1 1 1 1

Biform Structure	Biform Structure with patterns omitting task 3
Item: 1 2 3 5 6 7	Item: 1 2 3 5 6 7
0 0 0 0 0 0	0 0 0 0 0 0
0 0 1 0 0 0	0 0 1 0 0 0
0 1 1 0 0 0	0 1 1 0 0 0
1 1 1 0 0 0	1 1 1 0 0 0
1 1 1 0 0 1	1 1 1 0 0 1
0 0 1 1 0 0	0 0 1 1 0 0
0 0 1 1 1 1	0 0 1 1 1 1
1 1 1 1 1 1	1 1 1 1 1 1
	0 1 0 1 1 1
	1 1 0 1 1 1

Figure 11.5 Analyzed model structures for longitudinal samples 2.1–2.4 ($N = 45$).

creased. Hypothesis H_2 specified a changing structure over time. But with what structure does one begin and end in testing specific structure change hypothesis? Moreover, how does one control for α-errors in sequential testing of new hypotheses with the same data? Because of these ambiguities, the following results are presented only for their heuristic value to those who are initiating new studies and gathering new data.

Table 11.6 lists two additional structures (Model A — biform structure; Model B — biform structure with Task 3 omitted) which have only empirical support and no substantive interpretation. The latter is true especially for Model B.

The biform structure is a valid model only for children in the third grade. Therefore, one could assume that a significant change in cognitive development occurs before and after this grade. But, unfortunately, the types or models of structure that pertain before and after this grade are unknown. Further exploratory analysis with the structure of Model B could not answer this question in a satisfactory manner, because the model fits children from the second to the fourth grade. One could have accepted Model B for the

Table 11.6

Analysis of Longitudinal Samples by the Dayton &
MacReady Model: Probabilities for Model Fit[a]

Grade (sample)	Model		
	Guttman structure	Model A	Model B
1(2.1)	<.005	*.005*	.000
2(2.2)	<*.005*	<.005	.30**
3(2.3)	<.005	*.23***	.25**
4(2.4)	<.005	<.005	*.17***

[a] Double asterisk indicates fit.

second *and* the fourth grades if it had not held for the third grade, too. Therefore, no accurate identification and prediction of structural change is possible for these items and for the data under study. We require more sophisticated hypotheses to provide valid information from a design as sketched in Table 11.6. This will only be possible when there are good (i.e., nonsignificant) fitting values distributed over the cells of design in an interpretable manner (i.e., as sketched by those cells of Table 11.6 whose entries are printed in italics).

2. EXAMPLE 2.2: EVALUATING ASSUMED STRUCTURE IN CHILD DEVELOPMENT

In 1976 a sample of 121 children, roughly 7 years in age, from different social backgrounds was drawn as part of the longitudinal project "Child Development and Social Structure" (Edelstein, Keller, & Wahlen, in press).[3] The sample was followed up every second year. One objective addressed in the project was to establish a logical order and a developmental sequence according to Piagetian task groups representing the physical cognitive field of developmental change. To illustrate some fundamental methodological points of view, we will select observational data from the project collected for four different cognitive variables at three successive times of measurement.

Let us begin by assuming an underlying structure for these four different cognitive variables and fixing it over the three times of measurement. The ability to give judgments of invariance (IN) is assumed to be preliminary to solving tasks of class inclusion (CI) and/or class inclusion with verbal mate-

[3] We thank Wolfgang Edelstein and his coworkers at the Max Planck Institute for Human Development and Education in Berlin for cooperation and use of some of their data analyzed in this example.

rial (CV). Both CI *and* CV are preliminary abilities necessary for solving logical multiplication tasks (LM). This structure leads to the creation of 6 true patterns that are included in the 16 possible response patterns. All other patterns are not in accordance with this hypothetical structure, which is depicted at the left-hand (dependent variable) side of the contingency table in Figure 11.6. The points of measurement (T_1, T_2, T_3) constitute the categories of the independent variable.

The next step in modeling the design is to establish the "inner structure" of the contingency table. This inner structure should reflect one's theoretical constraints and expectations with regard to the observational frequencies for each specific response pattern at the different points of measurement. Our hypothetical knowledge about child cognitive development leads to the following predictions:

1. At T_1 children respond mostly in the pattern (0000) or (1000).
2. At T_2 children respond mostly in the pattern (1000) or (1100 and 1010).
3. At T_3 children respond mostly in the pattern (1110) or (1111).

These predictions define the "substantial cells" of the table with most of the observed data. Remaining cells are designated "error cells" (marked by

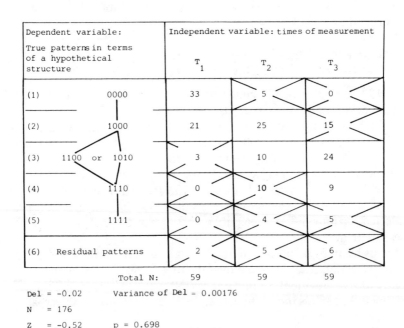

Figure 11.6 Design for aggregated group development.

a cross); no or only a few observations are expected in each. This design offers possibilities for modeling the expected empirical consequences of our theoretical ideas about developmental sequences and change. One possible hypothesis for an inner structure is given by the predictions made above and translated into the layout of the contingency table of Figure 11.6. After determining the actual frequencies for this table from the longitudinal data, the inner structure is assessed by the method of prediction analysis. The main purpose of prediction analysis is to apply a structural hypothesis to the cells of a contingency table and to evaluate the reduction in prediction error when this structure is taken as the basis for prognosis (Hildebrand et al., 1977; for further details see Example 3 and Figure 11.9). Computing the index of Proportional Reduction of Error leads to a value Del $= -.02.$; using the predictions made above, it follows that no reduction of error in prognosis is possible. Observed data do not correspond to our hypothetical expectations.

Let us try a "weaker" form of the prognosis:

1. At T_1 we expect (0000) or (1000).
2. At T_2 we expect (1000), (1100 and 1010) or (1110).
3. At T_3 we expect (1100 and 1010), (1110) or (1111).

This leads to a significant value of Del $= .53$; that is, using this inner structure in making predictions reduces by 53% the prediction error that is expected when knowledge about this inner structure is not used and only frequencies of the independent variables are taken into account.

The design presented so far only allows the evaluation of aggregated group development; the nature of developmental change can only be described on the basis of frequency distributions of the whole sample at each point of measurement. Analyzing individual development requires a modification of the contingency table design in the way depicted in Figure 11.7. In this special case two variables create the contingency table, each of which combines another point of measurement with the same underlying structure assumed for the task groups. In this modified design the observations inside the table receive another interpretation. Each frequency indicates the amount of individual change from the first point of measurement (T_1) to the following one (T_2); for example, at T_1, 33 children are classified with (000); at T_2, 5 are without measurable development (again 000), 18 step up to (100), another 5 to (110), and so on.

In modeling the inner structure of the cross-classification table one has to distinguish three different modes of development (see Figure 11.7): I_0 denotes identity, (i.e., no development); $D_1, D_2, \ldots, D_n$ denotes an i-step development ($i = 1, 2, \ldots, n$); and $R_1, R_2, \ldots, R_n$ denotes an i-step regression in development ($i = 1, 2, \ldots, n$). Next, one has to decide according to theoretical assumptions regarding cognitive development

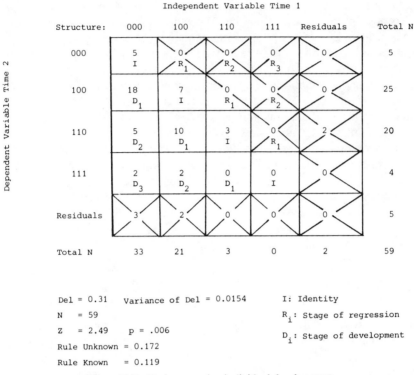

Independent Variable Time 1

Structure:	000	100	110	111	Residuals	Total N
000	5 I	0 R₁	0 R₂	0 R₃	0	5
100	18 D₁	7 I	0 R₁	0 R₂	0	25
110	5 D₂	10 D₁	3 I	0 R₁	2	20
111	2 D₃	2 D₂	0 D₁	0 I	0	4
Residuals	3	2	0	0	0	5
Total N	33	21	3	0	2	59

Del = 0.31   Variance of Del = 0.0154   I: Identity

N = 59 R_i: Stage of regression

z = 2.49   p = .006 D_i: Stage of development

Rule Unknown = 0.172

Rule Known   = 0.119

Figure 11.7   Design assessing individual development.

which mode and i-step amount of development should be evaluated; that is, which combination of substantive cells and error cells best represents the theoretical expectations. In the example under study (see Figure 11.7) the hypothesis "no regression" is supported using prediction analysis. A value of Del = .31 ($z = 2.49$; $p = .006$; one-sided) indicates a significant result; most of the observations can be expected to lie in the area of I_0 and $D_1, \ldots, D_n$ of the cross-classification table. More elaborate designs are discussed by Henning, Rudinger, Chaselon, and Zimmermann (1985).

C.   EXAMPLE 3: ANALYZING ERIKSONIAN PHASES

The data for this example come from a study by Lessing (1982).[4] Lessing was especially interested in the developmental task "first pregnancy, first

---

[4] We are grateful to Ellen Lessing, University of Bonn, for the use of her data in this secondary analysis.

child." Her conceptual starting point was the theory of psychosocial development created and elaborated by Erikson (e.g., 1959). Deriving a "meta-model" by interpreting Erikson's theory led to a hypothesis about the horizontal structure of the stages; that is, about their sequence. An unfavorable resolution within a preceding period of development precludes a favorable resolution in the following phase. A negative balance in phase K leads to unfavorable development (further negative balance) in phase $K + 1$. There exists a cumulative effect of negative components, facets, or aspects over the different life stages. In spite of Wohlwill's (1973) opinion that Eriksonian theory does not allow for a structural derivation, Lessing tried to build a testable, though very simple, model: a unilinear developmental sequence. Perhaps this is an oversimplification of the theory and there exist other, more admissible, sequences than those described by a unilinear progression model. We will return to this point later.

Lessing acquired her information through interviews conducted in a non-directive Rogerian manner with 46 women between 25 and 35 years of age who were expecting their first child. Four interviews were conducted in the following sequence: (1) the first within the initial 4 months of pregnancy; (2) the second 2 or 3 weeks before the end of pregnancy; (3) the third within the first 4 weeks after the birth of the child; and (4) the fourth after 6 to 8 months following the birth of the child. Lessing partitioned the life course of the mothers up to the 6 to 8 months following the birth of their children into four broad phases:

1. *Childhood,* which includes Eriksonian phases I (infancy — trust versus mistrust), II (early childhood — autonomy versus shame, doubt), III (play age — initiative versus guilt), and IV (school age — industry versus inferiority);
2. *Adolescence,* which is equivalent to Erikson's phase V (identity versus identity diffusion);
3. *Early adulthood,* which is equivalent to Erikson's phase VI (intimacy versus isolation);
4. *Adulthood,* which is equivalent to Erikson's phase VII (generativity versus self-absorption).

The four interviews of the mothers covered the four life-course phases in the following way:

1. Phases 1, 2, and 3, conducted in a retrospective manner;
2. Phases 1 and 2, conducted in a retrospective manner; and Phase 3, predominantly referring to the present situation;
3 and 4. Phase 4, referring to the present situation after birth of child.

The relation between the four levels of time (time of life course, interview timing, timing of Lessing's phases, timng of Erikson's phases) is shown graphically in Figure 11.8; this figure also makes it clear that the study was designed as a partly retrospective longitudinal investigation. The information gained in the interviews reflects the women's subjective interpretation of their individual life course. Thus, the study is concerned with the personal (re-) construction of the meaning of one's life.

According to Erikson's developmental stage theory, a necessary (but not sufficient) precondition for entering and successfully finishing a stage is to have finished the immediately prior stage without a negative balance. Therefore, data are needed that reflect the sign of this balance. For each of the four phases, Lessing elaborated a list of conditions describing facets of developmental tasks occurring within these periods of a person's life course. Too much space would be required to list all these facets: there were 17 for Phase 1; 32 for Phase 2; 70 for Phase 3 (one-third restrospective, two-thirds referring to the present situation); and 80 for Phase 4. Lessing coded the balance of a phase as positive if at least 50% of the task facets of a phase were reported as having been coped with successfully. A phase finished with a non-negative balance was coded 1, otherwise it was coded 0. Therefore, with four items (the four phases) one can construct 2^4 developmental sequences, as is depicted in Figure 11.8. The information about the phases obviously is highly condensed. The reader interested in more detail is encouraged to consult the sources cited.

Viewed sympathetically, all of these patterns seem plausible, understandable, and equally justified. They would serve as a description of some person's life course. But under the scope of the theory they are not all admissible. If we interpret the theory correctly, theoretically "normal" development in this group of women could be reflected by a unilinear sequence, so that only the five Guttman-like patterns would be allowed (see heavy lines in Figure 11.8). The other patterns are defined as "error" patterns. We tested this hypothesis by the Dayton and MacReady procedure (1976b), applying the Proctor option $\alpha = \beta$.

According to Eriksonian theory one would expect these data to fit a uniform scale that represents the hierarchy of developmental tasks and explains most of the variation in the observed frequencies of the various response patterns. The Dayton and MacReady model showed a goodness of fit for this uniform structure ($\chi^2 = 17.09$; $df = 10$; $p = .075$). But inspection of the estimated χ^2 values for all observed response patterns suggests that the response pattern (0011) with a partial $\chi^2 = 10.16$ has some special empirical contribution to the systematic variance, although there is only an observed frequency of 2 for this special pattern. Inclusion of this "critical pattern," even though it is not consistent with Eriksonian theory, in the former uniform scale improves the goodness of fit of the Dayton and MacReady model, thereby heightening the probability of this new and enlarged a priori struc-

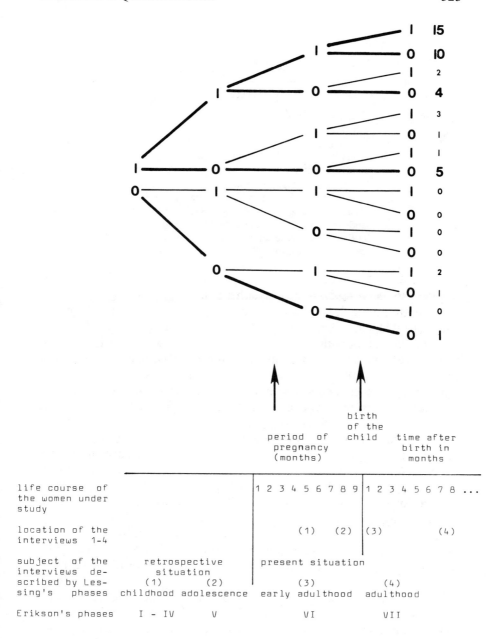

Figure 11.8 Design and data of the Erikson study by E. Lessing (1982).

Table 11.7

Multiple Contingency Table

Phases before pregnancy	Phases during–after pregnancy			
	(..00)	(..10)	(..01)	(..11)
(00..)	(1)	1	0	(2)
(01..)	0	0	0	0
(10..)	(5)	1	1	3
(11..)	(4)	(10)	2	(15)

[a] This table serves as input data for the analysis with *log-linear model* (frequencies in parentheses are set as structural zeros for quasi-independence model) and the *prediction analysis* by Hildebrand et al. (1977). Frequencies in parentheses are substantive cells, others are error cells.

ture ($\chi^2 = 5.35$; $df = 9$; $p = .80$). Neither structure yields a significant outcome (both models fit the data), but the second model, which includes the pattern (0011), has a significantly better goodness of fit value.

Validating the fit with another scaling model — the log-linear model — would give more confidence in the occurrence of that unexpected pattern (0011). For this purpose a long-linear model in the form of Goodman's quasi-independence model was applied, but the percentage of the "unscalable class" of persons was not estimated. If the assumption holds that most of the variance in the observed response patterns and their frequencies is concentrated on the "true score – a priori" patterns, the remaining patterns must be independent of the proposed structure. In this sense, true score patterns are defined as "structural zeros." A residual data matrix, reduced by the frequencies of the true score patterns, was tested for independence with the log-linear model (see Table 11.7). Model 1 (see Table 11.8), as the simplest, assumes only two outcomes. Only unfavorable (0000) or favorable (1111) phases form an all-or-nothing (i.e., concept attainment) approach, which of course is not confirmed by Erikson's theory. This model forms a point of reference for following hypotheses given by Models 2 and 3 (see Table 11.8).

Models 2 and 3 give evidence of a significant and sufficient goodness of fit for the quasi-independence model. The inclusion of the critical pattern (0011) in the former Guttman structure improved the fit of the tested independence of remaining observed patterns and their frequencies from 42 to 52%.

These results justify placing some theoretical importance on pattern

Table 11.8

Models and Results of Hypothetical Structures Tested for Independence by Log-linear
Models (Option: Quasi-independence Model)[a]

Model	Patterns as structural zeros	$\langle \chi^2 \rangle$	df	p
1	0000; 1111 (Concept attainment model)	15.99	9	.07
2	0000; 1000; 1100; 1110; 1111; (Guttman structure)	6.02	6	.42**
3	Same as Model 2 but including pattern 0011	4.20	5	.52**

[a] Double asterisk indicates substantial fit.

(0011). However, the results do not give sufficient justification for modifying the theoretical approach of Erikson. First, one would have to insure that adequate observational and interviewing techniques were used. Second, aggregation of all information and their transformation into response pattern data may yield information not sensitive enough to permit the detection of the properties relevant to Eriksonian developmental tasks. However, the scaling methods used seem to be sensitive in that they indicate substantive outcomes that we did not expect.

An alternate approach to the analysis of multiple contingency tables is given by a multinomial response model (see Table 11.1) developed by Hildebrand, Laing, and Rosenthal (1977). Applications of this kind of "prediction analysis" in developmental psychology are discussed by Henning (1979) and Froman and Hubert (1980) (see also Example 2.2 above). Whereas the constituent variables of a contingency table are not considered to be dependent or independent variables when the log-linear model is applied, in prediction analysis this distinction is necessary. The critical life event, pregnancy, provides a basis for treating the four categories before pregnancy as an independent variable and the four categories during–after pregnancy as a dependent variable (see Table 11.7). Prognosis then is based on a structural hypothesis mapped out onto the cells, and the design of that contingency table is formed by the variables. For example, if an indication of (10..) is observed in the phases before the period of pregnancy, we would expect in the phases after the period of pregnancy the pattern (..00), that is, observations in the cells without crosses.

The structural and qualitative hypotheses have to be derived from the theoretical framework underlying an investigation. In the case of Eriksonian theory we demonstrate testing two sets of hypotheses. The *first* one assumes the Guttman-like structure as the qualitative hypothesis. The *second* one includes the pattern (0011) in addition to the Guttman pattern. Only these patterns (i.e., their corresponding cells—see Figure 11.9) are substantive; all remaining cells are interpreted as "error cells." No observa-

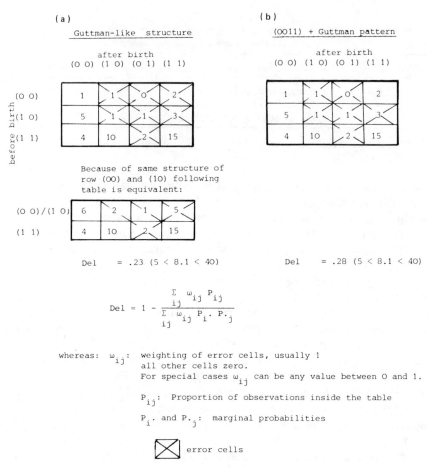

Figure 11.9 Contingency tables for two different qualitative hypotheses [(a), Guttman-like structure and (b), (0011) + Guttman pattern] about association of behavior patterns before and after the period of pregnancy (see also Figure 11.8 and Table 11.7).

tions are expected to fall in these cells. In this case the Del-value is 1. If there are observations in the error cells, Del decreases. A Del-value of zero means there is no prediction success at all; a negative Del-value indicates that a prediction made at random is better than a prediction made under the assumed structure in the contingency table.

The Guttman-like hypotheses (Figure 11.9a) led to a 23% reduction in prediction error. This Del-value differs significantly from a prognosis made at random (Del $= .23$; $z = 1.86$; $p = .03$ [one-sided]; Rule U $= .288$; Rule K $= .222$, where Rule U denotes the proportion of expected misclassifications and Rule K the proportion of observed misclassifications; Del = 1 − K/U). Taking the pattern (0011) into account we obtained the following results: Del = .28; z = 1.93; p = .03 (one-sided); Rule U = .248; Rule K = .178. The scope of prediction covered only 78% of the population, owing to the lack of an error cell in column (00). Thus, the results of prediction analysis correspond to our previous findings. The inclusion of pattern (0011) reduced prediction error by 28%. Of course, alternative qualitative hypotheses are possible in the context of Eriksonian phases. Some of them were discussed and evaluated by the statistical model of Dayton and MacReady.

However, this inductive procedure of model fitting is not at all in line with our previous arguments. It may be tempting to follow the recommendation given by the search algorithm of the program, but if one is interested, as we are, in changes of the "pure" developmental sequence brought about by critical events, it is necessary to consider all patterns that might reflect such effects. Why, for instance, should we treat pattern (0011) as admissible and declare the pattern (1011) to be an error pattern? Let us now consider more systematically how we are to detect changes in developmental sequences as a consequence of changes in the individual's social context.

Postulating that successfully finishing Phase 1 is a necessary prerequisite for success in Phase 2 is equivalent to defining (11), (10), and (00) as admissible combinations and the sequence (01) as an error cell in a 2 × 2 table defined by Phase 1 (+, −) and Phase 2 (+, −) classifications. In that framework all sequences with (01) transitions are not compatible with theoretical statements. However, the effect of a critical event such as pregnancy can be derived from these counter-theoretical inversions of the pattern. In other words, a change from 0 to 1 after the critical event permits us to deduce a positive effect.

Inferring an effect of a *critical event* is a quite different matter for the other transitions:

1. 1 1 : Definitely no negative effect, perhaps a positive one, but conclusion not unequivocal;
2. 1 0 : Definitely no positive effect, perhaps a negative one, but Conclusion not unequivocal;
3. 0 1 : Definitely a positive effect; and
4. 0 0 : Definitely no positive effect, perhaps a negative one, but conclusion not unequivocal.

For the patterns (11, 10, 00) one can certainly exclude the effect but one can draw only uncertain inferences about effects in the direction opposite to the excluded effects. Thus, the unilinear Guttman structure is a "no effect" structure because, given this pattern, it is not possible (and not necessarily for

explanatory reasons) to infer a definitely positive or negative effect of the
event pregnancy occurring between Phases 2 and 3.   This is illustrated in
Figure 11.10a.

In this pattern (Figure 11.10a) one cannot distinguish between pure theoretical sequences and sequences that are influenced by a critical event that is
confounded with the theoretical mechanism.

Then how is it possible to detect a "real" change in developmental se-

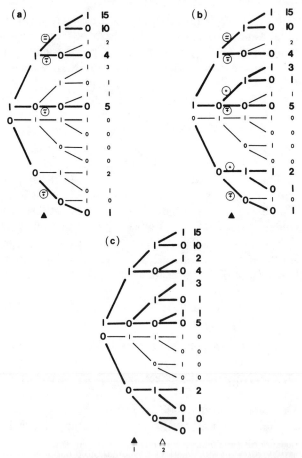

Figure 11.10   Erikson's stages (a) in a unilinear sequence with signs for effects of pregnancy
(▲), which can or cannot be inferred; (b) with the assumption of an effect of pregnancy; and (c)
with the assumption of effects of pregnancy and birth (△). ⊖ , no positive effect can be
inferred, definitely does not exist a negative effect; ⊕, no negative effect can be inferred,
definitely does not exist a positive effect; ⊕, a definitely positive effect.

quences as a consequence of some independent influence? According to our previous discussion under the hypothesis of a general effect of pregnancy on coping in the following phase, all transitions (00, 01, 11, *and* 01) from Phase 2 to Phase 3 have to be possible. This assumption leads to nine admissible patterns, as is shown in Figure 11.10b. Between Phases 1 and 2, with respect to 3 and 4, furthermore, only the "necessary" combinations are admissible. The test of this model yields a very good fit: $\chi^2 = 3.02$ ($df = 4$; n.s.). However, one should be aware that we tested a very "soft" hypothesis about the effect of pregnancy. We admitted the possibility of all kinds of effects of pregnancy: (uncertain) positive and (uncertain) negative ones. A more restricted hypothesis would involve assuming only positive effects of pregnancy. Thus, only patterns with the transitions (11) and (01) between Phases 2 and 3 would be admissible. The pattern (11) is included because a positive effect cannot be excluded, and (01) is included because it definitely is a positive effect, other things being equal. That is, between Phases 1 and 2, with respect to 3 and 4, there remain only the "necessary" combinations (00, 10, 11). This hypothesis leads to only six patterns. There is no fit for this model.

The idea of critical events can be extended to a second event terminating Phase 3 and defining the beginning of Phase 4: the birth of the child. If we again apply the considerations of the admissible transitions under the assumption of any effect at all, this leads to 12 (out of 16) admissible sequences. Only the sequences with the transition (01) from Phase 1 to 2 are excluded (see diagram). For this model the algorithm yields $\chi^2 = 0.00005$, a value not indicative of a good fit. As is shown in Figure 11.10c, all the admissible patterns have a frequency of zero. Before raising the objection that this result is trivial, one has to recognize that it is not at all trivial to find zeros exactly in the "forbidden" patterns with (01). At the same time, it is not too surprising that pregnancy and birth can have positive and/or negative effects within the life cycle of women, even when the life cycle is defined within a theory such as Erikson's.

III. Statistical Methodology

A.   CAUSAL AND SOFT MODELING

This chapter is mainly concerned with the evaluation of different types of hierarchical or branching structures, which should be explained as far as possible in terms of theory-dependent underlying processes. But initial theory building in developmental psychology seems to be more controversial than expected, witness the questioning of the stage theories of Piaget and

Kohlberg. As Campbell and Richie remark, "developmental sequences are far from being well understood. There is a growing awareness . . . that fundamental questions remain to be resolved" (1983, p. 156). Second, developmental research is increasingly involved in nonexperimental, quasi-experimental, or field research and design (e.g., Edelstein, Keller, & Wahlen, in press).

The contribution of methodology at this period of developmental research is to offer a great variety of methods and techniques useful in searching, describing, proving, testing, explaining, assessing, and evaluating empirical findings collected under theoretical expectations. Given these circumstances, the causal modeling approach (see especially Bentler, 1980; Jöreskog & Sörbom, 1981) seems to offer the greatest promise for psychological research. Two general approaches can be distinguished. The well-known covariance structure models (e.g., Bentler's causal modeling and Jöreskog's LISREL) should be used when theoretical knowledge can be expressed (i.e., specified mathematically) in structural equations.

The "soft modeling" data structure model PLS (Partial Least Squares, Wold, 1979) can be used when strong theoretical knowledge is scarce. The PLS model is a distribution-free estimation procedure for testing a system of specified structural relations between random variables, classified as latent variables. Wold and Bertholet (1983) developed the PLS approach for application to multidimensional contingency tables, as used in Section II of this chapter. Similar to the prediction analysis for cross classifications (Hildebrand et al., 1977), the PLS method provides predictive inferences that refer to the structural relations defined for purposes of searching for hierarchical or branching sequences. Furthermore, the relevance of predictions can be tested (see Lohmöller, 1983, p. 160). Application of the PLS method to developmental research problems will be introduced by Günther (1983) and Günther and Henning (1983).

B. UNIFICATION OF METHODS ANALYZING QUALITATIVE DATA

The various methods and techniques for analyzing qualitative data look very different but show similar, if not equivalent, results when applied to the data presented in the examples given in Section II. There is a basic model within which most of these apparently different scaling and evaluation models can be unified. This is of great theoretical and methodological importance for the sequential use of these methods in clarifying one problem and one data set. This fact enables one to make a consistent interpretation even of different empirical results, a situation that otherwise would not have

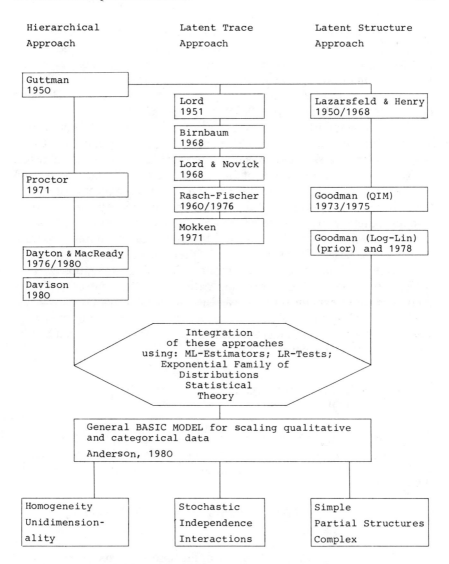

Fields of methodological applications

Figure 11.11 Sources and traditions of scaling and latent structure models.

been methodologically possible.   The purpose in this section is to show that most of the methods utilized are special cases of a general basic model.   The justification, both formal and statistical, for this basic model was developed by Andersen (1980a, pp. 235–295; 1980b).   Further developments were provided by Davison (1980, pp. 130–132), Dayton and MacReady (1980, pp. 344–345), Goodman (1978, pp. 403–405), Jöreskog and Wold (1982), and Mokken (1971, pp. 73–114). Empirical comparisons of alternative models for analyzing the scalability of response patterns—a representation of qualitative data—were presented by Clogg and Sawyer (1981), Henning (1981, 1984), and Rindskopf (1983).

In presenting some basic principles regarding the general model, the probability of the occurrence of an observed response pattern will be denoted by $p(u_h)$. Under the assumption of a nonobservable (i.e., a latent) variable θ, it is possible to estimate the values of this variable from the frequencies n_h of an observed pattern u_h. However, estimation requires the placing of restrictions (i.e., model assumptions) that admit only specific a priori (i.e., true) response patterns v_t to the data. In the case of a continuous latent variable, the assumptions concern the characteristics of the corresponding item trace lines (e.g., the Rasch–Mokken model). If the estimation is done with maximum likelihood methods, local stochastic independence is supposed. Furthermore, the structure of a response patterns data set is expected to be accounted for or explained by the variance of the latent variable.

The relationships among models that were used in computing and evaluating the examples from different fields of developmental research can be outlined as shown in Figure 11.11.

C. GENERALIZATION AND DERIVATION OF MODEL EQUATIONS

Basic Model. If the probability of making a positively scored answer to item i is written p_i ($i = 1, 2, 3, \ldots$, etc.) and if fixed θ-values for the latent variable are assumed, the response probability for a pattern of, say, four items is given by:

$$p(u_h)(\theta) = p_{abcd}(\theta) = p_1 p_2 p_3 p_4 \quad \text{with } p_i \text{ for } p_i(\theta)$$
$$\text{for } i = 1, \ldots, 4. \quad (1)$$

However, to estimate the probabilities for the observed response patterns u_h under the theoretical constraints given by the true response patterns v_t, the distribution function of the latent variable $\gamma(\theta)$ has to be taken into account. Defining the latent variable as a continuous one (as in the Rasch model), Equation 1 leads to:

$$p(u_h) = \int p_1 p_2 p_3 p_4 \gamma(\theta) \, d(\theta) \quad (2)$$

Defining θ as a discrete variable one gets:

$$p(u_h) = \sum_{t=1}^{s} p_{1t}p_{2t}p_{3t}p_{4t}\theta_t, \tag{3}$$

where θ_t indicates the discrete probability function with $t = 1, \ldots, s$ latent classes. Equation 3 presents a special formulation for a latent class model. Because we are primarily concerned with discrete models, Equation 3 should be generalized to Equation 4 and finally to the basic model in 5.

$$p(u_h) = \sum_{t=1}^{s} p(u_h \mid v_t)\theta_t \tag{4}$$

The product of the item response probabilities for the different latent classes $t = 1, \ldots, s$ can be interpreted as a conditional probability, connecting the u_h patterns with the true v_t patterns. Any particular specification or modification of this "recruitment probability" (Dayton & MacReady, 1980, p. 344) results in some type of model as pictured in Figure 11.11. All models can be derived from Equation 5.

$$p(u_h) = \sum_{t=1}^{s} \left[\prod_{i=1}^{n} (\alpha_{ijt})\theta_t \right], \tag{5}$$

with $i = 1, \ldots, n$ (number of items), $j = 2, \ldots, k$ (number of response categories for an item), $t = 1, \ldots, s$ (number of latent classes.) Finally, a goodness of fit test (χ^2 or likelihood ratio) compares the estimated frequencies to any response pattern u_h created by the constraints of the model assumption just concerned, with the observed frequencies of the response patterns u_h. The significance of this result is evaluated. The number of parameters to be estimated is of great importance. Estimation of parameters is possible only when their number does not exceed $(2^n - 1)$ for dichotomous response categories.

Guttman's Scalogram Analysis. This model needs no further specification of the recruitment probability beyond the specification in the basic model. Because Guttman's model is a deterministic one, the probabilities take only the values 0 or 1. The estimated probabilities for the specific a priori response patterns (i.e., 0000, 1000, 1100, 1110, and 1111) are identical to the θ_t-values corresponding to the different latent classes.

Proctor's Probabilistic Scale Analysis. This model includes response patterns that are not strictly linear or hierarchical, as is usually the case for a typical Guttman scale. Consider, for instance, the response pattern (1010). It is assumed that this pattern is either the result of a misclassification by the researcher or a response error on the part of the subject. As an alternative, Proctor (1970) defined a "guessing parameter (β)" to represent in the model the probability of giving a "wrong" answer to an item. The formula specifying the recruitment probability α is given in Table 11.9. Assuming only Guttman-like response patterns, the computation of the probability of occurrence for the "non-true" pattern (1010) is demonstrated in the following example:

$$p(1010) = \beta^2(1 - \beta)^2\theta_1 + \beta(1 - \beta)^3\theta_2 + \beta^2(1 - \beta)^2\theta_3 + \beta(1 - \beta)^3\theta_4$$
$$+ \beta^2(1 - \beta)^2\theta_5$$

To construct pattern (1010) from true pattern (0000) one has to invert the first and third answers (i.e., two items). To build (1010) from (1000) one has to invert only the third item, and so on. The misclassification or guessing parameter β then stands for the probability of incorrect responses to the items of a scale. But this model is more than just a probabilistic version of Guttman's scale analysis. With it, not only can one assess the pattern of a strict Guttman scale, but any response set can be taken as an a priori pattern, depending on the scope of a substantive theory.

Dayton and MacReady Model for A Priori Hierarchies. Proctor's model is a special case of this more general approach by Dayton and MacReady (1976a, 1976b, 1980). It includes both a guessing and a forgetting parameter and can be used to validate an a priori structure of response patterns and estimate their probabilities. The specification of the recruitment probability depends mainly on these locally independent parameters (see Table 11.9). The interpretation of these parameters leads to an assessment of the probability that some response pattern will not fit the a priori structure of patterns. Thus, from high parameter values it follows, for instance, that the set of a priori patterns being fitted to the observed patterns needs to be enlarged. Another advantage is the possibility of evaluating the explanatory power of different a priori structures, that is, alternative developmental sequences or sequential theories. A likelihood ratio test proves the significance of these identified differences. A useful application of this probabilistic model for qualitative data is in transforming the substantive assumptions about developmental processes into an adequate set of a priori response patterns (see also Price, Dayton, & MacReady, 1980).

Goodman's Quasi-independence Model. The models discussed so far have focused on deviations from a priori structure in formulating special parameters to explain some amount of deviation (error). Goodman, however, incorporated an additional latent class of respondents that we have called "intrinsically unscalable" (1975a, 1978). The group of scalable per-

Table 11.9

Taxonomy and Formal Integration of Several Scaling Models[a]

Model	Description
Basic model	$p(u_h) = \sum_{t=1}^{s} \left[\prod_{i=1}^{n} (\alpha_{ijt}) \theta_t \right]$
Guttman model	$\alpha_{ijt} = 0$ or 1
Proctor model	$\alpha_{ijt} = \beta^{x_{th}} (1 - \beta)^{n - x_{th}}$
Dayton & MacReady model	$\alpha_{ijt} = \beta_g^{x_{th}} (1 - \beta_g)^{m_t - x_{th}} \beta_f^{y_{th}} (1 - \beta_f)^{n - m_t - y_{th}}$
Goodman's QI model	$(\alpha_{ijt}) = \left(\sum_{t=1}^{s} I_{ht} \theta_t + \theta_0 \prod_{i=1}^{n} \alpha_{ijt} \right)$
Rasch model	$\alpha_{ijt} = [\exp(\theta - \beta_i)] / [1 + \exp(\theta - \beta_i)]$
Mokken model	$\alpha_{ijt} = f_{\mathrm{monotone}}(\theta, \beta)$
Log-linear model	$p(u_h) = \mu_{ij} = \gamma_{ij}^{12} \gamma_i^1 \gamma_j^2 \gamma^0$ for 2 by 2 table
	or
	$\ln \mu_{ij} = \theta_{ij}^{12} + \theta_i^1 + \theta_j^2 + \theta^0$

[a] See Table 11.1 for comparison. Here u_h is the observed response pattern; v_t, the expected (theoretical, "a priori") response pattern; $\alpha_{ijt} = p(u_h / v_t)$, the recruitment probability; $i = 1, \ldots, n$, the items; $j = 1, \ldots, k$ the response alternatives; $t = 1, \ldots, s$, the latent classes; β_g, the "guessing" parameter; β_f, the "forgetting" parameter; m_t, the number of zero codes in v_t; x_{th}, the number of "1" codes in u_h, when expecting "0" in v_t; y_{th}, the number of "0" codes in u_h, when expecting "1" in v_t; θ, latent variable subject parameter in Rasch model; β_i, the latent item parameter; and I_{ht}, the indication parameter, and which is 1 if $u_h = v_t$ and 0 if $u_h \neq v_t$.

sons coincides with the a priori structure that establishes several latent classes. The other group of persons is assumed to answer the items quasi-independently of the a priori structure (i.e., by chance). An accommodation of the quasi-independence model to the basic model needs further modification (see Table 11.9). Dayton and MacReady (1980, p. 347) provided a critical assessment of the model. For example, they pointed out that there exists no procedure to test the necessity of an "unscalable class." Consequently, they extended Goodman's approach to an "intrusion–omission error model," but that model is not reviewed here. The quasi-independence model has a close relationship to the log-linear model when it is applied to incomplete contingency tables or to those involving structural zeros. Our example with Eriksonian data (see Section II.C) emphasizes these relationships. The problem of incomplete tables is discussed more generally by Haberman (1979, p. 144) and Fienberg (1971).

Rasch Model. An interpretation of θ as a continuous variable leads to an alternative possibility for evaluating the unidimensionality and homogeneity of an item set as a uniform scale (i.e., as an ordered sequence). But the uniform scale type is the only one that is testable with the well-known Rasch model. The main property of this approach resides in the assumption of "nonoverlapping" item trace lines determined by the exponential equation (see Table 11.9). Indeed, the Rasch model is much too restrictive to be used to look for solutions to most problems in practical research. Moreover, it is not a good method for analyzing qualitative data even though it can be used for that purpose.

Mokken Model. The scale theory and procedure developed by Mokken (1971) overcomes some of the disadvantages of the Rasch model for practical use. However, the Rasch approach remains the more sophisticated measurement model. Mokken's scaling procedure relies on nonparametric tests to evaluate the monotonicity and homogeneity of items according to their response frequencies. All that is assumed is a monotonic function between latent variables and manifest frequencies (i.e., probabilities) of responses (see Table 11.9). A further important property of Mokken's scale analysis is *multiple* scalability. This means that an item set can be explored in terms of different (multiple) homogeneous scales which thus can be confirmed by more stringent scaling models. Mokken's model can also be used to select proper, that is, homogeneous, subsets of persons, variables, and occasions. For these subsets adequate structures can be defined (see von Eye, Chapter 5 this volume). The Mokken model is of inestimable heuristic value for an initial structuring of a complex set of responses, especially when hypotheses are lacking.

Log-linear Model for Contingency Tables. An alternative way to arrange the frequencies of response patterns is given by a multivariate contingency table (see the examples given earlier). The relationships between these items constitute simple or more complex structures, hierarchies, or sequences as they are specified by developmental hypotheses. By selection of adequate parameters (as shown for a simple 2×2 arrangement in Table 11.9), it is possible to identify structural hypotheses (i.e., models) that account for the variance of the cell frequencies of the contingency table. The log-linear approach is the most flexible one for constructing branching or other structures of response patterns that exceed in complexity the structures mentioned in the several scale forms above. Basically, most contingency tables can be analyzed by the log-linear model if they fulfill the condition of Poisson, multinomial, or product-multinomial sampling as tested and shown by Fienberg (1978, pp. 131–134). As was mentioned in the context of the

Dayton and MacReady model, it is possible both to prove different hypotheses about structures and to test the differences between these hypotheses.

Thus, there exists a hierarchy of models; in exploratory use the best-fitting model can be selected. Table 11.9 gives a taxonomic integration of all statistical models discussed in Section III of this chapter. This formal structure, which was initiated by Andersen (1980), is elaborated in the table and more formally organized. In relation to the general model and the many special cases derivable from it, the term of greatest interest is the recruitment probability α_{ijt}. Changing or modifying this term leads to the taxonomy of models depicted in Table 11.9.

Acknowledgments

We thank Friedrich Chaselon, Norbert Dommel, George Fennekels and Ejo Zimmermann for their invaluable assistance in data analysis and give special thanks to Doris Anderson and Amy Michele for their helpful support in preparing the text.

References

Aebli, H. A dual model of cognitive development. *International Journal of Behavioral Development,* 1978, *3,* 221–229.

Andersen, E. B. *Discrete statistical models with social science applications.* Amsterdam: North–Holland, 1980. (a)

Andersen, E. B. Latent structures analysis. University of København, Department of Statistics Research Report No. 64. København, 1980. (b)

Baltes, P. B., Reese, H. W., & Lipsitt, L. P. Life-span developmental psychology. *Annual Review of Psychology,* 1980, *31,* 65–110.

Bentler, P. M. Evidence regarding stages in the development of conversation. *Perceptual and Motor Skills,* 1970, *31,* 855–859.

Bentler, P. M. An implicit metric for ordinal scales: Implications for assessment of cognitive growth. In D. R. Green, M. M. Ford & G. B. Flamer (Eds.), *Measurement and Piaget.* New York: McGraw–Hill, 1971.

Bentler, P. M. The study of cognitive development through modeling with qualitative data. In R. H. Kluwe & H. Spada (Eds.), *Developmental models of thinking.* New York: Academic Press, 1980.

Benzécri, J. P. *L'analyse des données* (Vol. 2): *L'analyse des correspondances.* Paris: Dunond, 1973.

Birnbaum, A. Some latent trait models and their use in inferring an examinee's ability. In F. M. Lord & M. R. Novick (Eds.), *Statistical theories of mental test scores.* Reading, Mass.: Addison–Wesley, 1968.

Bishop, Y. M. M., Fienberg, S. E., & Holland, P. W. *Discrete multivariate analysis: Theory and practice.* Cambridge, Mass.: MIT Press, 1975.

Campbell, R. L., & Richie, D. M. Problems in the theory of developmental sequences: Prerequisites and precursors. *Human Development,* 1983, *26,* 156–172.

Christoffersson, A. Factor analysis of dichotomized variables. *Psychometrika,* 1975, *40,* 5 – 32.

Clogg, C. C., & Sawyer, D. O. A comparison of alternative models for analyzing the scalability of response patterns. In S. Leinhardt (Ed.), *Sociological methodology 1981.* San Francisco: Jossey – Bass, 1981.

Coombs, C. H., & Smith, E. K. On the detection of structure in attitudes and developmental processes. *Psychological Review,* 1973, *80,* 337 – 351.

Davison, M. L. Testing a unidimensional, qualitative unfolding model for attitudinal or developmental data. *Psychometrika,* 1979, *44,* 179 – 194.

Davison, M. L. A psychological scaling model for testing order hypotheses. *British Journal of Mathematical and Statistical Psychology,* 1980, *33,* 123 – 141.

Dayton, C. M., & MacReady, G. B. A probabilistic model for validation of behavioral hierarchies. *Psychometrika,* 1976, *41,* 189 – 204. (a)

Dayton, C. M., & MacReady, G. B. *Computer programs for probabilistic models.* Measurement and Statistic Research Report, College of Education, University of Maryland, June 1976. (b)

Dayton, C. M., & MacReady, G. B. A scaling model with response errors and intrinsically unscalable respondents. *Psychometrika,* 1980, *45,* 343 – 356.

Edelstein, W., Keller, M., & Wahlen, K. Structure and content in social cognition: Conceptual and empirical analyses. *Child development,* in press.

Erikson, E. H. *Identity and the life cycle.* New York: Norton, 1959.

Fienberg, S. E. *The analysis of cross-classified categorical data.* Cambridge, Mass.: MIT Press, 1977.

Fischer, G. Some probabilistic models for measuring change. In D. N. M. De Gruijter & L. J. Th. van der Kamp (Eds.), *Advances in psychological and educational measurement.* New York: Wiley, 1976.

Fischer, K. W. A theory of cognitive development: The control and construction of hierarchies of skills. *Psychological Review,* 1980, *87,* 477 – 531.

Froman, T., & Hubert, L. J. Application of prediction analysis to developmental priority. *Psychological Bulletin,* 1980, *87,* 136 – 146.

Gergen, K. J. Stability, change, and chance in understanding human development. In N. Datan & H. W. Reese (Eds.), *Life-span developmental psychology.* New York: Academic Press, 1977.

Gigerenzer, G. *Perceptual development and information integration.* Unpublished manuscript, Ludwig-Maximilians-Universität, München, 1982.

Gliner, G. S. A statistical paradigm to evaluation homogeneity within subjects and within tasks. *British Journal of Mathematical and Statistical Psychology,* 1982, *35,* 113 – 116.

Goldstein, H. *The design and analysis of longitudinal studies.* London: Academic Press, 1979.

Goldstein, H. Dimensionality, bias, independence, and measurement scale problems in latent trait test score models. *British Journal of Mathematical and Statistical Psychology,* 1980, *33,* 234 – 246.

Goodman, L. A. A modified multiple regression approach to the analysis of dichotomous variables. *American Sociological Review,* 1972, *37,* 28 – 46.

Goodman, L. A. Empirical evaluation of formal theory. *Journal of Mathematical Sociology,* 1974, *3,* 187 – 196.

Goodman, L. A. A new model for scaling response patterns: An application of the quasi-independence concept. *Journal of the American Statistical Association,* 1975, *70,* 755 – 768. (a)

Goodman, L. A. The relationship between modified and usual multiple-regression approaches to the analysis of dichotomous variables. In D. R. Heise (Ed.), *Sociological methodology 1975.* San Francisco: Jossey–Bass, 1975. (b)

Goodman, L. A. *Analyzing qualitative/categorical data.* London: Addison–Wesley, 1978.

Goodman, L. A. Three elementary views of log linear models for the analysis of cross-classifications having ordered categories. In S. Leinhardt (Ed.), *Sociological methodology 1981.* San Francisco: Jossey–Bass, 1981.

Grizzle, J. E., Starmer, C. F., & Koch, G. G. Analysis of categorical data by linear models. *Biometrics,* 1969, *25,* 498–504.

Gruen, G. E. Note on conversation: Methodological and definitional considerations. In I. E. Sigel & F. H. Hooper (Eds.), *Logical thinking in children.* New York: Holt, Rinehart & Winston, 1968.

Günther, P. Analysis of path models by partial least squares (PLS): A short story. In P. Günther & H. J. Henning (Eds.), *Current methodological issues in developmental psychology: A reader.* Bremer Beiträge zur Psychologie Nr. 22. Bremen: University Press: 1983.

Günther, P., & Henning, H. J. (Eds.). *Current methodological issues in developmental psychology: A reader.* Bremer Beiträge zur Psychologie Nr. 22 Bremen: University Press, 1983.

Guttman, L. The basis for scalogram analysis. In S. A. Stouffer, L. Guttman, E. A. Suchman, P. F. Lazarsfeld, S. Star, & J. A. Clausen (Eds.), *Measurement and prediction.* Princeton: Princeton University Press, 1950.

Haberman, S. J. *Analysis of qualitative data* (Vol. 2): *New developments.* New York: Academic Press, 1979.

Henning, H. J. Ein Verfahren zur Beurteilung qualitativer Hypothesen in Diagnose und Prognose. *Berichte aus dem Psychologischen Institut der Universität Bonn,* 1979, *5,* Heft 8.

Henning, H. J. Suche und Validierung kognitiver Strukturen, Entwicklungssequenzen und Lern-/Verhaltenshierarchien mit Hilfe probabilistischer Modelle. *Zeitschrift für Psychologie,* 1981, *189,* 437–461.

Henning, H. J. Skalierung qualitativer Daten und latenter Strukturen. In E. Roth (Ed.), *Methoden der Wirtschafts- und Sozialforschung.* München: Oldenbourg, 1984.

Henning, H. J., Rudinger, G., Chaselon, F., & Zimmermann, E. J. *Qualitative Forschungsmethoden in der Psychologie.* Bern: Huber, 1985.

Hildebrand, D. K., Laing, J. D., & Rosenthal, H. *Prediction analysis of cross-classifications.* New York: Wiley, 1977.

Hoppe, S., Schmid-Schönbein, C., & Seiler, T. B. *Entwicklungssequenzen.* Bern: Huber, 1977.

Hoppe-Graff, S. *Bedingungsanalyse zur Genese der Klasseninklusion.* Unpublished doctoral dissertation, University of Darmstadt, 1982.

Hubert, L. J. Matching models in the analysis of cross-classifications. *Psychometrika.* 1979, *44,* 21–41.

Hubert, L. J., Golledge, R. G., Costanzo, C. M., & Richardson, G. D. Assessing homogeneity in cross-classified proximity data. *Geographical Analysis,* 1981, *13,* 38–50.

Jöreskog, K. G., & Sörbom, D. *Lisrel v. Analysis of structural relationships by maximum likelihood and least squares methods.* University of Uppsala: Research Report No. 81-8: Uppsala, 1981.

Jöreskog, K. G., & Wold, H. (Eds.). *Systems under indirect observation* (Vol. 2). Amsterdam: North-Holland, 1982.

Keats, J. A., Collins, K. F., & Halford, G. S. *Cognitive development.* Chichester: Wiley, 1978.

Kluwe, R. H., & Spada, H. (Eds.). *Developmental models of thinking.* New York: Academic Press, 1980.

Krauth, J., & Lienert, G. A.   Multivariate nonparametric techniques in psychological research. *Psychologische Beiträge,* 1981, *23,* 226–241.

Krus, D. J.   *Order analysis of binary matrices.*   Los Angeles: Theta Press, 1976.

Lazarsfeld, P. F., & Henry, N. W.   *Latent structure analysis.*   Boston: Houghton–Mifflin, 1968.

Linder, A., & Berchtold, W.   *Statistische Methoden III.*   Basel: Birkhäuser, 1982.

Lessing, E.   *Eine E. H. Erikson-orientierte Follow-up-Studie über Frauen im Alter zwischen 20 und 35 Jahren.*   Unpublished doctoral dissertation, University of Bonn, 1982.

Lohmöller, J. B.   *Path models with latent variables and partial least squares (PLS) estimation.*   Unpublished doctoral dissertation, University of München, 1983.

Lord, F. M., & Novick, M. R. (Eds.).   *Statistical theory of mental test scores.*   Reading, Mass.: Addison–Wesley, 1968.

Mokken, R. S.   *A theory and procedure of scale analysis.*   The Hague: Mouton, 1971.

Muthén, B.   *Contributions to factor analysis of dichotomous variables.*   Uppsala: University of Uppsala, Department of Statistics, 1978.

Nagel, E.   Determinism and development.   In D. B. Harris (Ed.), *The concept of development.*   Minneapolis: University of Minnesota Press, 1957.

Nesselroade, J. R., & Baltes, P. B.   *Longitudinal research in the study of behavior and development.*   New York: Academic Press, 1979.

Nishisato, S.   *Analysis of categorical data: Dual scaling and its application.*   Toronto: University of Toronto Press, 1980.

Overton, W. F., & Reese, H. W.   Models of development: Methodological implications.   In J. R. Nesselroade & H. W. Reese (Eds.), *Life-span developmental psychology: Methodological issues.*   New York: Academic Press, 1973.

Pascual-Leone, J.   Constructive problems for constructive theories: The current relevance of Piaget's work and a critique of information-processing simulation psychology.   In R. H. Kluwe & H. Spada (Eds.), *Developmental models of thinking.*   New York: Academic Press, 1980.

Phillips, D. C., & Kelley, M. E.   Hierarchical theories of development in education and psychology.   *Harvard Educational Review,* 1975, *45,* 351–375.

Plewis, I.   A comparison of approaches to the analysis of longitudinal categorical data.   *British Journal of Mathematical and Statistical Psychology,* 1981, *34,* 118–123.

Price, L. C., Dayton, C. M., & MacReady, G. B.   Discovery algorithms for hierarchical relations.   *Psychometrika,* 1980, *45,* 449–466.

Proctor, C. H.   A probabilistic formulation and statistical analysis of Guttman scaling.   *Psychometrika,* 1970, *35,* 73–78.

Rasch, G.   An individualistic approach to item analysis.   In P. F. Lazarsfeld & N. W. Henry (Eds.), *Readings in mathematical social science.*   Cambridge, Mass.: MIT Press, 1966.

Rauh, H.   *Entwicklungspsychologische Analyse kognitiver Prozesse.*   Weinheim: Beltz, 1972.

Rauh, H.   Der Wandel von der traditionellen zur modernen Entwicklungspsychologie.   In H. Rauh (Ed.), *Jahrbuch zur Entwicklungspsychologie, 1978.*   Stuttgart: Klett, 1979.

Riegel, K. F.   The dialectics of human development.   *American Psychologist,* 1976, *31,* 689–700.

Rindskopf, D. A.   A general framework for using latent class analysis to test hierarchical and non-hierarchical learning models.   *Psychometrika,* 1983, *48,* 85–97.

Sheppard, J. L.   A structural analysis of concrete operations.   In J. A. Keats, K. F. Collins & G. S. Halford (Eds.), *Cognitive development.*   Chichester: Wiley, 1978.

Shye, S.   Partial order scalogram analysis.   In S. Shye (Ed.), *Theory construction and data analysis in the behavioral sciences.*   San Francisco: Jossey–Bass, 1978.

Singer, B., & Spilerman, S.   Mathematical representations of developmental theories.   In J. R. Nesselroade & P. B. Baltes (Eds.), *Longitudinal research in the study of behavior and development.*   New York: Academic Press, 1979.

Thomas, H.   Fitting cross-classification table data to models when observations are subject to classification error.   *Psychometrika,* 1977, *42,* 199–206.

van den Daele, L. D.   Qualitative models in developmental analysis.   *Developmental Psychology,* 1969, *4,* 303–310.

Wohlwill, J. F.   *The study of behavioral development.*   New York: Academic Press, 1973.

Wold, H.   *Model constructions and evaluation when theoretical knowledge is scarce.*   Cahier 79.06, Dept. of Econometrics, University of Geneva, 1979.

Wold, H., & Bertholet, J. L.   *The PLS (partial least squares) approach to multidimensional contingency tables.*   International meeting, Institute of Statistics and Social Research "C. GINI," University of Rome, 1981.   (Also: *Metron,* 1983, *41,* 105–126.)

Young, F. W.   Qualitative analysis of qualitative data.   *Psychometrika,* 1981, *46,* 357–388.

12

The Generalized Group
Effect Model*

DAVID A. KENNY

I. Introduction

The topic of linking individual development and social change presents a very difficult challenge. One can only approach the topic by simplifying it. In this chapter, I focus on the problem of how to interrelate the individual and the group and do not fully consider the dynamic aspect of the problem; the focus is on the level of analysis.

The problem of the level of analysis has an established tradition in methodology. However, most practitioners ignore the complexities and apply a naive and usually incorrect approach to the problem. For instance, they equate the unit of measurement with the level of analysis. Variables such as intelligence, extroversion, and attitude are all measured from persons and are, therefore, presumed to reflect only individual-level processes. Variables such as group size, productivity, and amount of resources are measured at the aggregate or group level and are presumed to reflect group-level processes. Thus, the origin of the measurements is presumed to define the

* Supported in part by grants from the National Science Foundation, BNS-7913820 and BNS-8210137. The MacArthur Foundation provided support during the author's sabbatical year at the Center for Advanced Study in the Behavioral Sciences, 1982–1983.

appropriate level of analysis. Such a strategy, while not totally unreasonable, is nonetheless flawed, as a simple example shows. One might measure group size by asking each individual how large the group is. Presumably one would obtain the same or nearly the same value for group size if one counted the members in the group. But, because group size was measured from individuals, does it become an individual-level variable? Of course not. One cannot simply equate the unit of measurement with the level of analysis.

Some have taken the position that there are no effects beyond the individual level. Group-level effects ae taken to be epiphenomenal. According to this position, when the proper analyses are undertaken, all the supposed group-level effects should be reducible to individual-level effects. This position is based not so much on empirical analyses as on an underlying belief in psychological reductionism. Proponents of this point of view are quick to point out that behavior is performed by individuals and so the appropriate level of explanation is at the individual level. To do anything else would invoke concepts such as group mind and the like. Others, like Cronbach (1976), have argued that higher-order effects are real and cannot be reduced to individual-level processes. The position taken in this chapter is nonreductionistic. However, I will take very seriously the contention of Hauser (1974) and others that proponents of group-level phenomena have the burden of proof on their shoulders. We must demonstrate group-level phenomena over and above individual-level processes.

In this chapter, I want to consider how one can study processes at two different levels—individual and group—simultaneously. Many developmental contexts embed the individual in a group: Persons are born into families, develop friendship networks, and learn in classes; later in life they work and play in teams. The chapter is divided into three sections. In the first section, the Generalized Group Effect Model, an approach, for studying the group–individual interface, is developed. This general model is shown to subsume analysis strategies that have been used by others. In the second section, the model is discussed in relation to the generations design in social psychology and the time-sequential design in developmental psychology. In the third section, the phenomenon of group polarization is discussed using the Generalized Group Effect Model. Although much of the discussion is necessarily quite technical, I have attempted to present the material as simply as possible. The formal rationale is presented elsewhere (Kenny, 1983; Kenny & La Voie, in press).

II. Hierarchically Nested Design

The most common design that is used to study the effects of some group on the individual is the hierarchically nested design. In this design each individual is a member of one and only one group and that person is measured on a set of variables. The number of persons in each group may be constant, as in juries, or it may vary, as in friendship groups. The usual practice is to perform two separate analyses, one for individuals and a second for groups. The individual analysis ignores the group structure in the data and examines individual scores, whereas the group analysis ignores individual-level processes and analyzes the group means. This naive analysis is inherently contradictory. Each analysis presumes that the other analysis yields no effects. For instance, the individual-level analysis ignores the group and must presume that there are no group effects. If there were group effects that were different from the individual-level effects, then the individual-level analysis would detail not only individual-level phenomena but also group-level phenomena.

This confounding of individual- and group-level processes had not gone unnoticed in the literature, and various methods have been developed to solve the problem. What follows is a synthesis of these methods; that is, a very general model for the hierarchically nested design is developed. The various analysis strategies proposed by others become special cases of the general model.

Threre are two variables X and Y, and it is presumed that X causes Y. The goal of the analysis is to measure the effect of X on Y simultaneously at the individual and the group level. The model will be called the *Generalized Group Effect Model* because other analysis strategies are special cases of it. Diagrammatically this model can be represented by

$$X = \text{individual} + \text{group}$$
$$\downarrow \qquad\quad \downarrow$$
$$Y = \text{individual} + \text{group}$$

At issue is how to measure the effects of X on Y at the two different levels represented by the two arrows.

It is useful to elaborate the model by expressing the individual effect as the sum of two components: first, the deviation of the individual effect from the mean of the individual effects, and second, the mean of the individual effects. The deviation score for persion i in group j will be denoted d_{ij}, the mean of the individual effects m_j, and the group effect g_j. Diagrammatically the model is now:

$$X_{ij} = d_{ij} + m_j + g_j$$
$$\downarrow \quad\ \downarrow \quad\ \downarrow$$
$$Y_{ij} = d_{ij} + m_j + g_j$$

There are now three different types of effects of X on Y: the group-level effect, the individual-level effect with mean subtracted out, and the mean individual effect on Y. We need to carefully distinguish the effect of m and g. The variable m is the average individual effect and so it refers to the group. The variable g is a pure group effect.

The variable d_{ij} equals $X - \overline{X}$ for the variable X and $Y - \overline{Y}$ for Y. Because d_{ij} can be directly measured, one can measure individual-level effects by regressing $Y - \overline{Y}$ on $X - \overline{X}$. The quantity $m_j + g_j$ equals the mean of the scores for group j, so the effects of both m and g cannot be estimated simultaneously. In the parlance of mathematical models, the general model is not identified. However, various special cases of the model are identified. Two important submodels are described next.

Fixed Effects. In this model, identification of the effect of X on Y is brought about by assuming that there are no group effects per se. The score is made up of deviation and mean effects only. The deviation and mean of X separately affect the deviation and mean of Y, respectively. In this model, the deviation scores exactly equal $X_{ij} - \overline{X}_j$ and $Y - \overline{Y}_j$ while the mean scores exactly equal $\overline{X}$ and $\overline{Y}$. Thus the deviation effect of X on Y can be measured by regressing $Y - \overline{Y}$ on $X - \overline{X}$ and the mean effect can be obtained by regressing Y and $\overline{X}$. If group sizes are unequal for the regression with group means, one should weight by group size. This analysis closely corresponds to the naive analysis strategy discussed in the first part of this section. However, there is one important difference: the individual analysis is not done on raw scores but on deviation scores.

The model is called a *fixed effects model* because it is compatible with the assumption that the researcher has set or fixed the level of X for each person or has fixed the level of $\overline{X}$ for each group.

Random Effects. In this model, all three effects of deviation, mean, and group remain. The deviation effects can be directly estimated by computing the mean deviation scores for the measures $X - \overline{X}$ and $Y - \overline{Y}$. However, the group means of $\overline{X}$ and $\overline{Y}$ now estimate both the average individual level effect for that group and the group effect. Thus, some of the variance in $\overline{X}$ and $\overline{Y}$ reflects individual- and group-level processes. To be able to separate these two components, two key assumptions must be made. First, individuals must be assumed to be randomly assigned to groups. The major consequence of this assumption is that the amount of the variance in the group means for variable X that can be attributed to individual-level effects is now known; it equals the variance of the deviation effects divided by the group size.[1] The remaining variance is attributed to group effects. Thus, group-level variance equals the variance in the group means minus the variance of

[1] As Kenny and LaVoie (in press) show, the estimate must be modified if group sizes are unequal.

the deviation effects divided by sample size. In a corresponding fashion, the group-level effect of X on Y can be estimated.

Second, it must be assumed that the effect of deviation and mean of X on Y is the same; that is, the effect of d and m must be assumed to be the same. Because these effects are assumed to be the same, d and m can be collapsed into a single variable. Thus, the model has an individual-level variable $d_{ij} + m_j$ and a group-level variable g_j. This model will be called the *random effects model* since persons are assumed to be randomly assigned to groups.

We now will consider how various researchers have studied the hierarchically nested design and how their model fits into the general framework that has been developed in this chapter. Before the details of applications are considered, a few rules of thumb will be presented. These rules concern the conditions governing when the fixed model should be applied and the conditions for the random model. The fixed effects model seems most appropriate for any variable measured before the groups were formed because group effects would not have had an opportunity to take effect. Also, variables that are not caused by group effects, such as sex and experimental condition, should be treated as fixed. Moreover, any variable that was used to form the groups should be treated as fixed. For instance, if groups were formed to have equal levels of ability, ability should be treated as a fixed variable. Finally, if for any variable the group means are constrained to be equal or nearly equal, this variable should also be treated as fixed.

Variables measured after the group was formed should be treated as random. Even if the groups were not formed randomly, it still seems advisable to treat such variables as random. In experimental research, it is quite common that persons are not randomly assigned to experimental conditions, but we still do t-tests and analyses of variance that presume random assignment. Granted, the consequences are more severe in this instance, but randomization still represents a reasonable starting point. If group-level effects net of individual-level effects are to be measured, it is not clear what assumption permitting estimation is more reasonable than randomization.

Contextual Analysis. Blau (1960) and Davis, Spaeth, and Huson (1961) developed a form of analysis for the hierarchically nested design that has become known as *contextual analysis*. As explained by Firebaugh (1978), contextual analysis consists of regressing Y_{ij} on X_{ij} and $\bar{X}_j$. This analysis strategy is essentially equivalent to the fixed effects model. The effect of X_{ij} in a contextual analysis is equivalent to the effect of $X_{ij} - \bar{X}_j$ in the fixed effects analysis, and the effect of $\bar{X}_j$ in the contextual analysis equals the group effect in the fixed model minus the individual-level effect (Firebaugh, 1978). Thus, a contextual analysis is a straightforward transformation of the fixed effects model.

Firebaugh (1980b) discusses the "frog pond effect," in which persons in groups compare their outcomes to the group average. For instance, a student's satisfaction in a course is determined not by absolute performance but by relative performance, that is, by the absolute performance of the individual minus the average performance of the group. This type of social comparison effect can be measured by a contextual analysis. A frog pond effect is indicated by large effects for X and effects of the opposite sign for $\overline{X}$. In terms of the fixed effects submodel, $X - \overline{X}$ has a large effect on Y, whereas $\overline{X}$ has little or no effect on $\overline{Y}$. As Firebaugh (1980b) notes, frog pond effects are usually accompanied by classical contextual effects and so may be difficult to identify uniquely.

Classroom Effects. Perhaps the most influential work in this area is the frequently cited unpublished paper by Cronbach (1976) on how to study students in classrooms. A thoughtful examination of the many issues in this area, the paper recommends an analysis that is essentially similar to the fixed effects model in this chapter. Cronbach is one of the few researchers who consider whether terms in the model are fixed or random. Also considered in the paper is the correlation between individual-level effects varying across groups, an issue not considered in this chapter.

Analysis of Covariance. In this analysis, individual scores are treated as the unit of analysis. A one-way analysis of covariance is done on the Y measure, the independent variable is group, the covariate X. According to Hauser (1974) and others who have used this analysis, there are no "true" group effects if group has no effect. That is, once the effect of X on Y within groups has been subtracted, if group means for Y do not significantly differ, there are no group-level effects.

This analysis strategy is a variant of the random effects model. The effect of the covariate is equivalent to the effect at the individual level in the random effects model. The test of the group's effect is equivalent to the test of whether there is group-level variance in the random effects model. However, this procedure does not measure the effect of X on Y at the group level directly (Firebaugh, 1980a); it only tells us whether there is statistically reliable variance in Y at the group level. The next procedure to be described yields the group-level effect of X on Y.

Kenny and La Voie. Kenny and La Voie (in press) have developed an analysis procedure that is equivalent to the random effects model outlined in this chapter. The individual-level effects are measured by regressing $Y_j - \overline{Y}_j$ on $X_j - \overline{X}_j$. The group-level effects require that the association between $\overline{X}_j$ and $\overline{Y}_j$ be over and above that expected by individual-level association. This analysis procedure is closely linked to a one-way analysis of variance in which group is the independent variable.

Experimental Studies. In these studies a variable is manipulated by the experimenter, as when a researcher varies the group size by having groups of size two and four. Anderson and Ager (1978) discuss the analysis of experimental data from the hierarchically nested design. The procedure they recommend is to determine first whether there are any group effects. In the terms of this chapter, an analysis is done using the random effects model and a determination is made as to whether there is group-level variance in Y. If there is, then group is the unit of analysis; if not, person is the unit of analysis.

In this analysis the experimental or *"X"* variable is entirely between groups. That is, persons within each group do not vary on X. Thus, there is no individual-level variance for X, only group-level variance.

Kraemer and Jacklin. These authors propose a general model for the study of variables in dyadic social interaction. For instance, one may study the effect of sex on dominance in interaction. Three different types of dyads can be created: male–male, female–female, and male–female. Kraemer and Jacklin's (1979) model includes the effect of a person's sex on his or her own behavior (the *subject effect*) and the effect of a person's sex on the behavior of his or her partner (the *partner effect*).

Sex is the *"X"* variable in a fixed effects model. Its individual-level effect is the subject plus partner effect; its group effect, the subject minus partner effect in a Kraemer and Jacklin analysis. The subject by partner interaction can be measured by comparing the same versus opposite sex dyads. Thus, a second *"X"* variable is created to measure the subject by partner interaction, and this variable varies only between groups.

The Generalized Group Effect Model thus subsumes quite a wide range of methods that have been used to analyze the hierarchically nested design. Interestingly, it can handle methods that have been proposed both for experimental as well as nonexperimental data.

At times within the same analysis, some variables are fixed and others are random. For instance, the variables X and Z cause Y, X is fixed, and Z is random. That is, one of the causes of Y operates under the fixed effects model and the other under the random effects model. Thus we have a model akin to the mixed model in the analysis of variance. One important complication in the analysis does arise. In measuring the group-level effects of the random variable on Y, the individual-level effect of Z on Y is subtracted out. In determining how much of the variance in Y occurs at the individual level, one must include only the unique variance due to the random variable Z net of X. This quantity is then used to determine the group-level variance. Recall that the group-level variance equals the variance in the group means minus the individual-level variance, adjusted for group size. Thus, the random effects variable net of the fixed variable enters this subtraction (see Kenny, 1983, for details).

Computations for the fixed effects, random effects, and mixed models can be performed by the computer program LEVEL (Kenny & Stigler, 1983). LEVEL handles up to twenty variables, unequal group sizes, and missing data. Moreover, regression equations can be directly estimated by the program.

III. Generations Design

In the previous section, a general approach to the simultaneous study of group and individual processes was developed. One drawback of that approach is that it does not explicitly consider the dynamic aspects of behavior at two levels. One way to make the approach more useful is to consider applying the model to other designs besides the hierarchically nested design. In this section the generations design is considered; it will be seen that this design is closely linked to the time-sequential design.

One of the landmark experiments in social psychology was Sherif's study (1935) of the autokinetic effect in a social setting. This experiment showed the existence of norms in subjects jointly judging the apparent motion of a stationary light. In an ingenious follow-up experiment, Jacobs and Campbell (1961) extended the work of Sherif. Like Sherif, they had subjects judge the apparent motion of a stationary light in a group situation. They then removed one subject from the group, added a new one, and had the group judge the light's apparent motion. Once again they repeated the procedure of removing and adding a subject.

In Table 12.1, a diagram of the design used by Jacobs and Campbell (1961) is presented. The crosses in the table represent data points. Initially, Persons 1, 2, 3, and 4 are in the group. Person 1 leaves the group and Person 5 enters. Persons 2 through 5 now make up the group. Person 2 then leaves the group and Person 6 enters. This design is called a *generations design*, since it mimics the birth and death process of generational turnover.

Jacobs and Campbell (1961) used the generations design to study whether an arbitrary belief could be passed on from generation to generation. Weick and Gilfillan (1971) and Zucker (1977) have extended this work. Insko and his colleagues (1980) have applied the design to study social evolution. The design has been infrequently applied, but it has given researchers answers to questions that could not be answered by other designs.

Although a series of investigators have used the generations design, they have not developed an analysis strategy for it. This is unfortunate because, as will be seen, a complete analysis of the design results in a rich understanding of social behavior. Moreover, an adequate analysis strategy might increase the frequency of the design's use.

Table 12.1

Generational Design

Group	1	2	3	4	5	6	7	8	9	10	11	12
							Person					
9									X	X	X	X
8								X	X	X	X	
7							X	X	X	X		
6						X	X	X	X			
5					X	X	X	X				
4				X	X	X	X					
3			X	X	X	X						
2		X	X	X	X							
1	X	X	X	X								

The model that will here be developed for the generations design is a modification of the model developed by Kenny and La Voie (in press) (i.e., the random effects submodel of the Generalized Group Effect Model). Each person's score is assumed to be a function of two terms, an individual-level term and a group-level term. In equation form the model is

$$X_{ij} = m_j + p_{ij}$$

where X_{ij} is the score of person i in group j, m_j is the group effect for group j, and p_{ij} is the individual effect for person i in group j. Let n be group size and g be the number of groups or generations. The total number of persons in the study is $g + n - 1$.

The estimation procedure for the model developed by Kenny and La Voie (in press) is based on the assumption that the groups are independent. However, this assumption is not tenable for the generations design, since each person is in $n - 1$ different groups. It seems reasonable that p_{ij} be correlated across the same individual. Also, the group effect m_j is correlated over time. In a sense, the group effect is a time series that has an autocorrelational structure. There are then two covariance structures: one for individuals, another for groups. Besides these covariances there are variances; again, one for individuals and another for groups. These variances and covariances should in principle be estimable.

The model for the generations design can be modified in several ways. One obvious modification is to differentiate the scores of persons within the groups. For instance, in groups of size four, persons may be assigned one of four roles, A, B, C, or D. As persons enter the group they are assigned role A; they then move on to B, C, and D. This change of roles is diagrammed in

Table 12.2

Generational Design with Roles A, B, C, and D

Group	1	2	3	4	5	6	7	8	9	10	11	12
									Person			
9									D	C	B	A
8								D	C	B	A	
7							D	C	B	A		
6						D	C	B	A			
5					D	C	B	A				
4				D	C	B	A					
3			D	C	B	A						
2		D	C	B	A							
1	D	C	B	A								

Table 12.2. The roles may be explicitly assigned (e.g., leader, second-in-command) or depend simply on the length of time in the group.

The generations model with roles requires modification of the model. The model now becomes

$$X_{ijk} = m_j + a_k + p_{ik}$$

where m_j is defined as before, a_k is the fixed effect for role k, and p_{ik} is the effect for person i in role k. The data can be viewed as a set of time series. For example, if $k = 4$, there are four time series $X_{ij1}, X_{ij2}, X_{ij3}$, and X_{ij4}, where the observations are temporally ordered by the subscript j. These four different time series can be seen in Table 12.2 as the observations designated A, B, C, and D. The intra- and interrelations of these four time series would yield estimates of role effect, variance due to person for a given role, variance due to group, autocorrelational structure for group, and autocorrelational structure for individuals. Presumably, all of these parameters could be estimated.

A. RELATION TO THE TIME-SEQUENTIAL DESIGN

One can view the generations design as being essentially equivalent to the time-sequential design (Schaie, 1965). The diagram in Table 12.1 is no different from Schaie's diagram for the time-sequential design: generation is equivalent to time, person to cohort, and role to age. Although diagrammatically similar, there are, however, two important differences. First, the generations design is for individuals, while the time-sequential design is for groups. Second, the time-sequential design as conceived by Schaie is not longitudinal, while the generations design involves the repeated measurement of the same individuals over time.

Many data structures are time sequential in nature. One example is any institution which keeps its clients for a fixed period and recruits new members while old members are still present. Colleges are one obvious example, as are other training programs.

It might be possible to adapt the models that have been developed for the generations design to the time-sequential design. Of course, there would have to be modifications to take into account the fact that group scores with varying group sizes are used in the time-sequential design, whereas the generations design presumes the sizes are one. To perform such an analysis one would need many more time points — at least 12 — than are ordinarily used in the time-sequential design. Since the analysis is essentially time series analysis, one can examine the effects of interventions as in the interrupted time-series design (Judd & Kenny, 1981).

It might seem anomalous that it is possible to estimate cohort, age, and time effects for the generations design (Mason, Mason, Winsborough, & Poole, 1973, maintained that these effects cannot be estimated). But there are two important differences between the model in this chapter and the analysis of Mason et al. First, the model for the generations design treats time and cohort as random rather than fixed factors. Second, these factors are assumed to be uncorrelated, something not assumed by Mason et al.

IV. Group Polarization

A second way to link the Generalized Group Effect Model to change and development is to consider an important but not well-known phenomenon of group polarization. Let us consider the history of this construct.

Stoner (1961) found that on a series of hypothetical life-choice questions, groups took riskier positions than individuals. This phenomenon, labeled the "risky shift," has generated more research in group dynamics than any other topic. Although the risky shift was demonstrable with the materials used by Stoner, it did not replicate well with other materials. In fact, a careful examination of Stoner's materials showed that not all items shifted toward risk: some consistently shifted toward conservatism. Thus the risky shift did not seem to be a reliable empirical phenomenon (Cartwright, 1973).

The phoenix arising out of the ashes of risky shift is group polarization (Myers & Lamm, 1976). As will be seen, group polarization explains why groups shift sometimes toward and sometimes away from risk. Moreover, group polarization refers to the effects of group discussion on virtually any topic, not just those concerned with risk.

What is group polarization? Basically, it is the fact that groups move in the direction of the pole toward which they are already leaning. For items about which individuals are already inclined to support moderate risk, the group will favor even greater risk. For items about which individuals are already inclined toward moderate conservatism, the group will become even more conservative. The same holds for political attitudes. Group discussion results in the group's taking a more extreme political position than the average individual's before discussion. Myers and Lamm (1976) reported tests of group polarization on a wide variety of topics with many subject populations and found it to be a very robust empirical phenomenon.

Although there are various social–psychological explanations of group polarization, there is to my knowledge no explicit formal quantitative model of group polarization, nor even a formal measure of polarization. What follows is a model of group polarization. Let us denote X_{ij} as the opinion of the ith individual in the jth group before discussion. Let $\overline{X}_j$ be the mean of the mean of X_{ij} for the jth group and $\overline{X}$ be the mean across all groups. Let k be the neutral point: for groups at the value of k, there is no polarization. Let us denote Y_{ij} as the opinion of the ith individual in the jth group after discussion. Let $\overline{Y}_j$ be the mean of the mean of Y_{ij} for the jth group and $\overline{Y}$ be the mean across all groups. At issue is how initial polarization in the group, $\overline{X}_j - k$, relates to postdiscussion polarization, $\overline{Y}_j - k$. The term $\overline{X}_j - k$ will be called prepolarization and $\overline{Y}_j - k$ will be called postpolarization.

Let us first consider linear polarization. Here $\overline{Y}_j - k = b(\overline{X}_j - k) + e_j$, where b is greater than one and e_j represents random group changes. If b is less than one then there would be depolarization. For this model, the fixed effects model of the Generalized Group Effect Model should be used; here, prepolarization is linearly related to postpolarization (i.e., the ratio of post- to prepolarization is constant). Given this model it follows that $\overline{Y} - k = b(\overline{X} - k)$. Thus, the overall amount of polarization is proportional to how initially polarized the members are. In this model, the overall amount of polarization is not dependent on how the groups are formed. If the groups are randomly formed or if the members are chosen to be relatively similar or dissimilar to each other, the same amount of overall polarization results.

The neutral point k can be solved for if b does not equal one. The neutral point equals $(\overline{Y} - b\overline{X})/(b - 1)$. If b equals one, there is no polarization of any type and so there is no need for any neutral point.

There is one major difficulty with the foregoing procedure in measuring the amount of polarization: it presumes that there is no measurement error in $\overline{X}_j$. The presence of measurement error in X will tend to produce attenuated estimates of b; that is, the estimates will be too close to zero. One result of this attenuation process is that depolarization might be indicated when it is not in fact present. Some type of correction for measurement error must be made so that the estimates of polarization and neutral point are not biased. These corrections can be accomplished if there are multiple indicators of X.

It is possible that group polarization is nonlinearly related to initial polarization. The curve could possibly be accelerating, decelerating, or first accelerating and then decelerating. For an accelerating function, the ratio of postpolarization to prepolarization would be greater for groups with high prepolarization. For a decelerating function, the post- to prepolarization ratio would be greater for groups with less prepolarization. The first accelerating then decelerating function would be shaped like an S curve. Properly constructed, these functions could still result in overall polarization when groups are randomly formed. However, with these nonlinear functions, if groups are nonrandomly formed it seems likely that different results would occur than when they are randomly formed.

Four different ways in which $\overline{X}_j - k$ is related to $\overline{Y}_j - k$ have been discussed: linear, accelerating, decelerating, and an S function. In what follows it will be presumed that the function is linear.

A. GROUP POLARIZATION AND MACROSOCIETAL INTERVENTIONS

In this section the effect of interventions at the societal level and their influence on individual attitudes will be considered. Among such interventions, I wish to consider mass media campaigns, the passage of laws, judicial decisions, and foreign affairs such as wars. While I cannot review the hundreds of studies that have been undertaken to investigate the effects of societal interventions on attitudes, I can summarize the views of Joseph Klapper (1960) on the effect of the mass media on attitudes. He has argued that the media do not change attitudes; they only strengthen existing attitudes. This reinforcing effect exists, Klapper argues, through the psychological process of selective exposure and attention. Klapper's view can be restated by saying that the media only push society in a direction it is already headed. Thus, media effects can be viewed as polarization effects, and so one can claim that societal interventions affect individual attitudes through group polarization.

What may be happening is that societal interventions play an agenda-setting role; that is, they induce persons to informally discuss the intervention. Group members discuss the issue and group polarization effects take place. If the group is already inclined in the same direction as the intervention, persons will move in the direction desired by those who produced the intervention. This analysis would also predict when interventions will produce no change. If the society is at or near the neutral point, the intervention will have no effect on attitudes. This appears to have been the effect of the Supreme Court's legalization of abortions in the United States in 1973. Opinion about abortion was evenly split before the decision, and so it remains today. The intervention produced no effect because the population was not initially polarized.

This view would also explain why some interventions have a boomerang effect in which the intervention increases negative attitudes. Perhaps this is what occurred in India when the government introduced a sterilization program. Because the population was already negatively disposed toward the intervention, the increased informal social communication resulting from the passage of the law resulted in polarization and increased negative attitudes.

V. Conclusion

The Generalized Group Effect Model represents a very general approach for studying the effects of individuals and groups simultaneously. The model subsumes various approaches to the study of groups that are used in such disciplines as sociology, educational psychology, and social psychology. There are two important submodels of the Generalized Group Effect Model. In the fixed effects model, there are no pure group-level effects; group effects are measured by the average individual-level effect. In the random effects model, persons are assumed to be randomly assigned to groups; individual-level effects are subtracted out of group means and correlations. The random effects model was applied to the analysis of the generations design in social psychology and the time-sequential design in developmental psychology, while the fixed effects model was applied to the measurement of group polarization.

Acknowledgments

Conversations with Thomas Pettigrew, Jeffrey Fisher, Lynn Gale, Reid Hastie, James Stigler, and Lawrence La Voie prompted many of the ideas in this paper. Special thanks are due Robyn Ireland for clerical assistance.

References

Anderson, L. R., & Ager, J. W. Analysis of variance in small group research. *Personality and Social Psychology Bulletin,* 1978, *4,* 341–345.

Blau, P. M. Structural effects. *American Sociological Review*, 1960, *25*, 178–193.

Cartwright, D. Determinants of scientific progress: The case of the risky shift. *American Psychologist*, 1973, *28*, 222–231.

Cronbach, L. J. *Research on classrooms and schools: Formulation of questions, design and analysis.* Unpublished paper, Stanford Evaluation Consortium, Stanford University, 1976.

Davis, J. A., Spaeth, J. L. B., Huson, C. A technique for analyzing the effects of group composition. *American Sociological Review*, 1961, *26*, 215–225.

Firebaugh, G. A rule for inferring individual-level relationships from aggregate data. *American Sociological Review*, 1978, *43*, 557–572.

Firebaugh, G. Assessing group effects: A comparison of two methods. In E. F. Borgatta & D. J. Jackson (Eds.), *Aggregate data: Analysis and interpretation.* Beverly Hills, Calif.: Sage, 1980. (a)

Firebaugh, G. Groups as contexts and frog ponds. *New Directions for Methodology of Social and Behavioral Science*, 1980, *6*, 43–52. (b)

Hauser, R. M. Contextual analysis revisited. *Sociological Methods and Research*, 1974, *2*, 365–375.

Insko, C. A., Thibaut, J. W., Moehle, D., Wilson, M., Diamond, W. D., Gilmore, R., Solomon, M. R., & Lipsitz, A. Social evolution and the emergence of leadership. *Journal of Personality and Social Psychology*, 1980, *39*, 431–448.

Jacobs, R. C., & Campbell, D. T. The perpetuation of an arbitrary tradition through several generations of laboratory microculture. *Journal of Abnormal and Social Psychology*, 1961, *62*, 649–658.

Judd, C. M., & Kenny, D. A. *Estimating the effects of social interventions.* New York: Cambridge University Press, 1981.

Kenny, D. A. Technical note on the generalized group effect model. Unpublished paper, University of Connecticut, Storrs, Conn., 1983.

Kenny, D. A., & La Voie L. Separating individual and group level effects. *Journal of Personality and Social Psychology*, in press.

Kenny, D. A., & Stigler, J. LEVEL: A FORTRAN IV program for correlational analysis of group–individual data structures. *Behavior Research Methods and Instrumentation*, 1983, *15*, 606.

Klapper, J. T. *The effects of mass communication.* Glencoe, Ill.: Free Press, 1960.

Kraemer, H. C., & Jacklin, C. N. Statistical analysis of dyadic social behavior. *Psychological Bulletin*, 1979, *86*, 217–224.

Mason, K. O., Mason, W. M., Winsborough, H. H., & Poole, W. K. Some methodological issues in cohort analysis of archival data. *American Sociological Review*, 1973, *38*, 242–258.

Myers, D. G., & Lamm, H. The group polarization phenomenon. *Psychological Bulletin*, 1976, *86*, 602–627.

Schaie, K. W. A general model for the study of developmental problems. *Psychological Bulletin*, 1965, *64*, 92–107.

Sherif, M. A study of some social factors in perception. *Archives of Psychology*, 1935, No. 187.

Stoner, J. A. F. *A comparison of individual and group decisions involving risk.* Unpublished master's thesis, Massachusetts Institute of Technology, 1961.

Weick, K. E., & Gilfillan, D. P. Fate of arbitrary traditions in a laboratory microculture. *Journal of Personality and Social Psychology*, 1971, *17*, 179–191.

Zucker, L. G. The role of institutionalization in cultural persistence. *American Sociological Review*, 1977, *42*, 726–743.

Author Index

Numbers in italics refer to the pages on which the complete references are cited.

Subject Index